A COMPLETE ILLUSTRATED HISTORY OF THE

CRUSADES

AND THE CRUSADER KNIGHTS

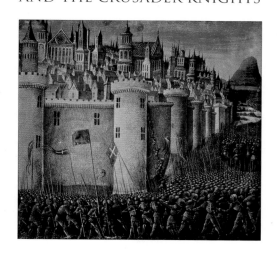

A COMPLETE ILLUSTRATED HISTORY OF THE
CRUSADES
AND THE CRUSADER KNIGHTS

THE HISTORY, MYTH AND ROMANCE OF THE MEDIEVAL KNIGHT ON CRUSADE, WITH OVER 400
STUNNING IMAGES OF THE BATTLES, ADVENTURES, SIEGES, FORTRESSES, TRIUMPHS AND DEFEATS

CHARLES PHILLIPS
CONSULTANT: DR CRAIG TAYLOR

HERMES
HOUSE

CONTENTS

Introduction 6

THE FIRST AND SECOND CRUSADES 12

Timeline 14
The kingdoms of Palestine 16

CHAPTER ONE: HOLY WAR 18

Fighting a holy war 20
Defenders of the faith 22
Muslim empires 24
Christians in the East 26
The Power of the papacy 28
The Holy City of Jerusalem 30
The penitential journey 32
Crusader pilgrims 34

CHAPTER TWO: A CALL TO ARMS 36

Constantinople under
  threat 38
Righteous warfare 40
God wills it! God wills it! 42
The quest for glory 44
Walking to the Holy Land 46

CHAPTER THREE: THE JOURNEY TO PALESTINE 48

More than the stars of
  heaven 50
Princes on crusade 52
The crusaders in
  Constantinople 54
The siege of Nicaea 56
Men of iron 58
Defender of Jerusalem 60
The march across
  Anatolia 62

CHAPTER FOUR: BOUND FOR JERUSALEM 64

The siege of Antioch 66
The capture of Antioch 68
Miracles at Antioch 70
The Prince of Antioch 72
The way to the Holy City 74
Robert of Jerusalem 76
Jerusalem! Jerusalem! 78
The Holy City captured 80
After the victory 82

CHAPTER FIVE: THE LAND OVERSEAS 84

The foundation of Outremer 86
Government of the crusader states 88
Life in the crusader states 90
Prince of Galilee 92
Krak des Chevaliers 94
By sea from Italy 96

CHAPTER SIX: MUSLIM RESURGENCE AND THE SECOND CRUSADE 98

The Field of Blood 100
The capture of Edessa 102
Soldiers of Islam 104
Call to a second crusade 106
Crusaders set out 108
Disaster at Dorylaeum 110
The Council of Acre 112
Despair and recriminations 114
Nur ed-Din and a unified Syria 116
The battle for Egypt 118
The chivalrous infidel 120
Crusaders destroyed 122
Jerusalem recaptured 124

THE LATER AND EUROPEAN CRUSADES 126
Timeline 128
The Catholic expansion 130

CHAPTER SEVEN: RICHARD THE LIONHEART AND THE THIRD CRUSADE 132
Once more to Jerusalem 134
Kings of Europe take the
  cross 136
Barbarossa's crusade 138
In Sicily and Cyprus 140
A sick winter 142
The capture of Acre 144
Atrocity at Acre? 146
Richard's march to Jaffa 148
An uncertain future 150
The Treaty of Jaffa 152
After the Third Crusade 154

CHAPTER EIGHT: CRUSADES OF THE EARLY 13TH CENTURY 156
Fighting for Venice 158
On to Constantinople 160
The sack of Constantinople 162
A new view of crusading 164

The Children's Crusades 166
The Fifth Crusade 168
Jerusalem regained 170
Kingdom of Jerusalem rebuilt 172

CHAPTER NINE: CRUSADES OF THE MID-13TH TO 15TH CENTURIES 174
Crusade in Egypt 176
A king's ransom 178
The Eighth Crusade 180
Saint Louis 182
The Ninth Crusade 184
The fall of Tripoli and Acre 186
The attack on Alexandria 188
Peter I of Cyprus 190
Crusade to Mahdia 192
Defeat at Nicopolis 194
The end of Byzantium 196
The Conqueror 198
The miracle of Belgrade 200

CHAPTER TEN: THE WARRIOR MONKS 202
Knights of St John 204
Hospitallers save Rhodes 206
Suleyman takes Rhodes 208

Knights of the Temple of
  Solomon 210
Knights Templar in the field 212
Templar builders 214
Downfall of the Templars 216
Teutonic Knights 218
Warriors of the Reconquista 220
Knights of St Thomas 222
The Order of St Lazarus 224

CHAPTER ELEVEN: THE EUROPEAN CRUSADES 226
The Reconquista 228
The Spanish Crusade of 1212 230
The conquest of Granada 232
The Albigensian Crusade 234
Massacre of the Cathars 236
The Cathar Inquisition 238
The Baltic Crusades 240
In Prussia and Lithuania 242
Crusades against the Hussites 244
Crusades in Italy 246

AFTERWORD 248

Index 252
Acknowledgements 256

INTRODUCTION

They bear weapons suitable for war, they have the cross of Christ on their right shoulder or between their shoulders, and with a unified voice they give issue to the cry, 'God wills it! God wills it! God wills it!' This was the description – according to an anonymous chronicle of the First Crusade, the *Gesta Francorum* (Deeds of the Franks) of *c*.1100 – given to the Norman lord Bohemond of Taranto when he asked for information about the army marching across Europe in 1096, bound for the Holy Land. The army had arisen in response to a call from Pope Urban II, in November 1095, for the fighting men of Europe to hurry to the aid of Christians in the East, who were being persecuted by Muslim Seljuk Turks, and to liberate the sacred places of Jerusalem. Bohemond was inspired to follow them.

Pope Urban's sermon at Clermont was one of the most powerful and influential in history. Its depiction of the humiliation of Christians by Turks and the Muslim

▼ *Fighting in the name and under the cross of Christ. Godfrey of Bouillon was the first ruler of the Latin Kingdom of Jerusalem.*

▲ *The Third Crusade (1189–92) achieved the Muslim surrender of Acre to King Philip II of France and Richard the Lionheart.*

possession of Jerusalem – represented as the taking 'into slavery of the Holy City of Christ' – inspired an outpouring of religious anger and energy sufficient to mobilize Christians in their thousands to leave their homes and march across continents risking all for Christ and the Church. Particularly persuasive was Urban's promise that participation made personal salvation almost certain – he said, according to an account of his speech by Robert the Monk: 'Take on this journey for the remission of sins, in confidence of the undying glory of God's kingdom.'

The speech launched the popular movement of pilgrims and soldiers described above – known as the People's Crusade by historians – and a second wave of armies led by leading nobles and minor royalty, called the Princes' Crusade, in which Bohemond of Taranto took part. These two waves of people converged on Constantinople, capital of the Christian Byzantine Empire, where they arrived between August 1096 and May 1097. A little over two years later, in July 1099,

after many gruelling marches, desperate sieges and brutal battles, and reportedly having been helped at Antioch by heavenly armies led by St George, the survivors of these crusader forces succeeded in capturing Jerusalem from Fatimid Muslims amid scenes of deplorable ferocity yet nevertheless in the belief that they were doing God's will. The crusade leaders reported to the pope: 'The Lord ... made a gift to us of the city, along with his foes ... in the portico of Solomon and in his Temple, our men rode in the blood of the Saracens even up to the knees of their horses.'

These events, celebrated as a glorious triumph in Europe, led to the establishment of a Christian Kingdom of Jerusalem in Palestine and Syria that survived in various forms until 1291, and inspired a whole series of crusading expeditions not only to the Holy Land but also to north Africa and within Europe itself.

CRUSADER PILGRIMS

The knights and men-at-arms who embarked on the crusade of 1095–99 in response to Pope Urban II's call did not believe that they were setting out on the first of a long series of religious–military expeditions. They were under the impression that this was to be a decisive, divinely blessed mission that would remove the need for future wars. If they succeeded, as they were sure they must, there would be no need for a repeat campaign.

Moreover, they did not call their journey a crusade or themselves crusaders. They envisioned the enterprise as a journey (*iter*), specifically as a kind of pilgrimage (*peregrinatio*) – each of them took a vow (*votus*) to reach Jerusalem and pray in the Church of the Holy Sepulchre. On their clothing they wore the sign of the cross (*crux*). They became known as those marked with the cross (*crucesignati*). The journey they undertook was also sometimes called the way (*via*) or the business

▲ *In the encounters between Christian crusaders and their Muslim enemies, both sides called on God to support their cause.*

(*negotium*). The travellers were also called the faithful followers of Saint Peter (the *fideles Sancti Petri*) or the knights of Christ (the *milites Christi*).

The taking of the cross initially referred to the actual ceremony of dedicating one-self to the expedition – a priest blessed the fabric cross and gave it to the participant who reverently had it attached to his clothing. Subsequently, the taking of the cross referred to the carrying out of the act of sacrifice – and so included travelling and fighting on the expedition. The word 'crusade' came into use gradually in the 12th and 13th centuries, first in old forms of French as *crozada* (in Spanish/Portuguese *cruzada* and in more modern French *croisade*), and passed into English.

MILITARY BROTHERHOODS

In the aftermath of the success of the First Crusade, the monastic order of the Knights Hospitaller of St John of Jerusalem was established in Jerusalem. It had responsibility for the defence of the Holy Land and had grown from a hospice (guesthouse) or hospital for pilgrims to Jerusalem. The brotherhood was recognized in 1113 by Pope Paschal II (ruled

1099–1118) as the Hospitallers of St John of Jerusalem. This was followed shortly afterwards by the establishment of the order of the Poor Knights of Christ and the Temple of Solomon – later known as the Knights Templar, recognized in 1129 by the Council of Troyes and confirmed by Pope Innocent III in 1139. More broth-erhoods followed, including the Teutonic Knights, the Knights of St Thomas Acon and the Knights of St Lazarus.

▼ *In November 1095, in the market place of Clermont, Pope Urban II makes the call to arms that results in the First Crusade.*

These monastic military brotherhoods won a reputation for great bravery and ferocity in crusading campaigns and in defence of the Christian settlements in the Kingdom of Jerusalem, where they built and garrisoned many great castles.

Later, the Knights Templar were charged with heresy and suppressed by the Catholic Church in the early 14th cen-tury, and most of their very considerable assets were passed to the Knights Hospitaller, who went on to win wide acclaim and admiration for their heroics in defending first Rhodes and then Malta against the Ottoman Turks. The warrior brotherhoods were an institution inti-mately connected with the crusading spirit and unique to the culture of chivalry. They are treated in a separate chapter.

THE NINE CRUSADES

Traditionally historians identified nine crusades. According to this reckoning, the First Crusade of 1095–99, which ended with the taking of Jerusalem and the estab-lishment of the Kingdom of Jerusalem, was followed by a second (1147–49), called by Pope Eugenius III (ruled 1145–53) in response to the capture by Muslim forces of Christian-held Edessa. Led by King Louis VII of France and Conrad III of Germany, it ended dismally in a humiliating failure to take Damascus.

The Third Crusade (1189–92) was called in 1187 by Pope Gregory VIII (ruled October–December 1187) following the devastating defeat of the army of the Kingdom of Jerusalem by Muslim general Saladin at the Battle of the Horns of Hattin in July 1187 and Saladin's subsequent capture of Jerusalem. The crusade was led by Holy Roman Emperor Frederick I, King Philip II of France and King Richard I Coeur de Lion ('the Lion Hearted') of England. Frederick died en route, Philip and Richard were delayed in Sicily and Cyprus and then quarrelled, and although Coeur de Lion performed a number of heroic acts and won a great victory over Saladin in the Battle of Arsuf, the crusade ended in a negotiated settlement without the hoped-for recapture of the city of Jerusalem.

▼ *At Nicaea, Antioch and Jerusalem, the armies of the First Crusade used siege equipment against the city fortifications.*

The Fourth Crusade (1202–04) was called by Pope Innocent III (ruled 1198–1216), with the aim of attacking the Holy Land by way of Egypt, but it fell under the control of the city of Venice, which provided the fleet for the crusader army, and diverted to attack the Christian city of Zara and then the Byzantine capital, Constantinople. The Fifth Crusade (1217–21) attacked Egypt and succeeded in capturing the port of Damietta, but then made an unwise attempt to attack Cairo that ended in defeat by the Egyptian sultan al-Kamil, bringing a humiliating end to what had been a promising campaign. In the course of this crusade, the papal legate Pelagius was offered possession of Jerusalem – indeed, the return to the borders of the Latin Kingdom of Jerusalem as they had stood before the disastrous defeat at the Battle of the Horns of Hattin – but declined on the grounds that the Holy City must be won by the sword and not by negotiation with the infidel.

The Sixth Crusade (1228–29) was led by Holy Roman Emperor Frederick II while he was excommunicated following a quarrel with the pope and was remarkably successful: through diplomacy rather than military might, he regained possession of Jerusalem, Nazareth and Bethlehem. The Seventh Crusade (1248–54) was led by King Louis IX of France in response to the fall of Jerusalem to the Khwarezmian Turks in 1244. Once again attacking Egypt and capturing Damietta, it ended in humiliating failure. Louis was captured and ransomed at enormous expense, after which he travelled to Acre in Palestine and remained there for some years.

The Eighth Crusade (1270) was again led by Louis IX. It set out for Syria but diverted to attack Tunis, where Louis died either of bubonic plague or dysentery and where the crusade came to nothing. The Ninth Crusade (1271–72) consisted of a campaign to the Holy Land led by the future King Edward I of England, in the course of which he made a few minor territorial gains – and famously survived an assassination attempt.

DISPUTES OVER NUMBERING

The labelling of the nine crusades is arbitrary. There were not only a large number of other smaller crusades between those summarized above, but also many other campaigns that were promoted as crusades with the grant of indulgences after 1271 – at least until the Battle of Lepanto in 1571, between the Christian 'Holy League' (of the papal states, Spain, Venice, Genoa, the Duchy of Savoy and the Knights of Malta) against the fleet of the Ottoman empire, if not even later.

Moreover, the nine crusades in the traditional list include: one (the Fourth) that got no farther than Constantinople, two (the Fifth and the Seventh) directed not at the Holy Land but at Egypt, and one (the Eighth) that diverted to Tunisia and ran out of steam there. There were many other crusades in Europe that do not make it into the traditional list. These were fought

in Spain and Portugal against Muslims, in the Baltic region against pagans, in southern France and Bohemia against Christians declared heretics by the Catholic Church, and in Italy against enemies of the papacy.

As a result of these complications, historians question the traditional numbering. Some identify the Sixth Crusade (1228–29), the campaign by Holy Roman Emperor Frederick II, on which he regained possession of Jerusalem and Bethlehem through diplomacy, as part of the Fifth Crusade (1217–21), the campaign to Egypt under the command of papal legate Pelagius – for Frederick was pledged to join the Fifth Crusade but did not arrive despite the fact that a German army was in Egypt awaiting his command. Some see the Ninth Crusade (1271–72) on which the future King Edward I of England campaigned briefly in the Holy Land, as part of the Eighth Crusade (1270), the all-too-brief campaign during which King Louis IX of France died during the siege of Tunis.

It follows that historians disagree as to the total number of crusades. In the 18th century some counted eight crusades while some insisted there were just five (the First, Second, Third, Fifth and

▲ *Louis IX's ships on the Nile battle against the Saracens during the 7th Crusade.*

Seventh). Many modern historians also limit the numbered crusades to just five, but usually number only the first five from the traditional list and then describe the rest by name.

In this book, for reasons of clarity and ease of comparison with other reference sources, we will follow the traditional numbering from the First to Ninth Crusades and refer to other campaigns by name (usually that of the destination or leader) and date. Minor (unnumbered) crusades to the Holy Land or those aimed at restoring Christian power in the Holy Land are treated in the progression of the main narrative, but the crusades directed against Muslims in the Iberian Peninsula, against pagans in central and northern Europe, against heretic Christians in France and Bohemia and against enemies of the Church in Italy are treated in a separate chapter.

◄ *The Knights of St John defend the island of Rhodes against Ottoman attack in 1480.*

INTERPRETATIONS OF
THE CRUSADES

Just as the number and scope of the crusades are not well defined, so their historical and cultural meaning is the subject of energetic debate. Historians disagree over which campaigns should be classed as crusades and over when the crusades ended, and argue over the effect and legacy of the crusades. Part of the continuing fascination with various aspects of the crusades lies in their almost chameleon-like quality, their accessibility to widely different interpretations.

The crusades have been cast as an attempt to defend the Christian faith, to protect the pilgrims travelling to the Holy Land and the pilgrim sites they visited. They have been represented as a more cynical effort to impose the authority of the pope in Rome across the Orthodox Church of the East. These wars have also been described as a brilliant intervention by the Church to control the aggression of the knightly class and provide an outlet for it, or else to give members of the laity an opportunity to express their piety and religious devotion.

Again, the crusades have been considered an expression of the military power of an international knightly class that was closely bound across countries and sought an external enemy. The conflicts have been represented as wars of opportunity, a chance for lesser members of royal and noble households, and for those lower down the social scale to make a name for themselves while seeking land and wealth. They have been seen as an outpouring of racism and hatred – merely an excuse for violence and religious persecution. It is clear in reference to this last point that the rhetoric used by Urban and later crusade preachers unleashed feelings of religious rage that were difficult to control, and that already in 1096 (and several times afterwards) gave rise to racist and religious attacks by crusader armies on Jewish communities in Europe.

RESONANCE

The crusades retain a great fascination and have a powerful resonance for modern readers. The word 'crusade' for this reason is a heavily loaded one. From the 17th century onwards, European writers began to use the word to describe a committed, worthy but not violent struggle – in this context, a crusade would be launched to counter a medical condition such as polio or a social ill such as drunkenness. But the term remained in use to describe a military campaign when a speaker wanted to mobilize feelings of righteous indignation (and perhaps provoke a feeling of moral

▲ Centuries of crusading campaigns against the Moors of Spain and Portugal came to a climax with the conquest of Granada by the armies of Ferdinand and Isabella in 1492.

superiority). On 6 June 1944, for example, US President Franklin D Roosevelt's prayer to mark the launch of the Allied forces' D-Day campaign in Normandy called the struggle against Nazi Germany 'our united crusade'.

More controversially, in September 2001, in the wake of the terrorist attacks on the United States, President George W Bush called his declared 'war on terror' a 'crusade'. He subsequently had to withdraw the label in the face of protest that it caused offence to Muslims and Jews because of the great violence against their communities during the crusading campaigns of the Middle Ages. The word's resonance remains so strong that supporters of Arab independence denounce the very presence of Western powers in the Middle East as a 'crusade'. In Islamic

◄ The Dominican friars sent to counter the Cathars in France were not welcomed.

communities the name 'crusaders' or 'Franks' (from the large Frankish, or French, contingent in the early crusade armies and among the settlers in the Christian Kingdom of Jerusalem) were for centuries a hate name, summoning the image of violent, boorish and unsophisticated foreigners.

There is no doubt that as a whole the crusaders came nowhere near any Biblical ideal of Christian behaviour, and that many were just as bloodthirsty, uncultured and brutal as their Eastern critics declared. Some of the crusaders were driven by greed and the lust for power – and exhibited cynical opportunism. They indulged in acts of barbarity, often driven by fear and group hysteria. We may think that some of their acts, goals and judgements were simply deluded.

Yet the extraordinary enterprise of the crusader armies retains an undeniable heroic element – and herein lies another part of the continuing appeal for modern audiences. A good number of those who participated may have merely professed to be taking the cross for religious reasons while secretly hoping to find land, wealth or simply adventure. But another large contingent of crusaders genuinely committed themselves to crusading for religious reasons, and for these people, taking the cross was an act of self-denial, of committing to a larger cause. In entering on a seemingly impossible enterprise

▲ *Continuing fascination with the crusades was reflected in the success of the 2005 movie* Kingdom of Heaven.

with faith, self-belief and a willingness to risk death, these crusaders exhibited human qualities that we still find broadly admirable in other contexts – for example, in a mountaineer determined to conquer a peak at all costs or in an explorer disappearing into the wilderness with a burning desire to reach his goal.

RELEVANCE

Accounts of the crusades inspired generations of Europeans in the Middle Ages, finding an audience eager for accounts of adventure, acts of sometimes foolhardy bravery and undying chivalry beneath the burning sun in deserts, mountains, towns and cities familiar from biblical history. This appeal remains alive today. At the same time, the bloody legacy of the events described in this book makes the subject of the crusades one of contemporary importance: the crusades had their noble and heroic side, but they also cast a deeply troubling shadow and left a lasting historical legacy. The study of the causes and events of these medieval wars of faith remains relevant at a time when religious and political leaders still seek to mobilize followers by summoning the memory of the crusades and the spirit of jihad.

◄ *Modern Jerusalem, three times a holy city: to Jews, as the City of David; to Muslims, as the city from which Muhammad ascended to heaven in his Night Journey; to Christians, as the scene of Christ's crucifixion, burial and resurrection.*

PART ONE

THE FIRST AND SECOND CRUSADES

When Pope Urban II finished the great speech at Clermont in 1095 in which he called knights to the First Crusade, those who rushed to obey his summons at once began to adorn their clothing with the sign of the cross – and the cross was soon established as the sign beneath which the crusader knights rode into battle. In its original biblical context the cross was a symbol of Christ's intense physical suffering, and of his refusal to foment violence and take up arms; through centuries it became emblematic of the power of God and of Christianity, and was worn by pilgrims. But in the hands of the crusade preachers and the knights they inspired, the cross turned into a symbol of dedication and military vigour – an icon that inspired faith, a badge of honour to be worn by those who signed up for the perilous journey to the Holy Land and a sign of the salvation they were seeking. It symbolized the faith and obedience embodied in the cry 'God wills it!' that arose following Urban II's speech, the shout that became the battle cry of the crusader knights on campaign.

▲ *Muslim horsemen often pretended to flee. Crusaders lost many a battle by charging recklessly in pursuit of a feigned retreat.*

▶ *The knights who responded to Urban's call to arms were inspired by tales of the religious campaigns of Charlemagne and his knights, seen here beseiging the walls of Pamplona in AD778.*

TIMELINE

March 1095 Byzantine Emperor Alexius Comnenus I sends envoys asking Pope Urban II for help against the Seljuk Turks.
27 November 1095 At Clermont, Pope Urban II calls Christian knights to arms, launching the First Crusade.
1095 Pope Urban declares that Christians fighting Moors in Spain would win full crusading privileges.
April 1096 The first two waves of the People's Crusade, one led by Walter Sans Avoir and one by Peter the Hermit, depart for the Holy Land.
May 1096 Crusaders under Count Emicho of Leisingen carry out attacks on Jewish communities in the Rhineland.
1 August 1096 The armies of the People's Crusade arrive in Constantinople.
21 October 1096 The People's Crusade is routed by Seljuk Turks in Anatolia.
November 1096–May 1097 Crusade armies led by Hugh of Vermandois, Godfrey of Bouillon, Bohemond of Taranto, Raymond of Toulouse and Robert of Normandy arrive in Constantinople.
6 May 1097 Crusaders begin siege of Nicaea, capital of the sultanate of Rum.
19 June 1097 Following secret negotiations, Nicaea surrenders – to Byzantine emperor Alexius Comnenus I.
1 July 1097 Crusaders defeat Seljuk Turks at the Battle of Dorylaeum.
21 October 1097 Crusaders begin the siege of Antioch.
December 1097 Bohemond of Taranto and Robert of Flanders defeat a Turkish army under Sultan Duqaq of Damascus.
January 1098 Morale is low among the crusaders, who suffer severe famine; many, including Peter the Hermit, desert.
9 February 1098 Bohemond of Taranto defeats a relief army under Radwan, Seljuk ruler of Aleppo at Harenc, 25 miles (40km) from Antioch.
10 March 1098 Baldwin of Boulogne creates crusader state: the County of Edessa.
April 1098 Embassy from Fatimid Egypt

▲ *Moors besiege a Christian castle in Spain.*

arrives at Antioch, offering crusaders possession of Syria if they agree not to attack Jerusalem. The crusaders decline the offer.
2 June 1098 Stephen of Blois begins march north to Constantinople.
3 June 1098 Crusaders capture Antioch. The citadel remains in Turkish hands.
6 June 1098 Relief army led by Sultan Kerbogha of Mosul arrives at Antioch and begins siege of crusaders within city.
14 June 1098 Peter Bartholomew claims to have discovered the Holy Lance in the city of Antioch.
28 June 1098 Crusaders defeat Sultan Kerbogha in battle outside Antioch. The citadel surrenders.
December 1098 Crusaders from Antioch capture nearby Maarrat an-Numan.
January 1099 Raymond of Toulouse leads the crusade army south from Antioch, bound for Jerusalem.
January 1099 Bohemond of Taranto establishes the second crusader state, the Principality of Antioch.
8 April 1099 Peter Bartholomew undergoes 'Ordeal By Fire' in an attempt to prove that his claimed discovery of the Holy Lance in Antioch was genuine. He is severely injured and dies on 20 April.
May 1099 Crusaders capture Tortosa and march down the coast as far as Arsuf.
5-6 June 1099 Tancred of Hautveille and Baldwin of Le Bourg capture Bethlehem, birthplace of Christ.

7 June 1099 Crusaders begin the siege of the city of Jerusalem.
13 June 1099 Crusade army fails in assault on Jerusalem.
7–9 July 1099 Crusaders hold a three-day penitential fast prior to renewing their assault on the city.
15 July 1099 The crusaders capture Jerusalem. For two days, 15–16 July, they run amok, killing and looting.
22 July 1099 Godfrey of Bouillon is elected Defender of the Holy Sepulchre.
1 August 1099 Arnulf of Choques is elected Patriarch of Jerusalem.
5 August 1099 Patriarch Arnulf announces he has found a piece of the True Cross (the cross on which Christ was crucified) in Jerusalem.
12 August 1099 Godfrey of Bouillon consolidates the victory in Jerusalem by defeating a 50,000-strong Fatimid relief army in the Battle of Ascalon.
1100 Pope Paschal II calls a new crusade in response to calls from crusader lords for reinforcements.
18 July 1100 Godfrey of Bouillon dies; his brother Baldwin of Edessa is elected his replacement.
September 1100 Crusader troops are mobilized in response to Pope Paschal's call to arms depart from Italy.
25 December 1100 Baldwin of Edessa is crowned King of Jerusalem.
1100 Patriarch Arnulf is replaced by Dagobert of Pisa, the new papal legate. Arnulf becomes Archdeacon of Jerusalem.
June 1101 The Italian crusaders, fighting alongside Byzantine troops commanded by Raymond of Toulouse and a French–Burgundian–German force under Stephen of Blois, are routed by Seljuks.
1101 The Kingdom of Jerusalem captures Caesarea and Arsuf.
May 1104 The Kingdom is further expanded with the capture of Acre.
1107 King Sigurd I of Norway embarks on crusade.

12 July 1109 After a long siege Tripoli surrenders to crusaders and Bertrand, illegitimate son of crusader lord Raymond of Toulouse, becomes ruler of the fourth crusader state, the County of Tripoli.

May 1110 The Kingdom of Jerusalem captures Beirut.

4 December 1110 King Baldwin I and King Sigurd I of Norway capture Sidon.

1110 Tancred of Hauteville, veteran of the First Crusade and regent of Antioch, captures the castle of Krak des Chevaliers.

15 February 1113 Pope Paschal II recognizes the monastic order of the Hospitallers of St John of Jerusalem.

1113 Paschal II recognizes the Equestrian order of the Holy Sepulchre of Jerusalem.

1114 In Spain Count Berenguer of Barcelona leads a crusade against the Muslim-held Balearic islands.

1118 Pope Gelasius II declares a crusade against the Moors in Spain.

2 April 1118 King Baldwin I of Jerusalem dies and is succeeded by his cousin Baldwin of Le Bourg as Baldwin II.

19 December 1118 Crusaders in Spain capture the city of Saragossa.

28 June 1119 Artuqid Turkish ruler Ilghazi inflicts crushing defeat on Christian army in the Battle of the Field of Blood.

1122 Pope Calixtus II calls crusades to the Holy Land and Spain. A large fleet sails for Jerusalem from Venice.

c.1123 The brotherhood of the Order of St Lazarus of Jerusalem is established.

1124 With the help of Venetian crusaders, the Kingdom of Jerusalem captures Tyre.

January 1128 Knights Templar recognized at the Council of Troyes.

21 August 1131 King Baldwin II of Jerusalem dies and is succeeded by his daughter Melisende and her husband Fulk of Anjou. They rule as Queen Melisende and King Fulk.

1135 Pope Innocent III offers crusade indulgences for those fighting antipope Anacletus II.

13 Nov 1143 King Fulk of Jerusalem dies and is succeeded by his wife Melisende, co-ruling with their son Baldwin III.

24 December 1144 Turkish general Imad ed-Din Zengi captures the capital of the crusader state of Edessa.

1 December 1145 Pope Eugenius III calls the Second Crusade.

1 March 1146 Eugenius III reissues his call to arms, authorizing Bernard of Clairvaux to preach the crusade.

Easter Day 1146 Bernard preaches the crusade at Vezelay in central France. King Louis VII takes the cross.

25 December 1146 Another crusade sermon by Bernard of Clairvaux inspires Conrad II of Germany to take the cross.

1146 While the Second Crusade is being preached, violence breaks out against Jews in the Rhineland.

13 April 1147 Pope Eugenius III guarantees full crusading privileges to those fighting pagan Wends in the Baltic.

May–June 1147 Armies of the Second Crusade set out for the Holy Land.

July–September 1147 German crusaders campaign against pagan Wends.

mid-September 1147 German crusade army arrives at Constantinople.

24 October 1147 Crusaders aid in the capture of Lisbon from the Moors.

25 October 1147 In Anatolia German

▼ *Kurdish general Saladin the Great.*

crusaders are defeated by Seljuk Turks.

8 January 1148 French crusaders are defeated by Seljuk Turks in Turkey.

19 March 1148 King Louis VII of France arrives in Antioch.

24 June 1148 The Council of Acre determines the future direction of the Second Crusade and decides to attack Damascus.

23 July 1148 Crusader armies arrive at Damascus and lay siege to the city.

28 July 1148 After the arrival of a relief army under Nur ed-Din, crusaders abandon the siege of Damascus. This marks the end of the Second Crusade.

29 June 1149 Nur ed-Din defeats and kills Raymond, Prince of Antioch.

1153 Baldwin III takes power in his own right as King of Jerusalem.

1154 Nur ed-Din captures Damascus.

10 February 1162 King Baldwin III of Jerusalem is succeeded by King Amalric I.

26 September 1164 Pope Alexander III recognizes the Spanish military brotherhood of the Order of Calatrava.

1164–69 A power struggle in Egypt ends in March 1169 with Salah ed-Din Yusuf (later called Saladin) as vizier of Egypt.

c.1170 Spanish military brotherhood of Order of Santiago is established.

11 July 1174 King Amalric I of Jerusalem is succeeded by his son Baldwin IV.

October 1174 Saladin takes Damascus.

25 November 1177 Baldwin IV defeats Saladin at the Battle of Montgisard.

1180 Pope Alexander III approves the establishment of the Knights of Our Lady of Mountjoie in Jerusalem.

1185 Baldwin IV dies and is succeeded by his nephew Baldwin V with Raymond of Tripoli as regent.

1186 Baldwin V dies and is succeeded by his mother Sibylla. She rules as Queen with Guy of Lusignan as her consort.

4 July 1187 Saladin wins a decisive victory in the Battle of the Horns of Hattin.

8 July 1187 Acre surrenders to Saladin.

4 September 1187 Saladin takes Ascalon.

20 September 1187 Saladin besieges the city of Jerusalem.

2 October 1187 Saladin succeeds in recapturing Jerusalem.

THE KINGDOMS OF PALESTINE

To understand the movements of the great crusading armies, and appreciate the drama of their adventures, it is helpful to know the routes they took and the boundaries they crossed.

Tracing the long and dangerous journey made on the First Crusade underlines the enterprise's vast ambition and daring (shown on the map below). From central and northern Europe, some from as far north as England, or from southern France, by a variety of routes – across the Holy Roman Empire and Hungary, or through Italy and by sea across the southern Adriatic – the great armies marched under the banner of the cross to Constantinople, capital of the Byzantine empire, then on across Anatolia and down the Mediterranean coast towards their glittering goal, the Holy City of Jerusalem.

Across these thousands of miles trailed many, many thousand men (and some women), first the somewhat ragged forces of the People's Crusade – according to Byzantine princess Anna Comnena, to see them was 'like looking at rivers flooding together from all directions' – then no fewer than five princely armies. The routes of the four main princely armies are detailed on the map. Faith and the inspirational words of Urban II and the crusade preachers drove them on and helped them keep their nerve: this was a great adventure but also a daunting and frequently terrifying challenge. In taking the cross many had cried 'God wills it!' and the belief that they were destined to achieve their goal bore the core of the crusaders onward in the face of hardship, defeats and the deaths of comrades. More than

three years elapsed between the departure of the first elements of the People's Crusade in April 1096 and the bloody capture of Jerusalem in July 1099.

JERUSALEM

With the Holy City in Christian hands for the first time since AD638, the crusaders began building. They erected a palace beside the al-Aqsa Mosque, in the place

▼ *The first of the main princely armies to depart was that of Godfrey of Bouillon, who left Lorraine in August 1096. Bohemond of Taranto set sail from Bari in October 1096. At the same time Raymond of Toulouse left southern France and Robert of Flanders set out from the north. Their combined forces took Nicaea in June 1097 and marched across the Sultanate of Rum.*

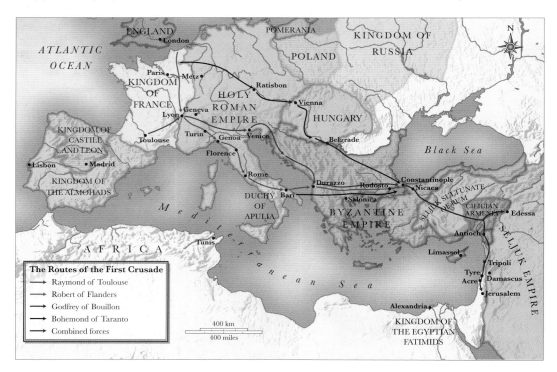

The Routes of the First Crusade
→ Raymond of Toulouse
→ Robert of Flanders
→ Godfrey of Bouillon
→ Bohemond of Taranto
→ Combined forces

400 km
400 miles

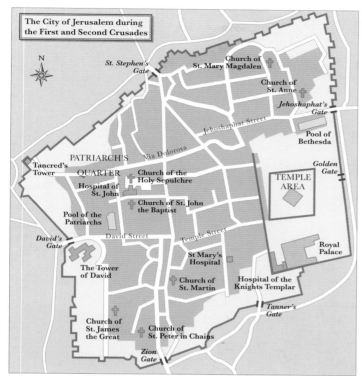

The City of Jerusalem during the First and Second Crusades

Saladin and his troops captured Acre and other strongholds along the Mediterranean coast: from Acre he headed north and took Sidon and Beirut, then marched south and took Jaffa and Ascalon before moving inland to capture Jerusalem on 2 October 1187. He campaigned again in 1188, in the north, and won several further victories, including the capture of the fortress of Saone. But he did not take Tyre, and this would be an invaluable foothold for a Christian revival in the Holy Land.

▼ *Saladin campaigned at great speed, determined not to allow the Christians to regroup. He took Acre just four days after the victory at the Horns of Hattin, then captured Ascalon, during a solar eclipse, exactly two months after Hattin. By 20 September he had marched inland to begin the siege of Jerusalem.*

The Conquests of Saladin

▲ *Pilgrims entered the city by David's Gate in the west and went directly to the Church of the Holy Sepulchre. Christ reputedly entered the city on Palm Sunday through the Golden Gate, beside the Temple Area.*

crucified, and the site of his tomb. Pilgrims visiting Jerusalem could follow the 'Way of the Cross' from the site of Pontius Pilate's palace on Jehoshaphat Street to the site of Christ's crucifixion and burial.

believed to be the site of the ancient Temple. Later this became the headquarters of the Knights Templar, and a new palace was built in the west of the city at the Tower of David, by David's Gate. In this place King David had reputedly written the Book of Psalms in the 11th-10th century BC. Under the Muslims, bells had been banned from churches, but now they were restored and rang out over the capital of a Christian kingdom in the Holy Land, a city perceived as the centre of the world.

In the course of 50 years to c.1150 the crusaders built the great Romanesque Church of the Holy Sepulchre, containing the rock of Calvary on which Christ was

THE CONQUESTS OF SALADIN

Less then a century later, beginning in July 1187, Muslim leader Saladin won a series of victories that brought the Christian Kingdom of Jerusalem close to extinction (shown in the map right). Crossing the River Jordan from the east with an army of around 30,000 on 30 June 1187, Saladin defeated Guy of Lusignan, King of Jerusalem, and a 20,000-strong army in the Battle of the Horns of Hattin on 4 July. Jerusalem was an easy target after this victory, in which the crusaders famously lost their treasured relic of the 'True Cross' on which Christ died, for the Kingdom's military force was all but wiped out.

CHAPTER ONE

HOLY WAR

Knights such as Godfrey of Bouillon and Robert of Flanders won enduring fame on the First Crusade of 1096–99, their exploits quickly embroidered in legends. Yet for every knight such as Godfrey or Robert there were many other crusaders who died uncelebrated and in wretched circumstances – of starvation, of disease, in battle or ambush – many having brought financial ruin on themselves after borrowing very heavily to make the trip. It can be difficult at a distance of several centuries to see why so many men (and women) were moved to risk so much on such a venture. A key explanation is that they were inspired to view the enterprise as a holy war – they saw themselves as the latterday counterparts of the Israelites, whose struggles against enemies of their faith were an inspirational prototype of the crusades. The biblical warrior Judas Maccabeus is said, according to the Second Book of Maccabees, to have gone into battle with a golden sword given to him in a vision by the prophet Jeremiah with words that could happily have given service as a blessing for medieval knights: 'Take this holy sword, a gift from God, wherewith thou shalt overthrow the adversaries of my people Israel'. Judas's soldiers followed him into battle in a manner that was equally suited as inspiration for the crusaders' assault on Jerusalem: 'Thus being exhorted with the words of Judas, which were very good, and proper to stir up the courage, and strengthen the hearts of the young men, they resolved to fight, and set upon them manfully; that valour might decide the matter, because the Holy City and the temple were in danger.'

▲ *The pope had the spiritual authority to judge even royal sinners.*

◄ *The army of Bohemond of Taranto comes under attack while trying to cross the River Vardar en route to fight in the First Crusade. The journey was long and arduous.*

FIGHTING A HOLY WAR
THEORIES OF JUST AND SACRED WARS

The Benedictine historian Guibert, Abbot of Nogent-sous-Coucy, author in the early 12th century of a chronicle of the First Crusade, declared that 'God has instituted in these days sacred wars, so that the body of knights … can find a means of winning their salvation'. Guibert may have suggested that holy wars were created in his era by a watchful God, but in truth the idea of fighting a just and divinely sanctioned war had its origins centuries earlier, and had roots as far back as the biblical era.

THE EXAMPLE OF THE OLD TESTAMENT

There are many examples in the Old Testament of the Bible of warfare waged on God's instructions or in his name. The God celebrated in the Old Testament appeared to use warfare to achieve his ends; he himself dealt in death. According to the Book of Exodus (Chapter 15), after

▼ *The anger of Israel's warlike God brought ruin on the Egyptians when the Red Sea closed over them, allowing the Israelites to travel on towards the Promised Land.*

escaping from captivity in Egypt the Israelites sang a hymn of praise in which they joyously celebrated their miraculous escape, the parting of the Red Sea and the death of their enemies in its waters: 'The Lord is a man of war: the Lord is his name … Pharaoh's chariots and his host hath he cast into the sea … the depths have covered them: they sank into the bottom as a stone. Thy right hand, O Lord, is become glorious in power: thy right hand, O Lord, hath dashed in pieces the enemy.'

The Old Testament God did call on his people to kill on his behalf – for example, when he instructed King Saul (David's predecessor as the king of Israel): 'Thus saith the Lord of hosts, I remember that which Amalek did to Israel, how he laid wait for him in the way, when he came up from Egypt. Now go and smite Amalek, utterly destroy all that they have, and spare them not; but slay both man and woman, infant and suckling, ox, sheep, camel and ass' (1 Samuel 15: verses 2–3).

A gallery of Israelite warriors, including David, Gideon and Joshua, were venerated as proponents of righteous warfare, even as exemplars of the knightly

▲ *'And I beheld when He had opened the sixth seal, and, lo, there was a great earthquake …' Martial language, such as this quote from the Book of Revelation encouraged Christians to believe that God sanctioned the use of violence.*

code of chivalry; chief among them and celebrated alongside David and Joshua among the 'Nine Worthies' of the biblical, classical and chivalric worlds was Judas Maccabeus, guerrilla fighter against Seleucid overlords of Jerusalem in the 2nd century BC.

Judas Maccabeus was said to have led his warriors into battle 'fighting with their hands, but praying to the Lord with their hearts' and in battle 'they slew no less than five and thirty thousand'; in the midst of this carnage they were 'greatly cheered with the presence of God'. This quotation is from Chapter 15 of the Second Book of Maccabees, part of the Old Testament for Roman Catholics and Eastern Orthodox Christians but in modern times usually considered by Protestant Christians to be in the Apocrypha, a selection of texts that is associated with the Bible but not seen as part of it.

▲ St Augustine, kneeling, was inspired by the preaching of St Ambrose, right, the Bishop of Milan. Both men were great intellectuals and rhetoricians who developed theories of a just use of violence.

VIOLENCE OF THE LAST DAYS

In the New Testament, Christian knights and their clerical supporters drew on the warlike imagery of descriptions of the Day of Judgement in the Book of Revelation, in which celestial armies gave expression to the righteous anger of God, which was likened to a winepress. Many of the knights, clerics and ordinary people who travelled to the Holy Land on the First Crusade had a strong sense that they were living in the last days before the Second Coming of Christ, which gave a great sense of urgency to the need to achieve remission of sins. Moreover a key

incentive for travelling to Jerusalem was that the events of the Last Judgement were expected to be played out in the city where Christ died and was buried.

JUSTIFICATION OF HOLY WAR

Theoretical justifications of holy war drew on 4th- and 5th-century AD Christian writers, such as St Ambrose, Bishop of Milan, and his pupil St Augustine, Bishop of Hippo. These theologians drew on classical philosophy: in particular those of the 4th-century BC ancient Greek philosopher Aristotle, who developed the notion of a 'just war' waged for the purpose of maintaining peace; ancient Roman ideas that wars could justly be fought to defend oneself, to recover seized territory or property, or to inflict punishment on a wrongdoer as long as the war was fought with proper authority (of the state); and the theory of

the 1st-century BC Roman statesman Cicero, who argued that a just war had to be fought using just means or in the right way – for example, with bravery. As developed by St Augustine, the Christian theory of a just or holy war required that it be fought in self-defence or to recover a seized territory or possession, on proper authority, and with the right intentions and means by all involved. Augustine added that wars fought on God's authority did not breach the commandment forbidding killing.

These ideas of sanctioned violence, of just and sacred war, applied to public bodies, such as State or Church. Individuals were required to be obedient to these public bodies, and to fight if commanded to do so. But in their individual lives violence was not sanctioned, and here Christ's troubling commands to love thy neighbour and to show forgiveness applied. Here was the distinction between sanctioned violence carried out in defence of the Church under vows to maintain the peace of God, and private wars, the secular clashes between knights that were condemned by the Church.

▼ Augustine urged Christians to focus on a mystical heavenly Jerusalem in his work The City of God, written shortly after 410.

DEFENDERS OF THE FAITH

CHRISTIAN WARRIORS IN A HOLY WAR

The great Norman crusader lord Tancred of Hauteville was filled with energy, according to his biographer Radulph of Caen, by Pope Urban II's call to the First Crusade. Before departing on crusade, Radulph writes, Tancred was disturbed by the disjunction between on the one hand the demands of life as a feudal knight, which required him to wage war, and on the other the teaching of Christ to turn the other cheek and act with generosity to the needy. The new idea of crusading, in which waging war against pagans was presented as a form of devotional penance for Christian knights, was tailor-made to address such a difficulty, and Tancred responded with enthusiasm: in Radulph's words, 'as if he had previously been asleep, he came awake, his energy was aroused, his strength increased, his seeing grew sharper and his bravery was born'.

In the context of energizing knights to fight for the Church in distant lands, Pope Urban's conflation of waging war and doing penance was a stroke of genius, and a new departure. But the idea of fighting a holy war – and of being a holy warrior – was not a new one: Radulph may well have been overstating Tancred's sense of discomfort at the disjunction between his life as a knight and his life as a devout Christian. For the knights who travelled on the First Crusade were descendants of Germanic tribes whose warrior-band philosophy, incorporating celebration of the military lord and of feats of martial vigour, had had a profound effect on thinking and writing about the Christian faith in the centuries since they had been converted in the 5th and 6th centuries AD.

▲ *In the 5th century, King Clovis of the Salian Franks began his people's long association with the Catholic Church when he converted to Christianity in order to marry Princess Clotilde. The faith became increasingly militarized.*

Figures such as Clovis I, the first Frankish king to convert to Christianity, and his successor, Charlemagne, were viewed as warrior heroes as much as they were Christian kings. Christian language and thought became infused with Germanic warrior imagery. For example, in the masterful 8th-century Anglo-Saxon poem *The Dream of the Rood*, the poet uses very military language in describing his dream of seeing Christ on the cross, calling Christ the 'young hero', 'the warrior', 'the Prince' and 'the Lord of Victories', and envisages Christ's actions on the cross as those of a fearless warrior.

HOLY WAR AND DIPLOMACY

One key divide between the westerners, or 'Latins', who travelled on crusade and the easterners, or 'Greeks', they went to help, derived from a distinctly different outlook on life, particularly when it came to diplomacy and war.

The Latins had a developed theory of the just, or holy, war and of the righteousness of combat, but the Greeks viewed conflict only as a last resort and preferred to settle disagreements through diplomacy and compromise. Many of the Latins were only a few generations separated from forebears among the Viking raiders, and the Greeks saw them as uncultured barbarians; for their part, the Latins viewed the Greeks as untrustworthy – particularly in their willingness to negotiate and sign treaties with Muslim powers.

FIGHTING TO PROMOTE CHRISTIANITY

Battle imagery invaded Christian thought, and Christian practices found a place on the battlefield. King Alfred of Wessex prayed with his commanders before battle and his warriors had Christian images on their weapons; in chronicles his wars were always presented as being for Christianity against pagans. Likewise, Charlemagne's battles against pagan enemies such as the Saxons were presented as holy wars. For the 'pagans', the price of defeat by Alfred or by Charlemagne was forcible conversion to Christianity. Such a war was self-evidently a holy one, fought in order to spread the faith. The empire that Charlemagne built was an explicitly Christian one.

FIGHTING TO DEFEND CHRISTIANITY AND THE CHURCH

From c.850 onwards when Charlemagne's empire began to fall apart, the chief foes were marauding pagans – Vikings, 'Saracens' (Muslim Arabs and Berbers) and Magyars. Fighting against these raiders

▲ *Christian Emperor Charlemagne leads his army at the walls of Pamplona, Spain, 778, from a 14th-century manuscript.*

was a defence of Christianity and the idea of 'Christendom' began to inform debate. The community of European peoples who had once been united under the Frankish empire were now bound by their common Christian faith and their opposition to non-Christian, pagan enemies.

In the 9th and 10th centuries, moreover, in increasingly lawless times, church authorities began to promote the theory that armed warriors had a responsibility to protect the weak, and particularly the Church. The churchmen promoted the Peace of God, under which warriors would swear to protect those who were not equipped to protect themselves – principally clergy and monks. In this context, fighting was a form of piety.

This initiative did more than condemn attacks on church property, going as far as to encourage violence in the interests of preventing lawless attacks. As with Urban's call to arms at Clermont, in the Peace of God initiative the Church was not simply giving its blessing to violence, it was rather bringing violence into being.

Throughout the period there were also those churchmen who resisted the glorification of violence, who continued to promote the monastic or clerical life as the ideal Christian one. Killing remained officially a sin. The Norman soldiers who fought at Hastings under William the Conqueror were required to do penance for the blood they had spilled, despite the fact that they were fighting under a papal banner (with the pope's backing) and the explicit approval of their clergy.

▼ *At Hastings in 1066 Christian Normans fought Christian Anglo-Saxons. Duke William's men were supported by the pope.*

MUSLIM EMPIRES
THE SPREAD OF ISLAM

In the late 11th century, prior to the First Crusade, control of the eastern Mediterranean was divided between the Christian Byzantine Empire based in Constantinople, the Sunni Muslim Seljuk Turks nominally ruled from Baghdad, rival Seljuk groups in Anatolia with a capital at Nicaea, and Shi'ite Muslim Fatimids from northern Africa. In eastern Anatolia the Muslim Turkish Danishmends were also a force to be reckoned with.

THE ISLAMIC EXPANSION

The great expansion of Islam began from the Arabian Peninsula in the 7th century AD. In the hundred years following the death of the Prophet Muhammad – founder of the faith – in 632, Muslim warriors created a vast empire stretching from Spain in the west to parts of China and India in the east, and encompassing Palestine, Syria and Mesopotamia.

▼ *Islamic warriors spread north, taking on the Persian and Byzantine empires, then eastwards across Africa to Spain by 711.*

THE PROPHET AND HIS TEACHING

The Prophet Muhammad was born in c.570 in the caravan city of Mecca, Arabia, a member of the Quaraish tribe. He began to preach in around 613 and established the new faith of Islam in exile from Mecca at Yathrib (later known as Medina, the City of the Prophet) in 620–30, before returning to Mecca from 630 until his death two years later.

Muhammad taught that there was one God, named Allah, Creator of all that existed, who demanded honour and submission from humans – the word *Islam* means 'surrender' (that is, to the will of Allah), while *Muslims* are so called from the Arabic for 'those who submit'. *Allah* was another name for the 'God of the Christians and the Jews'. Muhammad's teachings were gathered in the Koran, which his followers said completed and superseded the Christian and Jewish books; Muhammad was the final prophet in a sequence that also included Noah, Abraham and Jesus.

▲ *Angels Gabriel, Michael, Israfil and Azrail attend on the Prophet as he travels to Mecca. One of a set of 16th-century Ottoman illustrations on Muhammad's life.*

THE FIRST ISLAMIC LEADERS

Following the death of Muhammad in Mecca in 632, one of his followers, named Abu Bakr, a merchant and member of a minor clan in the Prophet's Quaraish tribe,

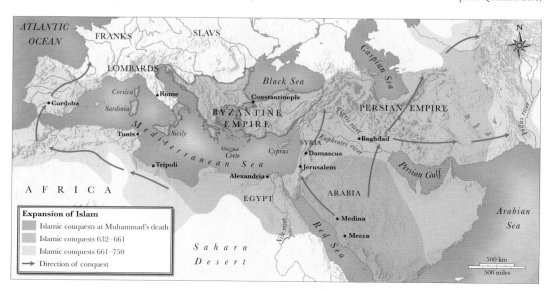

Expansion of Islam
- Islamic conquests at Muhammad's death
- Islamic conquests 632–661
- Islamic conquests 661–750
- → Direction of conquest

was elected as *khalifat rasul Allah* (Successor to God's Prophet) or 'caliph': the spiritual and political leader of the faithful. He died in 634, but before his death appointed a successor, another merchant and a member of the Quaraish, named Omar bin Khattab.

Under Caliph Omar's rule (634–44), Muslim Bedouin tribesmen won astonishing victories against the Byzantine and Persian empires, defeating the Byzantines in Syria and the Persians in Mesopotamia. They took Damascus in 635. In 637 they captured the Persian capital Ctesiphon. In 638 they took Jerusalem. In the 640s they established themselves in Egypt, capturing Alexandria in 646. By this time Omar was dead. Disputes over the succession gave rise to schism and centuries-long enmity between Sunni and Shi'ite Islam.

SUNNI AND SHI'ITE SPLIT

Omar was succeeded by Othman ibn Affan, another merchant and also one of Muhammad's original converts and once again a member of Quaraish tribe of Mecca. There was opposition to his appointment, gathered around the Prophet's cousin and son-in-law Ali, husband of Muhammad's daughter Fatima. When Othman was murdered in 656, two rival caliphs vied to replace him: on the

▼ *This image of a Moorish army is from a manuscript made for King Alfonso X of Castile and Leon (r.1252–84).*

one hand Ali, and on the other, Mu'awiyah, a member of Umayyad clan, who had earlier been appointed Governor of Syria by Othman. In 661 both Ali and Mu'awiyah were stabbed as they prayed in mosques in separate cities – Ali later died, but Mu'awiyah survived. Ali's supporters appointed his son Hassan caliph, but in a confrontation with Mu'awiyah he backed down; then when Mu'awiyah died in 680, Ali's second son Hussein claimed the caliphate. In an encounter with Mu'awiyah's son Yazid on 10 October 680, Hussein and all his followers were killed.

The split between Shi'ite and Sunni Muslims derived from this power struggle. Sunnis backed the descendants of Mu'awiyah – the Umayyad caliphs – as the rightful leaders of Islam, but Shi'ites declared them usurpers and argued that Ali had inherited the spirit of Muhammad and that leadership of Islam should be from his descendants. The Shi'ites' name came from that of the followers of Ali in the 7th century – the *shi'at Ali* (the party of Ali), whereas the Sunni were so called because they said they were following the *sunna* (example) of Muhammad.

AN ISLAMIC EMPIRE IN SPAIN

Muslim Arabs spread westwards from Egypt through northern Africa. Their advance was temporarily held up by the Berbers of the Atlas Mountains but after constructing the fortified city of Kairouan (in modern Tunisia) they subdued the Maghreb region of north and north-western Africa, then under the great Arab general Tariw ibn-Ziyad, crossed the Straits of Gibraltar and in just five years took virtually the whole Iberian Peninsula from its previous rulers, the Visigoths.

Arabs began to raid beyond the Pyrenees Mountains into southern and western France. In 732 at the Battle of Tours the marauding Arabs finally met their match in a redoubtable army commanded by Charles Martel ('the Hammer'), King of the Franks. Thereafter the Arabs withdrew into Spain and consolidated their possessions there.

▲ *St James makes a miraculous appearance in the legendary Battle of Clavijo in 844.*

UMAYYADS, ABBASIDS AND FATIMIDS

In the east the Umayyad descendants of Caliph Mu'awiyah ruled the Islamic empire from Damascus until they were ousted in 750 by their cousins and rivals the Abbasids, who established the capital of the empire at Baghdad in Iraq. The Abbasids came to power with Shi'ite support but ruled as Sunni Muslims. In 909 militant Shi'ite Muslims established a rival Fatimid dynasty (claiming direct descent from the Prophet's daughter Fatima) in Tunis and built their capital at Cairo.

By the second half of the 10th century the balance of power in the western Mediterranean was between a resurgent Byzantine empire, which had re-established itself in Syria; the increasingly weak Abbasid caliphate in Baghdad, which had nominal control over Iran, Iraq and the remainder of Syria; and the Fatimids of Cairo, who had extended their territory up through Palestine.

THE RISE OF THE SELJUKS

Then the Seljuk Turks erupted onto the scene. Originally from central Asia, these Turkmen tribes converted to Sunni Islam, conquered Afghanistan and eastern Iran, and in 1055 took control of Baghdad. In the 1070s the Seljuks delivered a crushing blow to the Byzantine army at the Battle of Manzikert, capturing Syria and most of Palestine from the Fatimids.

CHRISTIANS IN THE EAST
THE 'EMPIRE OF THE GREEKS'

The Latin Christians led by the pope in Rome, the faithful who were summoned by Urban II to the First Crusade, did not have a close or easy relationship with their counterparts in the Eastern Church and the Byzantine Empire.

CHRISTIAN ORIGINS IN THE EAST

Christian presence in the eastern Mediterranean dates back to the 1st century AD, when saints Peter, Paul and Barnabus established the first Christian community in Antioch – its members were the first people in history to be called 'Christians'. The origins of the Christian Byzantine Empire lie in the 4th century, when Constantine, the first Roman emperor to support Christianity, established the city of Constantinople as a new capital for the Roman Empire.

Constantine built the city as Nova Roma (New Rome) on the site of the trading city of Byzantium, according to legend created in 667BC by Greek colonists led by

▼ *According to tradition, St Peter was the first Bishop of Antioch, then Bishop of Rome – and, as such, was the first pope.*

King Byzantas (or Byzas); New Rome was renamed Constantinople (the city of Constantine) after Constantine's death in AD337. In contrast to previous Roman emperors, who had persecuted Christians, Constantine announced that Christianity would be tolerated in the empire in 313 – traditionally he had won power after a vision had inspired him to fight under the sign of the Christian cross. He then laid the groundwork for the establishment of a Christian culture in the empire, although he was not himself baptized until shortly before his death. He called the Church's first ecumenical meeting, the Council of Nicaea, in 325. This council drew up the first statement of uniform Christian doctrine, the Nicene Creed.

Situated on the Bosphorus between the Black Sea and the Sea of Marmara, at the intersection of the mercantile routes of Asia and eastern Europe, Constantinople grew fabulously wealthy on the profits of trade. After the death of Emperor Theodosius I in 395, the Roman Empire was permanently split into eastern and western halves, ruled from Rome and Constantinople, respectively. Following the sacking of Rome by the Visigoths in 410 and the collapse of the eastern empire in Europe culminating in the deposition

▲ *Constantine the Great (left) founded Constantinople, while his mother St Helena (right) played an important part in Jerusalem's rise as a centre of pilgrimage.*

of the last emperor in Rome, Romulus Augustus, in 476 by the Germanic king Odoacer, the city of Constantine was the capital of the Byzantine Empire.

EXPANSION AND DECLINE

In the 7th and 8th centuries the Byzantine Empire came under repeated attack by the swiftly expanding Muslim empire. Several times, from 674, the Arabs attempted to take Constantinople itself, but without success; they were finally driven back from the city when the siege of 717 was decisively defeated by the Byzantine emperor Leo III. In the period 863–1025 the Byzantine Empire expanded greatly and at one point in 976 the Arabs were driven back as far as the very gates of Jerusalem. But after the death of Emperor Basil II in 1025, the empire's fortunes declined once more, and in the mid-11th century the Seljuk Turks erupted into the region, culminating in the severe defeat of the Byzantine army by the Seljuks at Manzikert in Armenia in 1071. This defeat lost the empire all its lands in Anatolia.

▲ *St Mark, author of the Gospel of Mark, is revered by Christians in north Africa, and was Bishop of Alexandria.*

CONFLICT WITHIN

The name 'Byzantine Empire', it should be noted, dates from the 16th century, when it was first used by a German historian. The rulers and citizens of the empire called it 'Roman', whereas those in western Europe called it the 'Empire of the Greeks'. From the 9th century onwards the great powers of Europe were increasingly in competition with the Byzantine Empire to determine who was the successor of ancient Rome – as well as being in dispute over territories in Italy. In 800 Charlemagne was crowned *Imperator Augustus* (August Emperor) by Pope Leo III in Rome, in an attempt to revive the Roman Empire in the west; he also bore the title *Patricius Romanorum* (Protector of the Romans). In the 10th century Otto II of the Germans married a Byzantine princess – Theopanu, niece of the Byzantine emperor John I Tzimisces – but was in conflict with the eastern empire and declared himself 'Roman emperor'.

TENSION BETWEEN WESTERN AND EASTERN CHURCHES

There was also conflict between the Church hierarchies of west and east. In 1054, the leaders of the Churches – Pope Leo IX in Rome and Patriarch Michael Cerularius in Constantinople – excommunicated one another. The tension went right back to the 5th century, when, following the fall of Rome, the pope assumed the mantle of protector of Christians in the west. Rome was the burial place of the Apostle Peter and the popes claimed direct succession from him and ultimate authority over the entire Church; but the patriarchs of Constantinople claimed they were the highest authority, since Constantinople was the seat of the eastern Roman Empire.

Matters of doctrine also caused controversy: the Eastern Church allowed married priests but the Latin Church insisted officially on celibacy of the priesthood; the Latin Church allowed the use of unleavened bread in the Mass but the Eastern Church was against this. Another major disagreement arose over whether in the Christian Trinity of Father, Son and Holy Spirit, the Spirit derived from the Father or from both the Father and the Son. The Nicene Creed had declared 'I believe in the Holy Spirit, the Lord the giver of Life, who proceedeth from the Father', but western churches had added the words 'and the Son'. This *filioque* clause (so called from the Latin word meaning 'from the Son') had first been used in Spain in the 7th century, then had been backed by Charlemagne, and had finally been accepted by the papacy in 1014; but it was vehemently rejected by the Eastern Church as heresy. In 1089 Urban II sent an embassy to Constantinople asking for full relations to recommence between Western and Eastern Churches but the division – later known to historians as the 'Great Schism' – endured.

▼ *The Byzantine Empire held territory in Italy. At Ravenna, the basilica of San Vitale contains this beautiful mosaic of Christ.*

THE POWER OF THE PAPACY
POPES STRUGGLE FOR INDEPENDENCE

The second half of the 11th century saw concerted attempts by the papacy to establish the Church in a strong position independent of secular power. The idea of fighting as a form of Christian devotion was taken a stage further when popes presented struggles in support of the papacy as holy wars.

Pope Leo IX (ruled 1049–54) personally led troops to war against Norman adventurers in southern Italy in 1053. He set the precedent of promising his soldiers absolution of their sins and remission of penance as their reward. In this campaign the papal army was defeated at the Battle of Civitate by a Norman force led by Humphrey of Hauteville and containing Robert Guiscard. Ten years later the Normans were papal allies: after Pope Nicholas II (ruled 1059–61) invested

▼ *Pope Gregory VII grants absolution to German emperor Henry IV in 1077. This was an important but temporary victory for the papacy in the long struggle to establish its independence from secular rulers.*

▲ *Cluny Abbey in France was at the forefront of Church reform in the 10th to 12th centuries and its abbot was second in power only to the pope. Otho of Lagery, later known as Pope Urban II, was a prior there. As pope, he visited the abbey in 1095.*

Robert Guiscard as duke of Apulia, Calabria and Sicily, the Norman army fought under a papal banner in invading Muslim Sicily. Another branch of the Norman family also had a papal banner for William of Normandy's invasion of England in 1066.

GREGORY VII AND ST PETER'S SOLDIERS

Pope Gregory VII (ruled 1073–85) became embroiled in a long-running dispute with the German emperor Henry IV (reigned 1056–1105). The main issue of contention in what is known to historians as 'the Investiture Controversy' was whether Henry or Gregory should control

▶ *Pope Leo X and Patriarch Michael Cerularius of Constantinople excommunicated one another in 1054. The quarrel had begun centuries before in a dispute over which church had primacy.*

the church: it was focused on who should have control over bishops' investiture (appointment and presentation of symbols of office) in the German church; it followed a period in which the papacy had been very weak, and Henry IV's predecessor, Henry III, had appointed three German popes. Gregory set out to mobilize his own papal force, the *Militia Sancti*

Petri (the 'army of St Peter'). He told the knights in his service that they were 'vassals of Saint Peter' and as reward would receive Peter's blessing 'in this life and the life to come'.

Gregory and Henry IV clashed dramatically. In 1076 Gregory excommunicated Henry and declared him *anathema*, which meant he was excluded from the community of Christian believers and that none of his subjects had to keep oaths made to him. German nobles forced Henry to back down and in January 1077 he travelled to the pope's castle at Canossa in northern Italy, where Gregory made him wait outside, barefoot and clad in a hair shirt in the snow, before finally allowing him in to receive forgiveness. This decisively changed the balance of power between pope and emperor, but only in the short term: Henry and Gregory clashed again and Gregory excommunicated Henry again in 1080; Henry attacked Rome three times between 1081 and 1084 and on the third occasion Gregory had to be rescued from his castle of Castel Sant'Angelo in the city by his ally and vassal, the Norman adventurer Robert Guiscard.

REFORM AND PAPAL POWER

Gregory is remembered as a 'reforming pope', because he attacked such abuses in the church as simony (the sale of Church offices) and tried to impose celibacy on the priesthood. Both these campaigns were tied up with his efforts to establish the absolute supremacy of the papacy – simony was beneficial to secular leaders who used it to bring about the appointment of their own supporters in key positions, and he made use of the campaign for celibacy to counter the power of rebel bishops who allowed married priests. He was passionately committed to the spiritual renewal of the Church.

GREGORY VII'S 'CRUSADE'

Gregory is also notable for his attempt to launch a forerunner of the crusades – a military expedition to help Constantinople and the Christians in the East in 1074.

THE ISSUING OF INDULGENCES

Popes used the promise of forgiveness, the remission of penances and the granting of indulgences as a lure to mobilize armies in their support. The issuing of indulgences derived from the idea that a punishment remained due for a sinner even when he or she had won forgiveness for a sin through repentance and confession; a sinner might win God's eternal forgiveness through genuine repentance but still be liable for a temporal punishment.

In the early Christian Church 'canonical penances' were calculated to wipe a sinner's slate clean, to do away with the temporal punishment; then in the early medieval Church, parts of the canonical penance were commuted – a repentant sinner was told he or she would achieve the same benefit by donating a specified amount of money to the Church, by giving alms to the poor or by spending an allotted period of time in fasting or prayer. Indulgences were usually partial – they commuted part of the punishment. The first recorded instance of an absolute or plenary indulgence that promised the complete avoidance of temporal punishment was the speech by Urban II at Clermont in 1095, when he issued his call to arms in the First Crusade. He declared: 'Whoever, acting out of devotion and not for the sake of winning honour or riches, travels to Jerusalem to free the Church of God may substitute this sacred journey for all penance.'

▼ *Pope Urban II at Clermont, where he issued his call to take up arms.*

Gregory made the attempt in response to a call in 1073 from Byzantine emperor Michael VII for help against the Seljuk Turks. In a manner that would have many echoes in Urban II's declaration at Clermont in 1095, Gregory promoted the enterprise in 1074 as an act of charity on behalf of those he hoped to involve, and claimed that they would be following the example of Christ, acting under the mandate of God himself; he also offered the promise of 'eternal reward'. Gregory did manage to raise an army but the enterprise foundered and the expedition did not set out.

The First Crusade was a direct descendant of the holy wars that were fought in the name of the papacy, since it was launched by the pope and fought with the aim of establishing his supremacy over the Eastern Church and his rule over a united Christendom. From the outset it was conceived by those involved in it as an expression of papal power.

THE HOLY CITY OF JERUSALEM

PLACE OF CHRIST'S PASSION, SACRED TO THREE FAITHS

Several medieval maps survive to the present day in which Jerusalem is represented as the centre of the Earth, which was at that time believed to be flat. To Christians of this era, the city was the holiest spot in the world, the place where God, through his son Jesus Christ, had redeemed the fallen creation.

Jerusalem was and is sacred to Jews and Muslims, as well as to the followers of Christ. Jews revere Jerusalem as the city of David, founder of the united kingdom of Israel and Judah, and the place where his successor, Solomon, built a great temple. To Muslims Jerusalem is traditionally the third most sacred city in the world after Mecca, the Prophet's birthplace, and Yathrib, or Medina, the city in which he established the Islamic faith in AD620–30. Jerusalem is said to be the place from which the Prophet made an ascent into heaven – according to Muslim tradition,

▼ *The Church of the Holy Sepulchre, believed to be built on the spot where Christ was crucified, was the crusaders' goal.*

Muhammad was taken up from Mecca by the Angel Gabriel one night in 620 and transported to Jerusalem, from where he ascended a golden ladder to heaven.

REPEATED VIOLENCE

By the time of the First Crusade in the 11th century, the city already had a long and bloody history. Following the era of David and Solomon the city was sacked by the Egyptian pharaoh Sheshonk I in 922BC, and then both city and Temple were destroyed by Nebuchadnezzar of Babylon in 587BC. This cataclysmic event, which resulted in the exile of the Jews in Babylon, was followed eventually by their return under Cyrus the Great of Persia and the building of a second Temple in 515BC.

Under the rule of the Seleucids (the rulers of a kingdom that grew out of the empire of Alexander the Great) in the 2nd century BC, Judas Maccabeus led his celebrated revolt to reclaim the city and cleanse the Temple. In the era of chivalry he became an unlikely role model for the crusader knights as a religious warrior.

ROMAN CITY

At the time of Christ, Jerusalem was part of the province of Judea in the Roman Empire. A Jewish revolt in AD66 resulted in a devastating attack led by the future emperor Titus, in which the city was almost completely destroyed and the Temple once again reduced to ruins. A new city named Aelia Capitolina was built by Emperor Hadrian, provoking another revolt in 132–35, put down again by Roman might; at this time Hadrian renamed the Roman province of Judea 'Syria Palaestina' after the Philistines named in the Bible. Jerusalem remained under Roman rule until the 7th century, although from the 4th century onwards this was under Christian emperors. The city became a well-established site of pilgrimage for Christians.

▲ *Jerusalem was depicted as being at the centre of the world in this map from an English psalter c.1262. Christ and two angels preside. The east is at the top, Europe and Africa at the bottom.*

CHURCH OF THE HOLY SEPULCHRE

Built by Emperor Constantine in c.325, the Church of the Holy Sepulchre was said to mark the site of Golgotha, or the Hill of Calvary, where Christ was crucified and then buried.

The church consisted of three parts: a basilica named the *Martyrium* built over the place of crucifixion, a colonnade called the *Triportico* built around the Hill of Calvary, and a rotunda called the *Anastasis* (Resurrection) containing the actual cave in which Christ was said to have been buried. The tomb itself was enclosed in a special structure beneath the rotunda called the 'edicule' (from Latin *aediculum*, meaning 'small structure'), and visiting the edicule understandably became a major focus for Christian pilgrims and subsequently crusaders.

AN ARAB CITY

Jerusalem was captured by Bedouin Arabs under Omar bin Khattab, the second caliph, or leader, of Islam, in 638. His successors, the Umayyad caliphs of Damascus and their successors, the Abbasid caliphs of Baghdad, ruled over Jerusalem for more than 600 years, until 969. These regimes were both supporters of mainstream Sunni Islam, but in 969 the rival Fatimid caliphs of Cairo in Egypt, who were Shi'ite Muslims, took control of the city.

THE DOME OF THE ROCK

The city's principal Muslim holy site, the Dome of the Rock, was constructed in 685–91 by the Umayyad caliph Abd al-Malik. It was a mosque built as a *masshad* (pilgrimage shrine) for Muslims, on the reputed site from which Muhammad ascended to heaven on his Night Journey. The site was also sacred on three counts for Jews: as the place where the patriarch

▼ *The army of Nebuchadnezzar, king of Babylon c.605–562BC, brings death and destruction to the city of Jerusalem. The illustration is from the* Commentary on the Apocalypse *(c.776) by Spanish monk Beatus of Liébana.*

Abraham had readied himself to sacrifice his son Isaac to please God; as the rock on which Jacob had dreamt of a ladder ascending to heaven; and as the site of King Solomon's Temple. The al-Aqsa Mosque was built nearby at around the same time. In the crusader era, contemporary reports suggest that many Christian pilgrims, ignorant of their history, believed the Dome of the Rock to be the biblical Temple of Solomon.

▲ *Christ's empty tomb is visible within the Church of the Holy Sepulchre in this 14th-century view of pilgrims visiting Jerusalem.*

The Umayyad, Abbasid and Fatimid caliphs were mostly liberal towards Christian pilgrims. There was a major outbreak of persecution in the early 11th century, when the Fatimid caliph al-Hakim ordered the destruction of Christian shrines, including the Church of the Holy Sepulchre in 1010. This aggression proved to be short-lived, however, and in the 1040s the church was reconstructed by Byzantine builders with the permission of Fatimid caliph Ma'ad al-Mustansir Billah.

In 1071, however, the Fatimids were ousted from Jerusalem by the Seljuk Turks, who were far less tolerant of Christianity, and were unwilling to allow pilgrims to come and go unmolested. The reported attacks by Seljuk Turks on Christian pilgrims to Jerusalem was one of the provocations and justifications of the First Crusade.

Immediately prior to the First Crusade, Jerusalem was in the hands of the Seljuk Turks, but during the crusade (in 1098) it was recaptured by the Fatimid Muslims, so it was from the Fatimids that the crusaders took it in July 1099.

THE PENITENTIAL JOURNEY
A LONG HISTORY OF PILGRIMAGE

The religious tradition of the pilgrimage, or penitential journey, has roots that travel down deep into history. Christians in the 10th and 11th centuries enthusiastically embraced the crusade as a form of pilgrimage, as a means of expiating their sins.

The tradition of making religious journeys to visit shrines dates back to at least the world of ancient Greece, when people would travel to visit the Temple of Diana at Ephesus in Asia Minor (now western Turkey) and other sacred sites. Christ's birthplace, Bethlehem, and the scene of his Passion, Jerusalem, were places of pilgrimage for Christians from as early as the 2nd century AD.

FIRST CHRISTIAN PILGRIMS TO JERUSALEM

Eusebius, an early 4th-century Bishop of Caesarea, made references in his *Historia Ecclesiastica* (History of the Christian Church) to travelling Christians making

▼ *Devout pilgrims patiently wait to receive a papal blessing before embarking on their voyage to the holy places in the East.*

religious visits to Jerusalem. In truth, there was little for Christians to see in the city before Constantine the Great began a programme of identifying sacred sites and building churches.

Before Constantine's time the Jerusalem of Christ's era was almost entirely covered with the new city of Aelia Capitolina built by Hadrian following the near-total destruction of the earlier city by the future emperor Titus in AD70. The only known site associated with Christ's Passion was the cenacle, or supper room, reputedly the place in which Christ shared his last earthly meal with his disciples and gave them the basis of the Christian Mass, or Communion service. The cenacle was in the house said to have belonged to Mary,

▲ *The 'True Cross' is identified when it miraculously heals a sick woman during St Helena's pilgrimage to Jerusalem.*

mother of Saint Mark, author of the biblical Gospel of Mark; she was a prominent early Christian and the house was a meeting place for the disciples and followers after Christ's resurrection.

Constantine identified the site of Christ's burial in an area that, according to Bishop Eusebius, had been built up with earth and used as the site for a temple of the Roman goddess Venus, probably during Hadrian's rebuilding of the city. Constantine excavated the mound and found a cave that was then identified as the place where Joseph of Arimathaea placed Christ's body after it was taken down from the cross. There, Constantine constructed the Church of the Holy Sepulchre in c.AD325.

THE 'TRUE CROSS'

According to a tradition first recorded by the late 4th-century Christian writer Socrates Scholasticus, Constantine's mother Helena – who also converted to Christianity – made a pilgrimage to Jerusalem in c.312–30 and, under the guidance of a local Jew, found Christ's cross together with those of the two robbers who were crucified alongside him. A miracle revealed which one of the three was the cross used to crucify Christ: each of the crosses was laid on a very sick woman and one of them, imbued with divine power because Christ's blood had been spilt on it, brought about a cure. Helena also supposedly found the inscription hung above Christ's head on the cross, which identified him as 'King of the Jews', and the nails used to fix Jesus to the cross: the relics were sent to Constantinople, where the nails were beaten to form the emperor's bridle and helmet.

According to some accounts Helena also took the cross itself back with her to Constantinople, but other versions indicate that parts of the cross were kept in the Church of the Holy Sepulchre: pilgrims were venerating relics of the cross there by about c.380. Shortly afterwards, accounts of pilgrimages indicate that religious travellers were also being told that they could see the Holy Lance that pierced Christ's side, the crown of thorns He wore and the pillar at which He was whipped.

A fragment of the cross was taken from Jerusalem by Persian Sassanid emperor Khosrau II when he took the city in 614, then recaptured by Byzantine emperor Heraclius when he defeated Khosrau in battle. After keeping the relic briefly in Constantinople, Heraclius returned it to Jerusalem, where it remained. It was hidden by Christians early in the 11th century, and reputedly found in August 1099 by Arnulf of Choques, the city's first Latin Patriarch. The fragment became the principal sacred relic of the Kingdom of Jerusalem, kept in the Church of the Holy Sepulchre, and carried into battle by the crusader armies. This was the relic whose loss to Saladin's army during the Battle of Hattin in 1187 caused such lasting concern and consternation.

PILGRIMAGE AS PENANCE

The pilgrimage was a form of penitential discipline. Making a pilgrimage was a form of penance, that is an act performed to win forgiveness of sins. A priest, or in more serious cases a bishop, would specify the particular pilgrimage that a penitent must undertake in order to earn forgiveness. While travelling, the pilgrim might be required to wear a heavy chain or a hair shirt to add to the penance.

THE POWER OF RELICS

The institution of the pilgrimage was supported by the belief – already powerful as we have seen by the 5th century, and strong right through the Middle Ages – in the spiritual force of physical relics of Christ and his saints. In addition to fragments of objects such as the Cross or the Crown of Thorns, pilgrims travelled to venerate miraculously preserved body parts of sacred figures, such as fingers or hair clippings. These relics were believed to be imbued with divine power and regularly, like Helena's piece of the cross, effected extraordinary cures. Pilgrimages did not have to be to Jerusalem or the Holy Land: penitents could make journeys to a wide range of sites closer to home that were associated with the lives of saints or sanctified by the possession of a holy relic.

THE GOLDEN LEGEND OF THE TRUE CROSS

The pilgrims who venerated pieces of the True Cross in various locations were eager to tell and hear stories of its origin. A story developed linking the wood from which the cross was made to the Tree of Life that grew in the Garden of Eden; the form in which this tale has survived is the *Golden Legend* written by Jacopo of Voragine, Bishop of Genoa, in 1260. According to this story, the cross was made of wood grown from a seed of the Tree of Life: as he lay dying, Adam persuaded his son Seth to get the seed from the archangel Michael; when he returned with it, Seth placed it in Adam's mouth. Adam was buried after he died and a great tree grew from the seed and lived for many hundreds of years. Finally it was cut down: the wood was used to build a bridge. It happened that the biblical Queen of Sheba crossed the bridge on her way to visit King Solomon: she saw the wood's true nature and worshipped it, then told Solomon that a piece of the wood would be instrumental in the establishment of a new covenant between God and the Jews. Solomon was afraid and had the wood buried, but 14 generations later it was unearthed and made into the Holy Cross on which Christ died.

◄ *The Queen of Sheba kisses the wood of the Cross in a fresco of the story by Piero della Francesca in the Church of San Francesco, Arezzo, Italy.*

CRUSADER PILGRIMS
A SACRED ENTERPRISE

Access to Jerusalem was the ultimate prize for the crusader armies, for their journey was a pilgrimage as well as a military campaign. Each crusader who took the cross vowed to enter the Church of the Holy Sepulchre and pray there.

PILGRIMS BEARING ARMS

At low points during the First Crusade, such as the long siege of Antioch and the delay following its capture, the rank and file of the army were inspired to endure by their desire to fulfil their pilgrimage vows. Following the taking of Jerusalem, and their visit to the Church of the Holy Sepulchre, many felt that their enterprise was complete and took off for home, despite the fact that the crusaders' hold on Jerusalem was tenuous and that a formi-

▼ *Amid brutal violence, the soldiers who recaptured Jerusalem at the climax of the First Crusade celebrated ecstatically. Their pilgrimage had reached its goal.*

dable Egyptian relief army under the command of Fatimid vizier al-Afdal Shahanshah was marching on the city.

Before the crusades, there was already, as we have seen, a well-established Christian tradition of the pilgrimage as a form of penitential discipline. There was also a precedent for armed pilgrimage: in 1064, 7,000 armed German pilgrims under the command of two archbishops and two bishops marched to Jerusalem – some apparently wearing crosses. In 1095 Pope Urban II conflated the idea of a holy war fought in the name of God and the papacy with the benefits of a penitential journey. Part of the explanation for the response to his call to take the cross and travel on armed expedition to Jerusalem was that it met a keenly felt need – it allowed people to make their piety public and to seek expiation for their sins.

For many, the highest expression of Christian faith in action remained the monastic or clerical life. For example,

▲ *Preaching the Second Crusade in 1146, Bernard of Clairvaux urges Christians to take up the cross of Christ, and demonstrate their willingness to share in His suffering.*

Aelfric Grammaticus (the Grammarian), 10th-century abbot of Eynsham in southern England, declared that monks were the proper soldiers of Christ, those who fought with the words of prayers rather than with the metal of swords. But not all

THE GERMAN PILGRIMAGE OF 1064–65

Various chronicle accounts survive of the German pilgrimage of 1064. It was led by Siegfried, Archbishop of Mainz, and William, Archbishop of Trier, supported by Otto, Bishop of Regensburg and Gunther, Bishop of Bamberg. According to one report, Bishop Gunther cut such a splendid figure on this voyage that when the pilgrims came to Constantinople the people suspected that he must be the Holy Roman Emperor himself, travelling in disguise.

As they moved on towards Jerusalem, the pilgrims met returning travellers who told horror stories about the treatment of Christians by Arabs. On Good Friday 1065 the German pilgrims themselves were attacked by Arab bandits and then besieged at an isolated farmhouse over the entire Easter weekend. But, inspired by their archbishops and

bishops, the pilgrims trusted in God and in their weapons and drove back the besiegers on Easter Sunday, despite having gone three days without food or water. They captured some leading Arabs who had broken into the enclosure and used these men as hostages.

Another much-reported and horrific episode on the pilgrimage involved the rape of an abbess in full view of the travelling pilgrims by a gang of Arabs. The abbess was so badly injured that she died. One account of the pilgrimage, contained in the *Life of Bishop Altmann of Passau*, commented: 'Brought down by events like this and other humiliations in Christ's name, the travelling faithful won high praise in all quarters, from men and from angels above, because they elected to enter God's kingdom, suffering many tribulations.'

---

could follow this path. As Guibert, the Benedictine abbot of Nogent-sous-Coucy in France, wrote after praising the holy wars of the crusades as giving knights a chance to win their salvation: 'In this way they are not forced to give up secular affairs entirely by entering the monastic life of the clerical professions, as was once the normal practice, but can reach in some degree God's grace while following their own careers, with the freedom and in the dress to which they are used.'

THE CROSS OF SUFFERING

The men (and women) who took the cross did not call themselves crusaders. They were known by contemporaries as *cruces-ignati* – people marked with the cross. Nor did they call the enterprise a crusade. It was variously called a business, a journey or way and a pilgrimage. Urban principally promoted it as a military expedition.

When Bernard of Clairvaux came to preach the Second Crusade in 1146 – with such dramatic effectiveness that his sermons were viewed as a 'divine augury' and

a 'miracle' – he emphasized the expedition to Jerusalem he was urging as an opportunity for Christians to win salvation and, on an individual level, to demonstrate their repentance. In his vision, the cross worn by the crusaders was a sign that they

were willing to share in the suffering of Christ; what pain and difficulty they had to endure en route to victory would only improve the effectiveness of the enterprise in winning salvation for them.

In a sermonizing letter, which he despatched to the people of France and Bavaria in 1146, Bernard called the crusade 'Christ's business, in which is found our salvation' and called for urgency – 'now is the right time, now is the day of total salvation'. He summoned the vision of pagans defiling the Holy City, the place where so many Christian pilgrims had 'confessed their wrongdoings with tears and won forgiveness'; he said that the all-powerful God could of course cleanse the city with a battalion of angels, but that he preferred to test the mettle of his faithful Christian soldiers.

Bernard concluded with the following exhortation 'since your land is bursting with courageous men and is celebrated for the strength of its young warriors, gird yourselves like men and take up arms joyfully in the name of Christ.'

▼ *Bernard of Clairvaux and other crusade preachers painted a picture of terrible outrages perpetrated by Muslim 'Saracens' against the Christians in the East.*

CHAPTER TWO

A CALL TO ARMS

On 27 November 1095, in a stirring speech to a great crowd at Clermont in France, Pope Urban II set in motion preparations for the First Crusade, which was to prove the start of centuries of violence between European Christians and Eastern Muslims in the Holy Land. Of course, he did not know that his speech was the beginning of hundreds of years of religious conflict, and the pious knights and other European warriors who responded to his call to arms were not aware that they were embarking on the first of a series of wars of the cross – indeed, they were encouraged to believe that the war would be final, victory total and glorious. Urban made the claim that Christ offered the ultimate reward to the knights and infantrymen he was seeking to mobilize. According to the version of the speech recorded by eyewitness Fulcher of Chartres, Urban urged those who waged war to take their courage and martial vigour abroad and put it to good use in combating 'barbarians' and cleansing the Holy Land: 'Let those who have been used to fighting without justice in private wars against faithful men and women, now embark against the faithless infidel and bring to an end with a great victory this war which should have been launched long ago ... Let those who have been earning mercenary pay instead earn eternal reward.' This reward, promised by the pope on behalf of God, was the complete remission of sins, the glory of heaven.

▲ *The People's Crusade sets out for the Holy Land, led by Peter the Hermit.*

◀ *The wealthy and deeply devout Count Raymond IV of Toulouse was the first European nobleman to obey Christ's command – as relayed by Pope Urban – to take the cross. Many pilgrims travelled in his party.*

CONSTANTINOPLE UNDER THREAT

EMPEROR ALEXIUS'S CRY FOR HELP

In March 1095 Alexius I Comnenus, ruler of the Byzantine Empire, despatched envoys to the Council of Piacenza in Italy to ask Pope Urban II for help in fighting the Seljuk Turks. This appeal either convinced Urban to promote a holy war to come to the aid of Christians in the East and reclaim the Holy Land, or else gave him ammunition to justify a decision he had already made to ask the chivalry of Europe to fight for the cross in the East.

Alexius's appeal was one of a number he made in the 1090s. He wanted military help in launching a counter-attack against the formidable Seljuk Turks, who had defeated the Byzantine Empire at the Battle of Manzikert in 1071 and had established the Sultanate of Rum in central Anatolia in 1077. Since becoming Byzantine emperor in 1081, Alexius had succeeded

in halting the invasion of Byzantine lands in Greece by the southern Italian Norman lord Robert Guiscard in 1081–82, then in beating back the incursions of the Turkish Pecheneg nomads in the Balkans. He saw an opportunity in the death in 1092 of the Turkish sultan of Baghdad, Malik Shah, and the collapse of his empire in Iraq, Syria and Palestine. The time appeared to

▲ *Alexius made much of the barbarity of the Seljuk Turks. They were fierce warriors, but maintained a highly civilized court.*

be ripe to strike back against the Seljuks and to reassert Byzantine authority across many of its former lands.

To win the support of Western nobles, Alexius and his envoys emphasized the

▼ *Pilgrims arrive at Jaffa (top) and pay a toll before entering Tyre (bottom). Both cities attracted pilgrims because of their role in biblical and early Christian history, and became crusader strongholds.*

ALEXIUS I COMNENUS

Alexius I Comnenus, who ruled as Byzantine emperor from 1081 to 1118, proved himself one of the leading statesmen of his era. He came to power, by seizing the throne from Nicephorus III, just ten years after the empire's catastrophic defeat at the Battle of Manzikert by the Seljuk Turks, and ruled through the period of the First Crusade and the establishment of the crusader states of Jerusalem, Antioch, Edessa and Tripoli.

He made the crusader lords swear an oath to return to him the lands they gained on campaign and, although this was not honoured, by the crusaders' efforts he regained control of many cities including Nicaea, Sardis and Ephesus, as well as much of Anatolia. In his 37-year reign he restored the Byzantine Empire to a position of relative strength following its series of defeats at the hands of Normans and Turks. He founded the Comnenian dynasty of Byzantine emperors, who ruled until the late 12th century. In the words of an anonymous Greek biographer, he was a man 'great both in the power of his will and in deeds'.

◄ *The likeness of Alexius I Comnenus, Byzantine emperor between 1081 and 1118, adorns one side of this gold Byzantine soldo (penny coin).*

threat to Christians and their holy places posed by the pagan Turks. But he did not envisage a holy war – he wanted a mercenary army, whose soldiers he could control with financial incentives. He did not foresee the struggle for the Holy Land launched by the pope; fighting to recapture Jerusalem was never part of his plan – the city had, after all, been in Muslim hands since 638.

LETTER TO COUNT ROBERT OF FLANDERS

One of Alexius's appeals survives in the form of a letter dated 1093 written to Count Robert II of Flanders. Count Robert's father – Count Robert I of Flanders – had stayed with Alexius in Constantinople on his return from a pilgrimage and Alexius had reportedly been impressed by the strength of his escort. His letter tried to appeal on several different fronts, seeking to generate not only righteous anger but also a lust for riches.

The letter described how the Patzinaks (or Pechenegs) and Turks carried out forced circumcision of Christian babies and boys above the baptismal font, and forced them to urinate into its waters; it suggested that they not only abducted and raped Christian women (both virgins and

▲ *The crusaders were awestruck by the beauty and ancient treasures of the walled city of Constantinople. This map was made in c.1485 by the Italian cartographer Cristoforo Buondelmonti.*

venerable matrons), but also performed acts of sodomy on Byzantine men – including Christian clergy, monks and even bishops. He compared their acts to those of the 'impious Babylonians', who, according to biblical accounts, had mistreated the Jews in exile – suggesting

thereby that under the threat of the Turks, the Christian Byzantines were effectively in exile in their own lands.

Alexis lamented that the great expanses of the Byzantine Empire had been snatched away and suggested that the invaders were on the verge of capturing Constantinople itself, 'unless the help of God and faithful Latin Christians should come quickly to us'. He pointed out that the cities of the East – and notably Constantinople – were rich in holy relics and that God would punish any brave lord who refused to come to their protection; those who did come, he said, would win reward in heaven.

Later in the letter, however, Alexius also emphasized that these cities were additionally full of treasures and gold, and of beautiful women – 'Greek women possess a beauty beyond compare that would be a good enough reason to lure the brave armies of the Franks to Thrace'. The Latin Christian lords should not allow these beauties – neither treasures nor flesh and blood – to fall into pagan hands.

▼ *Byzantine forces besiege Messina in Sicily. In Italy, the Byzantines had for centuries been at odds with the Normans and other Europeans, whose help they now requested.*

RIGHTEOUS WARFARE

POPE URBAN II PREACHES THE FIRST CRUSADE

On Tuesday 27 November 1095 at the close of the Council of Clermont in central France, Pope Urban II issued a rousing call to arms, urging the Christian knights of Europe to travel to the aid of their brothers in the East and liberate the holy places of Jerusalem from unbelievers. The speech was the high point of a months-long tour of France promoting the crusade between August 1095 and September 1096.

The Council of Clermont, an assembly for church reform, had been running since 18 November and had been attended by around 300 prominent clerics. They had deliberated on clerical marriage, the elimination of simony (the practice of selling Church positions) and the excommunication of King Philip of France for committing adultery.

Word must have been circulated that the pope was planning to make a great announcement, for the crowd that gathered to hear him was too large to fit into the Cathedral at Clermont and the papal

▲ *In Fulcher of Chartres's account of the speech, Urban declared 'Let men who have grown used to waging private war against fellow Christians go now against the infidel and win a great victory in this war that should have been started long ago.'*

throne was therefore moved to a field just outside the city. There, Urban delivered the passionate address that launched the First Crusade.

URBAN'S SPEECH

We know that Urban was a highly intelligent man and a great orator and can tell from the response that the speech had an electrifying effect. But it is impossible to know for sure what he said. Five separate substantial accounts of Urban's speech survive, but all were written in the early 12th century in the light of later assumptions about the enterprise and after the First Crusade had ended in triumph at Jerusalem in 1099.

The earliest account was in the anonymous chronicle *Gesta Francorum* (Deeds of the Franks), probably written by a follower of Bohemond of Taranto in *c*.1100. This was used as a source by the other reports. Shortly afterwards, perhaps in 1101, Fulcher of Chartres, an ecclesiastic who travelled on crusade in the party of

Stephen of Blois and Robert of Normandy, wrote a history of the First Crusade that also included a major report of the speech; it is probable that Fulcher was actually present at the Council of Clermont. Another very important description of the speech was given by Robert the Monk, who reworked the *Gesta Francorum* in *c*.1106; he was almost certainly not present at Clermont.

A fourth account was written by the Benedictine historian Guibert, Abbot of Nogent-sous-Coucy, in his *Dei gesta per Francos* (Deeds of God carried out by the Franks) of *c*.1108. He used the *Gesta Francorum* as a principal source but also used material gleaned from discussions with crusaders he knew; he, too, was present at the Council of Clermont, so must have included his memories as an eyewitness in the report. A fifth version of Urban's speech was given by Balderic, Archbishop of Dol-en-Bretagne from 1107–30, who based his account – written 10–20 years after the speech – on the *Gesta Francorum*.

According to the account in the *Gesta Francorum*, Urban primarily focused on the instruction of Christ to his followers that they should take up the cross and follow him, and described how men should seek to save their soul and find reward in

▼ *Urban is escorted to Clermont, where he asked bishops and abbots to bring the leading lords in their areas to the council.*

heaven by finding the way to the Holy Sepulchre in Jerusalem.

In Fulcher of Chartres's report, Urban presented the expedition as an opportunity for secular warriors to become soldiers in Christ's service. He condemned lawlessness and the actions of robbers and urged that the Truce of God, the general peace agreed on Church authority, should be honoured. Then he called on all present to hurry to the aid of Christians in the East against 'Turks and Arabs', and to 'drive that vile race from the territories of our friends'. He said: 'All who die on the journey, overland or across seas, or in fighting against pagans, shall be rewarded with immediate remission of sins.'

In Robert the Monk's account, meanwhile, Urban emphasized the need to fight for the conquest of the Holy Land more than hurry to the aid of the Christians in the East. He repeated many of the descriptions of pagan infamy listed in the supposed letter of Alexis I to Count Robert II of Flanders – such as forced circumcision of Christian boys, spilling of human blood in the font and brutal rape of Christian women.

▲ *Robert the Monk described Urban calling on Christians to go to the aid of their brethren because, in the words that became the battle cry of the crusaders, 'God wills it!'*

▼ *According to Balderic, Urban called on knights to defend the Church of the Holy Sepulchre and other Eastern churches as they would defend their mother.*

In Robert's account, the pope also emphasized the great history of the Franks and their pedigree as a fighting race – they were above all other nations in arms, and should be inspired by the deeds of their ancestors, great warriors such as Charlemagne: 'O bravest of soldiers, the sons of invincible forebears, do not forget the valour of your ancestors.' He added that France was crowded with men, nd that inevitable competition bred conflict, but that the Holy Land to which he called them was – as noted in the Bible – one that 'floweth with milk and honey'; it was 'a paradise of many delights' and, moreover, a place consecrated by the suffering of Christ. He personified the city of Jerusalem, which he said lay at the centre of the world: 'from you,' he said, 'she asks for help!' He added: 'Take on this journey for the remission of sins, in confidence of the undying glory of God's kingdom.'

Balderic of Dol's version emphasized particularly the desecration of holy places in Jerusalem by pagans and called powerfully on Christian knights to stop fighting one another and, instead, to combat Turks and others in the Holy Land. In this account, Urban declared 'may you find it is a beautiful thing to give your life for Christ in the city in which he gave his life for us all'; fighting Saracens, he said, was 'righteous warfare', and would deliver 'everlasting glory'. He also pointed out, however, that worldly wealth would be an auxiliary prize – for the enemy was in possession of great riches.

The account of Guibert of Nogent emphasized the notion, current in the 10th and 11th centuries, that the 'Last Days' were at hand prior to the Second Coming of Christ as described in the biblical Book of Revelation and suggested that Christian knights should go to Jerusalem to oppose pagans as part of this final conflict. In this version, Urban described the many sufferings of Christian pilgrims to the Holy Land at the hands of pagans. He promised that knights fighting in the holy war would have Christ as 'standard bearer and inseparable leader'.

GOD WILLS IT! GOD WILLS IT!
THE RUSH TO TAKE THE CROSS

At the end of Urban's speech, a great shout went up among those in the crowd: 'God wills it! God wills it! God wills it!' Adhemar, Bishop of Le Puy, stepped forward and fell to his knees before Urban, and asked to be allowed to take part in an expedition to the East. Urban appointed him to serve on the pope's behalf as leader of the crusade. Some men trembled and wept in the crowd, and others discussed Urban's words earnestly: almost at once, many came forward in imitation of Adhemar to pledge themselves to undertake the task to which Urban called them.

TAKING THE CROSS

According to some accounts volunteers at once began to mark themselves out by attaching a cross to their clothes, in homage to the cross of Christ; clerics and monks surrendered their cloaks to provide

▼ A monk bestows the cross on a crusader. The symbol of Christ gave weight and meaning to each knight's journey eastwards.

material from which people cut the crosses. Fulcher of Chartres reported that as soon as people took the oath to go on the expedition, they made 'shining crosses' from cloth of gold or silk and attached them to their shoulders.

It seems obvious from contemporary accounts that the events at Clermont were carefully stage-managed: doubtless Urban had instructed a cleric to set up the chant of 'God wills it! God wills it!' and arranged in advance that Adhemar would step forward and be the first to take a vow. According to Robert the Monk, Urban whipped up the crowd further by claiming that the fact that they all chanted the one phrase was evidence that God was at work among them, in line with Christ's promise that 'Where two or three are gathered together in my name there am I in the midst of them': though the words were issuing from many mouths, they had their origin in one place, in God. And he proceeded to specify that these words should become the battle cry of the crusading armies when they went to war in the East.

▲ Crusader knights of the Minutolo family kneel in prayer, in a fresco from San Gennaro Cathedral, Naples. Over centuries families became associated with crusading as fathers and sons, uncles and nephews took the cross on different campaigns.

The visual drama of 'taking the cross' by attaching it to clothing was also seemingly prearranged, with clerics briefed beforehand to provide the necessary material for the eager men in the crowd.

The taking of the cross was a symbolic visual act that gave added physical weight to the verbal vow taken by the participants. The Gesta Francorum reported that the Franks who undertook to make the expedition sewed the cross of Christ on their right shoulders. According to Robert the Monk, Urban instructed all those taking the vow to mark themselves with the sign of Christ's cross either on their forehead or on their chest, and said that when they had accomplished what he asked them to do, they should wear the cross on their back between their shoulders. Guibert of Nogent also reported that it was

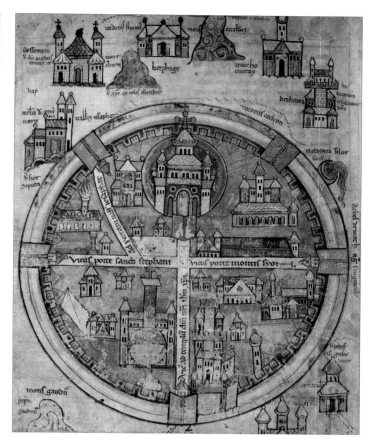

Pope Urban's order that people sew the cross, made of any material, on their shirt, cloak or chain mail tunic. In this version, Urban added that any person who took the vow and then did not travel would be an outlaw for all time.

THE REMISSION OF SINS

Although the accounts of the speech at Clermont vary, we can be certain that Urban's appeal did promise the remission of sins for those who took part – the journey itself would bring the same benefits as a pilgrimage to Jerusalem.

The issues of sin and forgiveness were very important for people of all classes at this time, not least because it was commonly held that the expected Second Coming of Christ was imminent, and that the 'Last Days' of the world as described in the Bible were at hand. This meant that the feared Day of Judgement was also imminent, and that it was a matter of even greater than normal urgency to find officially sanctioned ways of seeking forgiveness for wrongdoing.

FIGHTING WITH GOD'S BLESSING

Urban II, who came from the minor nobility of the Champagne region of France, knew how to address the knightly class, and his appeal at Clermont and throughout the preaching tour of which it was a part struck a note that rang true with the warriors in his audience. The Church's initial response to the emergence of knights

▲ *Jerusalem, the Holy City, and navel of God's creation, was said to be calling out in her distress to the knights of Europe, begging to be freed.*

had been to try to stifle their enthusiasm for fighting – in the Peace of God and Truce of God movements, to limit knightly conflict to prescribed periods. But on the expedition Urban proposed should take place to the East, knights would be encouraged to fight, and would do so with the full blessing of the Church and of God. Moreover, in doing so they would gain spiritual blessings as well as impunity – as Christ's soldiers they would win forgiveness of their sins and ultimately their salvation after death.

THE QUEST FOR GLORY

MOTIVES OF THE KNIGHTS WHO UNDERTOOK THE FIRST CRUSADE

The primary motivation of the knights who departed on the First Crusade was religious. Taking the cross was an act of piety, a statement of faith.

Taking the cross as a knight was likened to becoming a monk, which in this period was put forward as the spiritual ideal for a Christian life. Those who took the cross were treated like the clergy, and acquired certain associated privileges – while on crusade they did not, for example, have to pay taxes or settle debts or carry out feudal military service. It was understandably a matter of concern for those considering going on crusade that they were leaving their family and property behind, but the Church promised protection on their behalf. In the account of Urban's speech at Clermont given by Guibert of Nogent, the pope announced that anyone who molested the property or family of a soldier of Christ while he was on pilgrimage to the Holy Land would be subject to 'a fearful anathema' – that is, excommunication.

▼ Before embarking upon crusade a knight receives Holy Communion. Crusading was comparable to the quests in search of honour taken by knights in chivalric poems.

GLAMOUR AND HONOUR

But there were also secular attractions for the crusaders in addition to these primary religious motives. The knights were seeking honour and glory as well. Glamour was attached to the crusade proposed by Urban: it was an adventure and, as we have seen, it allowed the knights of Europe to indulge their taste for conflict.

The code of chivalry, which in the late 11th century was in the early stages of its development, taught that knights must seek opportunities to practise their martial skills and to prove themselves worthy of the honour of being a knight. In Europe they could be frustrated in doing this by the Peace of God and by secular or ecclesiastical authority, but on crusade they were encouraged to do so. The knights were – and saw themselves as – an international elite: the landowners of northern France and of England and of southern Italy had more in common with each other than they had with their countrymen; the crusade gave them an enemy and a target, and the opportunity to ride out among their peers seeking glory.

THE LURE OF WEALTH?

For many decades historians argued that the crusaders also rode eastward in search of a fortune. The accounts we have of the appeal that was made to the knights of Europe certainly included the promise of wealth. Alexius Comnenus's letter to Count Robert II of Flanders pretended that in Constantinople there was more gold than anywhere else in the world – and that the city's churches were overflowing with silver and precious stones and fine silks as well as gold; moreover, he claimed that the riches of all the emperors of the ancient Roman Empire were hidden in the palaces of the city. In Balderic of Dol's account of Pope Urban's speech at Clermont, the pope promised the crusaders the spoils of the enemy: 'the

▲ A knight offers his service to God. This celebrated crusading image is from the English Westminster Psalter of c.1250.

possessions of the enemy will be yours, too,' he said, 'since you will make their treasures your spoils'.

The knights, of course, were happy to take what spoils of war came their way in line with conventional practice in the medieval period. But they did not set out principally to seek their fortune.

At one time, historians argued that crusade armies contained many younger sons, men who seized on Urban's call to reclaim the Holy Land as a chance to make a place for themselves in the world and win a fortune. This traditional account pointed out that within the feudal system in northern France and England, younger sons in noble families could not inherit their father's wealth and had limited opportunities for self-advancement. And even in southern Europe, where inheritances were shared out among all sons, many found their prospects were poor because the property was split so many times among

▲ *Committing to crusade required bravery, a willingness to risk all fighting far from home. Most knights were sustained by their faith that they were carrying out God's will.*

descendants that it became insignificant. However, modern historians dismiss this argument, pointing out the great expense of equipping oneself to go on crusade. To travel on crusade cost a knight many times his annual income.

From surviving charters and other documents we can see that the great majority of crusaders intended to return, if they did not die on the adventure overseas, and were not deliberately setting out to make a new life in a strange land. Moreover, it is simply not true that younger sons rather

▶ *Knights had to equip themselves at great expense with a horse, weapons and finery. Crusading was a chance to demonstrate social standing and chivalric qualities.*

than their older siblings went on crusade – great lords and eldest sons travelled as well as their younger brothers. It is true that following the success of the First Crusade and the establishment of the crusader kingdoms of Jerusalem, Edessa, Antioch and Tripoli, a number of Europeans settled in the Middle East. But

historians now question whether these settlers were primarily crusaders, as was once assumed, or whether they were emigrants after the crusade taking advantage of the new opportunities.

There were certainly individual cases of young men who made their name and fortune on crusade, but they were not a general type among the crusaders. Many knights, in fact, made significant financial sacrifices to go on crusade – some had to mortgage their property to pay for the expedition – and pay high rates of interest on the loan; others sold their land – and often accepted a poor price because in France, for example, the 1090s were a time of agricultural depression. The fact that so many knights made substantial sacrifices to take the cross is testament to the power of Pope Urban's stirring appeal and runs quite counter to the proposal that knights travelled to the Holy Land out of financial self-interest.

WALKING TO THE HOLY LAND

THE PEOPLE'S CRUSADE

The sermon at Clermont may have been meticulously planned and the accompanying pageantry carefully staged, but the response to Urban's plea took him by surprise. In addition to a well-equipped military force of great princes, lords and knights of the kind Urban had hoped to mobilize, a vast army of peasants and poor townspeople also left their homes, determined to put their trust in God and make their way to the Holy Land.

PETER THE HERMIT

A monk and popular preacher from Amiens named Peter the Hermit toured northern France and Flanders on a donkey, calling for crusade volunteers. He was a small man, known as 'Little Peter' by his contemporaries, with a long thin face, like

▼ *Peter shows knights their duty. Byzantine princess Anna Comnena wrote that Peter had tried before to make a pilgrimage to Jerusalem, but had been tortured by Turks.*

that of his donkey, and eccentric habits – he dressed only in a cloak, was often unwashed and lived on nothing but wine and fish. Yet Peter had the orator's gift, the ability to transfix a large crowd; according to Guibert of Nogent, who met him, Peter's charisma was such that his acts and deeds seemed 'half divine'. Peter claimed that Christ himself had appointed him to preach the crusade – and even pretended that he had a letter from God to prove it. The crowds flocked after him.

This first wave of crusaders contained many hangers-on with little or no military equipment or experience of fighting, although the core of the group was adequately fitted out with horses and weapons. But remarkably there were only eight knights. The most notable of these was the experienced Walter of Sans Avoir in the Seine Valley. (He was not, as is commonly written, a penniless knight. This traditional reputation derives from a misunderstanding of his name – for

generations historians interpreted Walter Sans Avoir to mean he had nothing, that he was penniless; in fact, it refers to his feudal base, a place of that name in the Seine Valley.)

DEPARTURE FOR THE HOLY LAND

Pope Urban had declared the Feast of the Assumption of the Blessed Virgin Mary (15 August 1096) to be the starting point for the expedition, but the people who gathered to travel on what historians call the People's Crusade were impatient to depart. Peter the Hermit assembled his followers at Cologne, Germany on 12 April. His plan was to gather more followers by preaching among the Germans.

A French contingent of a few thousand under the leadership of Walter Sans Avoir could not brook even this minor delay and departed at once. They followed an overland route, and were in Hungary by 8 May. They then proceeded without incident as far as Belgrade, on the border of Byzantine lands. However, the governor of Belgrade refused them entry and the French crusaders looted the countryside – in the market town of Semlin, 16 of them were captured and stripped of their armour, which was hung from the walls of the castle there. Eventually the main group reached Nish (now in Serbia) and waited for a troop escort from the Byzantine emperor in Constantinople.

A second wave of around 20,000 left Cologne under Peter the Hermit's leadership on 20 April and followed the same route as the French pilgrims who had gone before. The first part of their journey was uneventful, but when they reached Semlin and saw the armour of the earlier crusaders hanging from the castle walls, they rioted and attacked the city, killing 4,000 locals. Afterwards, they crossed the River Save before attacking and looting Belgrade. At Nish, where they arrived on 3 July, the garrison commander was

▲ Faith drove them on. The unlikely looking forces of the People's Crusade march across Europe in an image from the 15th-century Les Passages faits Outremer.

the crusaders – especially in the Rhineland, where there were dreadful massacres in Worms, Mainz, Cologne and Trier. Count Emicho's troops massacred 800 Jews at Worms on 18 May and at least 1,100 at Mainz on 27 May.

Anti-Semitism had been current for centuries, but these were the first organized attacks against the Jews in European history. Some of the crusaders, including Count Emicho himself, felt that the Jews – culpable for the crucifixion of Christ – were just as much enemies of the cross as the Muslims, and believed that the crusading spirit could be given expression close to home. Feeling was also running high against the Jews among crusaders who had to borrow money to finance the crusade since, because money-lending was forbidden among Christians, they usually had entered into debts with Jewish lenders. Many of these crusaders now grew rich by stealing the Jews' money. Some historians refer to these attacks as the 'First Holocaust', linking them to the official attempt to exterminate the Jews by the Nazi government of Germany during the 1930s and World War II.

initially peaceable and promised an escort to Constantinople if the crusaders would move quickly on, but then a skirmish broke out between locals and some German crusaders and the commander unleashed the full force of his garrison, routing the motley crusader force and killing about 5,000 crusaders. Peter the Hermit and the chastened survivors carried on, and on 12 July arrived at Sofia (now in Bulgaria), where they awaited a military escort from Constantinople.

CRUSADES AGAINST THE JEWS

Some sections of the great population mobilized for a crusade did not travel to the Holy Land, but carried out attacks against Jewish communities in France and Germany. The most serious slaughter was carried out by a 10,000-strong army commanded by Count Emicho of Leisingen, who claimed that Christ had appeared to him and promised to make him emperor if he would convert the Jews of Europe. The Church authorities largely tried to protect the Jews, but Jews were forcibly converted or killed in their thousands by

---

WHY DID SO MANY PEOPLE JOIN THE PEOPLE'S CRUSADE?

In the late 11th century there was a resurgence of belief that the Second Coming of Christ was imminent. This fired a popular desire to make a mass pilgrimage to Jerusalem and to return the Holy City to Christian control. At the same time, a series of celestial events – including a comet, a lunar eclipse and a meteor shower – seemed to reinforce the sense that the enterprise preached by Pope Urban and Peter the Hermit had God's blessing. In addition, there had been an outbreak of ergotism, or 'St Anthony's fire', food poisoning (caused by long-term consumption of cereals containing fungi). This poisoning results in convulsions and gangrene, and it was interpreted as evidence of God's displeasure and made people desire to expiate their sins by making a pilgrimage. Some historians argue that in the years prior to 1096, the peasants of northern Europe had been suffering very severely as a result of the plague, drought and famine and were seeking escape from these terrible conditions.

► For most people in Europe, life was harsh. Some may have seen the crusade as a chance for a new beginning.

CHAPTER THREE

THE JOURNEY TO PALESTINE

The vast contingent of pilgrims and soldiers led by the monk Peter the Hermit and the knight Walter of Sans Avoir was followed to Constantinople by no fewer than five armies commanded by minor royals and some of the leading noblemen of Europe – including Duke Robert of Normandy, eldest son of King William I of England, and Hugh of Vermandois, younger brother of King Philip I of France, as well as counts and noblemen such as Raymond of Toulouse, Godfrey of Bouillon and Bohemond of Taranto. The second wave of armies, some of whom travelled overland and some by sea, is known to historians as the Princes' Crusade to distinguish it from the earlier People's Crusade, which was so called because it contained many unarmed pilgrims and peasants. As had the People's Crusaders before them, the Princes' armies endured their share of mishaps and disasters before they ever arrived at the glittering capital of the Byzantine Empire; and, arriving there confident in the knowledge that they were riding to the help of beleaguered Christians, their leaders faced an uncertain welcome from an emperor suspicious of their motives, who in particular feared that they aimed to establish themselves as rulers in his territory. In the event, the two crusades merged – after a catastrophic defeat at the hands of the Seljuk Turks in Anatolia, the chastened remnant of the People's Crusade returned to Constantinople, joined up with the still fresh and confident armies of the Princes' Crusade and set off for Jerusalem.

▲ *A messenger is sent for help at the siege of Antioch.*

◄ *The main strength of a crusader army was in its mounted cavalry bearing lances, but the soldiers were also a very effective force when battle broke down into hand-to-hand combat.*

MORE THAN THE STARS OF HEAVEN

THE PEOPLE'S CRUSADE ARRIVES IN CONSTANTINOPLE

The two main branches of the People's Crusade, one under the leadership of impoverished knight Walter Sans Avoir and the other following charismatic monk Peter the Hermit, had both arrived at Constantinople by 1 August 1096.

Anna Comnena, daughter of the Byzantine emperor Alexius I, described how the armed contingent was accompanied by a vast crowd of crusader-pilgrims 'outnumbering the grains of sand on the sea shore or the stars sparkling in the sky, carrying palms and crosses on their shoulders'. This group included many women, children and old people. She wrote that 'to look upon them was like watching powerful rivers flooding from all sides to a confluence'.

▼ *Peter the Hermit's charismatic preaching convinced many to abandon home and loved ones to honour the cross. Arriving in the East, they began to realize the immense difficulty of the task they had taken on.*

ACROSS THE BOSPHORUS

Alexius had expected a disciplined and cohesive army to be sent from Europe; instead he was confronted with a motley band of largely ill-equipped travellers who expected to be fed and given assistance. He refused them entry into the city, and made them camp outside the city walls. Within five days he had ferried them all across the Bosphorus into Anatolia.

It may be that the emperor simply wanted to be rid of them, and sent them on without much help to face almost certain death; on the other hand, it is possible that the crusaders insisted on marching on towards Jerusalem despite his best efforts to dissuade them. Anna Comnena – whose account in the *Alexiad* (c.1148), a biography of her father, understandably cast Alexius in a sympathetic light – claimed that the emperor tried to persuade Peter to await the arrival of reinforcements before moving on, but that Peter insisted on crossing into Anatolia and pressing on

towards Jerusalem. Alexius also warned the hermit not to be drawn into battle, because he saw that the crusaders were evidently no match for the Turkish army.

The crusaders were joined by several contingents of Italians, newly arrived from home. The group marched on, pillaging the towns they came to until they reached Nicomedia (now Izmit in Turkey), where they quarrelled. The Italians and Germans, under the command of an Italian by the name of Rainald, separated themselves from the French under Geoffrey Burel. Peter the Hermit and Walter Sans Avoir were no longer in control of events.

RAIDS IN ANATOLIA

The crusaders established a camp at Civetot, on the Sea of Marmara (the inland body of water that connects the Black and Aegean seas). Groups set out from the main crusader camp, competing with one another in attempts to progress the crusade. A French contingent marched as far as Nicaea, wealthy capital of the Turkish sultanate of Rum, and looted the edge of the city – according to Anna Comnena's colourful version of events, they committed atrocities there, torturing venerable old men, killing children and even cooking babies over spits and eating them.

Meanwhile, a 6,000-strong German troupe took the city of Xerigordon. In response the Turks sent an army to lay siege to Xerigordon, which captured the only source of water, located outside the city walls. The Germans lasted eight days, and surrendered only after they were reduced to drinking their own urine and the blood of their donkeys to survive. In defeat, they were slaughtered, or forced to convert to Islam and sold into slavery.

CRUSADERS MASSACRED

The Turks then set a trap for the remainder of the crusaders. In the main camp at Civetot, Turkish spies spread a rumour

▲ *The dreams of glory summoned by Peter the Hermit fell apart in the unfamiliar territory of Anatolia, where the crusaders were ravaged by the Seljuk Turks.*

that the Germans had not only triumphed at Xerigordon, but had also taken Nicaea. The rumour spread like wildfire, and generated a clamour to travel swiftly on to Nicaea and share in the looting. Peter the Hermit was absent, having travelled back to Constantinople to negotiate for supplies; Geoffrey Burel convinced the entire remainder of the force, some 20,000 strong, that they should move out at once.

On 21 October at dawn they marched out of the camp towards Nicaea. Anna Comnena commented at this juncture that the 'Latins' (Italians and Europeans) were known for their love of money, and that when they went on a military campaign

their lust for wealth grew even stronger, becoming so overpowering that it robbed them of their judgement and made them rush headlong, as here, into trouble. In her account, they simply ran out of the camp towards Nicaea, without arming themselves, clamouring for money, with no semblance of discipline: they were entirely unprepared for what followed.

The Turks had laid an ambush in a narrow valley just 3 miles (5km) from the crusader camp. There they set on the army led by Geoffrey Burel, provoking a wave of blind panic among them. The slaughter was most terrible. Anna Comnena reported that when after the battle men went to clear the battlefield they gathered together the corpses of the fallen crusaders and made not merely a mound or a hill but a grisly flyblown mountain. Only 3,000 crusaders survived, and they took refuge in an abandoned castle. The Turks pursued them there and laid siege, but in time a Byzantine force sailed across from Constantinople, chased the Turks off and freed the crusaders.

A RABBLE OR AN ARMY?

The conventional view of the People's Crusade has been that the people who made this long and fruitless pilgrimage were little more than a rabble roused by an unscrupulous charismatic preacher, and that their 'armies' contained no more than a handful of properly equipped and trained soldiers. However, it is worth considering that this first wave of crusaders maintained their discipline sufficiently to march all the way across Europe as far as

▲ *Peter distributes crosses to eager volunteers. He convinced many of his poorer followers that a host of angels would defend them if they came under attack.*

Constantinople and that in Anatolia they did win military victories before their ultimate defeat. Even granted this, however, the ill-conceived People's Crusade cannot ultimately be adjudged anything more than a disaster. Scores of thousands of people lost their lives – the 3,000 crusaders who survived defeat in Anatolia were the only survivors of the crusade.

After they were freed by the Byzantine relief force from the castle in which they had taken refuge, the survivors made their way slowly back to Constantinople, where they eventually joined up with the better equipped armies that had followed them from Europe.

▼ *The crusaders arrive in Constantinople. A significant proportion of the peasants on the People's Crusade died of starvation or were sold into slavery.*

PRINCES ON CRUSADE

THE LEADERS OF THE FIRST CRUSADE

The European princes and nobles who responded to Pope Urban's call to crusade travelled in five main armies to Constantinople by different routes. They began to leave in mid-summer 1096 and arrived at Constantinople at various times between November 1096 and May 1097.

The first army to arrive was that of Hugh of Vermandois, who as younger brother of King Philip I of France was a prince of a royal house and one of the highest-ranking of the crusaders. He was reputedly convinced to embark on the crusade by an eclipse of the moon in February 1096, which he interpreted as divine guidance. The chronicler William of Tyre called him 'Hugh Magnus' (Hugh the Great), but despite high birth Hugh did very little of note, being an ineffective soldier and leader. He certainly had a high opinion of himself, however: according to Anna Comnena, he sent a breathtakingly arrogant letter to Alexius, in which he declared: 'Be advised, O Emperor, that I am the King of kings, highest-ranking of

▲ *Bohemond of Taranto's crusading feats won him the hand of Constance, daughter of King Philip I of France, in 1104.*

all beneath the sky. My will is that you should attend me upon my arrival and give me the magnificent welcome that is fitting for a visitor of the noblest birth.'

Hugh's army travelled by way of Italy, where they were joined by a number of soldiers previously under the command of Count Emicho, leader of the German Crusade against the Jews – soldiers who had been dispersed by a Hungarian army. The army set sail from Bari across the Adriatic Sea, but were shipwrecked off the Byzantine 'port of Dyrrhachium (now Durres in Albania) and had to be rescued by the Byzantine governor of that locality before being escorted to Constantinople, arriving in November 1096.

GODFREY OF BOUILLON

The second army was from northern France and Belgium, led by Godfrey, Lord of Bouillon and duke of Lower Lorraine, with his younger brother Baldwin and his older brother Eustace III, Count of Boulogne. The army, perhaps 40,000 strong, set out from Lorraine in August

1096 bound for Constantinople: they followed largely the same route as the People's Crusade, through Hungary and the Balkans (part of the Byzantine Empire), where they crossed the River Danube at Belgrade and proceeded via Sofia and Adrianople (modern Edirne in Turkey) and arrived at the Sea of Marmara in mid-December. On 23 December they pitched their camp beneath the walls of Constantinople. In some accounts, this army was referred to as 'the Lorrainers'.

BOHEMOND OF TARANTO

The third army was made up of Normans from southern Italy and led by Bohemond of Taranto. Bohemond was the son of Norman adventurer Robert Guiscard and was an old enemy of Emperor Alexius, having fought against him during his father's failed invasion of the Byzantine Empire in the early 1080s. In his company

▼ *Godfrey of Bouillon. The crusade made him into a figure of legend, celebrated in literature as one of the 'Nine Worthies'.*

was his nephew Tancred, the son of Bohemond's sister, Emma of Apulia.

Bohemond did not hear Pope Urban's call to arms. He joined the crusade only in October 1097 after he encountered knights making their way towards the Holy Land by way of southern Italy, where he and his army – including Tancred – were besieging the town of Amalfi, which had rebelled against his authority. Among these knights was Tancred's brother William: learning of the purpose of their journey, the Normans under Bohemond elected to join the crusade. The army set sail in October 1096, crossing the Adriatic from Brindisi to Avlona (a seaport now in Albania) and marched overland to Constantinople, where it arrived on 9 April 1097.

RAYMOND OF TOULOUSE

The fourth army belonged to Raymond, Count of Toulouse, Duke of Narbonne and Margrave of Provence. He was the first noble knight to take the cross after Pope Urban's speech at Clermont, and was profoundly religious: according to one account in an Armenian chronicle, he had made a pilgrimage to Jerusalem before the First Crusade, and during the course of this journey lost an eye; he had also fought in Spain against Muslim armies. He was 55, the oldest and also the wealthiest of the crusading lords, and he might have expected to be named leader of the expedition, but Pope Urban gave no special position to any of the secular lords, vesting his authority in the papal legate Adhemar, Bishop of Le Puy, who travelled in Raymond's party.

Raymond, in the company of his third wife Elvira (the illegitimate daughter of King Alfonso VI of Castile) and Bishop Adhemar, departed from Toulouse with a large army and a significant contingent of unarmed pilgrims in October 1096. They took an overland route by way of Genoa and Venice and along the coast as far as Dyrrhachium, before heading inland. They arrived at the gates of Constantinople on 27 April 1097.

DUKE ROBERT OF NORMANDY

The fifth main army was jointly led by Duke Robert of Normandy, his brother-in-law Stephen, Count of Blois, and Count Robert II of Flanders.

Duke Robert of Normandy was the eldest son of King William I of England, who, on his deathbed, had bequeathed the duchy of Normandy to Robert and the English throne to his second son, William Rufus. The two brothers had been at war on and off since William Rufus had become King of England on the Conqueror's death in 1087: in September 1096, Robert pawned the duchy of Normandy to William Rufus in return for 10,000 silver marks, which he used to fund his part in the crusade.

Stephen, Count of Blois, was married to Robert's sister, the formidable Adela of Normandy, and according to contemporary accounts went on the crusade only because he was ordered to do so by his wife. (He was to be father of a king of England, for his son Stephen – born at

▲ *Robert II, Count of Flanders, was one of the co-leaders of Robert of Normandy's section of the crusading army.*

Blois in 1096 before the crusade – was King Stephen of England from 1135–54.) Count Robert of Flanders was an experienced campaigner and skilled knight, who had proved his worth by governing Flanders while his father had been away on a pilgrimage to Jerusalem from 1085–91. Also in this army was Bishop Odo of Bayeux.

This fifth army left northern France in October 1096, but was waylaid in southern Italy where Duke Robert and Count Stephen settled for the winter, enjoying the hospitality of local lords. But Count Robert of Flanders pressed on with his force, sailing from Brindisi and marching overland to Constantinople. The remainder of the army followed in the spring, leaving Brindisi in April and arriving in Constantinople in May 1097, just a month behind Raymond's army.

THE CRUSADERS IN CONSTANTINOPLE
NEGOTIATIONS WITH EMPEROR ALEXIUS

Alexius quite naturally viewed the princely crusaders with suspicion. The princes and lords had mobilized great armies and brought them on to imperial Byzantine territory officially to supply help to Christians in the East, but it was difficult to be sure of their true motives.

The emperor could not be certain that the Latin lords were not plotting to capture pieces of his empire for themselves. In any case, the crusaders were also talking of capturing Jerusalem, which Alexius still viewed as a possession of the Byzantine Empire, even if one that was temporarily in Muslim hands. Moreover, among the leaders was a major former adversary, Bohemond of Taranto.

Alexius determined to make each of the crusader lords swear an oath of allegiance to him, under which they would pledge to be his vassals and would promise to return any Byzantine lands that they won in the course of the crusade. In return, he would supply the crusade with provisions, money, horses, guides and a supporting

▲ *Constantinople had formidable defences. Its magnificent double walls, with 142 fortified towers and 11 gates, were built in 412–22 during the reign of Theodosius II.*

military force. In demanding personal oaths of loyalty, Alexius adopted the established practices of Europe: in his own domain he could expect the total obedience of his subjects, but in the feudal lands from which these lords had come, he knew, great men generally held they were bound only by oaths they swore in person to an emperor, a king or a suzerain (feudal superior).

HUGH OF VERMANDOIS

The first of the princely crusaders to arrive, Hugh of Vermandois, expected a grand welcome; Alexius was happy to provide gifts and to spout honeyed words, but he kept Hugh under close supervision – virtually as a prisoner – in a monastery. For all his self-aggrandizement, Hugh did not object when asked to swear an oath of loyalty as vassal to the emperor.

GODFREY OF BOUILLON

When the second main army arrived under Godfrey of Bouillon and his brothers, Alexius made them camp outside the

THE IMPACT OF CONSTANTINOPLE

The city of Constantinople amazed the crusaders. Emperor Alexius had decided to make the armies camp outside Constantinople's great city walls, but he allowed small groups of five or six at a time to enter the city in order to pray in the churches and see the sights. They were astonished by what they found – by the

city's size and wealth, by its baths and sanitation and by the beauty of the churches and the rich collections of treasures and of sacred relics. Fulcher of Chartres wrote: 'Oh what a splendid and noble city! What fine monasteries, what elegant palaces we saw, what superb workmanship! How many superb works … It would take too long to describe the richness of all kinds of goods, of silver and gold, fine clothes and sacred relics.' The Frankish lords were also suspicious of, and perhaps a little intimidated by, the courtly ritual of the Byzantine Empire.

◄ *Constantinople retained its great beauty through centuries of conflict.*

▲ *Godfrey of Bouillon and his army praise God as they make the passage across the Bosphorus into Anatolia, moving closer to their ultimate destination, Jerusalem.*

city walls. Godfrey was unwilling to swear the proposed oath of loyalty, maintaining that he could not became a vassal of Alexius since his feudal lord was the German emperor Henry IV. He attempted to play for time, since he wanted to wait for the other European lords to arrive. Alexius, on the other hand, was concerned about what might happen if Godfrey, Bohemond of Taranto and other lords marshalled their armies at Constantinople at the same time: he was absolutely determined to move on Godfrey's troops before Bohemond arrived, but he could not do so until Godfrey agreed to swear the oath. Alexius cut off the food supplies to the crusader camp, but when this provoked an outburst of looting and then scavenging he began to provide food once more.

The waiting game continued until, growing desperate, Alexius cut off the food to the camp again. This time Godfrey and his army launched a military attack on Constantinople, which provoked panic among the citizens. Alexius decided to move the army on without requiring Godfrey to swear the oath but the men he sent with this message were attacked by the crusaders before they could deliver the information. Finally, Alexius lost his patience and unleashed the imperial military on the crusader camp. This was enough to bring Godfrey and his brothers to heel and on Easter Sunday, 5 April 1097 they swore the required oaths, recognizing Alexius as their overlord and promising to return to him any conquests they made in former Byzantine territories. The next day, Godfrey and his troops were transported across the Bosphorus.

THE NORMAN CONTINGENT

Three days later, on 9 April, Bohemond of Taranto arrived. According to contemporary sources, Bohemond declared 'I come by my own free will to be a friend to your Majesty'; Alexius housed him in magnificent quarters and gave him splendid gifts. Contemporary accounts report that Bohemond asked to be named as deputy or chief commander to Alexius in Asia, but Alexius was noncommittal. Bohemond was happy to swear the oath that Alexius suggested, although he set little store by it and had no intention of keeping it. They moved on: on 26 April the Norman army was transported across the Bosphorus and joined the troops of Godfrey of Bouillon in Anatolia. Bohemond's nephew Tancred, however, had refused to swear the oath and slipped out of Constantinople by night to escape having to do so.

RAYMOND OF TOULOUSE AND ROBERT OF NORMANDY

That very same day saw the arrival at Constantinople of the army of Raymond of Toulouse. It had not had an easy march, and had even come under attack from imperial forces. Raymond refused to swear an oath to Alexius as his overlord, but promised to return conquered lands.

The final groups of arrivals, Duke Robert of Normandy, his brother-in-law Stephen, Count of Blois, and Count Robert II of Flanders agreed to swear the oath. According to chronicler Fulcher of Chartres, who travelled in their company, swearing the oath was 'essential to make good our friendship with the emperor, for without his advice and help we would not be able to make the journey we planned'.

THE SIEGE OF NICAEA
THE CRUSADERS MAKE THEIR MARK

The princely and noble leaders of the First Crusade were now gathered in Anatolia at the head of an army of perhaps 60,000 men. They agreed that they should move first against Nicaea, the capital of the Turkish sultanate of Rum, for it was clear that the crusade could not safely advance beyond Nicaea towards Jerusalem if the city remained in Turkish hands.

The crusaders were not a united force, for there were many rivalries between lords, and regional, cultural and linguistic differences among the knights and soldiers. In addition to the main army there were many non-combatants – women and children, some of them families of crusaders, as well as aged pilgrims and clergy – and the battered remnants of the People's Crusade. There was also a Byzantine force, around 2,000 strong, supplied by Alexius and under the command of an experienced general named Taticius; Alexius's order was that the crusaders would give the command of cities and territories they captured to Taticius.

CRUSADERS ENCAMP AT NICAEA
The crusader army arrived at Nicaea in instalments – the first groups, under Godfrey of Bouillon, Robert of Flanders,

▲ *During the siege of Nicaea, the crusaders lobbed the heads of corpses into the city.*

Tancred and Taticius arrived on 6 May and were reinforced a few days later by Bohemond of Taranto. On 14 May a large force under Raymond of Toulouse swelled their numbers, and the final contingent, under Robert of Normandy and Stephen of Blois, joined the camp on 3 June.

The city of Nicaea, on the eastern side of Lake Iznik, was an ancient Christian town, where, in AD325, the Church's first General Council had agreed the statement of Catholic Christian beliefs still known as the Nicene Creed. Situated just 50 miles (80km) from Constantinople, it was for centuries part of the Byzantine Empire, but had been captured by the Seljuk Turks in 1077. The crusaders surrounded it on three sides and settled in for a siege; they were unable, however, to blockade the lake approaches so the city could still bring in supplies. Emperor Alexius provided the crusader army with supplies and siege equipment.

ABSENT RULER RETURNS
Kilij Arslan, the Sultan of Rum, was not present to defend his capital. Not expecting any greater threat from the new wave of crusaders than he had experienced from the ineffective armies of the People's Crusade, he had departed to fight rival ruler Ghazi ibn Danishmend in Sivas (also

▼ *Under heavy attack by the forces of the Seljuk sultan, Kilij Arslan, the crusaders' rally was later attributed to heavenly aid.*

known as Sebastea), several hundred miles away at the eastern edge of his territory. (The Danishmends were named after dynastic founder Ghazi ibn Danishmend; he had captured the Roman city of Sebastea and renamed it Sivas, making it his capital in *c*.1080.) When Kilij Arslan received messages to the effect that a large and apparently well-equipped army was besieging Nicaea, he made a hurried peace with Danishmend and rushed back.

By mid-May Kilij Arslan was in the vicinity of Nicaea, viewing the crusader forces with dismay. On 16 May he launched a surprise attack on the recently arrived army of Raymond of Toulouse, which was still setting up camp to the south of the town. It was a fierce clash, in which Raymond showed great skill to hold his force together until reinforcements sent by Godfrey of Bouillon arrived and decided the conflict in the crusaders' favour. A notable casualty, according to the account in a letter written by Stephen of Blois, was Baldwin, Count of Ghent. Kilij Arslan withdrew and gathered his forces in the hills to fight another day.

The siege of Nicaea lasted six weeks. The crusaders had only lightweight siege equipment and were unable to do significant damage to the town walls; they were

▼ Nicaea's walls, about 32ft (10m) tall, ran for a total of 3 miles (5km). The west wall gave directly on to the lake.

limited to hurling small rocks, flaming missiles, beehives, the heads of corpses and other foul objects at the defenders. They could not smash their way into the town and since the town garrison could bring in supplies across the water of the lake, there was no hope of starving them out. There seemed to be no end in sight.

OUTMANOEUVRED BY ALEXIUS

Emperor Alexius was keeping a close watch on events from a camp at Pelecanum nearby. He wanted to regain control of Nicaea in good condition for the Byzantine Empire, and so wanted to prevent the crusaders destroying its defences, overrunning the city and looting its wealth. With typical cunning, he went behind the backs of the crusaders, opening secret negotiations with the Turks in Nicaea. He promised them good treatment if they would surrender to him; if they did, he would protect them with his own troops against the crusaders.

On the morning of 19 June the crusaders prepared to launch a major attack on the town and saw to their initial puzzlement and then dismay that the Byzantine standard was flying above the walls. The Byzantine troops were in control of the city. They acted as guards, only

▲ Nicaea was an important city for Christians, where a groundbreaking council had taken place in AD325 to formulate what became known as the Nicene Creed.

allowing the crusaders inside the walls in small groups. Alexius laid on food and wine for the crusading army and made gifts of jewels and gold to the leaders, but the crusaders remained deeply unhappy at having been outmanoeuvred and denied the riches they had expected to gain from looting.

In the aftermath, Alexius had a stand-off with Tancred: he refused to give Tancred his share of the gold unless the prince swore an oath of fealty. Tancred insisted that his loyalty was to Bohemond, not to Alexius; and he demanded as much gold as all the other lords put together, plus the amount it would take to fill Alexius's campaign tent. The tense situation was only resolved when Bohemond persuaded Tancred to give way.

Despite the crusaders' disappointment at the outcome in Nicaea, the future looked bright. Stephen of Blois wrote to his wife Countess Adela declaring they would be in Jerusalem in just five weeks. In fact, the crusaders' journey to the Holy City was to take more than two years.

MEN OF IRON
THE BATTLE OF DORYLAEUM

Near Dorylaeum (modern Eskiehir) on the Anatolian plateau, the crusaders were attacked by a Seljuk Turkish army led by Kilij Arslan, Sultan of Rum. The battle, on 1 July 1097, was fierce and long – from the third hour to the ninth, according to the Frankish chronicle the *Gesta Francorum*. After weathering a Turkish assault, the crusaders were reinforced when the rear of their army caught up and turned the tables to win a great victory.

BUILD-UP TO THE BATTLE
Following the capture of Nicaea, the crusaders set out eastwards across the Anatolian plateau towards their ultimate goal, Jerusalem. In the vanguard of the army were around 20,000 Normans under Bohemond of Taranto, his nephew Tancred and other noblemen; in the rear, around a day behind, were some 30,000 Franks led by Raymond of Toulouse, Godfrey of Bouillon and other lords. Kilij Arslan, who was smarting at the loss of his

capital city Nicaea, had retreated to the mountains and, in alliance with Ghazi ibn Danishmend, prepared an ambush for the Christian invaders. The Turkish army was probably about 20,000–30,000 strong – although the contemporary crusader accounts claim it was much bigger, with Raymond of Aguilers suggesting 150,000 and Fulcher of Chartres reporting 360,000 men under Kilij Arslan's command.

Bohemond noticed that Turkish scouts were watching the crusaders' vanguard, and on the evening of 30 June, three days' march out of Nicaea, set up a defensive camp near the town of Dorylaeum. At once, he sent a messenger riding at breakneck speed back to the army's rearguard, with an urgent summons for the Franks to come to the rescue of their comrades.

DAWN ONSLAUGHT
The Turks attacked at dawn the next day, 1 July. Bohemond ordered his knights to form a defensive line, while the foot

soldiers and women took refuge in the camp. He ordered that no one was to try to charge the attackers – they were to put all their efforts into holding them at bay. The plan was to defend the camp until the rest of the army caught up.

Rather than engaging the crusaders in a pitched battle of foot soldiers and cavalry of the kind fought in Europe, the Turks surrounded the camp and attacked from all sides. The Turkish army was all cavalry: its horsemen swept in from every direction, then swerved away at the last moment, sending a storm of spears and arrows into the camp. The attack was strange and terrifying for the crusaders – as Fulcher of Chartres wrote, 'this form of warfare was not known to us'. The *Gesta*

▼ *Heavily armoured crusaders clash head on with the Turks. At Dorylaeum the Franks were amazed at the size of the Turkish army, while the Turks marvelled at the ferocity of the crusaders' charge.*

▲ *When properly deployed, a fully armoured cavalry backed up by foot soldiers and archers was a formidable force.*

Francorum reported, 'the Turks were attacking us from all sides … we were not able to resist or weather the force of so many'. The defence was brave, but seemed ultimately hopeless.

Many of the pilgrims who accompanied the soldiers were killed, and those huddled in the camp feared that they would be slain. According to contemporary accounts, while some women ran tirelessly back and forward bringing water to the cavalry, others seem to have been quickly convinced that defeat was inevitable and set about making themselves as attractive as possible as a way of averting death by winning admirers among the Turks.

REINFORCEMENTS TO THE RESCUE

For six hours the army of Kilij Arslan and his allies kept up the assault. They were breaking through the crusaders' defences and an end to the battle was in sight. But at this moment, the rear of the crusaders' army rode in to the rescue.

On their arrival, a group of knights under Raymond of Toulouse attacked the Turks from the flank. Then the crusader cavalry drew up swiftly in battle formation, with Godfrey of Bouillon and Hugh

of Vermandois aligning themselves to the right of Bohemond, and Stephen of Blois and Robert of Normandy to the left. They attacked, a great wall of cavalry, bristling with lances, thundering across the field.

THE LURE OF RICHES

The battle continued. The crusaders were no longer in desperate straits, but they were unable to drive the Turks off. According to the *Gesta Francorum*, the crusaders marvelled at the size of the Turkish army and knowing that these essentially nomadic men carried their riches with them, they looked forward to seizing some of the wealth they had missed out on when they had been denied the chance to sack Nicaea. They declared: 'Let us all be one in faith in Christ and in the victory of the Holy Cross because this day, God willing it, we shall become rich!'

Then knights under the papal legate Bishop Adhemar of

Le Puy launched a surprise attack on the Turks from the rear, having ridden round under cover of some low hills. The army of Kilij Arslan, now tiring, and fearing being surrounded, broke and fled. The crusaders rode in triumph through the enemy camp, setting it afire and looting the riches in its tents.

VICTORY FOR THE 'MEN OF IRON'

The Turks' casualties were very heavy. Probably around 4,000 crusaders died; among them was Tancred's brother, William. Disaster had been very close at Dorylaeum: defeat would have brought the crusade to a premature end, but victory reinforced the crusaders' belief in their holy mission.

▼ *The Turks were astonished by the determination of the Norman and Frankish knights. Impressed by the chain mail armour that allowed the knight to withstand the blows of swords and points of arrows, and their indomitable strength under attack, they dubbed the crusaders the 'men of iron'.*

DEFENDER OF JERUSALEM
GODFREY OF BOUILLON

French knight Godfrey of Bouillon did not play a leading role in the First Crusade until its final stages, when he was one of the first Christians into Jerusalem on 15 July 1099 and after its capture became the first ruler of the Latin Kingdom of Jerusalem. He died only a year later, but he succeeded in consolidating the kingdom, and within a century of his death had become a hero of medieval legend, celebrated in chansons about the crusade that were told by *trouvères* (troubadours) at the noble courts of Europe as early as the 12th century.

Born in 1060 in northern France or Belgium, perhaps in Boulogne-sur-Mer, Godfrey was lord of Bouillon, a castle and village in the Ardennes forest of France, and from 1087 duke of Lower Lorraine. Most of Godfrey's life before he left in his mid-30s on crusade was spent asserting his right to the lordship of Lower Lorraine against attempts by Henry IV, King of Germany and ultimately Holy Roman Emperor, to take these territories away.

FINANCING THE CRUSADE

In 1095, inspired by Pope Urban's call to crusade, Godfrey either sold or agreed loans against his substantial landholdings and thereby raised a large force of knights. He also accepted money from Jewish communities in the Rhineland who were desperately attempting to buy safety in the face of repeated atrocities by crusaders. With his brothers Baldwin and Eustace, Godfrey embarked with an army of perhaps 40,000 from Lorraine in August 1096. They reached Constantinople in November, the second of the princely armies to arrive, following that of Hugh of Vermandois, brother of Philip I of France.

When the following year the crusaders set out for Jerusalem, Godfrey and his knights played only a supporting role in the conflicts en route, such as the capture of Nicaea and Antioch, while in between those two events, he and his contingent were part of the force that rode to the rescue of the beleaguered vanguard of the crusader army at the Battle of Dorylaeum. After Antioch, he took part in the march on Jerusalem and the siege of the city and was one of the first knights to climb the walls when it was taken on 15 July 1099.

DEFENDER OF THE HOLY SEPULCHRE

A week later, in a meeting of the crusade leaders in the Church of the Holy Sepulchre in Jerusalem on 22 July, Godfrey was elected ruler of the newly established Latin Kingdom of Jerusalem. He did not accept the title of king in a city where the crusaders believed that Christ himself was the only true ruler, and was known either as *Princeps* (Prince) or as *Advocatus Sancti Sepulchri* (Defender of the Holy Sepulchre).

According to the *Gesta Francorum*, Godfrey's task as ruler was to 'subdue the pagans and defend the Christians'. He set about ensuring the survival of the new kingdom, which was by no means certain, for the great majority of the crusaders departed, leaving him with a force of only 300 knights and 2,000 infantry and without a fleet with which to mount naval blockades of Muslim cities along the coast. He agreed truces with the cities of Acre, Ascalon and Caesarea and, most important of all in the short term, succeeded in defeating the Egyptian army in the Battle of Ascalon.

DEATH AND LEGACY

On 18 July, less than a year after his election, Godfrey died in Jerusalem. He was around 40 years old. Accounts of how he died differ: the Muslim chronicler Ibn al-Qalansi reported that Godfrey was shot by an arrow while besieging Acre, but

▼ *At Jerusalem Godfrey and the crusaders emulate the example of Joshua and the Israelites at Jericho in marching around the city prior to launching their attack.*

Christian chroniclers wrote that he fell ill in Caesarea in June and succumbed to the illness on 18 July in Jerusalem – some versions allege he was poisoned by the emir of Caesarea.

Godfrey was succeeded by his younger brother Baldwin – according to the chronicler Radulph of Caen, before he died he called the Patriarch of Jerusalem and leading secular lords and warned them, saying they needed to consider formally who should succeed him, but they asked him to nominate his successor and when he named Baldwin they were pleased and pledged to be loyal subjects to him.

THE LEGEND OF GODFREY OF BOUILLON

It was Godfrey's position as the first ruler of Jerusalem and his achievement in securing the future of the Latin kingdom there that established his towering reputation in medieval legend. In the stories that

▼ *The enduring fame and memory of Godfrey of Bouillon is honoured by a fine equestrian statue in Place Royale, Brussels.*

▲ *The clergy, knights and citizens of the young Kingdom of Jerusalem mourn Godfrey at his funeral on 23 July 1100.*

quickly began to circulate, he was presented as an exemplar of fearless chivalry and a man of immense strength – in one story he wrestled a bear into submission, in another he beheaded a camel with one skilful stroke of his sword. William of Tyre, whose chronicle of the Kingdom of Jerusalem was written in the late 12th century when the myth of Godfrey was already established, described him as taller than average, with solid limbs, a brawny chest and 'strong beyond any comparison'; William reported that the hero was good-looking, with blond hair and beard. Godfrey was certainly an intelligent man and a forceful character, but there is little evidence that he was truly devout, and he was certainly not the paragon of Christian virtue that he became in his legend.

THE MARCH ACROSS ANATOLIA
AND THE ESTABLISHMENT OF THE COUNTY OF EDESSA

Following their victory in the Battle of Dorylaeum, the crusaders rested for two days and then marched onwards to the south. They headed across the Anatolian plateau bound for Antioch in Pisidia and thence on to Iconium.

A HELLISH SUMMER

It was summer and the gruelling heat took a heavy toll on the army. According to chronicler Albert of Aix, the suffering was terrible: children, women, animals and soldiers died at the roadside from thirst and heat exhaustion; some women gave birth in the dust and were too weak to do anything but stagger on, abandoning their babies in the roadway; when a river was reached, many more people and their ani-mals died from drinking too much. Albert claims that 500 people died in a single day from the effects of the heat. It seemed to the crusaders that far from arriving in the paradise of a land flowing in milk and honey, as promised by Urban II, they had arrived in hell.

Near Heraclea, the crusaders had to muster the strength to fight a Turkish army under two emirs from Cappadocia; the battle was soon over, for the Turkish army – perhaps made nervous by reports of the crusaders' exploits at Dorylaeum – dispersed and fled when Bohemond gathered his finest knights and charged at speed with couched lance.

In September the crusaders arrived at the Cilician Gates, the daunting pass

▲ *The people of Edessa pay homage to Baldwin I, King of Jerusalem.*

through the snow-covered Taurus Mountains that lay between the Anatolian plateau and the Mediterranean coast. By this stage almost all the travellers' pack animals had died and many knights were without horses, having to ride on oxen and force dogs to pull carts.

The weather was still hot and dry and the crusaders decided that if they took the pass, they would be vulnerable to guerrilla attacks from the Turks. The main body of the army now marched north-east, away from the Cilician Gates, into easier wooded country towards Armenian lands. In these territories, the crusaders could expect a welcome: the Armenians were Christians who had been evicted from their lands in the southern Caucasus by Byzantine forces and so had little affection for the emperor of Constantinople. They were also enemies of the Turks.

FIGHTING OVER TARSUS

A smaller force of around 100 knights and 200 foot soldiers under Tancred elected to split off from the main army, risk the passage through the Cilician Gates and attempt an assault on the Turkish-garrisoned town of Tarsus on the plain beyond. At Tarsus, Tancred succeeded in driving out the Turks and raising his own banner, with the help of reinforcements of 500 knights and 2,000 foot soldiers led by

---

FIRST-HAND ACCOUNTS OF THE FIRST CRUSADE

Such was the impact made by the crusaders' success in librating Jerusalem that several histories were written soon afterwards. *Gesta Francorum* (Deeds of the Franks) was written almost immediately after the capture of Jerusalem in c.1100 by an anonymous follower of Bohemond of Taranto. Fulcher of Chartres, a churchman who travelled in the party of Stephen of Blois, also wrote a history of the crusade perhaps as early as 1101–06. The history of Raymond of Aguilers, chaplain to Raymond, Count of Toulouse, is rich in accounts of visions and miracles – including the discovery of the Holy Lance at Antioch. Radulph of Caen was chaplain to Bohemond of Taranto and he wrote a biography of Bohemond's nephew, Tancred, in c.1112. Albert of Aix (also known as Albert of Aachen) wrote a 12-volume history of the First Crusade and the early history of the Latin Kingdom of Jerusalem in c.1125–50; Albert's is the most detailed chronicle of the First Crusade. Among other first-hand accounts of events of the time are Anna Comnena's biography of her father, Emperor Alexius, and the writings of Armenian Christian Matthew of Edessa. There are also later accounts of events of the First Crusade written by Muslim chroniclers, including Ibn al-Athir and Sibt Ibn al-Jawsi.

▼ *In the aftermath of the crusade, churchmen recorded God's triumphs.*

Baldwin of Boulogne, brother of Godfrey of Bouillon. The two knights then disputed the spoils: Baldwin had led his men through the Cilician Gates not to help Tancred but in order to prevent him (and thereby his uncle Bohemond) from taking control of the coast.

Rival lords were coming into open and bitter conflict as they disputed control of captured territories. In this instance, Baldwin had many more knights and soldiers than Tancred, so Tancred gave way. When more of Bohemond's knights arrived at Tarsus, Baldwin refused to open the city gates and they were put to the sword in an attack by Turkish troops. Tancred moved on and took control first of Adana and then of Mamistra. Baldwin followed. The two armies fought, but finally agreed to withdraw from the coast.

ON TO ANTIOCH

The main army had a terrible time crossing the Anti-Taurus Mountains that stood inland, behind the Taurus range. By this time it was October and heavy rains had begun – in wet conditions, the steep tracks were almost impassable. The army limped across the mountains and moved on

▼ *During the lengthy siege of Antioch, various plots to take the city by stealth were attempted, and rumours of secret truces and intercepted messengers were rife.*

towards the city of Antioch. Tancred, meanwhile, had captured Alexandretta, crossed into Syria and was reunited with the main army as they prepared to besiege Antioch in October 1097.

BALDWIN ESTABLISHES THE COUNTY OF EDESSA

For his part, Baldwin headed north-east to the town of Edessa, an important and wealthy Armenian town to the east of the River Euphrates, while the main army settled in for the siege of Antioch. Edessa was governed by an Armenian Christian

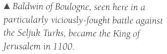

▲ *Baldwin of Boulogne, seen here in a particularly viciously-fought battle against the Seljuk Turks, became the King of Jerusalem in 1100.*

named Thoros, who had only two years earlier captured it from the Turks. Thoros's position was far from secure: he was surrounded on all sides by Seljuk emirs who were all too keen to depose him. He was happy to welcome a fellow Christian in Baldwin, and to accept the support of his fighting men. Baldwin, clearly sensing possibility, demanded that Thoros adopt him as his son and heir, which he did in a public ceremony.

Shortly afterwards, Thoros was killed during a revolt by the townspeople, who were said to hate him because he was a Greek Orthodox rather than an Armenian Orthodox Christian. Baldwin became ruler, calling himself Count of Edessa. Thoros's death was highly convenient for Baldwin, but we do not know for sure that he masterminded it – indeed, his contemporary supporters vehemently denied that he had any involvement.

Baldwin thereby established the County of Edessa, the first of the crusader territories that would be created in the course of the First Crusade.

CHAPTER FOUR

BOUND FOR JERUSALEM

The extraordinary events of June 1098 at Antioch were the turning point of the First Crusade. In that month the crusaders twice went from despair to wild elation. At the start of June they were bogged down in a siege of the city that they had been enforcing since October 1097 with little progress, and were expecting the arrival within days of a vast Seljuk Turkish army led by Sultan Kerbogha of Mosul, who had every intention of lifting the siege.

One of their leaders, Stephen of Blois, abandoned the enterprise and departed for home. They were starving, and frightened, and desperate. Then they took the city through cunning and subterfuge on the night of 2 June, and rejoiced wildly and raucously. But within three days they were plunged into despair again, when Kerbogha arrived and besieged them. Within the city they wondered if the entire crusade would come to nothing, but after visions of St Andrew and the discovery of what was purportedly the Holy Lance – the spear with which Christ's side was pierced on the cross – morale soared. On 28 June the crusaders threw open the gates of Antioch and rode out behind Bishop Adhemar bearing the Holy Lance to take on the huge army of Sultan Kerbogha. Despite being vastly outnumbered, they won, and claimed it as a miracle. Antioch was safe, and as soldiers of Christ riding in a divinely ordained mission to liberate Jerusalem; the crusaders must triumph.

▲ *The town of Latakia was one of the key ports in Syria. The crusader armies were dependent on it for the delivery of supplies.*

◄ *The crusaders at last reach Jerusalem, and give thanks and praise to God for a hard-won achievement that has taken so much longer than expected.*

THE SIEGE OF ANTIOCH
A LONG STRUGGLE TO WEAR DOWN THE CITY'S DEFENCES

The crusader army drew up before Antioch in October 1097. The city lay in a vital position on the route from Anatolia into Syria, and the crusader lords knew that they had to capture it before moving southwards through Syria and on down the Mediterranean coast towards the city of Jerusalem.

FORBIDDING DEFENCES
At once the crusader lords saw that capturing Antioch was a daunting task, for it had 400 towers set in 25 miles (40km) of defensive walls running across very hostile terrain. A siege would be difficult – the city stood on the bank of the River Orontes, so was very well supplied with water, and there were even areas of pasture set safely within the forbidding walls. Military attack was impossible from the north, because of the river, and from the south because of the forbidding bulk of Mount Silphius, site of Antioch's citadel. Writing home, Stephen of Blois called the city 'unassailable' and by general consensus the city was deemed to be impossible to take by force: the Arabs had captured it in AD637, and since that time it had only been taken twice – by the Byzantine Empire from Arabs in 969 and by Seljuk Turks from the Byzantines in the 1080s – both times by treachery.

In October 1097 when the crusaders set up camp before the city, Antioch was in the hands of a Turkish governor, Yaghi-Siyan, ruling on behalf of the Seljuk sultan in Baghdad, Barkiyaroq. The citizens were mostly Christians, a combination of Orthodox Greeks, Armenians and Syrians, most of whom disliked their governor heartily. Taking a precaution against possible treachery, Yaghi-Siyan made himself more unpopular by expelling the leading Christian citizens and jailing the Patriarch of Antioch, a very senior ecclesiastic on a par with the patriarchs of Constantinople and of Jerusalem.

TO ATTACK OR TO BESIEGE?
The crusader lords discussed how to proceed: Raymond of Toulouse argued for a military assault, but Bohemond urged a siege and an attempt to foster treachery within the city. Caution prevailed, and the army settled in for a siege. As autumn passed into winter, they had to deal with dwindling food supplies, regular sallies by the garrison and the taunting behaviour of Yaghi-Siyan, who put the Patriarch of Antioch in a cage, and hung it from the walls to enrage the Christians without. Stephen of Blois wrote to his wife, reporting that: 'We have lived through great

▲ *Like the cities of Nicaea and Jerusalem, Antioch was surrounded by massive walls that demanded the construction of siege towers for any attack to be successful.*

suffering and evils beyond counting. Many people have exhausted their finances, and others were saved from starvation only by the kindness of God. The cold is excessive and there are terrible deluges of rain.' In these months, having come so far, thousands of the poorer crusaders died of starvation; some people ate their horses, while there were even reports of cannibalism among the most desperate.

TWO RELIEF ARMIES ROUTED

The need for food grew so severe that in late December Bohemond and Robert of Flanders risked riding out on a foraging expedition up the fertile valley of the River Orontes. There they encountered a large Turkish army under Sultan Duqaq that was marching from Damascus to raise the siege of Antioch. In a tense battle, the crusaders recovered from a disastrous start, in which Robert of Flanders and his men were almost defeated, to launch a powerful counter-attack that drove the Turks off. Bohemond and Robert returned safely to Antioch, but without the supplies they had been seeking.

The New Year brought little comfort. Godfrey of Bouillon and Raymond of Toulouse fell ill. Robert of Normandy left the siege, withdrawing to Laodicea in Anatolia (near modern Eskihisar in Turkey). In February the Byzantine general Taticius took his troops north, either in search of supplies or else because he judged it more important to consolidate Byzantine gains in Anatolia than continue

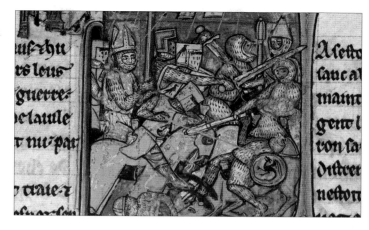

▲ *Wearing his mitre in battle, papal legate Adhemar of Le Puy takes the battle to the Seljuks at Antioch. He carries the Holy Lance discovered within the city.*

▼ *During the long months of the siege at Antioch, the crusaders spent a great deal of time building siege equipment to drive home their assault, but they made little progress.*

a hopeless siege. Many began to despair, losing their faith in what they were doing; some deserted, including Peter the Hermit who was caught and forcibly brought back to Antioch by Tancred.

Then a fresh threat emerged: news arrived that a large relief army under Radwan, Seljuk ruler of Aleppo, had approached and had set up camp at Harenc, only 25 miles (40km) from Antioch, in preparation for launching an attack on the besieging army. The crusaders struck first: Bohemond led a company of knights out by night and surprised Radwan's army, winning a stunning victory despite being vastly outnumbered.

SIEGE EQUIPMENT

In March an English fleet under Edgar the Atheling, a claimant to the throne of England, arrived at St Symeon, the port of Antioch, with supplies, siege equipment and building materials. The crusaders tightened their grip on the city by building tall siege towers and a fort called the 'Castle of Raymond' opposite the city's Bridge Gate; Tancred established a position in a monastery opposite St George's Gate. Spring turned to summer and although the city was almost entirely encircled, the crusaders were no closer to taking it by force. It was clear that they would need to find someone in the city who was willing to betray his masters.

THE FALL OF ANTIOCH
THE CRUSADERS CAPTURE THE CITY

In May 1098 the crusading army encamped around Antioch received news that a mighty relief army was approaching under the command of the powerful Sultan Kerbogha of Mosul. It was clear that they needed to take the city before Kerbogha arrived, otherwise his force would either destroy the crusader army or drive it away – and all their efforts and suffering during the eight-month siege would have been wasted.

THE CRUSADERS ABANDONED
At this crucial moment Stephen of Blois, who had been elected commander-in-chief of the besieging army, abandoned the crusade. Deciding that the enterprise was doomed to failure and taking a sizeable contingent of French soldiers with him, he marched back towards Constantinople to take a ship for Europe.

▲ *Betrayed to its besiegers, Antioch is overrun. The city has a European look in this 15th-century French illustration.*

His timing could not have been worse, for Bohemond had found the ally he had been seeking within Antioch. This man was an Armenian, a Christian convert to Islam named Firuz, who commanded key defence towers overlooking the Gate of St George. Firuz had been fined for hoarding foods and according to some versions had discovered that his wife had been seduced by his superior officer. He was happy to have his revenge and profit by it.

BOHEMOND TAKES THE CITY
On the night of 2 June 1098 the crusading army feigned a retreat from the city walls. To Antioch's Turkish governor, Yaghi-Siyan, it looked as if the news of

Sultan Kerbogha's imminent arrival had forced the invading Christians to take fright and abandon the enterprise, or else to lift the siege in order to fight Kerbogha's army in open countryside.

But in the middle of the night, the treacherous watchman Firuz let down a rope beside the Gate of St George and allowed Bohemond to climb into the city. At the top, in the darkness, Bohemond felt his hand seized by another and heard a voice whisper: 'Long life to this hand.' He was followed in by a group of 60 knights. They succeeded in surprising the watchmen and guards and at dawn opened the Gates of St George and of the Bridge.

LOOTING AND DESTRUCTION
Meanwhile the main army had returned under cover of darkness and now they swept into the city. Terrible scenes followed, as the starving crusaders gave vent to their fear and greed, raping and killing, looting and burning. Many of the Christian citizens burst out from their houses into the streets to seek revenge against the Turkish overlords, but were killed in the confusion and lawlessness by the blood-crazed crusaders.

A few Turks survived by taking refuge in the citadel under the command of a son of Yaghi-Siyan. As for Yaghi-Siyan himself, he escaped on horseback, but fell and was knocked unconscious during his flight to the mountains; his companions left him for dead, but some Armenians found him and, recognizing his face, cut off his head. They brought the corpse and its head to Bohemond in Antioch and were given a substantial reward.

The crusaders, when their heads cleared, praised God. Another victory had been achieved that had seemed impossible. They had taken the impregnable city of Antioch. It was beginning to seem as if their success in the crusade truly was to be guaranteed by God.

THE TAFURS

The most intense members of the crusader army were the Tafurs, poor soldiers originally part of the People's Crusade who were fired with wild religious fanaticism. According to Guibert of Nogent they marched barefoot and without weapons, living on the roots of plants, as a kind of holy army, and led by their own king of the Tafurs. They were notorious among the enemy – their name comes from the Arabic *tafuria*, meaning 'poverty-stricken'. They were always associated with the most extreme behaviour of the army, for instance performing acts of cannibalism during the siege of Antioch or later at Maarrat an-Numan, and were said to have urged on soldiers to acts of cruelty against the enemy at Antioch and in Jerusalem. The Tafurs were later celebrated as the deserving poor in the crusade chanson, the *Chanson d'Antioch*, which suggested that God had led the crusaders to victory because of the Tafurs' religious devotion.

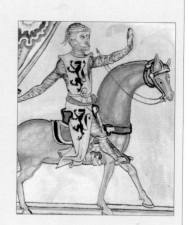

▶ *The 'king' of the Tafurs was reputedly a wealthy Norman knight, who took pity on their plight and gave up his position and comforts to become their leader.*

TRAPPED INSIDE THE CITY

But in the days following their victory, the Christians' delight turned to fear once more. Sultan Kerbogha arrived on 6 June and set his army before the city. The besiegers became the besieged.

There was little food within Antioch. Kerbogha's troops took possession of the citadel and the crusaders had to fight determinedly to prevent them flooding over its walls into the city.

The crusaders pinned their hopes increasingly desperately on relief from Emperor Alexius, who had set out with an army from Constantinople in the spring. But these hopes were empty: Alexius had met the fleeing Stephen of Blois, who had described the critical situation at Antioch. Alexius, convinced that the crusaders' cause was lost, had turned back.

The crusaders' numbers were cut further by desertions – those who fled were derided as 'rope-danglers', presumably because they used ropes to climb from the city walls. By this stage, the Christian army probably numbered no more than 30,000. The crusaders' position was desperate.

▶ *Flooding into the city after months of frustration, the crusaders ran amok. Terrified citizens jumped to their deaths to avoid being torn limb from limb.*

MIRACLES AT ANTIOCH

FIRED WITH BELIEF, THE CRUSADERS DEFEAT SULTAN KERBOGHA

In early June, as we have seen, the crusaders were at the lowest of ebbs. Once the euphoria of breaking into Antioch had died down, they found themselves besieged and starving in the city.

Then, on 11 June, a priest named Stephen of Valence reported to the papal legate Bishop Adhemar that he had had a vision of the Blessed Virgin Mary and of Christ himself and that Christ had promised to come to the army's aid. Around the same time, a Provençal peasant named Peter Bartholomew reported that he had had a whole series of visions of St Andrew, who had revealed that the Holy Lance – the spear with which Christ's side was pierced on the cross – was within Antioch, buried beneath the Church of St Peter. There were other portents, including a meteor that seemed to fall directly on to Sultan Kerbogha's besieging army.

▼ *Soldiers fall to their knees in awe as Peter Bartholomew presents the Holy Lance (the spear that pierced Christ's side on the cross). The illustration is from an edition of William of Tyre's crusade history made for King Edward IV of England.*

THE DISCOVERY OF THE HOLY LANCE

On 14 June an excavation was carried out in the Church of St Peter: at first the digging soldiers found nothing, but then Peter leapt into the hole, dressed only in a shirt, and triumphantly brandished a length of metal that he declared to be the lance. A few sceptics doubted, but most were swept up in a wave of delirious rejoicing. Here was proof that God was on their side. They need fear no more.

THE DEFEAT OF KERBOGHA

The leaders prepared for battle and on 20 June elected Bohemond commander-in-chief. Bishop Adhemar ordered a three-day fast (not much of a challenge, since most were already without food) in repentance of their sins and preparation for battle. At first light on 28 June the soldiers attended Mass then flung open the city gates and marched out to take on the army of Sultan Kerbogha.

They marched behind Bishop Adhemar holding the Holy Lance and priests dressed in white and carrying crosses

▲ *Reported visions of the Blessed Virgin Mary and of Christ himself in Antioch, together with the discovery of the Holy Lance, raised feelings among the crusaders to such a fever pitch that they came to believe themselves invincible.*

while they prayed aloud. Their chances of success seemed to be nil. The encircling army was vast. The crusaders were weak from hunger. In previous encounters on crusade, their strength had been the mounted charge of knights with couched lances, but now they had only around 200 horses left alive. Many of the knights had to fight on foot.

According to the *Gesta Francorum*, as the crusaders emerged from the city they saw a great host on white horses and bearing pure white banners charging to their aid. This was – they afterwards reported in awe – nothing less than a heavenly army commanded by saints George, Demetrius and Mercury riding in to ensure that God's will was done. This was in line with the prophecies of the Last Days in the biblical Book of Revelation,

▶ At Antioch the crusaders built this façade
in front of a cave believed to have been used
as the very first Christian place of worship
by St Peter and followers in c.AD40–50.

which declared that the heavenly armies
following the Word of God 'were upon
white horses, clothed in fine linen, white
and clean'.

The crusaders, calling on God's name,
charged the Turkish army. Amazingly, the
Turks broke up and fled. A letter written
by the leaders of the crusade to Pope
Urban II, describing the victory, declared
'from the very first clash on the battlefield
we drove the enemy back'.

Kerbogha had split his force between
an advance group near Antioch's Bridge
Gate and a main camp no less than
3 miles (5km) away. Charged by the crusaders, the advance group fled just as
Kerbogha arrived with the main army
from the camp. The main force then also
abandoned the battle – perhaps partly
because they were surprised by the discipline and ferocity of the crusaders' assault
but principally, according to Islamic
sources, because the sultan's rivals in the
army wanted to prevent Kerbogha capturing Antioch and so called off their men
at the very last moment.

Finally Kerbogha set fire to the
sun-dried battlefield in a last desperate
attempt to change the course of the conflict, but to no avail. The crusaders were
afire with belief, and fought like men possessed; they had no desire to flee since
behind them was only the empty city
where they had been starving to death. In
the citadel above the city, the Turkish garrison watched Sultan Kerbogha's army flee
and knew that their chance had gone.
They sent a message of surrender to
Raymond of Toulouse. The crusaders had
complete control of the city. The letter to
Pope Urban II continued: 'the right hand
of God fought on our side … our Lord
Jesus Christ brought the entire city of
Antioch to the Roman religion and faith.'

THE HOLY LANCE AND ITS EFFECT ON THE CRUSADERS

In the medieval era Christians had a
deep and powerful belief in the miraculous powers of relics of the life of
Christ and other biblical figures. The
astonishing effect of the Holy Lance on
the crusaders can partly be explained as
an effect of this belief. In addition, the
majority of the crusaders were under
extreme mental and physical stress –
starving and desperate for hope – which
would increase the likelihood of mass
hysteria. The relic supposedly discovered by Peter Bartholomew was
presented as the lance used by a Roman
soldier to pierce the side of Christ while
he was hanging on the cross, an event
described only in the Gospel of St John
and said to be the fulfilment of a prophecy
in the Book of Psalms concerning the
Messiah. Many crusaders in Antioch must
have known and chosen to forget that a
spear said to be the Holy Lance had been
found in Jerusalem, where it was seen by
many Christian pilgrims in and around
the 5th–6th centuries AD; by the time
of the First Crusade, this other spear was
being kept in Constantinople.

▶ In John's Gospel, the soldier was said to
have pierced Christ's side with the lance
rather than break his legs, which was
normal practice with the crucified.

THE PRINCE OF ANTIOCH

BOHEMOND OF TARANTO

Bohemond of Taranto, the Calabrian-born Norman knight who established himself as Prince of Antioch, was an inspirational leader of men and by far the most effective general among the knights of the First Crusade. He was also powerfully ambitious and primarily self-interested; the realization of his dream of establishing a personal principality meant far more to him than the official aims of the First Crusade. He did not even take part in the triumphant conclusion of the crusade, the capture of Jerusalem, having remained in Antioch to consolidate his position there.

BOHEMOND'S APPEARANCE AND CHARACTER

Anna Comnena, daughter of the Emperor Alexius, met Bohemond in Constantinople at the start of the First Crusade and left a vivid portrait of the man. She reported that Bohemond was astonishingly tall – she claimed he was 18 inches (45cm) taller than the tallest men; he had a narrow waist but broad chest and shoulders and very strong arms; he had a sturdy frame, she said, but a slightly stooping stance. His skin, she reported, was noticeably white, but his cheeks were red; his hair was light brown and worn shorter than was normal among the crusaders, cut just above the ears. He had grey eyes, which suggested (according to Anna) that he was a man of indomitable courage and great dignity. People were astonished at the sight of him.

Anna noted that Bohemond's size and strength made him frightening – even his laugh, she remembered, caused people to be nervous; in fact the mere mention of his name made people jittery. But he certainly also had charm. It was clear that courage and love ran deep in him, and he found expression for both these qualities in warfare. His intelligence was sharp – he always made ambiguous, non-committal replies to questions, and his mind 'ran

▲ *Bohemond climbs into Antioch on the night of 2 June 1098 after the watchman let down a rope ladder. He then threw the gates open to admit his fellow crusaders.*

over all possible outcomes' and 'dared all things'; his actions were often unpredictable, for he rushed into undertakings. Overall, he was 'like no other man ever found in the Byzantine Empire, whether a foreigner or a Greek'. It is a measure of the impression that Bohemond made that Anna's account, with its vivid details, was written around 40 years after she met him and that he was the only one of the crusader lords she described so closely.

THE YOUTHFUL GENERAL

Bohemond's father was the powerful Norman adventurer Robert Guiscard. As a baby, the future prince of Antioch was christened 'Mark' but as he grew was given the name 'Bohemond' by Guiscard in tribute to a legendary giant of that name. In 1080–85, in his early 20s, Bohemond proved himself a great general during Guiscard's daring invasion of the Byzantine Empire, and in 1082–84 while commanding the Norman army when

Guiscard was recalled to Italy, he won two major victories over Emperor Alexius. Bohemond was forced to abandon the campaign in 1084 through illness, and returned to Italy. Guiscard's death in 1085 was followed by a succession conflict in which Bohemond fought his half-brother Roger; this was ended by a settlement, favourable to Bohemond, imposed by Pope Urban II.

In 1096 Bohemond joined the First Crusade: in some accounts, he was besieging the rebel town of Amalfi (near Naples) when he encountered knights riding to the crusade and, impressed by their zeal, opted to join them. In other versions, such as that of the 11th-century Benedictine chronicler Geoffrey Malaterra, Bohemond saw the crusade from the start as a chance to continue his father's attack upon the Byzantine Empire and to carve out a principality there for himself.

A LEADER OF MEN

Throughout the early part of the First Crusade, Bohemond was the effective commander of the enterprise, an inspirational general and leader for the crusaders. At Dorylaeum through his quick thinking and tactical nous he averted disaster and held off the Turkish attacks until the main force of the crusader army could arrive. During the difficult months of the siege of Antioch Bohemond again proved his excellence as a general – not only defeating a large force under Sultan Duqaq that he encountered during a foraging mission, but also routing and driving back a substantial relief army under Radwan, Seljuk ruler of Aleppo.

Bohemond then almost single-handedly brought about the capture of Antioch through clandestine negotiations with the rebel Firuz within the city and a daring night-time raid. Afterwards, when the crusaders were besieged within the city by Sultan Kerbogha, when despair was

▲ *The crusader army had feigned a retreat but turned around and flooded into Antioch after Bohemond had opened the gates.*

mounting and desertions were common-place, he remained inspirationally upbeat, touring the defensive positions, making sure that they were manned and lifting the spirits of the defenders with the example of his courage and self-belief.

After the discovery of the Holy Lance, Bohemond was privately sceptical that a miracle had occurred, but he knew well enough how to marshal the outpouring of emotion among the rank and file: he was elected commander-in-chief of the army by the lords, and in this capacity planned the army's tactics and oversaw the aston-ishing victory over the besiegers on 28 June 1098.

SEEKING CONTROL IN ANTIOCH

Throughout this period, however, Bohemond was also plotting to outma-noeuvre the other crusader lords and establish a private holding in his name at

Antioch. He was even apparently willing to put this objective above the success of the crusade itself: during the siege his men spread discontent within the crusader camp, suggesting that a military assault would never succeed and that their cause was hopeless, so that when he established contact with an ally within the city and with the news that Sultan Kerbogha was approaching fast, he could negotiate hard, knowing that he held all the cards. From the other leaders he wrung the concession that he could keep Antioch if they won it. He proceeded with the capture of the city only when he knew that it would be his.

Bohemond remained in Antioch when the main crusading force marched on towards Jerusalem in January 1099. He watched the conquest from afar, and then visited Jerusalem at Christmas 1099 to ful-fil his vows. On this occasion, wily as ever, he engineered the election of Dagobert of Pisa as Patriarch of Jerusalem to counter-act the strength of the Lorrainer faction under Godfrey of Bouillon, who was by that time the effective king of Jerusalem.

AFTER THE CRUSADE

In 1100 Bohemond launched an attack on Danishmend, the warlike emir of Sivas (Sebastea), but was captured and thrown in jail. He stayed there for three whole years until being ransomed in 1103 by Baldwin of Le Bourg, at that time Count of Edessa and later King Baldwin II of Jerusalem. In the following year, Bohemond was heavily defeated by a Seljuk army after he attacked and besieged the city of Harran. After this setback Bohemond returned to Europe, where in 1105–06 he was hailed as a conquering hero for his part in the crusade.

Now Bohemond felt that he was poised for enduring greatness and after raising a large army he launched an attack on the Byzantine Empire. The enterprise failed, and Bohemond was forced to accept a peace treaty in 1108 by which he became the emperor's vassal. He died, humiliated and with his dream of creating a powerful independent principality broken.

However, he was able to pass Antioch on to his heirs, and was assured of everlasting fame for his reputation as a charismatic diplomat and general. Without his leadership, the crusade would have foundered at Dorylaeum or Antioch before it ever reached Jerusalem.

▼ *On his death in 1111, Bohemond was buried in this mausoleum at the Cathedral of San Sabino in Canosa di Puglia, Italy.*

THE WAY TO THE HOLY CITY
DELAY IN ANTIOCH PRECEDES THE MARCH SOUTH

The capture of Antioch appeared to open the way to Jerusalem. The army's morale was sky high, bolstered by the conviction that with the Holy Lance in their possession they were invincible because they fought with God's blessing. But this impetus and energy was wasted, allowed to drain away, while the princely and noble leaders of the crusade were locked in dispute over what should be done with Antioch.

Raymond of Toulouse insisted that Antioch be returned to Alexius in order to honour the vow that he and other lords, including Bohemond, had made while in Constantinople, to return captured lands to the Byzantine Empire. Bohemond claimed the city for himself and, as we have seen, before beginning the assault he had negotiated an agreement with the other lords that he should keep it; he argued that because Alexius had not come to the crusaders' aid when they were besieged in Antioch, and left them to God's mercy, that the vow no longer held. Nevertheless, Raymond sent a message to Alexius with Hugh of Vermandois to the effect that they would return Antioch to the empire if the emperor now agreed to bring an army to help them in the conquest of Jerusalem.

THE UNTIMELY DEATH OF BISHOP ADHEMAR

Just over a month after the capture of Antioch, the crusaders lost their spiritual leader when Bishop Adhemar, the papal legate, died of a plague that swept through the city. Adhemar's death was a great setback, for he had been a guiding presence, presiding over councils of leading lords, reminding all involved of the original purpose of the undertaking and attempting to restrain the leading lords from personal conflicts that might derail the crusade.

He had also been a visible leader of the army and played a major part in determining battle tactics. For example, prior to the siege of Antioch a crusader force under Robert of Normandy captured the Iron Bridge across the River Orontes 15 miles (24km) from Antioch, defeating a garrison sent from the city to do so; in this battle, on Bishop Adhemar's advice, they used a tortoise formation – the crusaders held their shields above their heads to form a protective barrier to hold off arrows fired by the defenders, and were able to advance largely unscathed and overpower the garrison. The formation was inspired by the *testudo* formation of the ancient Roman army, which the bishop probably read about in a Roman military treatise.

▲ *The crusader army finally began its march southwards from Antioch towards Jerusalem. Rank and file soldiers were convinced Heaven was lighting their way.*

THE ATTACK ON MAARRAT AN-NUMAN

The months dragged on, with little happening. Groups of crusaders raided the countryside around Antioch; some went north to join Count Baldwin in Edessa. In December an expedition was mounted to take the strategically significant town of Maarrat an-Numan to the south of Antioch. The army captured the town and slaughtered its 20,000 population and then, finding little or no food, they were allegedly reduced to cooking and eating some of the freshly slain inhabitants.

JERUSALEM BECKONS

The Holy City to which the crusaders were ultimately headed was no longer in the hands of the Seljuks. In 1098, while the crusaders were occupied at Antioch, an army of the Fatimid Vizier of Egypt, Al-Afdal Shahanshah, had retaken Jerusalem and Palestine as far north as Beirut – lands which they had only lost to the Seljuks in the early 1070s. The Fatimids had

---

CANNIBALISM AMONG THE CRUSADERS

According to accounts by Tancred's biogapher Radulph of Caen, and in a letter to Pope Urban II, the troops at Maarrat an-Numan were driven by desperation and maddening hunger to commit acts of cannibalism. Guibert of Nogent, who discussed incidents of cannibalism in his *Historia Hierosolymitana*, reported that perhaps because of incidents such as this or perhaps because of wild rumour and speculation, the Turks and other 'Saracens' became convinced that it was common practice among the crusaders, whom they regarded as savages, to eat the flesh of their dead enemies. He then described an act of provocation by the Tafurs, who openly spit-roasted a slain Turkish prisoner in view of the Turks in order to madden and anger them – they had no intention of eating the man's flesh. It is probable that accounts of crusaders eating flesh were propaganda on behalf of Christian writers seeking to make the crusaders seem fierce.

---

declared that the city was open to Christian pilgrims, who could come and go safely – the city's holy places did not need rescuing.

Although the crusaders did not know this, the Byzantine emperor Alexius had effectively disowned them, declaring to the Vizier that he could not control and did not support them, and renewing an alliance with Fatimid Egypt. Yet the bulk of the crusaders were desperate to march on Jerusalem, determined to fulfil their vows to reach the city and worship in the Church of the Holy Sepulchre, and driven by the conviction that they were engaged in a divinely inspired war fighting for Christ and his saints.

While the leading crusaders continued to hesitate, the lesser lords and knights – together with members of the army's rank and file – urged the continuation of the crusade. They offered to recognize Raymond of Toulouse as leader of the crusade if he would command them on the way to Jerusalem. Raymond accepted, giving way in the stand-off and allowing Bohemond to keep Antioch.

Finally, in mid-January 1099, walking barefoot as a pilgrim, Raymond finally left Antioch and began the journey southwards towards Jerusalem, leading a force of 5,000 crusaders. Tancred and Robert of Normandy followed with their troops almost immediately, while Robert of Normandy and Godfrey of Bouillon caught up around a month later.

PROGRESS SOUTHWARDS

The crusaders encountered little opposition as they marched south, partly because local lords – following the defeat of Kerbogha and the advance of the Fatimids – thought that dealing with the Christians was a way of exploiting the changing balance of power to their own advantage, and partly because the rulers simply wanted

▼ *As the crusader army advanced through the Holy Land, its reputation for ferocity and acts of barbarity preceded it.*

▲ *Local lords were willing to make deals with the crusaders so they would pass by and become someone else's problem.*

to keep the crusaders moving on, avoiding the devastation that would follow from conflict, and making the bedraggled army another ruler's problem.

The crusaders captured the port of Tortosa, strategically important for maintaining their supply line, and then passed Tripoli on the coast of Lebanon on 16 May without attacking, after its emir agreed to pay them protection money and supplied them with horses and provisions. They proceeded down the coast past Beirut and into Fatimid-held territory, past Acre and Caesarea to Arsuf, about 50 miles (80km) north-west of Jerusalem, from where they headed inland towards the Holy City.

They stopped for four days at the town of Ramla, which they found deserted of its Muslim garrison but well supplied with food. Here, according to Fulcher of Chartres, they installed a bishop in the Church of St George and left a Christian garrison holding the fortress before setting out once more for Jerusalem on 6 June.

ROBERT OF JERUSALEM

CRUSADER KNIGHT COUNT ROBERT II OF FLANDERS

French knight Robert of Flanders fought bravely in the major sieges and battles of the First Crusade, including the capture of Jerusalem in 1099, and when he returned to Europe after fulfilling his vows he won acclaim and adulation for his part in events that were quickly becoming the stuff of legend. Hailed as Robertus Hierosolimitanus (Robert of Jerusalem) and as 'Robert the Crusader', in the ensuing decades his fame was almost equal to that of Godfrey of Bouillon.

THE 'ARDENT WARRIOR'

The eldest son of Robert I, Count of Flanders (the nobleman known also as Robert the Frisian), Robert the younger had ruled the county as regent while his father had undertaken a pilgrimage to Jerusalem in 1085–91. After his father's death in 1093 he took power as Count Robert II, but within two years had committed to the First Crusade. He was already an experienced knight, and on the crusade he proved himself a great general and soldier, often in close association with Bohemond of Taranto. *Gesta Francorum* described Robert as an 'ardent warrior'.

EXPLOITS ON CRUSADE

Robert travelled on crusade in the company of Godfrey of Bouillon, leaving northern France in October 1096. In Constantinople he was easily persuaded to swear the oath of loyalty to Emperor Alexius in the company of Bohemond and Godfrey. After taking part in the siege of Nicaea, Robert marched on in the vanguard of the crusader army with Bohemond of Taranto – the part of the

THE CULT OF ST GEORGE

Robert played a significant part in the establishment of the cult of St George in Europe, for on his return he brought with him a precious relic, supposedly the arm of St George, which had been given to him as a gift by Emperor Alexius. Robert gave the relic to the Church of Anchin in Flanders, which established the church as a pilgrimage centre. He also founded the Monastery of St Andrew at Betferkerke near Bruges.

▼ *An artist's impression of Count Robert and Godfrey of Bouillon depositing trophies, supposedly won in the Battle of Ascalon, in the city of Jerusalem.*

army that came under attack in the Battle of Dorylaeum. He and his men fought bravely to keep the Seljuk Turks under Kilij Arslan at bay until the arrival of the main part of the crusader force, then fought on in the centre section of the crusader army alongside Raymond of Toulouse, when it launched the counter-attack that managed to decisively break the Turkish advance.

In the long siege of Antioch, Robert took part in key manoeuvres at the side of Bohemond of Taranto. In December they rode out to forage for food in the fertile valley of the River Orontes and, on 30 December, they together encountered and defeated a relief army sent by Duqaq, the Seljuk ruler of Damascus. As at Dorylaeum earlier, the charge of the Frankish and Norman knights riding with lances couched was too much for the Turkish horsemen to endure. When Antioch was subsequently taken, Robert was among the first of the crusaders to enter the city with Bohemond.

Then on 28 June 1098, when the Christian army broke out of the city to attack Sultan Kerbogha's besieging force – behind the Holy Lance, to the sound of prayers chanted by priests and in the face of a blinding vision of heavenly warriors under St George riding to their rescue – Robert together with Hugh of Vermandois commanded the first regiment to emerge, which deployed along the riverbank in a line. Contemporary accounts of the battle suggest that leadership was exemplary, for the crusader deployment and tactics were highly disciplined. After this battle, Robert took part with Bohemond in the capture of the citadel of Antioch, which had held out against the crusaders when the rest of the city had fallen.

LOYAL TO BOHEMOND OF TARANTO

Subsequently, Robert backed Bohemond in the dispute with Raymond of Toulouse over whether the crusaders could keep the city or must return it to Alexius. In December that year he rode out with

Raymond of Toulouse to attack the strategically important town of Maarrat an-Numan to the south of Antioch: Robert took part in the siege and capture of the town and presumably also in the massacre of its 20,000 inhabitants. He probably did not become involved in the alleged instances of cannibalism in which, according to Radulph of Caen, the starving crusaders cooked and ate the freshly slaughtered locals, both adults and children – this was most likely limited to the rank and file, while the nobles and commanders would have had the resources to buy scarce and overpriced food.

The crusaders recommenced their movement towards Jerusalem in January 1099, led by Raymond of Toulouse. Robert of Normandy and Tancred swore oaths to become Raymond's vassals and marched in his army, but Robert of Flanders and Godfrey of Bouillon refused to swear and initially remained in Antioch with Bohemond, subsequently joining the army at the siege of Arqa in March.

Robert largely remained with the army all the way down the coast to Jerusalem, except that at one point he and Tancred made a diversion into Samaria to find wood for building siege engines to use in the expected siege of Jerusalem. Robert then took part in the siege and capture of Jerusalem and in the subsequent Battle

▲ The ancient port of Latakia in Syria, taken by Count Robert and Raymond of Toulouse in 1099, became an important holding of the Principality of Antioch.

of Ascalon, in which the crusaders drove off a Fatimid army commanded by al-Afdal Shahanshah, Vizier of Egypt. Having been warned of the approach of the Fatimid army, the crusaders rode out to meet them and caught them by surprise in their camp near Ascalon. In this battle, he fought in the centre of the crusader force with Tancred, Robert of Normandy, Eustace of Boulogne and Gaston of Bearn, while Godfrey of Bouillon commanded the left wing and Raymond of Toulouse led the right flank. The crusaders triumphed despite being outnumbered by as many as five to one.

HOMEWARD BOUND

Robert of Flanders left Jerusalem in the company of Robert of Normandy and Raymond of Toulouse at the close of August 1099. On route to Constantinople, they conquered the Syrian port of Latakia, which became part of the crusader Principality of Antioch. In Constantinople, both Roberts declined an offer from Emperor Alexius to remain there in his service and took ship for Europe and a wildly enthusiastic homecoming.

JERUSALEM! JERUSALEM!
ARRIVAL AT AND BESIEGING OF THE HOLY CITY

As spring turned to summer in 1099 the crusaders neared their goal day by day. They were encountering little opposition, and even receiving a welcome of sorts, but they got an inkling of the locals' true attitude when a carrier pigeon was killed by a hawk above their camp and was found to have been carrying a message from the governor of Acre calling on faithful Muslims to take up arms and repel the Christian invasion.

A WELCOME IN BETHLEHEM

Christian inhabitants of Bethlehem sent out envoys begging the crusaders to liberate them from Egyptian occupation. Tancred and Baldwin of Le Bourg accepted the call and were welcomed as a liberating army by citizens and priests. The sight of their banner flying above Christ's birthplace was an enormous boost to the crusaders. They were further cheered by an eclipse of the Moon that occurred at that very time – they interpreted it as portending the imminent eclipse of the crescent, the symbol of Islam.

'MOUNT JOY'

On 7 June 1099, the very day after the taking of Bethlehem, the crusader force crossed the hill known as Mountjoie ('Mount Joy') to generations of pilgrims and saw the walls of Jerusalem before them. 'Jerusalem!' went up the cry, and echoed down the lines. According to William of Tyre, the crusader-pilgrims fell to their knees and sobbed tears of joy, offering prayers of gratitude that God had led them to their destination; they cast off their shoes and bowed low to the ground in order to kiss the earth of the Holy Land. It had taken them three years to get there,

▲ At last the crusaders see the cherished city of Jerusalem. They offer prayers to God for having delivered them to their goal.

a long period of suffering and desperate exertions in which the pull of the Holy City and of their pilgrims' vows had inspired them to carry on. Now Jerusalem's walls were spread out before them. But their task remained a daunting one, for this city was one of the world's most strongly fortified, in a commanding position with deep valleys on two sides, to the east and west.

Assault was really only feasible from the north, for in the south on Mount Zion conditions could not support anything other than a small encampment. Expecting a siege, its governor, Iftikhar al-Daula, had prepared well, bringing in provisions and poisoning wells around the city, and sending urgent communication to Cairo calling for a Muslim relief army. He also expelled the city's Christian inhabitants to prevent any of them betraying Jerusalem to the crusaders.

AN ATTACK IN FAITH

The crusader army was not large enough to surround the city fully. On the northern wall, Godfrey of Bouillon arrayed his troops, alongside those of Robert of Flanders and Robert of Normandy, while to the south was the army of Raymond of Toulouse. In the gruelling heat of the summer and with very little water available, the crusaders decided to act quickly. They launched an attack on 13 June, although they had insufficient siege equipment. They had been spurred on by a hermit who reported that he had been told in a vision that if they proved their faith by attacking at once even without the necessary equipment God would grant them instant success. The attack failed, and brought home to the besiegers their urgent need for wood and other equipment with which to build proper siege towers.

Then, as if in answer to their prayers, Tancred found a hidden collection of

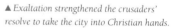

Exaltation strengthened the crusaders' resolve to take the city into Christian hands.

timber in a cave, and six English and Genoese ships put in at Jaffa bearing wood, nails, bolts, ropes and other supplies. Hidden from sight of the Jerusalem garrison, the crusaders set to work building two siege towers. They even took apart two ships to get more wood.

THE EXAMPLE OF JOSHUA

As at Antioch, they were working against time, for they received a warning that Governor Iftikhar al-Daula's cry for help had been answered, and a large relief army

was on its way from Egypt. But they found time to mount a penitential procession around the city. A crusader priest named Peter Desiderius had been visited by the late Bishop Adhemar in a vision, and been instructed that if the army marched barefoot around the city walls Jerusalem would fall within nine days. This was inspired by the example of Joshua, Israelite leader in *c*.1200BC, who, according to biblical accounts, led his army seven times around the city of Jericho – and, as promised by God, the walls of the city fell down and the Israelites captured it. The entire crusader army held a three-day fast and on the second day, Friday 8 July, marched barefoot around the city, singing hymns. Members of the garrison gathered on the walls to jeer at the soldiers, who proceeded to the Mount of Olives to hear sermons by Peter the Hermit and others.

Five days later, the siege towers were ready. The plan was to mount the main assault on the north wall, using the two towers, one commanded by Godfrey of Bouillon and the other by Robert of Normandy, while a second assault was led by Raymond's force from the south side.

Godfrey rallies foot soldiers and knights at Jerusalem. Victory now seemed as certain as that of Joshua at Jericho.

THE HOLY CITY CAPTURED

THE CRUSADERS' TRIUMPH – AND SHAME

After dark on the night of 13 July, the crusaders began to move their siege towers up to the walls of Jerusalem. They worked beneath a murderous storm of arrows, missiles, pitch and Greek fire. All night and all the next day, while behind them the mangonel hurled great rocks at the walls of Jerusalem, sweating and toiling beneath a searingly hot sun and through great clouds of dust, they laboured at hauling the machines forward.

At last, on the morning of 15 July, Godfrey of Bouillon's tower was close enough to the wall to make a bridge across on to the city ramparts near Herod's Gate. Godfrey and his brother Baldwin fought bravely on the tower. At around noon, despite the defenders' desperate attempts to repel them using fire and boiling water, the first crusaders made it on to the ramparts from Godfrey's tower. Among the first across were two brothers from Flanders, Lethold and Gilbert of Tournai. Just afterwards, the second tower under Robert of Normandy established a bridgehead to the wall.

THE CITY TAKEN

The defenders on the north wall retreated in order to take refuge in the al Aqsa mosque. Crusaders clambered over the walls and opened gates from within, and their comrades flooded into Jerusalem, unleashing a frenzy of bloodletting.

During the long struggle to get the towers up to the walls, according to the author of the *Gesta Francorum*, the crusaders had been surprised by how difficult it was, 'numbed with astonishment and extremely frightened'. Now, in the moment of triumph they had dreamt of for years, they unleashed their pent-up emotions in a bloodbath. According to the same author, 'the defenders of the city fled … and our men, following Lethold, ran after them, slaughtering them and dismembering them all the way to the Temple of Solomon. And in that place there was so much killing that the blood

▼ *The besiegers endured a heavy assault from the battlements as they moved their siege towers, little by little, up to the walls.*

came up to our ankles.' According to the Provençal chronicler Raymond of Aguilers, 'in the streets and squares of the city, piles of heads, hands and feet could be seen. People were making their way over the corpses of men and horses. But this is only to describe the minor horrors …'

The defenders of the north wall were pursued by Tancred and his men, and surrendered to him, promising to pay a large ransom. They took refuge in the al Aqsa mosque praying for their lives. Tancred claimed the Temple quarter in his name, and set his banner flying above the building. The Jews of the city also fled for their lives, taking refuge in their main synagogue, by the Western Wall.

The *Gesta Francorum* account goes on to describe how the pilgrims followed the soldiers into the city and also slew 'Saracens' indiscriminately to left and right. At the Temple of Solomon, it reports, attackers and defenders 'fought a furious battle all day so that their blood flooded all over the Temple. At last the pagans were defeated and our men took a good number of men and women prisoner in the Temple. They killed whichever prisoners they wished and chose to allow others to live.'

THE HONOUR OF RAYMOND OF TOULOUSE

On the south wall, meanwhile, the defenders kept Raymond of Toulouse's attack at bay until they saw that behind them the city had been lost. Then they made a swift retreat to the citadel, the Tower of David, and finally surrendered there to Raymond. He gave his word that they would have safe passage out of the city – and, remarkably, amid such chaos was able to honour it, escorting them from Jerusalem as far as the Muslim garrison in the port of Ascalon. This honourable enactment of the safe escort was a brief interlude of restraint.

THE CITY IS STRIPPED

The account given by Fulcher of Chartres describes how crusaders ran into deserted houses and seized whatever they found. Whoever was first into a building was able to claim it – 'in this way, many poor folk became rich'. For it was a frenzy of greed, as well as of bloodletting. According to the *Gesta Francorum*, 'the crusaders seized silver and gold, mules and horses, and buildings full of all manner of riches'.

A VIOLENT CLEANSING

It was normal practice in 11th-century warfare for an army to loot a city it had conquered after a long siege. The attack on the inhabitants of Jerusalem had an extra intensity, fuelled as it was by papal and priestly rhetoric about the need to sweep the city clean of 'Saracens'. After the killing, the soldiers and pilgrims piously gave thanks to God in the Church of the Holy Sepulchre. Fulcher of Chartres presented this dreadful slaughter as a purgative cleansing: 'O day so fiercely longed for! ... O deed above all other deeds! ... [the crusaders] desired that this place, for so long made unclean by the pagan practices of its inhabitants, should be cleaned of its filth.' Raymond of Aguilers declared that: 'after the city had

▼ *In the 15th century, when this illustration was drawn, the battle for Jerusalem was reimagined as a civilized encounter.*

been taken, it was a rich reward to see the devotion of the pilgrims at the Holy Sepulchre; the manner in which they clapped in their exulting, singing a new song to the Lord.'

The slaughter continued for almost two days. Tancred was not able to protect the Muslims in the al Aqsa mosque. On 16 July the crusaders forced their way into the building and killed every man, woman and child. The synagogue, filled with refugees, was burned to the ground. A letter from the crusade leaders to the pope declared proudly that in the portico of Solomon and in his Temple, 'our men rode in the blood of the Saracens even up to the knees of their horses'. A reference, perhaps, to the Book of Revelation, whose apocalyptic accounts of the Last Judgement were familiar to the crusaders: 'And the winepress was trodden without the city, and blood came out of the winepress, even unto the horses' bridles.'

▲ *The crusaders dedicated their attack to Christ and proclaimed a desire to win Jerusalem for God.*

▼ *In the heat of the moment, bloodlust took over from pious righteousness, and one act of barbarity was followed by another.*

AFTER THE VICTORY
THE CITY SECURED WITH TRIUMPH AT ASCALON

In the immediate aftermath of the slaughter of 15–16 July, the crusaders had had to deal with cleaning the city, since the piles of corpses made such a terrible stench. The *Gesta Francorum* reports that the bodies of the Saracens were dragged out of the city and burned in huge pyramids. The smoke hung over the city in a dreadful pall.

DEFENDER OF THE HOLY SEPULCHRE

On 22 July, the eighth day after the taking of Jerusalem, the crusaders elected Godfrey of Bouillon to rule the city as Defender of the Holy Sepulchre. The first choice had been Count Raymond of Toulouse as king, but he declined the offer saying no mortal man should wear a crown in the city that belonged to Christ. Godfrey agreed with this statement, but came up with a compromise title that allowed him to take power.

▼ *With the city of Jerusalem secured, normal rules of pillage did not apply, and the victors became rich overnight.*

In many ways, Godfrey was an understandable choice. He had proved himself pious, steadfast and brave. Among the other lords, Bohemond had established himself in Antioch and Baldwin in Edessa, while Robert of Normandy had truly joined the crusade in order to liberate Jerusalem and was now set on returning to France. Raymond's refusal of power in Jerusalem is less easy to understand, given that he had shown himself elsewhere to be ambitious and not averse to putting political ambition above Christian piety. It is possible that his refusal was a ploy to prevent any of the lords claiming the kingship or that he considered Jerusalem too difficult a prize to defend and was planning to establish a principality in Tripoli.

JERUSALEM'S FIRST LATIN PATRIARCH

Then on 1 August Arnulf of Choques, the chaplain in Robert of Normandy's army, was elected Patriarch of Jerusalem. Arnulf had been one of the most prominent sceptics voicing doubts about the validity of Peter Bartholomew's claims that he had

▲ *When the Church of the Holy Sepulchre gave up a piece of the True Cross it was seen as a further validation of the attack.*

discovered a piece of the Holy Lance in Antioch, and his opposition had played a major part in forcing Peter to undergo a trial by fire in April during the march south, after which the visionary had died. During the siege of Jerusalem, Arnulf had made a statue of Christ to stand on one of the siege engines. Then, on 5 August, he announced that he had discovered a piece of the True Cross (the cross on which Christ had been crucified) in the Church of the Holy Sepulchre. This became one of the most treasured possessions of the Kingdom of Jerusalem.

Arnulf's election was supported by Godfrey, and in return Arnulf backed Godfrey's decision to make the Kingdom of Jerusalem a secular state rather than one under Church – and ultimately papal – rule. He imposed the Latin form of Christianity, barring the priests of other denominations, such as the Orthodox Greeks and the Coptic, Armenian or Georgian Christians, from the Church of

the Holy Sepulchre. He also reportedly authorized the torture of other Christians to force them to reveal where they had hidden other parts of the True Cross. The events of these first weeks of the Kingdom of Jerusalem created a fierce hatred in the Eastern churches for the Latin Christians that would endure for centuries.

BATTLE OF ASCALON

Godfrey's first job as ruler was to repel the Fatimid relief army summoned from Egypt by Jerusalem's governor, Iftikhar al-Daula, before the fall of the city. The Fatimids had raised a force of perhaps 50,000 men under the command of Vizier al-Afdal Shahanshah, who intended to mount a siege of Jerusalem. On 10 August, Godfrey received reports from scouts that the Muslim army was massing in the vicinity of Ascalon, a port about 35 miles (55km) east of Jerusalem. Godfrey led his army out of Jerusalem to confront the Fatimid force, with Robert of Flanders and Arnulf; they were followed the next day by Raymond of Toulouse and Robert of Normandy. On the way, at Ramla, they met up with Tancred and Eustace of Boulogne, Godfey's brother.

In total, the crusader force numbers totalled around 10,000, with probably as few as 1,200 knights and the rest infantry. They were severely outnumbered by the Fatimids, although not as badly as is suggested in the *Gesta Francorum*, which claims the Egyptian army was 200,000-strong. The crusaders had their relics to comfort them: they marched behind Arnulf carrying the piece of the True Cross he had found and Raymond of Aguilers carrying the relic of the Holy Lance.

On 11 August the crusaders discovered a large number of goats, cattle, sheep and even camels grazing near Ascalon: they presumed the creatures were intended as a source for food for the large Fatimid army, although a few captives taken in a small encounter by Tancred indicated that the animals were intended as a decoy in the hope that the crusader army would lose its discipline and begin pillaging.

When the crusader scouts discovered the precise location of the Fatimid force, the Christian army marched on with the animals in tow, making their army seem larger than it otherwise would have done.

The two forces met in open conflict outside Ascalon. Most contemporary accounts suggest that the crusaders caught the Fatimids unprepared and that the battle was quickly over. It began with an exchange of arrows, and then the two main contingents fought at close quarters with lances, the kind of battle in which the crusaders were at their best. The Fatimids broke and fled, some into the city, some into the sea. They abandoned their camp, and all its treasures, which were claimed by Tancred and Robert of Normandy.

QUARREL OVER ASCALON

The crusaders rejoiced, but prepared for a second battle. However, after spending the night in the abandoned Fatimid camp, they discovered the next day that the Fatimid survivors had begun a retreat to Egypt. The city lay at their mercy, but its garrison declared that it would only surrender to Raymond of Toulouse – doubtless because he had behaved honourably in providing safe escort for Iftikhar al-Daula and his troops during

▲ *The crusaders rejoice as the symbol of Christ's Passion is raised at the end of their long and desperate campaign.*

the capture of Jerusalem. Raymond and Godfrey quarrelled over the spoils: Godfrey refused to accept the surrender on these terms, declaring that the city should come to him as ruler of Jerusalem, Raymond, furious at being thwarted again by Godfrey; marched back to Jerusalem, with Robert of Normandy. Godfrey alone was not strong enough to capture Ascalon, and so it remained in Muslim hands. Allowing this to happen was a grave mistake, for taking Ascalon would have been an important step towards consolidating the fledgling Kingdom of Jerusalem.

CRUSADE COMPLETED

For the great majority of the crusaders, the enterprise was now at an end and most went home. At the end of 1099 Godfrey remained in Jerusalem with only around 2,000 foot soldiers plus perhaps just 300 knights – in the estimation of William of Tyre. Robert of Normandy and Robert of Flanders were among those who departed for Europe and with them Godfrey sent word that the Kingdom of Jerusalem needed reinforcements.

CHAPTER FIVE

THE LAND OVERSEAS

The many settlers who stayed after the First Crusade in 1099 created an outpost of Latin Christendom in the East. The land in which they made their homes became known as *Outremer* – from the French word meaning 'overseas'. Outremer encompassed the four crusader states established during or as a result of the First Crusade: the County of Edessa; the Principality of Antioch; the Kingdom of Jerusalem; and the County of Tripoli.

The settlers organized life along familiar lines, introducing the feudal system and imposing the rites of the Latin Church on other Christians. But in many respects, also, they went native. Fulcher of Chartres, who became chaplain to King Baldwin I of Jerusalem, wrote: 'We were once Westerners, but now we are men of the East. You may once have identified yourself as a Roman or a Frenchman, but here, in the present, you are a man of Galilee or of Palestine.... For we do not remember the lands of our birth; to the majority of us they are unfamiliar, foreign lands.' He went on to describe how the lords of the new estates came to appreciate local customs and food and married local women, whether Armenians, Syrians or even 'Saracens' – of course, he added, 'only to those who have been baptized'. It is clear that for the settlers life in Outremer represented the start of something permanent. When the soldiers of the Second Crusade arrived in 1148, they were shocked to find that the leading men of Outremer in their eyes were more like 'Saracens' than Christian princes.

▲ *The coastal crusader citadel of Sidon, in Lebanon.*

◄ *The impressive remains of Krak des Chevaliers at Qal'at al-Hisn in Syria are an enduring symbol of the might of the military orders and the kingdoms of Outremer.*

THE FOUNDATION OF OUTREMER

EDESSA, ANTIOCH, JERUSALEM AND TRIPOLI

The first crusader states had been established in 1098 en route to Jerusalem, when Baldwin of Boulogne created the County of Edessa based on the ancient city of that name (now Urfa, Turkey), and Bohemond of Taranto established the Principality of Antioch in Syria.

THE KINGDOM OF JERUSALEM

The third state, the Kingdom of Jerusalem, did not technically come into existence until 17 months after the Christian conquest of Jerusalem on 15 July 1099. As we have seen, Godfrey of Bouillon, refused to be called king in the city where Christ wore a crown of thorns and took the title 'Defender of the Holy Sepulchre'. But following Godfrey's death in July 1100 his brother Baldwin, no longer 'of Boulogne' but 'of Edessa', had no such qualms, and was crowned king on 25 December 1100 by Daimbert, Patriarch of Jerusalem.

Daimbert had arrived in Jerusalem from Rome in 1099. The Archbishop of Pisa, he had been sent from Italy as the new papal legate, the replacement for Bishop

▼ *Baldwin of Boulogne became Baldwin of Edessa and then, on the death of his brother Godfrey, King Baldwin I of Jerusalem.*

Adhemar of Le Puy, who had died of the plague in Antioch. Daimbert engineered the removal from office of the recently elected Patriarch of Jerusalem, Arnulf of Choques, on the grounds that Arnulf's election had been illegal, and took his place. He allowed Arnulf to occupy the lesser position of Archdeacon.

Then Daimbert set to work to bring about the creation of the papal state in the Holy Land that had been Pope Urban II's dream. He recognized the rule of Bohemond as Prince of Antioch and Tancred as Prince of Galilee, thus guaranteeing their independence from Jerusalem. From Godfrey he won the assurance that on his death the church would inherit control of Jerusalem – according to William of Tyre, Godfrey's plan was to cede rule to the Church in the Kingdom of Jerusalem and to carry on crusader conquest as far as Egypt, where he would establish his own secular kingdom.

But when Godfrey died unexpectedly, fate and conspiracy among the secular lords combined to prevent Daimbert achieving his and the papacy's wish of establishing a theocracy (a state ruled by God through churchmen). At the time of Godfrey's death, Daimbert was away on a campaign with Tancred against Haifa, and Baldwin was secretly summoned to come to Jerusalem and take power. When

▲ *The crusaders called this fortress on Mount Hermon 'L'Asibebe'. In English it is called Nimrod Fortress after the biblical hunter – and 'Citadel of the Mosquitoes'.*

Daimbert heard that Godfrey had died and that Baldwin was marching on Jerusalem, he wrote to Bohemond offering him rule of Palestine under Daimbert's authority – and asking him to prevent Baldwin reaching Jerusalem. The letter was intercepted, however, and Bohemond was captured while attempting an attack on Danishmend, emir of Sivas (Sebastea).

Baldwin marched into Jerusalem and secured his power base. Daimbert was forced to crown him king. Baldwin gave his previous holding, the County of Edessa, to his cousin Baldwin of Le Bourg. Early in 1101 Tancred abandoned his rule as Prince of Galilee, moving to take up power in Antioch – he reigned as regent for Bohemond, who was in Danishmend's jail (where he remained until 1103).

THE FOURTH CRUSADER STATE

The crusader state of the County of Tripoli was created in the course of the war waged by Raymond of Toulouse, from 1102 onwards, against Fakhr al-Mulk, emir of the coastal city of Tripoli (now in Lebanon), in power there as a vassal of the Fatimid caliphs in Cairo. Raymond died in 1105, before the city fell, naming his cousin William-Jordan as regent and his infant son Alfonso-Jordan as heir; but subsequently, one of his illegitimate sons, Bertrand, who had been serving as regent of Toulouse in his father's absence, arrived in the Holy Land. Bertrand and William-Jordan agreed, as a result of King Baldwin I's intervention, that they would each keep the conquests they individually made. Bertrand was the main beneficiary, for he captured Tripoli and became sole ruler when William-Jordan died a little while afterwards; Alfonso-Jordan meanwhile returned to France with his mother.

Bertrand ruled the County of Tripoli as a vassal of the king of Jerusalem. Within his realm, the castle of Krak des Chevaliers was given to the military order of the Knights Hospitaller in 1142.

THE GEOGRAPHY OF OUTREMER

The County of Edessa was the farthest north of the crusader states and set in a remote, landlocked position, with half of its territory lying far away from the Mediterranean, on the east bank of the River Euphrates; the other three states were all coastal domains. The Edessa territory west of the Euphrates was governed from the castle of Turbessel, strongly fortified against attacks from the Seljuk Turks of the Sultanate of Rum, which lay to the north. To the west lay Armenian Cilicia, parts of the Byzantine Empire where the crusaders had made conquests, including the city of Tarsus.

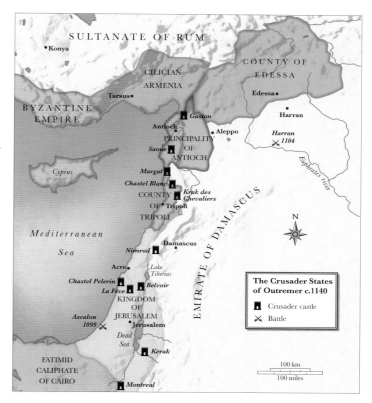

▲ The majority of Outremer territories were coastal, and the Christian lords grew rich on trade passing through their ports.

▼ Krak des Chevaliers, the 'Castle of the Knights', in the County of Tripoli, was the foremost crusader fortress of Outremer.

The Principality of Antioch bordered the County of Edessa to the south-west, and ran down to the Mediterranean coast. When Tancred was regent in 1100–03 he expanded the Principality north-west to take the cities of Tarsus and Latakia from the Byzantines. To the south was the County of Tripoli, leading south again to the Kingdom of Jerusalem. By the mid-1100s, when the Kingdom was at its largest, it extended north to south from Beirut (now capital of Lebanon) to Rafia (modern Rafah in the Gaza Strip). In the north it was separated by the district of Lebanon from the Emirate of Damascus; in the south-east it ran all the way to the Arabian desert and even encompassed the Red Sea port of Aïla (modern Elat). After the First Crusade, some parts of Cilicia remained in European hands, but they never formed into a state or principality.

GOVERNMENT OF THE CRUSADER STATES

THE FEUDAL HIERARCHY IS EXPORTED TO OUTREMER

The crusader states were governed on the lines of the feudal system. The crusaders imported this social system from Europe because in their eyes it had God's blessing as the perfect way to create stability within a hierarchy of duties and responsibilities. Each man had his place, by divine plan, beneath the king. Detailed accounts of the government of the Kingdom of Jerusalem survive, and we know that the other crusader states had a parallel system.

THE KING OF JERUSALEM

Within the Kingdom of Jerusalem, the king was paramount. Great lords held land as his tenants in chief – men such as Tancred, Prince of Galilee, or Eustace Grenier, Lord of Caesarea. These lords in turn packaged land out to their tenants or rear-vassals. Only Catholic Christians were permitted to hold fiefs – Jews, Muslims and all other Christians were excluded from the system.

As in Europe, the lords and their vassals were required to provide military service – for example, Caesarea was required to provide 100 knights, as was Galilee; even the inhospitable lordship of

▼ *The port of Caesarea, a major crusader possession on the Mediterranean coast, dates back to around the time of Christ. It was built by Herod the Great in c.25BC.*

Oultrejourdain (the land east of the Jordan river containing the Negev Desert) had to raise 60 knights.

In 1166 the second tier of tenants, the rear vassals, took vows of liege homage to the king – at that time, Amalric. The chief city of Jerusalem was naturally reserved for the king himself, part of a royal domain that he governed directly.

THE KING'S POWER STRUCTURE

The king's most senior officers were: a seneschal, with control of royal castles and the treasury; a butler, in control of the royal household; and a constable, in charge of the military establishment. The collection of revenue from the countryside largely used pre-crusade methods, and then the moneys were passed via scribes and bailiffs, through local treasuries to the Grant Secrete, or principal treasury.

The king's power was limited by the great lords as tenants-in-chief and the rear-vassals, in their capacity as members of the High Court. The king took an oath in its presence, and was forbidden to seize any lord's fief-holding unless the decision was approved by the Court. The High Court, and not the king, made the kingdom's laws or assizes – the Assizes of Jerusalem. (These are sometimes wrongly said to have been drawn up by Godfrey of Bouillon.) Under these assizes, if the king broke his oaths, his feudal dependants had the legal

right to resist. In addition, if two members of the royal family came into dispute over succession to the throne, the Court had the power to determine the new king. However, the Court met only when summoned by the king so, if necessary, he was able to sideline its powers.

The High Court also functioned as the kingdom's highest legal tribunal, and there was no appeal against its judgements. Beneath it was a network of burgess courts to judge cases involving Western settlers; these courts had the power to impose the death penalty or to send offenders into exile. In addition, within the larger fiefs there were courts of knights and burgesses. These courts were limited to Latin Christians. Other Christians used a separate group of port and market courts. For Muslims and Jews, cases were divided into spiritual or secular: spiritual cases were judged by the existing religious authorities of qadis or rabbis, while secular ones went to newly established native courts called the Courts of the Syrians.

Assemblies of leading citizens – including senior churchmen, top members of the military orders and prominent townsmen as well as the king and nobles – were occasionally held to debate matters of consequence such as the necessity of levying taxes to pay for wars or policy problems such as where help could most profitably be requested among western lords. These meetings were called *parlements*.

THE INDEPENDENCE OF MAJOR LANDOWNERS

As in feudal Europe, the king often struggled to impose his will on the most powerful lords, who possessed strongly fortified castles and their own military forces – for example, Reynald of Châtillon, lord of the important fief of Montreal from 1174, was largely a law unto himself and waged a private war against Muslims, ignoring the royal policy of his king,

Baldwin VI. The lordship of Montreal was a wealthy one, for its main castle, Al-Shaubak (also known as Montreal) controlled lucrative caravan routes from Damascus to the Red Sea and Egypt.

THE RICHES OF THE KING

This difficulty was balanced by the fact that the king's domain made him richer than any of his lords: it contained the ports of Tyre and Acre as well as the city of Jerusalem. The king imposed customs duties at ports along the Mediterranean coast, and taxed overland trade caravans; he also had a monopoly on some local industries and was the only lord permitted to coin money in the realm; he had the right to claim shipwrecks; he could also, with the approval of his *parlement* or the High Court, levy one-off taxes – as when, in 1182, Baldwin IV imposed a tax of 2 per cent on all incomes, including those of the Latin Church, in order to raise money to fight Saladin. These large and varied incomes made the kingship of Jerusalem very profitable indeed: the king of this small eastern kingdom was probably richer than most European princes in the 12th century. And he was able to use his wealth to hire mercenaries.

THE POWER OF THE CHURCH

After the king, the Patriarch of Jerusalem was the most important person in the kingdom. The Latin Church in Palestine quickly became powerful, establishing a number of monasteries on land donated by wealthy crusaders and ruthlessly

▲ The prosperity of Outremer depended on trade. The king of Jerusalem amassed great wealth from taxes on desert caravans.

sidelining other Christians, such as the Coptic, Syrian, Greek Orthodox and others. The Patriarch was elected by the clergy, then acclaimed by the people: his position was subject to the approval of the pope, who would confirm the Patriarch's powers after the election.

▼ The city of Tyre, an important port on the Mediterranean coast, had a Christian community from the 2nd century onwards. Its Muslim rulers surrendered in 1124.

THE MILITARY ORDERS

One of the principal difficulties for the crusader authorities was the low number of settlers. They made repeated attempts to attract immigration from Europe, but they remained vastly outnumbered – a ruling minority with a very large subject population of Syrians, Greeks and Muslim Arabs who could not be relied on if the kingdom came under attack. By the 1180s, only an estimated 35 per cent of the population was European in origin.

The establishment of the military orders such as the Knights Hospitaller, the Knights Templar and the Teutonic Knights helped to boost the Kingdom's strength. The increasingly wealthy orders, funded by lavish donations in Europe, were able to buy castles and land from impoverished noblemen among the settlers and were an important means of maintaining order.

However, the ultimate loyalty of the military orders was to the papacy; they were not bound by feudal ties to the king, and technically did not owe military service in the defence of the kingdom, although in practice they fought in all the major campaigns. They also had the right to negotiate directly with Muslims.

LIFE IN THE CRUSADER STATES

THE RICH ENJOY LOCAL LUXURIES

In Jerusalem and other cities of the crusader states, the great lords and many of their retainers lived in fine style. They had their pick of the cargoes of Chinese silk, rare stones and spices that were brought to the Mediterranean coast overland from central Asia by camel caravan; in addition, they chose from the finest locally produced cotton and glassware.

In their city dwellings and their castles, they surrounded themselves with the finest luxuries, including silk wall hangings, woven carpets and beautifully carved Arabian furniture; the richest even used gold and silver plates. They adapted to the local diet, learning to enjoy dates, olives, watermelons, lemons, oranges and sugar cane, and to spice up their foods with pepper, ginger and cinnamon; they dressed in flowing robes, and began to wear open-toed sandals; some even adopted the turban. They married beauties among the local womenfolk – often in addition to European wives. Many lords kept elaborate Arabian-style gardens as havens from the dust and heat.

▲ *In this image of Bertrand of Saint-Gilles receiving submission from Seljuk qadi Fakhr al-Mulk it can be seen how the Westerners adapted their lifestyle to the climate and landscape of Outremer.*

LIFE IN THE COUNTRYSIDE

The majority of the Europeans lived in the cities and castles but there was some settlement in the countryside. Some occupied existing villages and towns. In the Mediterranean port of Caesarea, for example, the crusaders who captured the town in 1101 simply drove out the Muslim population and made their homes in the existing city. Initially they just adapted mosques to use them as churches. In the longer term, they dismantled the Great Mosque and built in its place the Catholic Cathedral of St Peter.

There were also new settlements, in which land was given to European peasants in return for a 10 per cent tithe paid to the local secular or religious landowner. For example, the village of Magna Mahumeria (modern day al-Bira) north of

Jerusalem was established on these lines in 1120 by canons of the Church of the Holy Sepulchre on land bequeathed to them by Godfrey of Bouillon.

For poor Eastern Christians and Jews in the parched countryside, however, life probably seemed to have changed very little as a result of the crusade: their Muslim landlords had been replaced by Christian lords, but little else was different. The Muslims, of course, had to come to terms with being cast among the poor.

One way in which the feudal system in the East was different to that in Europe was that the Christian lords were largely absentees, for they chose to live in Jerusalem or other cities rather than on their estates. Although technically they were the property of the Latin Christian master who owned their land, the Muslims, Jews and Eastern Christians had a significant amount of freedom. There was freedom of religion in that in the countryside, Jews, Muslims and Eastern

---

THE KING'S ARMY

The king's feudal subjects were required to perform military service, but unlike in Europe there was no time limit set on this; as a result, knights and soldiers were rewarded with pay. But the feudal army, given the small Western population of the kingdom, was always likely to be too small to mount an effective defence of Jerusalem and its environs. In addition to perhaps a few hundred knights, the king of Jerusalem used his immense wealth to hire a large force of mercenaries, including Seljuk or Greek mounted archers called *Turkopoles* (from the Greek for 'offspring of Turks'), Lebanese archers and Armenian and Syrian infantry. This force numbered around 20,000.

▲ *The crusaders drove the local inhabitants out of Caesarea in 1101 and simply took what they found for their own use.*

Christians could follow their own faith and in religious matters at least were subject to their own authorities.

The farmers grew cereals and summer crops such as maize and millet. They kept vineyards, orchards and olive groves, and a few grew sugar and cotton. They paid a tax of up to one-third of their arable crops and one-half of the produce from olive groves and vineyards.

RELIGIOUS FREEDOM

In the cities, Muslims, Jews and Eastern Christians had their freedom – except that Jews and Muslims were allowed only to visit Jerusalem and were officially not permitted to live there. The Armenians, Jacobites and Maronite Christians were allowed to worship according to their own rites, but as we have seen were excluded from the Church of the Holy Sepulchre.

The degree of tolerance that developed between the Catholic Christians and other groups was a matter of necessity. For example, trade connections had to be made with Muslims and Jews. The Catholics' treatment of Jews was considerably better in the crusader states than in 11th–12th-century Europe, and there were no pogroms against the Jews in the crusader states.

MERCHANT ENCLAVES

Within the cities – particularly the coastal ports, such as Tyre and Acre – were colonies of merchants from the cities of Genoa, Venice, Pisa, Marseille, Narbonne and so on, who lived in independent, self-contained districts under the control of their own consul; they were not subject to the feudal system and did not have to perform military service. These merchant colonies had landholdings on the edges of cities, where they grew sugar cane and cotton. They were allowed a monopoly on trade between the Kingdom and Europe and sent home ships heavily laden with highly profitable cargoes. Ships from European ports brought goods necessary to the settlers' way of life, although most adapted quickly to local conditions.

The ports grew very rich. Traders from the Byzantine Empire, Syria, Iraq and north Africa worked alongside those from the European mercantile cities of Europe. Taxes imposed by the authorities could be as high as 25 per cent. The most valuable trade of all was in spices leaving the Mediterranean ports bound first for Constantinople and then on to the towns and cities of western Europe. Among the richest and most profitable of the ports was Acre. The Muslim geographer Ibn Jubayr, born in Valencia, described Acre in 1185 as 'a trading stop for all ships. It is a major attraction for vessels and caravans, the meeting place for Christian and Muslim traders from all around the area. Its streets are hard to walk, so crowded are they by men from all countries.'

▼ *Acre was a key crusader city, which was taken, lost and recaptured many times.*

PRINCE OF GALILEE

TANCRED OF HAUTEVILLE

A Norman lord from southern Italy, Tancred of Hauteville rode on the First Crusade with his uncle Bohemond of Taranto and afterwards established himself first as Prince of Galilee and then as regent of the Principality of Antioch and the County of Edessa. Through his feats of bravery leading up to, during and after the capture of Jerusalem in 1099, and his staunch defence of the independence of the crusader state of Antioch against the Byzantine Empire, Tancred won enduring fame as a knight that made his name resonate down the centuries.

Grandson of the great Norman–Italian adventurer Robert Guiscard, Tancred shared his name with the founding father of the Hauteville clan, the relatively minor 11th-century nobleman from near Coutances in Normandy, whose sons – including William Iron-Arm, Guiscard himself and Roger, Count of Sicily – travelled south to achieve greatness. Tancred

▼ Tancred (right) meets King Philip I of France prior to marrying the king's daughter, Cecile.

the Crusader certainly lived up to the expectations that such ancestry aroused. His life was recorded in the *Gesta Tancredi in Expeditione Hierosolymitana* (The Deeds of Tancred on Crusade to Jerusalem), written in Latin by Norman churchman Radulph of Caen in the years after 1112, based on eyewitness accounts.

IN CONSTANTINOPLE AND CILICIA

Tancred took part in the early episodes of the crusade. Notably in Constantinople, when other crusader princes swore oaths to Alexius in which they promised to return any conquered lands to the Byzantine Empire, doubtless with the full intention of breaking them, Tancred avoided taking the oath at all by slipping out of the city at night.

He took part in the siege of Nicaea and the Battle of Dorylaeum, but Tancred first made his name on the crusade when taking Tarsus during an excursion in Cilicia in 1097; in this part of the crusade he came into open conflict with Baldwin of Boulogne (later King Baldwin I of

Jerusalem). Tancred went on to capture Adana, Mamistra and Alexandretta, before taking part in the siege of Antioch.

In the course of the siege at Antioch, when spirits in the camp were very low and members of the crusader armies were sorely tempted to abandon the adventure, Tancred encountered no less a figure than Peter the Hermit attempting to flee and make his way back to Constantinople. Peter was the itinerant French monk who had preached the crusade so enthusiastically in Europe and become one of the leaders of the 'People's Crusade'. Tancred forced him to return to the crusaders' camp before Antioch.

A BROKEN PROMISE TO PROTECT MUSLIM PRISONERS

During the capture of Jerusalem in 1099 Tancred took hundreds of Muslim prisoners and famously pledged to protect them from the rampaging soldiers who had taken over the city, in return for the offer of a large ransom. He flew his banner over the al Aqsa mosque where the prisoners were gathered, but on the second day of looting he allowed the Muslims to be slain – man, woman and child.

AFTER THE FIRST CRUSADE

In the aftermath of victory, Godfrey of Bouillon, newly elected as Defender of the Holy Sepulchre, gave Tancred the title Prince of Galilee. Then, in the following year, when his uncle Bohemond was taken prisoner during an ill-fated military expedition against Danishmend, the emir of Sivas (Sebastea) in eastern Anatolia, Tancred became regent of the Principality of Antioch. He extended its territories by seizing land from the Byzantine Empire, and resisted attempts by Emperor Alexius to bring him to heel.

In 1104 Tancred also became regent of the County of Edessa, when its ruler Baldwin of Le Bourg was taken prisoner

▲ *Tancred raises his banner above Bethlehem. He and Baldwin of Le Bourg established a crusader presence in Christ's birthplace before the attack on Jerusalem.*

by the Seljuk Turks at the Battle of Harran. In 1105–06 when Bohemond, having been released, returned to Europe to raise reinforcements, Tancred remained as regent in Antioch. He attempted to hold on to the regency of Edessa when Baldwin was released in 1107, but later agreed to relinquish his claim.

HUSBAND OF A PRINCESS

Around this time, Tancred married Cecile, daughter of King Philip I of France; she had travelled to the Holy Land to become the wife of Bohemond of Taranto, but that marriage had not taken place. He remained very powerful in Antioch and staunchly defended the Principality's independence from the Byzantine Empire – despite the fact that Bohemond, having been defeated in battle by Emperor Alexius, had signed the humiliating Treaty of Devol in 1108, in which he agreed that Antioch should be a vassal state of the empire. In 1100, moreover, Tancred gained a foothold in the crusader state of Tripoli when he gained possession of the powerful castle of Krak des Chevaliers.

DEATH AND REPUTATION

Just two years later, however, Tancred died of typhoid while still in power in Antioch. He had no children, but his memory was kept alive in Radulph of Caen's *Gesta Tancredi*. In addition to his status as a warrior in the key engagements of the crusade, Tancred demonstrated considerable strength of purpose and political nous, as he carved out a position for himself as the pre-eminent Catholic Christian magnate in northern Syria.

AFTERLIFE OF A CRUSADER

In the 16th century, Tancred was a hero of the epic poem *La Gerusalemme Liberata* (Jerusalem Delivered) by Italian poet Torquato Tasso. The poem used historical events from the First Crusade as a frame on which to hang a chivalric romance, and borrowed many narrative elements from the *Orlando Furioso* of Tasso's fellow-Italian, Ludovico Ariosto. In Tasso's work, the character of Tancredi falls in love with a Muslim warrior maiden, Clorinda, a character based on Bradamante in the *Orlando*; Tancredi himself is loved by Princess Erminia of Antioch, who betrays her city to the crusaders because of her love for him.

Italian composer Claudio Monteverdi used parts of Tasso's poem in his operatic dialogue *Il Combattimento die Tancredi e Clorinda* (The Fight Between Tancred and Clorinda), composed in 1624. In 1759 French writer Voltaire wrote a tragedy about the hero called simply *Tancrède*, and this, together with Tasso's poem, formed the basis of the opera *Tancredi in Siracusa* by Gioacchino Rossini in 1813.

▼ *In* La Gerusalemme Liberata *the distraught Erminia finds Tancredi heartbroken by the death of Clorinda.*

KRAK DES CHEVALIERS
AND OTHER GREAT CRUSADER CASTLES

The crusaders built a string of formidable castles in Outremer. Like castles in Europe, these functioned both as garrison points from which to dominate the surrounding countryside and as strongholds to which troops could retreat when under attack; they were either maintained as lordly residences or were garrisoned by the military brotherhoods. The foremost of all the crusader castles was Krak des Chevaliers (Castle of the Knights), built at Qal'at al-Hisn in Syria, and today celebrated as one of the finest surviving medieval castles in the world.

The first fortress on the site, which occupied a commanding position 2,300ft (700m) above sea level and dominating the valley between Tripoli and Homs, was built in 1031 for the Muslim emir of Aleppo. It had a Kurdish garrison and in Muslim chronicles was known as the 'Castle of the Kurds'. During the First Crusade, Raymond of Toulouse captured it in 1099 then abandoned it when he headed southwards with the rest of the

▼ *The inner enclosure at Krak des Chevaliers, enlarged by the Knights Hospitaller, incorporated some of the stonework of the original structure.*

crusader force to Jerusalem; Tancred, Prince of Galilee, then took the fortress in 1110 when he was regent of Antioch. Raymond II, Count of Tripoli, gave the castle to the Knights Hospitaller in 1144.

It was during its time under the care of the Hospitallers, who held it until it was taken by the Mamluk Sultan Baibars in 1271, that Krak was developed into the largest crusader castle in Outremer. The Hospitallers built an outer wall with a thickness of 10ft (3m) and with seven guard towers to make the fortress a con-

▲ *According to legend the crusaders found the Holy Grail at Caesarea. They built a castle there, but in 1265 the Mamluks razed it after taking the city.*

centric castle. (A concentric castle has two sets of defensive fortifications, a lower outer wall enclosing an outer bailey overlooked by a higher inner wall protecting the inner bailey. Its garrison would initially man the outer walls, but under heavy attack could retreat to the inner bailey and then any attacking force would have to

WELSH CRUSADER CASTLES
The future King Edward I of England visited Krak des Chevaliers when he travelled on crusade in 1271–72. He was impressed with its formidable concentric defences and, with the help of architect Master James of St Georges, reproduced them where possible in the castles he raised in Wales. Master James was so called after the castle of St Georges d'Espéranches that he built, but his masterpiece is considered to be Beaumaris, the concentric castle on the isle of Anglesey.

▲ *At Krak des Chevaliers the Knights Hospitaller built a vast central keep with a superb vaulted stone roof. The castle is one of the best-preserved crusader fortresses.*

cross the outer walls and outer bailey under heavy attack from the garrison before even beginning their assault on the formidable walls of the inner bailey.)

The Hospitallers refashioned the buildings of the inner ward in the Gothic style. They included a storage chamber almost 400ft (120m) in length and stables with the capacity to hold 1,000 horses, in addition to a well, bakery and a sizeable meeting hall and chapel.

Historians have estimated that there was room in the fortress for a garrison of up to 60 Hospitaller knights and around 2,000 infantrymen and that the storage chamber, supplemented by further storerooms that had been excavated in the cliff beneath the fortress, could hold enough supplies to enable the garrison to survive a siege of five years.

After Krak was rebuilt by the Hospitallers it never fell to military assault: the one time it was captured was through trickery, when Sultan Baibars forged a letter purporting to be from the garrison's commander in Tripoli, which commanded the defending knights to resign.

OTHER CRUSADER CASTLES

Belvoir, another concentric Hospitaller stronghold, was situated around 12 miles (20km) south of the Sea of Galilee and controlling the Jordan Valley. Following the Battle of the Horns of Hattin in July 1187, Belvoir withstood a siege by Saladin's forces for 18 months, before finally surrendering on 5 January 1189.

Margat, on the route between Tripoli and the port of Latakia and overlooking the Mediterranean, was the Hospitallers' headquarters in Syria. Originally an Arab fortress, it was captured by the Byzantines in 1104, then taken by Tancred and made part of the Principality of Antioch before being passed to the Hospitallers in 1186.

Montreal in the Transjordan (on the eastern side of the River Jordan) was built by King Baldwin I of Jerusalem on a hill dominating the plain of Edom and overlooking Muslim pilgrimage and caravan routes from Syria to Arabia. Reynald of Châtillon gained possession of the castle on his marriage to Stephanie, daughter of Philip of Milly, in 1183. From this stronghold Reynald emerged to raid Muslim caravans, and even planned an attack over

▼ *The 90ft (27m)-deep ditch at Saone Castle near Latakia in Syria is a powerful deterrent to attackers. But Saladin succeeded in taking the fortress in 1188, and it is also called 'the Castle of Saladin'.*

▲ *Steps lead to an inner retreat at the Castle of Saint-Gilles in Tripoli, named in honour of crusader lord Raymond of St Gilles, Count of Toulouse and of Tripoli.*

the Red Sea on Mecca; his repeated provocations reputedly enraged Saladin. After defeating the crusaders at the Horns of Hattin, Saladin personally executed Reynald; then, after taking Jerusalem in October 1187, he made it his business to capture Montreal. It took him almost two years, but the castle fell at last in May 1189 – after a devastating siege in which the defenders reputedly went blind from a severe lack of salt in their diet, and also were said to have sold their children and their wives to obtain food.

Saone, around 15 miles (24km) northeast and inland of Latakia in north Syria, was one of the biggest of the crusader fortresses, covering 12 acres (5ha) in a triangular fortification atop a rocky outcrop surrounded by precipices. On the eastern side, the crusaders dug an extraordinary defensive ditch 90ft (27m) deep, 60ft (18m) wide and 450ft (140m) long. In its construction, they shifted an estimated 2.4 million cubic feet (70,000 cubic metres) of rock, which they used in raising the castle's great towers and walls. Saone was besieged and captured by Saladin.

BY SEA FROM ITALY

CRUSADING PILGRIMAGES OF THE EARLY 12TH CENTURY

Several expeditions were mounted from Europe to Jerusalem in the aftermath of the First Crusade. Some were armed pilgrimages, others were called by the pope and preached as military crusades.

THE CRUSADE OF 1101

The first of these, generally known as 'the Crusade of 1101', set out almost immediately after the end of the First Crusade in response to calls for reinforcements from the original crusader lords. After the capture of Jerusalem and the defeat of the Egyptian army at Ascalon in 1099, the crusaders sent word back to Europe that they needed strengthening if they were to hold on to what they had won.

According to Genoese soldier and historian Caffaro di Caschifellone, two Genoese traders named William and Primus Embriaco had in the summer of 1099 sailed to Jaffa with two galleys, which were broken up to provide wood for making the siege machines used to take Jerusalem. Afterwards, they acquired vast riches at the Battle of Ascalon from the abandoned camp of al-Afdal Shahanshah, vizier of Cairo, and with this treasure and messages calling for reinforcements had sailed for Europe, arriving in Genoa on Christmas Day 1099.

▼ *The exploits of the crusaders were depicted proudly all over Europe, but the disastrous failure of the Crusade of 1101 in Anatolia brought a change in attitude.*

As a result of the call for help, a new crusade was called by Pope Paschal II, the successor to Pope Urban II. In particular, he urged the crusade on those who had taken part in the First Crusade but turned back, and those who had taken the vow in 1096, but not departed. The crusade had three main parts, all of which were crushed by Turkish armies in Anatolia.

The first phase began when an army consisting largely of Lombard peasants under Archbishop Anselm IV of Milan departed Milan in September 1100. On arriving in the East, the army pillaged Byzantine territory and even parts of Constantinople itself, so Emperor Alexius swiftly moved them on across the Bosphorus, where they waited for reinforcements. In May 1101 this first army was joined by a French–Burgundian–German force under Stephen of Blois (the same count who had travelled on the First Crusade) and a Byzantine army under Raymond of Toulouse, who was now in the service of Emperor Alexius. The combined crusader force suffered a devastating defeat at the hands of a Seljuk army at the Battle of Mersivan in June 1101; Raymond and Stephen of Blois both escaped and fled back to Constantinople.

▲ *The establishment of the Kingdom of Jerusalem, and in particular its capture of Mediterranean ports, opened a sea route from Europe to the Holy Land. It was taken by pilgrims and later crusaders.*

Meanwhile, a second crusader army from Nevers in France had arrived, but failed to meet up with the first; the second army was trounced by Seljuk leader Kilij Arslan at Heraclea Cybistra. A third army under Hugh of Vermandois and William IX of Aquitaine then arrived: around half of the force was again slaughtered by the Seljuks, although the other half travelled by ship directly to Palestine; Hugh of Vermandois was mortally injured in the battle with the Seljuks and died at Tarsus in October 1101.

Survivors of all three waves united and pressed on, but the expedition was by this stage more pilgrimage than crusade. They arrived in Jerusalem at Easter 1102. Many then went home, but some remained to fight with King Baldwin I of Jerusalem against an Egyptian army at Ramla, a battle in which Stephen of Blois was killed.

The First Crusade had given the crusader armies an aura of invincibility, but the Seljuk Turks' devastating victories in

1101 proved to the Muslim world that the armies of Europe were in fact far from unbeatable. The major consequence of the defeats was that the land route to Jerusalem from Constantinople could no longer be made safe, and so passage to the crusader states had to be by sea. With Jerusalem under Christian rule, ever larger numbers of Europeans wanted to make a pilgrimage there, and merchants from the Italian cities such as Venice and Genoa grew rich transporting them there.

THE EXPLOITS OF 'SIGURD THE CRUSADER'

In 1107–11 King Sigurd I Magnusson of Norway led an armed expedition to support the Kingdom of Jerusalem. Sailing with 60 ships, en route to the Holy Land he visited Lisbon and fought Moorish pirates off the Balearic islands; after arriving in Jerusalem, he fought alongside Baldwin I in 1110, helping the crusaders capture the coastal city of Sidon (modern Sayda, Lebanon). He returned home the following year, taking as a gift from Baldwin a piece of the True Cross that he housed in a castle at Konghelle (modern Kungälv, Sweden). Sigurd's adventure

▼ *Sidon, an ancient city on the coast of Lebanon, became a major lordship within the Kingdom of Jerusalem following its capture by crusaders including King Sigurd I Magnusson of Norway in 1110.*

earned him the title of Sigurd Jerusalemfarer (the Crusader), although his expedition was really more pilgrimage than crusade.

BOHEMOND'S 'CRUSADE' OF 1107–08

Around the same time, Bohemond of Taranto led a military expedition from Europe that is sometimes identified as a crusade. Bohemond was one of the leaders of the First Crusade who had established himself as Prince of Antioch, but after defeats at the hands of Muslim powers he had returned to Europe to raise an army in 1105–06. He led a military expedition to the East in 1107–08, but rather than using it to consolidate the position of Antioch he launched an attack on Emperor Alexius and was again defeated. The episode was ended in 1108 by the Treaty of Devol, in which Bohemond became a vassal of Alexius and agreed to allow a Greek Orthodox Patriarch to have authority in Antioch.

Two further crusades took place in the 1120s. The first was proclaimed by Pope Calixtus II in 1122 and is also known as the 'Venetian Crusade' because the main response came from the city of Venice. The city sent a large fleet, which was waylaid at Corfu before finally reaching the Holy Land, where it took part in the siege of Tyre. Tyre was captured in 1124 and became one of the key trading posts for

▲ *In a highly-charged atmosphere, Doge Dandolo of Venice forced the crusade leaders to swear an oath to support an attack on Zara. From this point, Venice rose to wealth and prominence on through trade with the Byzantine Empire.*

the Kingdom of Jerusalem. Calixtus also offered Christian soldiers fighting Muslims in Spain 'the same remission of sins we have offered to the defenders of the Church in the East' and the crusade he called had also found expression in campaigns against Spanish Islam waged by Alfonso I of Aragon in 1125.

Another crusade was launched in 1128, partly recruited by Hugues de Payens, the French knight who was a co-founder of the Knights Templar. This expedition attacked Damascus in November 1129 but failed to take the city.

CONTROL OF THE COAST

Partly with the help of these expeditions and partly by their own strength, the armies of the crusader states won control of the key ports along the Mediterranean coast of what are now Syria, Lebanon, Israel and Palestine in the quarter century after 1099. In 1101 they took Arsuf and Caesarea, Haifa and Acre in 1104, Beiry and Sidon in 1110 and Tyre in 1124. The only significant port left was Ascalon.

CHAPTER SIX

MUSLIM RESURGENCE AND THE SECOND CRUSADE

The Europeans who fought in the First Crusade and subsequently established the crusader states of Jerusalem, Antioch, Edessa and Tripoli benefited from division among their opponents. Fierce rivalries between Muslim lords meant that in many cases, they preferred to ally themselves with the crusaders than with their countrymen. But in the 12th century great Muslim generals such as Ilghazi, Zengi, Nur ed-Din and Saladin began to develop unity and inflict great defeats on the Christians. These men mobilized their armies and people with the call to jihad, or holy war. The capture of Edessa at Christmas 1144 provoked European Christians to mount the Second Crusade of 1147–49; the abject failure of that enterprise only boosted Muslim morale and inspired Nur ed-Din to further great exploits of jihad. Then, in 1187, Saladin annihilated the strength of the crusader states at the Battle of the Horns of Hattin, and later that year recaptured Jerusalem. According to his biographer Imad ed-din al-Isfahani, Saladin envisaged an even more sweeping holy war. After Hattin he declared: 'When Allah grants me possession of the rest of Palestine I shall divide my lands, make a will laying down my wishes, and then embark by sea to the Franks' faraway lands, and pursue them there, so as to clean the earth of all those who do not believe in Allah.'

▲ *Qalaat ar-Rahba in Syria was built by the great Muslim general Shirkuh.*

◄ *The culmination of the Islamic fight back in the Holy Land was the recapture of Jerusalem by Saladin's army on 2 October 1187, seen here through the eyes of a 19th-century artist.*

THE FIELD OF BLOOD

A GREAT TURKISH VICTORY NEAR ALEPPO

The first major victory in the Muslims' fightback against the crusaders came in 1119, when a vast Turkish army assembled by the emir of Damascus and the Artuqid Turkish ruler and general Ilghazi entirely devastated a Christian army commanded by Roger of Antioch. The defeat was so heavy that it became known to Western chroniclers as *Ager Sanguinis* (Field of Blood).

BACKGROUND TO THE CONFLICT

Things looked very grim for the Muslims of northern Syria at the close of the 12th century's first decade. In 1109 the crusaders captured and sacked Tripoli after a siege of five years. In May 1110 they took Beirut. On 4 December Sidon also fell and was sacked. In Baghdad the Seljuk Turkish sultan, Muhammad, faced calls to mount a jihad, or holy war, against the invaders.

Muhammad sent his general Mawdud, who was also governor of Mosul, to attack the crusader state of Edessa. The attack failed but there were many Christian

▼ *Imposing city walls embody the power of the Artuqid dynasty at Diyarbakir, Turkey.*

casualties. In 1113 Mawdud raised another army to mount a new wave of jihad, but the enterprise came to a premature end when he was murdered in Damascus by a militant Shi'ite assassin. Fulcher of Chartres recorded Christian relief – 'the Lord had allowed this man to be a scourge unto us for some time, but afterwards His will was that the general should die a lowly death by the actions of an unimportant man.'

Mawdud's place as leader of jihad was taken by Ilghazi, a highly gifted general who had fought in Mawdud's army. The Artuqid dynasty to which Ilghazi belonged had been established in the late 11th century by Artuq ibn Ekseb. Starting out in the service of the Seljuk Turkish sultanate, Artuq's descendants built an independent powerbase in the province of Diyarbakir (now south-eastern Turkey).

Ilghazi took power at Mardin in that province in 1108. In 1118 the citizens of Aleppo asked Ilghazi to become ruler of their city, which was in turmoil: Aleppo's ruler Alp Arslan had been assassinated by his eunuch, who had seized power and then been killed himself.

THE BUILD-UP TO THE BATTLE

The following year Ilghazi marched on Antioch. The Principality of Antioch was in the hands of Roger of Salerno, nephew of Tancred; Roger had succeeded his uncle as regent when Tancred died in 1112.

Roger brought trouble upon himself: when Ilghazi marched into the Principality, Roger and his army were safely ensconced in the fortress of Artah, near to the city of Antioch, and he overconfidently ventured forth to meet Ilghazi, ignoring orders from King Baldwin II to wait for reinforcements from Jerusalem, and advice from the Latin Patriarch of Antioch, Bernard of Valence, that they should remain in Artah. As a result, the Christian army was vastly outnumbered by the Turks. Roger established himself in the mountain pass of Sarmada, while Ilghazi was engaged in besieging the fortress of al-Artharib. Roger sent a contingent under Robert of Vieux Pont to try to lift the siege but they were outmanoeuvred when Ilghazi feigned a retreat and were easily defeated.

On the morning of Saturday 28 June 1119 Roger's army awoke in their camp at the Pass of Sarmada to find themselves

Western historians suggest the more sober figure of around 3,700, but accept that only a handful of Christians survived.

THE AFTERMATH OF AGER SANGUINIS

Although the city of Antioch had been left wide open to attack, Ilghazi failed to press home his advantage by advancing, and instead, he returned to Aleppo to celebrate his victory. Yet the total victory at the Field of Blood was of major significance: it delivered a great shock to the crusaders, and it proved to the Muslim world that their armies did not have to rely on the might of the Seljuk forces to defeat the European soldiers.

entirely surrounded by Ilgahzi's men. They may have suspected that this day might be their last and went to their deaths after the archbishop of Apamea had heard the confessions of the whole army.

▲ *The power of mounted soldiers – especially the devastatingly effective Turcopole archers – was decisive at the Battle of the Field of Blood.*

▼ *Armies on the march in crusader-era Syria relied on roads and bridges built by the Romans. This bridge, across the River Afrin in northern Syria, dates to c.3AD.*

THE BATTLE

Descriptions of the battle survive from both sides. The Christian perspective was given in an account by Walter the Chancellor, the Norman crusader who served as chancellor of the Principality of Antioch, in his *Bella Antiochena* (Antioch Wars); the Muslim view was recorded by Kamal ad-Din, a Muslim historian of Aleppo. When battle was joined, the crusaders began well but then fell into disarray when their Turcopole mounted archers were driven back into the main line under Roger's command. Roger, who was fighting under a great jewelled cross as his standard, was slain, slashed in the face with a sword and his head sliced open down to the nose. His army fled – according to ad-Din 'the arrows flew thick as a locust swarm, falling on cavalry and infantry alike' and forced the Christians into disorganized retreat. They were pursued without mercy, and cut down in the hillside vineyards nearby.

Ad-Din claims that Roger's army numbered 15,000 and that all but 20 were killed in the battle and the ensuing chase.

THE CAPTURE OF EDESSA
THE RISE OF IMAD ED-DIN ZENGI

Turkish general Imad ed-Din Zengi stunned the Christian world on Christmas Eve 1144 when he succeeded in capturing the capital of the crusader state of Edessa. In the 25 years since the defeat of Roger of Antioch by Ilghazi at the devastating *Ager Sanguinis*, there had been defeats for the crusader lords, notably at the hands of Ilghazi's fearless nephew Balak, but always the status quo was more or less maintained in the crusader states. Now Zengi's triumph at Edessa cast doubt on the very survival of Outremer, the Christian kingdom overseas. Among Muslims, Zengi was hailed as *al-Malik al-Mansur*, the 'victorious king'.

BALAK

Ilghazi did not long survive his triumph at the Ager Sanguinis – he died three years later, in 1122, having never risen to those heights of military success again – but his nephew Balak took up the torch and swiftly became a scourge of the crusader kingdoms. In 1122 he captured Joscelin of Courtenay, Count of Edessa, and the following year took captive no less a person than Baldwin II, King of Jerusalem.

In 1124 Balak became ruler of Aleppo and began to retake territory from the crusaders in northern Syria. But he died the same year, having been shot in the chest with an arrow while besieging the castle of Manbij. In a few years he had made a great impression on the crusaders – after recording the news of his death, Fulcher of Chartres wrote in his chronicle: 'Then we all gave thanks to God because Balak, the furious dragon who had stamped on Christianity, was brought low at last.'

THE ORIGINS AND EMERGENCE OF ZENGI

In Balak's wake, Imad ed-Din Zengi leapt to prominence. Zengi was the son of a governor of Aleppo who, after his father's execution for treason against the Seljuk sultan Malik Shah in the late 11th century, had been raised in Mosul. According to legend, Zengi was the son of Ida of Austria, mother of Leopold III, who had travelled with the Crusade of 1101 and disappeared, presumed dead, during the crusaders' defeat at Heraclea Cybistra by Kilij Arslan. The legend recounted that rather than being killed she was carried

▲ *The formidable citadel of Aleppo. The city was Imad ed-Din Zengi's base when he established his power after 1128.*

off to life in a harem, where she later gave birth to Zengi. However, this tall story is impossible on grounds of chronology, and cannot be true.

Zengi established himself as ruler in Mosul in 1127, then in Aleppo the following year. Over the next 15 years or so he worked tirelessly to extend his power in the region, fighting whoever came his way – his Turkish rivals, the Byzantine emperor or the crusader lords. Zengi repeatedly attempted to gain control in Damascus and in 1137, when the Damascenes allied with the crusaders, he ambushed the army of King Fulk of Jerusalem and then besieged them in the fortress of Barin, north-east of Tripoli, before allowing Fulk to buy his freedom and return home to Jerusalem.

ATTACK ON EDESSA

King Fulk's death in 1143 led to a joint succession by his wife Melisende (daughter of King Baldwin II) and his son

Baldwin III, but Melisende effectively ruled alone, with the help of the Constable of Jerusalem, Manasses of Hierges, and initially largely excluded Baldwin III from power. Zengi sought to take advantage of this situation and in 1144 turned against the County of Edessa.

Joscelin II, Count of Edessa, had made an alliance with Kara Aslan, the Artuqid Turkish ruler of Diyarbakir and had marched the bulk of his army out of Edessa to support Kara Aslan in a campaign against Aleppo. Zengi moved swiftly, mounting a siege of the city of Edessa in November 1144. Within its walls Hugh II, the Catholic archbishop, and Basil, the Armenian bishop, combined to lead the defence; Count Joscelin II, hearing of the developments, went to the town of Turbessel, (now Tilbesar in Turkey) and sent out a plea for help from the other crusader states. Queen Melisende sent an army led by Manasses, but Raymond of Antioch was unable to help.

At Edessa, Zengi built siege engines and set to work undermining the walls of the city. The defences were poor, for the population of the city, according to chronicler William of Tyre, were traders who 'knew

▼ *Fulk of Anjou became King of Jerusalem when he married Melisende, daughter of King Baldwin II, on 2 June 1129. Fulk was closely associated with the Knights Templar.*

THE FIRST FIVE KINGS OF JERUSALEM

Godfrey of Bouillon is regarded as the first king of Jerusalem although he was known as Defender of the Holy Sepulchre. Godfrey was succeeded in 1100 by his brother, Baldwin of Boulogne, who ruled as Baldwin I until he died in 1118. Baldwin's cousin, Baldwin of Le Bourg, then Count of Edessa, became Baldwin II of Jerusalem. He died in 1131 and was succeeded by his son-in-law, Fulk of Anjou, who ruled as King Fulk of Jerusalem. He died in 1143 following a hunting accident while on holiday in Acre, and was succeeded by his

▲ *Baldwin III, King of Jerusalem at the time of the disastrous Second Crusade.*

wife Melisende (Baldwin II's daughter) and his eldest son, who ruled as Baldwin III of Jerusalem until 1162.

nothing of using weapons and understood only the business of buying and selling'. They had to rely on mercenaries to man the walls, and their numbers were dwindling because Archbishop Hugh was a miser who hoarded the city's great wealth rather than put it to sensible use in paying for the defence of the walls.

On Christmas Eve 1144, Zengi's mining operations were complete and he gave the command to set fire to the wooden posts that supported the tunnels beneath the walls near the Gate of the Hours. The tunnels collapsed, the walls fell down, and Zengi's troops poured into the city.

THE ENEMY OF LATIN CHRISTIANS

Thousands were killed in the taking of Edessa before Zengi intervened, ordering his men to stop the slaughter. He made it very clear that his war was only against the Latin Christians or Franks: and he went on to execute all the Latin Christians who had been taken prisoner, but spared all the other Christians, whom he allowed to live on in the city as before. He appointed one of his commanders, Zayn ad-Din Ali Kutchuk, as the city's governor and allowed the Armenian bishop, Basil, to continue in his position. He destroyed the Latin Christian church buildings, but allowed the remainder to stand.

Subsequently Zengi captured Saruj (now Suruç in Turkey) but then retreated to Mosul when the army of Jerusalem at last arrived. He did not attempt to consolidate his power in the County of Edessa nor to attack Antioch, as many had feared. But his capture of Edessa sent shockwaves through Christendom and led to the calling of the Second Crusade. Zengi himself died in 1146, when he was stabbed to death by his eunuch slave during a siege at Qalat Jabar. He was remembered by Muslims as 'the great, the just, the helper of God … the pillar of religion, destroyer of infidels, rebels and atheists'.

SOLDIERS OF ISLAM
WEAPONS AND TACTICS

Many of the Muslim armies faced by the crusaders in the late 11th and 12th centuries were enormously large and contained a wide range of troops, including untrained, poorly armed peasants alongside professional soldiers with the finest equipment. The core of the armies was made up of crack Turkish troops.

The Turks were famous for their cavalry. They were quick and lightly armed. They wore lighter chain mail than the crusaders and conical helmets that were often inscribed with inspirational words from the Koran. They carried small, round shields that were much less burdensome than the elongated kite-shaped shields used by the crusaders.

They fought with clubs, swords and lances, but their principal weapon was the bow and arrow. They were highly skilled and trained horsemen who had entirely mastered the art of shooting from the saddle – they could fire off arrows while

▼ *Two Turkish cavalrymen practise the use of sword and lance while on horseback. Both also carry a bow and a sheath of arrows. Wearing light armour, they were generally no match for the crusaders in close fighting.*

riding at full speed, and could even fire over their shoulders as they rode away, a version of the famous Parthian shot. The arrows they loosed were not highly penetrative, but they were fired in such numbers that they caused panic and disarray among the Christian armies – various accounts of battle liken the arrows to a plague of locusts, a storm of rain or a thick cloud that blocked out the sun.

SPEED AND MOBILITY

The use of long-range weapons, such as the bow and arrow, and the mobility of the cavalry were the key to the Turkish tactics. Typically they attacked in the rear and the flank of the crusader army. According to contemporary accounts, the Turkish horses were quicker and lighter than the crusader's animals; their speed and movement were a constant threat.

They tried to avoid encountering the European knights' mounted charge, since they were not heavily enough armed to fight on these terms; however, they saw that once the crusader knights had charged the line they tended to dissolve in disarray, leaving them vulnerable to counter-attack and leaving the European

JIHAD

The Islamic faith places a religious obligation on Muslims to spread their faith by waging jihad (which means 'battle'). Mainstream Islam teaches that jihad is intended to be carried out by fighting against sin. Traditionally there are four types of jihad: in the heart, with the tongue, by hand and using the sword. Jihad in the heart is interpreted as meaning fighting evil in one's inner self, jihad by tongue and hand are usually said to mean avoiding wickedness and promoting righteousness. Jihad by the sword involves waging war against enemies of Islam. A key idea behind jihad is that the world is divided into two, one that belongs to Allah, and the other subject to chaos; it is the Muslim's duty to combat the rule of chaos by extending submission to Allah's will, within the self but also in the wider world.

infantry open to assault. A favourite stratagem, used effectively again and again, was to pretend to retreat, leading the European knights on and encouraging them to charge. The Muslim cavalry would then either draw the crusaders on into an ambush or turn quickly to launch a devastating counter-attack.

The heavily armoured and armed crusaders were stronger than the Muslims in close combat, so the Muslim tactics tended to avoid hand-to-hand fighting if they could by holding off and using the lightning cavalry attacks and bombardment with arrows to punish the Europeans; they would only commit to close-quarters combat when they could be confident of success. Eyewitness accounts of the Battle of Dorylaeum in 1097, during the First Crusade, reveal that the crusaders' long chain mail body armour provided a very

▲ *The crusaders were feared for their cavalry assault, but the Muslim warriors, on light and fast horses, were often able to outmanoeuvre them and drive them back.*

effective defence against the light swords carried by the Seljuks – and also against their arrows, unless these were fired from straight ahead when they were able to pierce the armour. If the crusaders were able to draw any of the attackers into close combat, they found they could usually get the upper hand.

FIGHTING IN GOD'S NAME

The Muslim armies were fighting to spread Islam through jihad, or holy war, just as the Christians had gone to war in the name of Christ. Eyewitness accounts of the Battle of the Field of Blood in 1119 reveal that prior to the battle the ra'is, or mayor, of Aleppo, Abu al-Fadi ibn al-Khashshab, rode out before Ilghazi's army and delivered a stirring speech, urging the soldiers to fight jihad without fear. His words reduced hardened soldiers to tears. Meanwhile, Prince Roger addressed his men as 'soldiers of Christ' and urged them to fight to the death if that were God's will.

Likewise, Norman eyewitness accounts of the earlier Battle of Dorylaeum in 1097 report that Seljuk Turks shouted as they came forward, 'calling in great voices in their own language a devilish word that I could not understand'. We know from Radulph of Caen, biographer of Tancred, that this word was 'Allachibar!' – far from devilish, it was a form of the Muslim holy words *Allah Akhbar* (God is Great). For their part, again according to eyewitness accounts, the crusaders were calling out 'God wills it!' 'God wills it!' as they fought.

◄ *The Turkish cavalrymen were renowned for their ability to fire arrows as they rode at full speed in battle. Feigning retreat, they often lured crusaders into rash charges.*

CALL TO A SECOND CRUSADE
BERNARD OF CLAIRVAUX APPEALS TO THE RULERS OF THE WEST

On 1 December 1145 Pope Eugenius III responded to the news that Turkish general Imad ed-Din Zengi had captured Edessa by calling a new crusade.

THE LOSS OF EDESSA
The first news of Edessa's fall had been brought back by pilgrims and then had been confirmed by Bishop Hugh of the Syrian town of Jabala, who was sent as part of an official embassy to Rome by Raymond of Antioch. In Italy, Bishop Hugh had an audience with the pope; he also informed the historian Otto of Friesling that a Christian king of India was ready to come to the aid of the crusader states – this was the first documented appearance of the enduring medieval myth of Prester John (*see* box).

▼ *'I opened my mouth; I preached; and the crusaders have multiplied beyond counting!'* Peerless orator Bernard of Clairvaux casts his spell over a vast crowd at Vézelay.

A CALL TO ARMS
Eugenius issued his rallying call in a bull, or papal letter, known as *Quantum praedecessores* and addressed to King Louis VII of France and his people. (Papal bulls were untitled and are named from their first words. In this case, *Quantum praedecessores nostri Romani pontifices* is the beginning of a phrase that translates 'The extent to which our predecessors the pontiffs of Rome did work to free the Eastern Church, we have learned from the accounts of older writers and by studying their deeds.') The bull recalled the heroic achievements of the crusaders of 1096–99 and offered remission (forgiveness) of sins for those who took the cross together with church protection of their possessions and relatives while they were away on crusade.

In France, King Louis was already planning a crusade, or perhaps a pilgrimage, and announced his plans at his court at Bourges at Christmas 1145, probably before hearing of Eugenius's bull. He encountered opposition at home, but after liaising with French preacher Abbot Bernard of Clairvaux, who referred him to the pope, Louis received Eugenius's enthusiastic blessing on the enterprise. The papal bull was reissued on 1 March 1146 and Bernard was authorized by the papacy to preach the crusade through Europe.

BERNARD PREACHES THE CRUSADE
On Easter Day 1146 Bernard preached before a vast crowd at Vézelay in central France. He was a great orator and he succeeded in whipping the crowd up into an absolute frenzy of enthusiasm. At the conclusion of his sermon, they leapt up almost to a man, shouting 'Crosses! Give us crosses!' Bernard had these prepared in advance, but even so he ran out – and reputedly then tore off his own clothing to make more crosses for the eager knights and infantrymen.

▲ *Frederick, Duke of Swabia, seen here being crowned emperor in 1155, took the cross at Spires in south-west Germany.*

Louis VII and his nobles were among those who took the cross: Louis received a cloth cross blessed by the pope, and people also flocked to the cause. Bernard wrote to the pope: 'I opened my mouth; I preached; and the crusaders have multiplied beyond counting. The countryside is deserted. You will hardly find one man for every seven womenfolk. In every place you will find widows whose husbands are far from dead.'

He continued the tour, preaching in Switzerland and Germany. Conrad III of Germany was initially unmoved by Bernard's pleas, but on Christmas Day at the Diet of Spires the abbot preached a second sermon to the German king, in which he took the part of Christ himself and asked Conrad directly: 'O Man, what should I have done for you that I have not

▼ *Louis VII, depicted here on his royal seal, was another head of state persuaded by Bernard of Clairvaux to take the cross.*

PRESTER JOHN

Legends of Prester John, a priest-king ruling over a Christian realm somewhere in the Orient, were popular from the 1100s until the 17th century.

The first mention of the king is found in the *Chronicon* of 1145 by Bishop Otto of Friesling, who reported that he had heard of the king from Bishop Hugh of Jaballa at the papal court in Viterbo, Italy, in that year. According to this version, the priest-king was a descendant of the Three Wise Men, or Magi, and after defeating the Muslim rulers of Persia had intended to free Jerusalem but had been waylaid by trouble crossing the River Tigris. The origin of the legend may have been in reports of successes against Muslim Persia by Central Asian Mongol rulers, one of whose queens and many of whose subjects were Christians.

The king soon became the subject of colourful legends that placed him in 'the three Indies' as ruler of a peaceful realm, sometimes said to contain the Fountain of Youth and to be adjacent to the Garden of Eden. One 12th-century document identified him as guardian of a

▲ *Prester John was still a legend around 1550 when he appeared as one of the wonders of the Orient on this mariners' chart of the Indian Ocean.*

shrine to the biblical apostle St Thomas at Mylapore, India. Later versions of the legend located Prester John's realm in Ethiopia. The goal of finding Prester John's kingdom inspired generations of eastbound adventurers, including the 13th-century Venetian, Marco Polo.

done?' Conrad was so deeply moved that he burst into tears: he and several of his noblemen, including Frederick, Duke of Swabia (later Emperor Frederick I Barbarossa), took the cross on the spot. Many ordinary Germans also joined up for the expedition.

As at the time of the First Crusade, the crusade sermons provoked anti-Jewish rioting in Germany. They were particularly inspired by an anti-Semitic monk named Rudolf who whipped up popular feeling by declaring that the Jews were not making any contribution to the rescue of the Holy Land. Abbot Bernard was eventually able to bring this outburst of violence to an end, persuading many of the rioters to join the official crusade, and ordering Rudolf to return to his monastery.

THE KINGS' CRUSADE

The departure date for the crusade was set for the summer of 1147. Bernard had recruited an impressive cast of Europe's royalty and nobility. In addition to two kings, Louis VII of France and Conrad III of Germany, Louis's wife, the celebrated Eleanor of Aquitaine and his brother Robert I of Dreux travelled on the crusade; other leading figures were William II, Count of Nevers; William of Warennes, 3rd Earl of Surrey; and Hugh VII 'the Brown' of Lusignan.

Another notable participant on the Second Crusade was Alfonso Jordan, a son of Raymond of Toulouse; Alfonso was born in Tripoli in 1103 but returned to Europe with his mother at the age of five and became Count of Toulouse.

CRUSADERS SET OUT
FROM EUROPE TO CONSTANTINOPLE

The armies of the Second Crusade set out in three waves in May and June 1147. The first departure in mid-May was from England and consisted of Norman, English, Scottish, Flemish and a few German crusaders. They were followed later the same month by a larger, mainly German army under Conrad III and then in June by a French force led by King Louis, containing armies from Aquitaine, Brittany, Burgundy and Lorraine.

EUROPEAN CRUSADES
In addition to its main theatre in the Holy Land, the Second Crusade had two European fronts, for Pope Eugenius also authorized holy wars in Germanic territories against the pagan Wends and in Spain against Muslims. He promised the knights

▼ *The first part of this itinerary to Jerusalem guides a prospective crusader from London to Dover. On the Second Crusade, many English knights travelled no farther than Lisbon in Portugal.*

and infantrymen who fought in these wars the same crusading indulgences he had offered for the war in the Holy Land.

The first wave of crusaders left England by sea, sailing around Brittany and the Iberian Peninsula, and were driven by bad weather to make landfall in June in Porto, where the local bishop persuaded them to make a diversion to Lisbon. There they backed King Alfonso I of Portugal in a four-month siege of the city, and looted it raucously after it fell on 24 October. Thereafter, some elected to remain in Portugal, and an English priest named Gilbert of Hastings was named the first Bishop of Lisbon, but most of the crusaders travelled on by sea to the Holy Land, departing in February 1148.

VIEW FROM THE EAST
In the Byzantine Empire memories of the First Crusade 50 years earlier were naturally still strong. When the new crusade was being planned, Emperor Manuel I Comnenus had given permission for its armies to pass through the empire, but he did not trust them – fearing that they had designs on his territories. He broke off a war against the Seljuk sultanate of Rum in spring 1147, signing a peace treaty with Sultan Mesud I, so that he could give his full attention to defending his lands against the crusaders.

The Muslim scholar and writer Ibn al-Qalanisi, mayor and chronicler of Damascus, described the sense of mounting fear in Syria as news filtered through that another wave of crusaders was about to break in the Holy Land. He wrote: 'The news was coming in from Constantinople, from the lands of the Franks and from neighbouring countries, too, that the kings of the Franks were travelling from their homeland to attack the land of Islam. They had left their own lands empty, without defenders, and brought with them great wealth.'

▲ *Manuel I Comnenus managed the Second Crusade's passage through his lands very successfully. He was reputedly a great jouster and fearsome warrior.*

THE PROGRESS OF THE GERMANS
The German army travelled by land through Hungary without much incident. Alongside Conrad in the royal party were his nephew, the haughty Frederick, Duke of Swabia, and the kings of Poland and Bohemia. Some contemporary accounts reported excitedly that this force numbered as many as one million, but in truth it was probably only about 20,000 strong. Before passing into Bulgaria, then part of the Byzantine Empire, Conrad swore an oath of loyalty to Byzantine emperor Manuel I Comnenus, pledging that he would do nothing likely to harm the emperor or his territory.

The army was given a Byzantine military escort, but this did not prevent it pillaging and looting as it went. At Philippopolis (modern Plovdiv, Bulgaria) a riot erupted after crusaders accused a local of witchcraft, and the outer part of

▲ *Kneeling humbly, King Louis VII receives a pilgrim's staff from Pope Eugenius III in the abbey church of St Denis in June 1147.*

the town was burned to the ground; then at Adrianople (modern Edirne, western Turkey), local robbers killed a German noble outside a monastery and Frederick of Swabia launched murderous reprisals, burning down the monastery and killing all the monks. Conrad then ignored the emperor's request to pass into Anatolia by the Dardanelles, and instead marched the ill-disciplined troop to Constantinople, where they arrived in mid-September.

KING LOUIS THE PILGRIM

On 8 June 1147 King Louis VII formally handed control of France to Abbot Suger of St Denis in a candle-lit service at the abbey church attended by the pope. Dressed as a pilgrim in a black tunic with red cross, Louis received the pope's blessing and, before a cheering congregation, was handed a pilgrim's staff and wallet. Leaving from Metz, the French army marched in the wake of Conrad's German force across Hungary, with the contingent from Lorraine marching ahead of the main force. The Provençal army under Alfonso of Toulouse waited behind, having decided to depart in August and go by sea.

In early October the French army arrived at Constantinople. There was some trouble at first, when the contingent from Lorraine clashed with the rear of Conrad's army outside the walls of Constantinople. But the Germans were already in the process of moving on, at the emperor's insistence, into Anatolia. In addition, some of the French wanted to attack the city on the grounds that the emperor had made a truce with the Seljuks, but the papal legates restored peace. King Louis was royally welcomed and entertained within the city. Manuel prevailed on him to swear an oath under which the crusaders would return to the Byzantine Empire any lands they captured on the crusade.

Troops from Savoy, Montferrat and Auvergne joined up with Louis at Constantinople. They had come overland through Italy, then by sea from Brindisi to Byzantine territory. Thus bolstered, the French army travelled across the Bosphorus into Anatolia. Unlike his grandfather Alexius at the time of the First Crusade, Manuel did not provide the crusaders with an army. The French marched on, accompanied only by a few Byzantine scouts, to meet their fate.

▼ *Abbot Suger acted as co-regent during the reign of Louis VII, when the king was absent on the Second Crusade.*

DISASTER AT DORYLAEUM

AND THE CRUSADERS' DIFFICULT PROGRESS TO ATTALIA

At Dorylaeum, the scene of the European armies' first victory in 1097 during the First Crusade, the bulk of the German army suffered a devastating defeat at the hands of the Seljuks, led by Kilij Arslan II, the son of the Seljuk ruler defeated there in 1097.

▼ *Warrior of the cross. Conrad survived defeat at Dorylaeum and a serious illness to take part in the final stages of the crusade.*

DIVIDED AND DEFEATED

When the German army reached Nicaea, Conrad decided to split it in two. He sent the largely non-combatant contingent of pilgrims led by Bishop Otto of Friesing, along a safer, but longer, route through Byzantine territory, while he and his army headed straight across Anatolia towards the Seljuk realm. Meanwhile, Seljuk scouts were keeping close tabs on the German progress. The main German army stopped to rest at Dorylaeum after a gruelling march and were ill-prepared for the Seljuk attack when it came out of the blue.

In the battle, the Europeans were out-thought and outmanoeuvred. The Seljuks once again tricked the European warriors by feigning retreat, luring the German knights into what they thought was a tri-umphant charge – only to be surrounded and utterly defeated by the Seljuks. The German army was virtually wiped out at a stroke. Conrad, Frederick and a few survivors, at most a tenth of the original army, began the retreat to Constantinople.

FRENCH PROGRESS

At Nicaea the German survivors joined up with the French army under Louis. They then marched along the western, largely coastal route already followed by Bishop Otto of Friesing as far as Ephesus. Conrad fell badly ill and was forced to return to Constantinople to convalesce; he was cared for there under the personal supervision of Manuel.

The French force marched on and succeeded in defeating a Turkish army in a minor skirmish outside Ephesus. As they pressed on through difficult winter con-ditions, under constant harassment by the Turks, discipline became ragged and morale very low.

In the region of Laodicea (near modern Denizli, in south-western Turkey) on 8 January 1148 the French army suffered a heavy defeat at the hands of the Turks. This setback came just a few days after a similarly damaging defeat nearby for the pilgrim contingent under Bishop Otto von Friesing.

RAYMOND OF ANTIOCH

Raymond of Poitiers took power as Prince of Antioch in 1136 on his mar-riage to the 10-year-old Constance, daughter of and heir to Bohemond II of Antioch, and was co-ruler with Constance. Raymond was the second son of William IX, Duke of Aquitaine and Count of Poitou, the French noble-man celebrated as the first troubadour poet, and was uncle to Duke William's granddaughter, Eleanor of Aquitaine. His rule in Antioch was not successful, for he was twice forced to pay homage to the Byzantine emperor and was unable to contain the threat of Nur ed-Din. Moreover he failed to divert the Second Crusade towards an attack on Nur ed-Din's powerbase at Aleppo.

Raymond was, however, one of the greatest courtly noblemen of his time. William of Tyre described him as being 'of noble descent, tall and stylish in fig-ure, the finest-looking of earthly princes, a man of great charm and wit, generous and magnificent beyond measure.' Raymond was also a patron of literature – he was responsible for funding the composition of the crusade poem the *Chanson des chétifs*. He was a most gen-erous host when Louis VII and Eleanor of Aquitaine made their visit during the Second Crusade – to the extent that rumours ran rife that he was Eleanor's lover. William of Tyre rehearsed this story, but modern historians tend to discount it as being unfounded.

BY SEA FROM ATTALIA

Louis and the survivors pressed doggedly on until they reached the port of Attalia (modern Antalya), close to where Byzantine territory gave way to Seljuk lands. Food was short, the army starving and desperate. The plan had been for the whole army to embark by sea from Attalia for Syria, but the fleet supplied by Emperor Manuel was far too small.

Louis took the available ships for himself, his household and the leading knights and essentially abandoned the remainder of the army to its fate. Although he left money with the Governor of Attalia to feed them, the soldiers and pilgrims had little alternative but to press on by land largely unprotected by knights through dangerous Seljuk territory to Tarsus. Most of the army's remnant was killed before reaching Tarsus.

Meanwhile Louis and his elite corps reached St Simeon, and were received with lavish hospitality by Raymond of Antioch. Escorted by Raymond, they arrived – exhausted and weary of both battles and voyaging – at the capital of the principality on 19 March.

▼ *King Louis, Conrad and the leading lords of Outremer arrive in Antioch. Here they took time to recover from the hardships of campaign, and debate the crusade's future.*

IN ANTIOCH

Louis considered what to do next. Raymond was keen to divert what force remained in the crusade against the rising power of Nur ed-Din, the Zengid ruler of Aleppo in Syria. Joscelin of Edessa, meanwhile, urged Louis to make the reconquest of Edessa his primary goal, arguing that the fall of Edessa had precipitated the crusade and therefore its recovery should be the expedition's primary goal. Louis

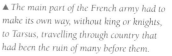

▲ *The main part of the French army had to make its own way, without king or knights, to Tarsus, travelling through country that had been the ruin of many before them.*

himself was preoccupied by his pilgrim's vows and wanted to press on to Jerusalem.

For a while the French lords and their ladies enjoyed the comforts of court life. Louis's wife, the intelligent and fiercely independent Eleanor of Aquitaine, was a keen advocate of her uncle Raymond's policy; in later years it was alleged that she was having an incestuous love affair in Antioch at this time with Raymond. But Louis was not minded to listen to her and when Fulk, the Patriarch of Jerusalem, arrived with an invitation from Queen Melisende and King Baldwin III, urging Louis's presence in Jerusalem, the French king began to make preparations for his departure. The royal couple argued – Eleanor stating that she would remain behind in Antioch and ask for a divorce. Louis reportedly dragged Eleanor forcibly out of the palace and made her come with him to Acre. Eleanor was not the only one who was angry – Raymond refused to take any part in the remainder of the crusade.

THE COUNCIL OF ACRE
AND THE HUMILIATING SIEGE OF DAMASCUS

When King Louis VII and Eleanor arrived in Acre, a great council was convened there on St John's Day (24 June) 1148 to discuss the future direction of the crusade. At this council the assembled lords agreed to attack Damascus, and the abject failure of this expedition was to bring the Second Crusade to an end.

CRUSADERS IN JERUSALEM

By the time Louis reached Acre, the remnants of the German pilgrim contingent under Bishop Otto had reached Jerusalem. Also in the Holy City was their king, Conrad III, who had recovered in Constantinople from his sickness and sailed directly as far as Tyre before travelling on to Jerusalem.

Other crusader groups had also made it to the Holy Land. Those who remained of the first wave of crusaders who had fought in the siege of Lisbon had arrived by sea, and the Provençal army that had

▼ *On three thrones, Louis VII of France, Conrad III of Germany and Baldwin III of Jerusalem hold court at the Council of Acre.*

▲ *This illustration from William of Tyre's History of Outremer (c.1280) shows the three kings at Acre and, below, the siege of Damascus that they decided to attempt.*

departed under Alfonso Jordan, Count of Toulouse, had landed. Alfonso almost immediately met his end, reputedly poisoned while at Caesarea by Raymond II, Count of Tripoli, who was fearful that Alfonso had come to claim the lands in Tripoli he had held in his infancy as the legitimate son of Raymond of Toulouse. (Count Raymond II was, in fact, Raymond

of Toulouse's great-grandson, descended through an illegitimate brother of Alfonso Jordan named Bertrand of Toulouse. This made him Alfonso Jordan's great-nephew.)

The council in Acre was officially a meeting of the High Court of the Kingdom of Jerusalem. In attendance were: Queen Melisende and her son King Baldwin III of Jerusalem; Manasses of Hierges, the constable of Jerusalem; Patriarch Fulk of Jerusalem; Louis VII; Conrad III; Bishop Otto of Freising; Duke Frederick of Swabia; and Henry II, Margrave of Austria. In addition, the masters of the military orders were there – Robert of Craon, master of the Knights Templar, and Raymond du Puy of Provence, master of the Knights Hospitaller. Other leading nobles of Outremer at the council included Walter Grenier, lord of Caesarea, Philip of Milly, lord of Nablus and Humphrey II, lord of Toron; but none of the lords of Antioch, Tripoli or Edessa were in attendance.

King Baldwin and the Knights Templar urged an attack on Damascus. Several local lords argued against this line of action, particularly on the grounds that

Mu'in ad-Din Unur, emir of Damascus, was an ally of the Christians against the Zengid lords of Syria – including the increasingly formidable Nur ed-Din of Aleppo. King Louis and King Conrad, however, were persuaded to back the attack on Damascus; the European lords, unversed in local politics and diplomacy, could not readily accept arguments in favour of making alliances with Muslim rulers and wanted principally to pursue a holy war against 'the infidel'. Moreover, while Aleppo meant nothing to them, Damascus was a city they knew from the Bible. An army was raised and in July assembled at Tiberias.

THE ORCHARDS OF DAMASCUS

The crusader lords decided to attack Damascus from the west, where a thick band of orchards would provide them with a steady food supply. They arrived there on 23 July, with the troops of the Kingdom of Jerusalem leading the way, followed by Louis and the French and then Conrad and the remainder of the German contingent in the rear. Emir Unur was warned of their approach, and had poisoned water sources, taken steps to strengthen his fortifications and sent out appeals for help to rival Muslim lords.

Taking the orchards was the crusaders' first task, but it was not an easy one: according to William of Tyre, they stretched for more than five miles 'like a dense, gloomy forest', the trees growing close together and accessible only by way of narrow footpaths between mud walls; in addition, there were defensive towers set at regular intervals. The crusaders poured into this difficult terrain, losing many men to arrow shots from the towers or to sudden attacks with spears from the darkness between the trees. They also had to face the city defenders who poured out of Damascus across the Barada river.

Both sides fought fiercely – according to a contemporary account, Conrad III made himself the talk of the entire army by dealing an overwhelming blow to a Turkish warrior that sliced through his

entire body, cutting off his head, neck and left shoulder. By the end of July 24 the crusaders had prevailed, taking control of the orchards and driving the Damascene defenders back behind their city walls.

Within the city, the people began to build barricades in the streets, fearing that they would be overrun. But at this point the crusaders paid the price for not encircling the city, for a relief army began to arrive from Aleppo in response to Emir Unur's cry for help – and this force, approaching from the north, was able to march right up to the city and enter through its North Gate. They began to launch counter-attacks on the Christian position in the orchards.

EASTERN APPROACHES

On 27 July the crusader lords took the fateful decision to move the army around the city to its open east side. Here they thought they might better be able to defend their camp. But – as they discovered the moment they arrived – there was

▲ The crusader armies fought bravely at Damascus, but were undone by their leaders' bad tactical and strategic decisions.

little or no food or water available there, and the eastern section of the city wall was very heavily fortified.

The crusaders and their leaders must have looked about in dismay. They could not return to the orchards, for by this stage Nur ed-Din himself had arrived and encamped his army there. In the burning heat of July, with insufficient water and the city strongly reinforced, their chances of taking Damascus had melted away; their position became untenable.

At dawn on 28 July, the Christian army began to abandon the siege, retreating in despair and disarray, harried all the way by the Turks. They lost many more men and horses during this humiliating retreat, and according to local chroniclers the human and animal corpses that lined the road sent up a stench powerful enough to make birds fall from the sky.

DESPAIR AND RECRIMINATIONS
THE AFTERMATH OF THE SECOND CRUSADE'S FAILURE

The crusaders' shambolic retreat from Damascus spelled the end of the Second Crusade, which fell apart in bitter recriminations. The failure of this enterprise had important and enduring consequences for the crusader states of Outremer and for their relations with the kingdoms of Europe.

In the immediate aftermath of Damascus, unity among the Christian forces was destroyed. Conrad took his troops to Ascalon, with the plan of taking that important port, but when none of the other parts of the army came to his aid he had to make another retreat. He headed home in September, but broke his journey to spend Christmas 1148 as a guest of Emperor Manuel in Constantinople. Louis, meanwhile, returned to Jerusalem. He did not embark for Europe until June 1149, then stopped on the way with King Roger of Sicily in Calabria, and with Pope Eugenius in Rome, before arriving back in Paris on 11 November.

THE FAULT OF OUTREMER LORDS

The crusaders felt bitterness towards both the native lords of Outremer and the Greeks of the Byzantine Empire. They asked how it was that the army had abandoned its hard-won position of strength in the orchards of Damascus, with the city almost at their mercy, to occupy an exposed and badly supplied position on the city's east side. They blamed the decision on bad advice from local lords, and began to circulate allegations that these lords had deliberately thrown away the military advantage.

One theory was that the lords had been outraged on discovering that the crusaders planned to grant the city to Count Thierry of Flanders and had secretly plotted to scupper the attack for this reason; another was that the lords were in league with Emir Unur of Damascus and had received payment for their part in making the siege

▲ *St Bernard of Clairvaux was a great teacher and inspiring preacher, but his reputation was ultimately damaged by the failure of the enterprise that he had done so much to instigate.*

fail. A third theory was that the lords had been plotting with Raymond of Antioch, who was still fuming at Louis's decision not to help him against Aleppo.

One of the central complaints of the crusaders was that both the lords of Outremer and the Byzantines had entered into alliances with Muslim rulers – in the case of Jerusalem with Emir Unur of Damascus, in the case of the Byzantine Empire with the Seljuk sultan Mesud I. This was inexplicable to the crusaders, fired as they were by the rhetoric of Bernard of Clairvaux.

BYZANTINE TREACHERY

The crusaders also had a string of complaints against Emperor Manuel and the Greeks of the Byzantine Empire. Some claimed that Byzantine scouts had deliberately led the German army into a Seljuk ambush at Dorylaeum – they asked whether perhaps Emperor Manuel had agreed this deal as part of the treaty he signed with Seljuks in 1147. In addition, they bemoaned the lack of support from Constantinople during the march of the French army across Anatolia and the fact that the fleet sent to King Louis in the port of Attalia was too small even for the much reduced army that had made it that far. Odo of Deuil, Louis VII's chaplain on the crusade, claimed that Manuel had betrayed the crusaders because Louis was an ally of Manuel's enemy Roger of Sicily.

CRITICISM IN EUROPE

In Europe Bernard of Clairvaux was at a loss fully to explain how the enterprise he had promoted as being devised and blessed in heaven could end in such abject failure. He attempted to blame the treachery of the Byzantines, but also said that the failure must have occurred because the sins of the crusaders had caused God to withdraw his support. Bernard participated in an attempt, driven by Abbot Suger of St Denis, to start a new crusade; at a meeting in Chartres in 1150, Bernard himself was elected leader of the enterprise. However, it came to nothing. Bernard was by now around 60 years old and having undergone many severe austerities as part of his spiritual life was far too frail to become a warrior monk.

Wider attempts to understand the crusade's failure led to criticism of almost all its aspects in Europe. There was denunciation of those, including Bernard, who had preached the enterprise. The anonymous Annalist of Wurzburg in Germany declared that the crusade preachers were 'witnesses of anti-Christ' who had misled good Christian folk. Other critics blamed the crusade leaders or the greed of Frankish lords in Outremer.

One idea with important consequences was that the considerable number of non-combatant pilgrims who had accompanied the crusade had been a major hindrance. The preaching of later crusades was focused more narrowly on mobilizing knights and infantry and avoided stirring up the passions of the people; indeed, after this crusade attempts were made to prevent pilgrims who could not fight or support themselves from travelling with armies to the East.

A WEAKENED OUTREMER

In the wake of the crusade's failure, the Kingdom of Jerusalem was in a far weaker position. The attack on Damascus had destroyed a valuable alliance, boosted Muslim morale and greatly strengthened the position of Nur ed-Din.

Moreover, the souring of relations between the crusader kingdoms and Europe meant that the leading knights among the European nobility were far less willing than previously to come to the aid of Outremer. Crusading and making a pilgrimage to the Holy Land suffered a severe decline in popularity. The success of the First Crusade had give the idea glamour and force, but these were dissipated by the failure of the Second. William of Tyre commented that after the Second Crusade Europeans 'looked askance at our leaders' ways' and 'showed complete indifference about the business of the kingdom'; this attitude spread – 'their influence caused others who had not been there to loosen their love for the kingdom' and so 'fewer folk, and those less committed in spirit, made the pilgrimage after this time'.

A QUARREL WITH CONSEQUENCES

The violent quarrel between Louis VII and his wife, Eleanor of Aquitaine, in Antioch during the Second Crusade had consequences that were still being felt in Europe in the 15th century. Eleanor tried but failed to get Pope Eugenius to grant a divorce on the couple's way home, but in March 1152 an annulment was granted on the basis of consanguinity (they were third cousins, once removed, as common descendants of Robert II of France). Just six weeks later, Eleanor married Henry, Count of Anjou and Duke of Normandy, who would become King Henry II of England in 1154. Because under Aquitaine law women would inherit property and her father's will had specified that the duchy should remain in the hands of her heirs, Eleanor brought vast and wealthy possessions in south-western France into the hands of the English crown.

▶ *Louis VII was both learned and devout. His wife, Eleanor, is said to have declared that she had thought she was marrying a king but found she had married a monk.*

Disputes over this land between England and France led to centuries of conflict, running right down to the Hundred Years War of 1337–1453. The royal couple had certainly begun to be estranged before travelling on the Second Crusade, but the quarrel in Antioch appears to have been a decisive moment, marking a split from which they did not recover.

NUR ED-DIN AND A UNIFIED SYRIA

MUSLIMS UNITE IN JIHAD

Buoyed by the abject failure of the Second Crusade, Nur ed-Din, whose personal reputation was enhanced by his part in driving back the crusaders at Damascus, prepared a new attack on the Principality of Antioch. His ultimate goal, however, was to capture Damascus and so unite Syria.

THE RISE OF NUR ED-DIN

Nur ed-Din was born in 1118, the second son of the great Turkish Muslim general Imad ed-Din Zengi, ruler of Aleppo and Mosul in Syria. On his father's death in 1146, Nur ed-Din took power in Aleppo while his brother Saif ed-Din became the ruler of Mosul. Nur ed-Din was already establishing himself as a scourge of the crusader lords, capturing a number of castles in the Principality of Antioch and also in November 1146 defeating an attempt by Joscelin of Courtenay, the ousted count of Edessa, to recapture his capital. In 1147 he formed an alliance with Emir Unur of

▼ *Knights ride out to battle in Syria. Nur ed-Din plotted his rise to power carefully, using diplomacy as much as warfare.*

Damascus as part of an attempt to create a united Muslim front against the advancing crusaders, but the two leaders were suspicious of each other's motives. Nevertheless, in 1148, as we have seen, Nur ed-Din came to Emir Unur's rescue when he brought his army to relieve the ill-conceived siege of Damascus that had been mounted by the crusader lords.

In the wake of the events at Damascus, Nur ed-Din's name was trumpeted far and wide. It was proclaimed that the crusaders had fled at the approach of his army. The victory of the city's defenders was recorded and celebrated as a triumph of jihad.

VICTORY IN ANTIOCH

In 1149, with help from Emir Unur of Damascus, he moved against Antioch, attacking the crusader castle of Inab in the Principality. Raymond, Prince of Antioch, rode out with an army to defend the citadel and was heavily defeated on 29 June 1149. Raymond was killed during the battle; afterward his head was cut off by Nur ed-Din's general Shirkuh and despatched by Nur ed-Din in a silver casket to the Abbasid caliph of Baghdad.

▲ *A wall painting depicts Templar Hugh IX the Brown of Lusignan, who died at Damietta on the Fifth Crusade. Nur ed-Din's campaigns had strengthened the Muslim defence for 40 years after his death.*

This victory put much of the territory of the principality in Nur ed-Din's hands and he marked his triumph by marching as far as the sea and having a celebratory swim in the Mediterranean. He did not move against the city of Antioch itself, however. He possessed the Principality east of the Orontes River and seemingly was happy for the capital of the state to remain in crusader hands: perhaps he did not want to get drawn into conflict over its possession with the Byzantine Empire, for Emperor Manuel Comnenus claimed it as his possession.

In 1149 Nur ed-Din's brother Saif ed-Din died and was succeeded as ruler of Mosul by another brother, Qutb ed-Din. The new ruler recognized Nur ed-Din as overlord of Mosul. Nur ed-Din's main concern was now to take control of Damascus and so create a united Muslim Syria.

TRIUMPH IN DAMASCUS

He besieged Damascus four times in 1150–54 without launching an assault on the city. By this time, Mu'in ad-Din Unur had died and been succeeded by a weaker ruler, Mujir ad-Din, who agreed to pay tribute to the king of Jerusalem. Finally, in 1154, the people and the garrison turned against their ruler, who they felt had betrayed Islam by making a demeaning treaty with the Christians, and opened the city gates to Nur ed-Din.

For once, the end of a siege was not marked by rioting and bloodshed. Nur ed-Din promised the leading citizens that he would protect their livelihoods; he provided food for the poor. He even cut taxes, and began a public building programme.

Nur ed-Din proceeded with caution. He did not march on Jerusalem, in fact he reaffirmed the treaty that had caused controversy and continued to pay tribute. He went on chipping away at the crusaders, in 1157 besieging the Knights Hospitaller at the Castle of Banias and trouncing a

▲ *Nur ed-Din beseiged the formidable walls of Damascus four times. A map from 1620 shows what a challenge this was.*

▼ *The leaning minaret, 170ft (52m) high, is all that remains of the mosque of Nur ed-Din at Mosul in Syria.*

relief army despatched from Jerusalem. In 1160 he captured Reynald of Châtillon, Prince of Antioch, who he kept in prison for 16 years. He also became involved in conflicts to the north, in 1159 agreeing an alliance with the Byzantine emperor Manuel Comnenus against the Seljuk Turks and the same year mounting an attack on the Seljuk sultan Kilij Arslan II.

THE RULE OF NUR ED-DIN

Nur ed-Din was celebrated for his piety and his just rule. A staunch follower of Sunni Islam, he did not make personal use of the wealth he generated through conquest, but poured it into the building of mosques, madrasas (religious schools), hospitals, public baths and caravansaries (lodges for Islamic travellers). He established fairer taxation and an effective civil service and justice system. He also built a network of khanqas, centres for Sufis, followers of a mystical branch of Islam. And he improved communication by introducing the use of carrier pigeons.

SUFISM

This branch of Islam outlines a path to God through self-purification, inner exploration and mystical experience. It probably developed at some time under the Umayyad caliphate in AD660–750, although all Sufi traditions trace their history right back to the time of the Prophet Muhammad (c.AD570–632); teachings were reputedly passed down the generations from master to pupil. Early Sufis were careful to stress their path as a complementary way to God alongside the Shariah (religious law), but from the late 12th century onwards Sufism and Shariah began to separate. Sufism is known for its magnificent collections of religious love poetry.

THE BATTLE FOR EGYPT
SYRIA LOOKS TO EXTEND MUSLIM POWER

In 1162, with Syria secure against intervention from the crusader lords, Nur ed-Din went on pilgrimage to Mecca. He had achieved his ambition of uniting Syria. His eyes – and those of his nominal masters, the Abbasid caliphs of Baghdad – began to turn to Egypt, and to view the possibility of overthrowing the Shi'ite Fatimid caliphate there and establishing a united Sunni Muslim state of Syria and Egypt. The same year, a new king mounted the throne in Jerusalem – Amalric I, brother of Baldwin III.

POWER STRUGGLE IN CAIRO
In Egypt, although rule was nominally by the religious leader or caliph, real power lay in the hands of the chief administrator, or vizier. In 1163, at a time when the caliph was the inexperienced 14-year-old al-Adid, the vizier Shawar was ousted and replaced by Dirgham. King Amalric of Jerusalem, seeing an opportunity, mounted an expedition into Egypt claiming that the Fatimids were not paying tribute that had been pledged during the reign of Baldwin III. This campaign failed and he was forced to withdraw to Jerusalem. Meanwhile, Shawar visited the court of Nur ed-Din begging for military help to restore himself to power, and offering lavish rewards.

In 1164 Nur ed-Din sent an army under his leading general Asad ed-Din Shirkuh bin Shadhi to Egypt. Shirkuh had risen from relatively humble origins by dint of his energy, leadership qualities and military excellence. His name, of Kurdish-Iranian origin, meant 'Mountain Lion'. William of Tyre described him as a short and 'very stout' man, and already in the early 1160s 'advanced in years', with a cataract in one eye; he presented him as a formidable leader, experienced in military affairs, possessed of 'great endurance in the face of hardships' and beloved of his men because of his profound generosity. With him to Egypt rode his nephew, Salah ed-Din Yusuf (later known as Saladin).

Shirkuh did his job: Dirgham was killed and Shawar reinstated. But at once Shawar reneged on his promises and entered an alliance with Amalric against the Syrians. Amalric invaded Egypt once more and with Shawar's troops besieged Shirkuh in the fortress of Bilbeis.

CRUSADERS HUMILIATED IN ANTIOCH
In response, Nur ed-Din launched an attack on the Principality of Antioch, where he besieged the castle of Harim and won a crushing victory against the crusader armies of Tripoli and Antioch. He

▼ *Qalaat ar-Rahba in Syria was one of the strongholds of the 'Mountain Lion' Asad ed-Din Shirkuh, general in the service of Nur ed-Din and uncle of the great Saladin.*

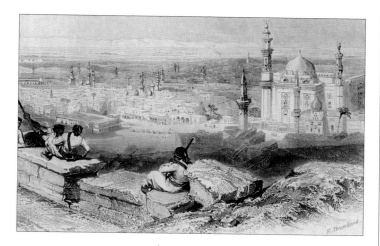

▲ *View of Cairo and the valley of the River Nile from the citadel constructed in the city by Saladin after he became vizier of Egypt.*

captured a roll-call of crusader lords: Bohemond III, Prince of Antioch; Raymond III, Count of Tripoli; Joscelin III, Count of Edessa; and French nobleman Hugh VIII of Lusignan, who had recently arrived on pilgrimage. Nur ed-Din had them all led in chains into Aleppo and cast into jail there. As many as 10,000 were killed in the crusader army, according to the Arab historian Ibn al-Athir.

But Nur ed-Din did not capture Antioch itself; it remained officially a Byzantine possession and he did not want to provoke Emperor Manuel Comnenus, with whom he had lately agreed a treaty. He did, however, capture Banias, and then kept up a constant harrying of the crusader states for the following two years. Meanwhile in Egypt, Amalric and Shirkuh made terms, agreeing to lift the siege and return home.

EGYPTIAN BATTLES

But in 1167 Shirkuh and Saladin invaded Egypt again. They were followed by Amalric's army in 1167. Initially there was a stand-off between the Christians and Shirkuh's army at Cairo. Shirkuh offered Shawar the chance to make a deal and unite against the crusaders, but he turned it down and instead renewed his alliance with Amalric. Shirkuh then led his men south, followed by the crusader army. The

two sides fought without clear result: Shirkuh occupied Alexandria, where he was welcomed by the largely Sunni Muslim population, but was then besieged by the crusader army.

Shirkuh broke out of the city in the hope that the crusader troops would follow him and engage in battle. But they sat tight, and Saladin was left in control of a starving population within the besieged city. Finally the standoff was broken not by a battle, but a truce; Saladin played no small part in brokering a deal under which both leaders took their armies home.

THE TAKING OF CAIRO

In 1168 Amalric entered an alliance with the Byzantine Empire and invaded Egypt once more. He captured Bilbeis, massacred the inhabitants and then besieged Cairo. Shawar changed sides once more, turning to Nur ed-Din and the great Shirkuh for help. Shirkuh and Saladin responded with all speed to the summons, marching south with an army containing 8,000 cavalry. The crusader army, badly outnumbered, withdrew once more and Shirkuh entered Cairo in triumph on 9 January 1169.

THE KURDS

Originally a pastoral people living in the mountains to the north and north east of what is now Iraq, the Kurds were subjects of the Abbasid Empire who established independent warrior principalities when the power of Baghdad waned in the 11th century. These states were overwhelmed by the invasion of the Seljuk Turks, but in the 12th century the Kurds rose to prominence again as soldiers of fortune in the pay of the Syrian rulers Imad ed-Din Zengi and Nur ed-Din. The brothers Najm ed-Din Ayub and Asad ed-Din Shirkuh made their names under Nur ed-Din: Ayub was governor of Damascus while Shirkuh was Nur ed-Din's leading general. Saladin was Ayub's son.

▼ *Kurdish mounted warriors battle against Arab counterparts.*

At first Shirkuh dealt amicably with Shawar, but then, ten days later, Shawar was killed after Saladin and his associates dragged him from his horse and had him beheaded – notionally on the orders of the caliph. Shirkuh then became vizier of Egypt. But within thee months Shirkuh had died, reportedly from overeating, and Saladin was in power in his place.

THE CHIVALROUS INFIDEL

SALADIN

Saladin was undoubtedly the leading Muslim figure of the entire crusading era. He inspired fear and awestruck admiration among the Westerners he repeatedly defeated in battle, while his magnanimous behaviour in victory won him a reputation as a chivalrous infidel, a seeming contradiction in contemporary Christian terms. He rose from relatively humble origins to become ruler of Egypt and Syria, and won undying fame in the Muslim world as the man who recaptured the Holy City of Jerusalem from the crusaders.

SALADIN'S YOUTH AND RISE TO PROMINENCE

The son of Najm ed-Din Ayub, governor of Damascus, Saladin lived as a young man at the splendid court of Nur ed-Din in that city, studying Islamic law, rhetoric and Arabic grammar, and developing a reputation as a brilliant all-rounder. Hee was a refined courtier who was skilled in debate, elegant in conversation, well versed in the traditions and military achievements of the Arab tribes, knowledgeable about the genealogies of the finest Arabian horses and a superb player of polo. This game was the equivalent at

▼ *Saladin was reputed to be equally at home pursuing learned discussion at court as he was directing armies in battle and making strategic decisions on campaign.*

Muslim courts of the chivalric tournament in Europe, a proving ground for young lords and a way of making a reputation among the political–military elite: Saladin achieved the distinction of being invited to join Nur ed-Din's own polo team.

He served his military apprenticeship in the service of his uncle Shirkuh, already established as Nur ed-Din's foremost general. Alongside Shirkuh he invaded Egypt three times, in 1164, 1167 and 1168–69. On the second of these occasions, Saladin was in command of the city of Alexandria while it was besieged by the crusader army – he later recalled: 'I endured many hardships at Alexandria that I can never forget.' Subsequently he took a leading role in the negotiations that brought the siege to an end and allowed both the Syrian and the crusader armies to go home with heads held high.

During these negotiations, Saladin's skill and nobility of character greatly impressed the crusader lords; he spent some time in the crusader camp after the siege was lifted, and according to some accounts was knighted by Humphrey II of Toron, Constable of the Kingdom of Jerusalem. The enduring myth of Saladin the infidel knight was born at this time.

VIZIER OF EGYPT

During the invasion of 1168–69, Saladin killed the vizier of Egypt, Shawar, and General Shirkuh became vizier in his place. When Shirkuh died on 22 March 1169 Saladin triumphed in politics within the Syrian army and took power for himself.

Saladin had triumphed in Egypt as a soldier of Syrian ruler Nur ed-Din, but his relationship with his nominal overlord became increasingly strained as it grew clear that Saladin was determined to rule in Cairo on his own terms, independently of influence from Damascus. In particular, he refrained from immediately removing the Shi'ite Fatimid caliph, while Nur ed-

▲ *Saladin gives thanks to Allah after his conquest of Jerusalem returned the city to Muslim control.*

Din was impatient for Sunni Islam to be imposed on Egypt. Finally, in September 1171, when the Fatimid caliph al-Adid died, Saladin abolished the Fatimid caliphate and proclaimed the name of the Abbasid caliph of Baghdad, Al-Mustadi.

Saladin's barely concealed ambition was to unite Egypt and Syria in an Islamic empire. He had been joined in Egypt by his father, a trusted intimate of Nur ed-Din, and on his advice did not make open moves against Syria and publicly behaved as if he were no more than Nur ed-Din's servant. But Nur ed-Din was not fooled and his anger with Saladin grew, especially when Saladin twice retreated from invasions of the crusader Kingdom of Jerusalem that his overlord had ordered. In 1174, Nur ed-Din was preparing to invade Egypt when he died of a fever resulting from a throat infection.

The heir to Damascus was Nur ed-Din's

ten-year-old son, al-Salih, and Syrian emirs began a scramble for power. Saladin marched on Damascus, according to some accounts following an invitation from local lords. His reputation went before him: when he arrived in October 1174, he was welcomed into the city by the people. He bolstered his position by marrying Nur ed-Din's widow and reinforced his popularity among his devoutly Muslim populace by vigorously promoting himself as a committed leader of jihad against the crusaders. Initially he did not have authority over Syria's other leading centres of power, but he imposed his authority on Aleppo in 1176 and on Mosul in 1186. By this stage he was close to his ultimate victory over the Kingdom of Jerusalem.

CONFLICT WITH JERUSALEM

Saladin had been reluctant to attack the Kingdom of Jerusalem while Nur ed-Din was alive: he was well aware that if he attacked from Egypt in the south while Nur ed-Din invaded from Syria, their combined force could wipe the crusader state off the map – but the outcome would then have been that Nur ed-Din, officially still Saladin's overlord, would have become

immeasurably more powerful. But after Nur ed-Din's death, any victory over Jerusalem was only going to boost Saladin's own power base; moreover, he had committed himself to attack the crusaders by public proclamations of his enthusiasm for jihad.

In November 1177 he marched north from Egypt against the Kingdom of Jerusalem. The new king of Jerusalem, Baldwin IV, who had succeeded his father Amalric I in 1174, had installed himself with 375 knights at Ascalon expecting a siege; but Saladin bypassed the city, sending a force to surround it, and moved on towards Jerusalem itself. Baldwin bravely broke out through the surrounding army and rode with a force of about 80 Knights Templar and a few thousand infantry to intersect Saladin's progress.

DEFEAT AT MONTGISARD

The Christian knights took Saladin's much larger army entirely by surprise near the fortress of Montgisard on 25 November and inflicted a devastating defeat on them that was celebrated for years; the Old French translation of William of Tyre's chronicle said that the Christians found St

George riding into battle at their side. Saladin lost his entire bodyguard and only just escaped with his life – according to contemporary accounts, because he was mounted on a racing camel and was able to outrun his pursuers. Only around 3,000 Muslim troops from an army of 30,000 or more limped back to Egypt.

Two years later Saladin had revenge of sorts. In a show of defiance, Baldwin had begun constructing a great castle at Jacob's Ford at the only crossing of the Jordan on the route from Damascus towards the Kingdom of Jerusalem. The king's men managed to complete the castle's outer walls, which stood 32ft (10m) in height, before Saladin marshalled his resources to attack. When the onslaught began Baldwin was in Tiberias: Saladin managed to breach the walls and killed 800 members of the castle's vast garrison, captured another 700 crusader soldiers and poisoned the water sources.

▼ *With an inferior force Baldwin surprised and defeated Saladin at Montgisard. The king fought left-handed since his leprosy had affected his right arm.*

CRUSADERS DESTROYED
SALADIN'S VICTORY AT THE HORNS OF HATTIN

In July 1187 Saladin moved again against the Kingdom of Jerusalem. On 4 July he annihilated the crusader army at the Battle of the Horns of Hattin, on one day destroying the Kingdom's united military capability and making inevitable his triumphant capture of Jerusalem later in the same year.

THE PROVOCATION OF REYNALD OF CHÂTILLON

Following Saladin's defeat at the Battle of Montgisard in 1177 and his revenge at Jacob's Ford in 1179, conflict between Saladin and the crusaders continued throughout the 1180s. A constant provocation was Reynald of Châtillon, a highly controversial figure in his own lifetime and beyond, the former Prince of Antioch (1153–60) who had spent 16 years in jail in Aleppo after being captured by Nur

▼ *Guy of Lusignan was crowned King of Jerusalem in 1180. He came to the throne as consort of Sibylla, daughter of Amalric I and sister of the leper-king Baldwin IV.*

ed-Din in 1160. Following the death of his wife, Reynald had made a powerful second marriage in 1183 when he wed Stephanie of Milly, heiress of the lordship of Oultrejordain, which included the powerful fortress of Montreal. From here, Reynald repeatedly attacked Muslim trade and pilgrim caravans, provoking Saladin to besiege the castle without success in 1183 and 1184. Reynald briefly practised restraint, but he was soon back to his old ways, attacking a caravan of pilgrims making the *hajj* (pilgrimage) to Mecca in 1185. (According to the 13th-century Old French *Continuation of the Chronicle of William of Tyre*, in this attack Reynald captured no less a figure than the sister of Saladin, but this is probably an invention since it is not confirmed in any of the contemporary accounts.) In May 1187 he attacked again, sweeping down from Montreal to attack a Muslim trade caravan from Cairo headed for Damascus. Saladin decided to act. He reputedly swore then that if he were ever to capture Reynald, he would kill him with his own hand.

THE SUCCESSION DISPUTE IN JERUSALEM

Saladin was also encouraged to attack by the weakness of the regime in Jerusalem, which had been undermined by a succession dispute. The dispute had begun in the reign of Amalric I's son, Baldwin IV, who, although a great military commander, was also a leper and was often too ill to govern and was unable to leave an heir. Two factions fought over the succession: on one side was Baldwin's eldest sister Sibylla and her ambitious husband Guy of Lusignan, supported by (among others) Reynald of Châtillon; on the other side was Raymond of Tripoli and the powerful Ibelin family, who backed the cause of Baldwin and Sibylla's half-sister Isabella, whose mother, Maria Comnena (widow of Amalric I), had married Balian of Ibelin.

▲ *Guy of Lusignan was banished from France by the future King Richard I of England. Guy arrived in the Holy Land some time after 1174, and can be seen here at his coronation as King of Jerusalem.*

Baldwin IV had Sibylla's young son Baldwin V crowned as co-ruler and heir in 1183 and when Baldwin IV died in spring 1185 the boy became king at the age of 8, with Raymond of Tripoli as regent. Baldwin V lasted less than 18 months: he died in summer 1186, and in the aftermath, Sibylla and Guy won the power struggle and Sibylla was crowned Queen with Guy as her consort.

A RECKLESS ADVANCE

Saladin gathered his army in May–June 1187 and on July 2 attacked Tiberias. The Christians gathered their forces at Sephoria under the leadership of Guy of Jerusalem (as Guy of Lusignan was known following the coronation of his wife Sibylla as Queen of Jerusalem). The army numbered around 1,200 knights and perhaps 20,000 infantry, representing the entire military strength of the Kingdom of Jerusalem. In attendance was the Bishop of Acre carrying a piece of the True Cross, the Kingdom's most sacred relic.

The position at Sephoria was a strong one, but Saladin was hoping that by his attack on Tiberias he could lure the crusaders out into open country. He got his way. Guy ignored advice from Raymond of Tripoli who counselled him not to risk a pitched battle against Saladin, and – urged on by the hot-headed Reynald of Châtillon – advanced towards Tiberias on 3 July. This was desert country, and the crusaders marched for hours without food or water, being harassed by Saladin's advance troops, until in the evening they encamped just to the south of the twin-peaked hill known as the Horns of Hattin.

SURROUNDED IN THE DESERT

In the morning they found that they were surrounded. Ahead of them, within sight, was a green valley and a lake, but Saladin's army barred the way. Saladin's men set fire to the dry grass around the crusaders, increasing the searing heat. Thirst maddened the crusaders, smoke billowed around them and arrows rained down on them from the sky. Saladin's secretary and chronicler Imad ed-din al-Isfahani later

▼ Knights of the Kingdom of Jerusalem lie dead on the battlefield following the defeat at Hattin. By tradition, a heavenly light shone over them for three nights.

recalled that: 'the people of the Trinity were eaten up by a worldly fire of three kinds, each irresistible and overwhelming: the fire of racing flames, the fire of raging thirst and the fire of whistling arrows.'

The crusaders tried to drive back the advancing army of Saladin, but without success. Only one sortie succeeded: Raymond of Tripoli, Reynald of Sidon and Balian of Ibelin broke out but were then unable to rejoin the battle; they rode away, knowing that Guy's rashness had brought the Kingdom to the brink of extinction.

Back in the heat of battle, the crusader army was driven up the hill towards the tent of King Guy, visible on the summit. To the despair of all, while fighting, the Bishop of Acre was robbed of the relic of the True Cross. Templars and Hospitallers fought bravely but they could not prevent the inevitable and eventually King Guy's tent fell and the battle was over.

HONOUR AND REVENGE

Guy and Reynald of Châtillon were still alive and were brought to Saladin's tent. Saladin gave the thirst-maddened Guy a drink of iced rosewater and the king

▲ The crusaders were overrun and all but wiped out by Saladin's army at the Battle of the Horns of Hattin. Fires set by Saladin's men swept smoke across the battlefield.

handed it to Reynald. Saladin grew angry, and made it clear that he had not offered the drink to his enemy Reynald – for by the Muslim warriors' code of war if a prisoner were offered food or drink by his captor his life had to be spared. Saladin did spare Guy, but slew Reynald by his own hand. 'Kings do not kill kings,' he said to Guy, but looking at Reynald added, 'that man's insolence went beyond what can be tolerated.'

On the following day Saladin ordered the execution of the surviving warriors among the Knights Templar and the Knights Hospitaller. Muslim holy men and Sufi mystics, who had joined the army in answer to the call to take part in jihad, begged to be allowed to perform the deed. Saladin seated himself on a mounted platform and watched, with his assembled soldiers, as the Christian warriors were put to death agonizingly slowly by these inexperienced swordsmen.

JERUSALEM RECAPTURED
SALADIN TAKES THE HOLY CITY

On 2 October 1187 Saladin and his army recaptured Jerusalem, ending almost 90 years of Christian rule.

CONTROL OF THE KINGDOM
Defeat at the Horns of Hattin had wiped out the crusader states' military strength and Saladin proceeded through the Kingdom virtually unopposed. Acre surrendered within days of the battle, and shortly afterwards Saladin's brother Al-Adil captured Jaffa. Nazareth, Caesarea and Haifa were taken and on 4 September Saladin captured Ascalon. Darkness fell by day because there was an eclipse of the sun; Christians who had heard of the eclipse of the moon witnessed before the capture of Jerusalem in 1099 may have seen this as an omen – and shuddered.

On 20 September 1187 Saladin began a siege of Jerusalem. The city's defence was

▼ In triumph the Muslim army was highly disciplined. Saladin had his enemies at his mercy but treated them respectfully. There was no repeat of the lawlessness of 1099.

the responsibility of Balian of Ibelin, one of the knights who had broken out of the Muslim encirclement at the Horns of Hattin; he had returned to the city in order to rescue his wife Maria Comnena (the city's former queen and widow of Amalric I). He did not have sufficient manpower to mount an effective defence of the city walls – according to one contemporary account, there were only two other knights and a limited number of men-at-arms. Nevertheless, he inspired the defenders to hold out for nine days.

TERMS OF SURRENDER
On 30 September, after the Muslim siege equipment had made a breach in the wall near the Gate of the Column, Balian rode out to Saladin's camp to discuss terms under which the city might be given up. At first Saladin did not want to negotiate. He reminded Balian of the terrible behaviour of the Christian knights in taking Jerusalem in 1099. He wanted nothing less then unconditional surrender.

Balian responded by threatening that if they could not agree a truce and ransom, he would order the Christians within the city to slaughter the 5,000-odd Muslim slaves and prisoners, then to kill their own wives and children, destroy their valuable

▲ Within Jerusalem, Balian of Ibelin led a few knights in desperate resistance to the siege, but they were vastly outnumbered. The Holy City passed into Saladin's hands.

possessions, attack the Muslim holy places and then fight to the death on the city walls. The city would be a bloodbath, loot would be destroyed, sacred places desecrated, and many of Saladin's soldiers would be killed unnecessarily in taking the city by force.

Saladin wanted to capture the city intact and did not want to cause the deaths of his fellow Muslims, so he agreed a ransom deal with Balian: ten dinars for each man, five for each woman and one for each child, with a lump sum of 30,000 dinars payable for 7,000 of the population who were too poor to pay their own ransom, the remainder of the unransomable poor were to be sold into slavery.

THE REOCCUPATION OF JERUSALEM
On 2 October 1187 Saladin and his disciplined army took the city peacefully. He was true to his word and the Franks were allowed to leave unmolested. Saladin sent groups of armed soldiers into the city to ensure that there was no looting or

SALADIN'S CHARACTER

Saladin was celebrated for his lively mind and sense of honour. Crusaders praised him for his generosity in victory and his wit in negotiation. His Muslim biographer Baha ed-Din ibn Shaddad wrote of him that he was a mine of fascinating information in conversation, a caring leader who would always ask after friends, and attempt to raise people's spirits. He would not allow fellow Muslims to be criticized in his presence, wanting to hear of people's good qualities instead. When he encountered orphans he always made sure that they were helped. Baha ed-Din ibn Shaddad recounted the story of how a distraught crusader woman demanded to see Saladin after her daughter had been stolen by Muslim soldiers: Saladin not only saw her and listened to her, but also sent men to scour the markets to see if they could find the girl; they did and he reunited her with her mother.

▼ A monument to Saladin in Damascus.

▲ An illustration of c.1400 looks back to the fight for Jerusalem in 1187. The besieging Islamic army has been reimagined as a conventional European force.

to pilgrims. The manner in which they reoccupied Jerusalem was a great and lasting credit to Saladin and his men, and should have shamed the Christian knights of 1099 had they been alive to see it.

Saladin's reputation for magnanimity and piety were enhanced by his treatment of the ransomed prisoners. Forty days were allowed for the Christians to raise the necessary ransoms. Throughout, Saladin behaved with the utmost generosity: when his brother, growing distressed at the vast numbers of captives, asked for some to be spared, Saladin freed 1,000; he gave another 700 their freedom in response to a request by the Patriarch of Jerusalem; and set another 500 free as a tribute to Balian. He then went even further, freeing the elderly and the infirm and all the husbands of women already freed.

MUSLIM JOY

According to Imad ed-din al-Isfahani, Saladin held a joyful court in the days after his retaking of Jerusalem, and was visited by many leading Muslims who 'covered his carpet with kisses'. He maintained a sober and dignified bearing, but his face was 'bright with joy' and 'his expression shone'; the great triumph he had achieved, Imad ed-din wrote, appeared to give him a halo of moonlight.

CHRISTIAN DESPAIR

The Kingdom of Jerusalem appeared to be close to extinction. In the two years following the Battle of the Horns of Hattin, Saladin captured more than 50 crusader strongholds. He did not move against Tripoli or Antioch and Tyre remained in Christian hands, but the taking of Jerusalem was a great propaganda victory that suggested there was no future for the Christians in Palestine.

News of the defeat at the Horns of Hattin and the loss of Jerusalem reached Europe in the autumn of 1187 and Pope Urban III is reported to have died of grief. Writers and preachers lamented the terrible turn of events. One declared: '... on that day, October 2, 1187, the queen among all the cities in the world was cast into slavery.' It was an end, but also a beginning – within weeks, Urban's successor Pope Gregory VIII issued a call for a fresh military expedition to the Holy Land and a new crusade began.

rampage. He then set about cleaning up the city, restoring the al Aqsa mosque and the Dome of the Rock to sacred use for Muslims. Although he was urged by his compatriots to destroy the Church of the Holy Sepulchre, he merely ordered it to be closed for three days, then reopened

PART TWO

THE LATER AND EUROPEAN CRUSADES

The kings, princes and knights who conducted the Third Crusade of 1189–92 – and those of the ensuing centuries – were inspired by tales of the heroic deeds of Christian warriors on the First and Second Crusades (1096–99 and 1147–49). In particular, they were driven by a desire to repeat the extraordinary achievement of the knights of the First Crusade, who succeeded against all odds in capturing Jerusalem for Christ and for the Western Church. They had little political or economic motive in fighting in the East – they were inspired principally by religious motives. The later crusades in the Holy Land were paralleled by wars of the cross fought against pagans of middle and northern Europe, against the Muslim 'Moors' of the Iberian Peninsula, against enemies of the Catholic Church in Italy, and against the French dualist Cathars and other Christians denounced as 'heretics' – a collection of campaigns characterized by historians as Baltic or European Crusades to distinguish them from those in the East. These crusades were different in character: while the Eastern Crusades remained essentially wars of religion, the European Crusades were mostly political or economic struggles, in which the powerful religious rhetoric was merged with political agendas and causes.

▲ *Holding key ports was essential in the crusading era so that vital supplies could be shipped in to maintain the long sieges.*

▶ *In 1249, on the Seventh Crusade, an army led by Louis IX of France landed in Egypt, aiming to destroy Muslim power in north Africa before attacking Syria.*

TIMELINE

29 October 1187 Pope Gregory VII calls the Third Crusade.

January 1188 Kings Philip II of France and Henry II of England take the cross.

March 1188 Frederick I of Germany takes the cross.

11 May 1189 German crusaders under Frederick I depart.

6 July 1189 Henry II of England dies; his successor Richard I sets about raising money to go on crusade.

27 August 1189 King Guy of Jerusalem begins siege of Acre.

17 May 1190 German crusaders defeat Seljuks and capture Iconium.

10 June 1190 Frederick I drowns in River Saleph (modern Göksu).

25 July 1190 Queen Sibylla of Jerusalem dies, sparking succession dispute.

20 April 1191 Philip II arrives at Acre.

8 June 1191 Richard I arrives at Acre.

12 July 1191 Acre surrenders.

7 September 1191 Richard I defeats Saladin in the Battle of Arsuf.

April 1192 Sibylla's sister Isabella and her husband Count Henry II of Champagne take power in Jerusalem.

5 August 1192 King Richard I defeats Saladin at Jaffa.

2 September 1192 Richard I and Saladin agree a peace treaty that brings an end to the Third Crusade.

4 March 1193 Saladin dies.

25 July 1195 Pope Celestine III calls a new crusade; German emperor Henry VI takes the cross and a crusade sails in 1197 but melts away following Henry's death in Sicily in September 1197.

August 1198 Pope Innocent III calls the Fourth Crusade.

October 1202 The armies of the Fourth Crusade set off.

24 November 1202 Crusaders sack the Christian city of Zara in Hungary (modern Zadar in Croatia).

1202 The military order of the Livonian Brothers of the Sword is established.

12–15 April 1204 Forces of the Fourth Crusade sack Constantinople.

16 May 1204 Count Baldwin of Flanders is crowned emperor of the new Latin Empire of Constantinople in the Church of Haghia Sophia, Constantinople.

1208 Pope Innocent III declares a crusade against the Cathars, a heretical Christian sect of southern France.

July 1209 A crusade army takes Béziers from the Cathars, killing 20,000.

15 August 1209 The crusaders capture Carcassonne and evict the Cathars from the city.

1212 Pope Innocent III proclaims a crusade in Spain against the Almohad caliphs.

16 July 1212 A Christian army led by Alfonso VIII of Castile and Sancho VII of Navarre defeats the Almohads under their caliph Muhammad al-Nasir in the Battle of Las Navas de Tolosa.

April 1213 Pope Innocent III proclaims the Fifth Crusade.

November 1219 The Fifth Crusade army captures and sacks Damietta, Egypt.

July 1221 The Fifth Crusade army is defeated by Ayyubid sultan al-Kamil after

▼ *Soldiers at the gates of Jerusalem, from 13th-century manuscript* Velislavovy.

its attempt to march on Cairo is stopped by the flooding of the River Nile.

*c.***1228** The Prussian Cavaliers of Christ Jesus are established to maintain a permanent military presence in Prussia.

1228 Despite having been excommunicated, Holy Roman Emperor Frederick II embarks on the Sixth Crusade.

17 March 1229 At the climax of the Sixth Crusade Frederick II takes possession of Jerusalem for Christendom. He triumphs through diplomacy rather than military force.

1233 Pope Gregory IX establishes an Inquisition to counter the continuing activity of the Cathars in southern France.

1233–34 Pope Gregory IX calls a crusade against pagan Prussians, led by the Teutonic Knights. The knights build fortresses at Marienwerder and Rehden.

1236 King Ferdinand III of Castile and León captures the city of Córdoba from the Moors as the Christian Reconquista in Spain continues.

March 1244 The Cathar stronghold of Montségur castle is taken by French royalist forces.

August 1244 Khwarismian Turks take Jerusalem. Only 300 Christians escape.

17–18 October 1244 In the two-day Battle of La Forbie, a Turkish–Egyptian army commanded by Baybars (the future Mamluk sultan of Egypt) crushes a Christian–Syrian army.

1245 Pope Innocent IV grants the Teutonic Knights the right to issue crusading indulgences to those fighting on their behalf.

1248 King Ferdinand III of Castile and León captures Seville.

25 August 1248 King Louis IX of France embarks on the Seventh Crusade.

6 June 1249 The armies of the Seventh Crusade capture Damietta, Egypt.

6 April 1250 After a failed advance, the crusade army surrenders and Louis IX is captured by Ayyubid sultan Turan Shah.

May 1251 Louis IX is released from captivity in Egypt after payment of a large ransom. He sails to Acre.

April 1254 After three years in the Holy Land, Louis returns to France.

1255 The Cathars abandon their last stronghold at Quéribus in southern France, and flee.

3 September 1260 Mamluk general Baybars defeats a Mongol army in the Battle of Ain Jalut in Galilee. Later the same year, he seizes power as sultan.

1265 Baybars invades Outremer, taking Caesarea and Arsuf.

24 March 1267 Responding to Baybars' attacks, Louis IX of France takes the cross once more.

May 1268 Baybars captures Antioch.

July 1270 Louis IX and the army of the Eighth Crusade besiege the city of Tunis, in north Africa.

25 August 1270 Louis IX dies during the siege of Tunis.

30 October 1270 The army of the Eighth Crusade lifts the siege of Tunis.

May 1271 Prince Edward (the future King Edward I of England) lands in Acre leading the Ninth Crusade, causing Baybars to abandon the siege of Tripoli.

May 1272 King Hugh of Jerusalem agrees a truce with Baybars.

16 June 1272 An assassin sent by Sultan Baybars fails in an attempt to kill Prince Edward in Acre.

24 September 1272 Edward quits Palestine and departs for England.

1289 Tripoli is captured by Mamluk sultan Qalawun.

11 April 1291 Mamluk sultan Khalil begins the siege of Acre.

18 May 1291 The Christians are driven out of the Holy Land as Acre is captured by Khalil.

22 November 1307 King Philip IV of France orders the arrest of Jacques of Molay, Grand Master of the Knights Templar, and other French Templars.

1309 Having left the Holy Land following the fall of Acre in 1291, the Teutonic Knights build a new headquarters at Marienberg, Prussia.

▲ *Copies of Albigensian books are burned by monks of the Dominican order, under orders from the Inquisition.*

1312 With support from King Philip IV of France, Pope Clement V dissolves the Order of the Knights Templar.

1330 King Alfonso IX of Castile defeats Sultan Muhammad IV of Granada in the battle of Teba in Andalusia; Sir James Douglas, boon companion of the late Robert the Bruce, dies in this battle.

1332 King Alfonso founds the chivalric Order of the Sash.

30 October 1340 King Alfonso defeats a Marinid army in the Battle of Rio Salado.

1344 King Alfonso captures Algeciras from the Moors.

27 June 1365 King Peter I of Cyprus leads a crusade against Mamluk Egypt.

9 October 1365 King Peter's army captures and sacks Alexandria. Shortly afterwards, the army melts away as many of its leading members return home, and Peter has to abandon the city.

1390 Count Louis of Bourbon leads a crusade against Mahdia, Tunisia, a base for Muslim pirates attacking Genoan ships. It ends in a profitable settlement.

25 September 1396 Ottoman Sultan Bayezid I trounces a European crusading army at the Battle of Nicopolis.

1420 The First anti-Hussite Crusade is mounted against the followers of executed preacher Jan Hus, in Bohemia.

6 January 1422 Jan Zizka leads a Hussite army to defeat the Second anti-Hussite Crusade at the Battle of Nemecky Brod.

1422–31 The Third, Fourth and Fifth anti-Hussite Crusades are mounted but come to nothing.

10 November 1444 At the Battle of Varna Sultan Murad II's Ottoman army defeats a European Christian army.

29 May 1453 Ottoman sultan Mehmed II captures Constantinople. This marks the end of the Byzantine Empire.

21–22 July 1456 In the 'miracle of Belgrade', a vast army commanded by Sultan Mehmed II fails to capture the city. Belgrade's Christian defenders are led by Janos Hunyadi of Hungary and Italian monk Giovanni da Capistrano.

26 September 1459 Pope Pius II calls a new crusade, but it comes to nothing.

28 July 1480 Mehmed II abandons his attempt to capture Rhodes having been repulsed by the Knights Hospitaller.

1485 As part of a final push to drive the Moors from Spain, the army of King Ferdinand II of Aragon and Queen Isabella I of Castile takes Ronda.

1487 Ferdinand and Isabella capture the island of Malaga.

1491 Ferdinand and Isabella besiege the Muslim stronghold of Granada.

2 January 1492 King Ferdinand II of Aragon and Queen Isabella I of Castile take possession of Granada, marking the end of the centuries-long Reconquista.

22 December 1522 The Knights Hospitaller surrender Rhodes to Ottoman sultan Suleyman I 'the Magnificent' after a six-month siege.

Sept 1565 The Ottomans fail to take Malta from the Knights Hospitaller.

7 October 1571 The Christian Holy League defeats the Ottoman fleet in the naval Battle of Lepanto in the Ionian Sea.

1588 Spanish forces fight for English Roman Catholic insurgents against the ruling Protestant establishment, with the support of crusading privileges.

THE CATHOLIC EXPANSION

The sense of glorious achievement felt by the Christian world after the success of the First Crusade was never to be repeated. Later crusades in the Holy Land and Europe were more complex and often severely compromised by mixed or deliberately duplicitous motives. The Fourth Crusade spiralled out of control amid political machinations and ended in the sacking and looting of Constantinople. In Europe, the crusading model was applied both to the fight against Muslim power in the Iberian peninsula and to campaigns waged against enemies both religious and political. The religious exaltation felt in 1100 did not accompany these events.

THE FOURTH CRUSADE

The Fourth Crusade was called by Pope Innocent III in August 1198. Its forces, which took some time to gather, departed from Venice in October 1202, bound initially for the former Venetian colony of Zara, which had become part of Hungary in 1186. (Today the city, on the Adriatic coast of Croatia, is called Zadar.) The crusade was vastly in debt to the city of Venice after negotiating an extravagant deal to supply a crusade fleet, and paid off part of the money owed by attacking and capturing Zara; from this point on they lost papal backing, for Zara was under the protection of a Roman Catholic monarch, King Emeric of Hungary, and Pope Innocent III had outlawed attacks on Christian cities. Some crusaders wanted no more to do with the enterprise and sailed directly from Zara to the Holy Land, but the bulk of this now badly flawed expedition became embroiled in the attempt by exiled Byzantine prince Alexius Angelus to oust Emperor Alexius III and claim the throne for himself.

Promised great wealth – nominally to help fund the recapture of Jerusalem – the crusaders left Zara on Easter Monday 1203 and arrived at Constantinople on 24 June that year. They landed on the far side of the Bosphorus but on 5 July crossed in transports and began a siege of the city. They took the Byzantine capital on 17 July, but then were forced to wait in their encampment for several months while the former Prince Alexius (now Emperor Alexius IV) raised the money he had promised them. Before he could do so, Alexius was deposed and a courtier named Alexius Doukas took power as Alexius V. A new siege began. The crusaders captured the city on 13 April 1204 and looted it wildly over three days. They established the Latin Empire of Constantinople; Count Baldwin of Flanders was elected Emperor Baldwin I. The crusade did not move on to the Holy Land.

RECONQUISTA

The *Reconquista* (Reconquest) of the Iberian Peninsula from its Muslim rulers was regularly promoted as a crusade from the 1090s onwards. The war against Islam in what became Spain and Portugal had

▼ *The papacy lost control of the Fourth Crusade, an enterprise in which religious crusading rhetoric was used to mask nakedly political motives. After the capture of the Byzantine imperial city, and the establishment of the Latin Empire of Constantinople, a large part of southern Greece was captured in winter 1204–05.*

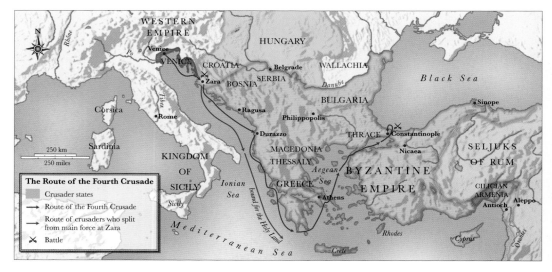

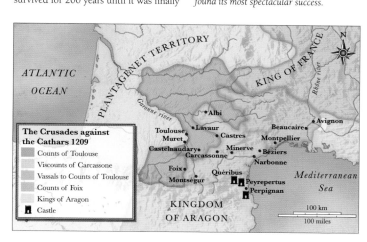

conquered by King Ferdinand and Queen Isabella of a united Castile and Aragon in 1482–92. With the capture of the city of Granada on 2 January 1492 the monarchs of the fledgling Spain ended 750 years of reconquest.

CATHAR CRUSADES

The first major battle of the decades-long Albigensian Crusade against the Cathar heretics of southern France was at Béziers on 21 July 1209: around 20,000 were killed. Carcassonne surrendered the next month. A Cathar fightback, supported by Peter II of Aragon, was defeated at Muret near Toulouse in September 1213. After 1216 the Cathars under Raymond VI of Toulouse and his son, Raymond VII, did win back a good deal of territory.

The war ended in 1229 but the fight against heresy continued through the often brutal activities of the Dominican Inquisition. The final Cathar strongholds in the hills and mountains east of Perpignan were captured in 1240–55.

▼ *The Cathars were especially numerous in what is now western Mediterranean France, then part of the Kingdom of Aragon. Although Cathar ideas did not originate in Languedoc, one of the most urbanized and populated areas of Europe at the time, it was there that their theology found its most spectacular success.*

▲ *The final war waged by Ferdinand and Isabella was explicitly a Christian crusade, and their army – as well as being equipped with the latest artillery – was reinforced by Christian troops from around Europe.*

actually begun almost 400 years earlier, not long after Arabs and north African Berbers seized most of the Christian kingdom of the Visigoths in AD711–716. Catalonia was recaptured in the late 8th century and became known as the 'Spanish March'. By the late 9th century Christian territory extended right across the north of the Iberian Peninsula; the remainder of what is now Spain and Portugal was ruled by a Muslim caliph from Córdoba.

After the Caliphate of Córdoba collapsed in 1002, the 30 or so independent Muslim kingdoms that succeeded it proved vulnerable to Christian advance: King Alfonso VI of Léon took Toledo in 1085 and looked set to recapture the entire peninsula but was defeated by the Almoravids of north-west Africa in the Battle of Sagrajas in 1086. They made southern Spain and Portugal part of the

Almoravid Empire, but this too collapsed after 1140 and was succeeded by the Almohad Caliphate, which held roughly the southern third of the country. The Muslims were pushed farther and farther south by the expansion of Christian Castile, Aragon and Portugal – until by the last quarter of the 13th century the Muslims held only the small Kingdom of Granada in the far south. This territory survived for 200 years until it was finally

CHAPTER SEVEN

RICHARD THE LIONHEART AND THE THIRD CRUSADE

On 7 September 1191, during the Third Crusade, King Richard I of England won a stunning victory over the great Saracen general Saladin at the Battle of Arsuf. Richard's battle tactics, which demanded total discipline from his knights in holding back from attacking under enormous provocation, were almost spoiled by a hasty charge led by the Knights Hospitaller, but ultimately were triumphantly vindicated as the Christians swept the Saracens off the battlefield in three unstoppable mounted advances.

The Third Crusade is forever associated with Richard I and his encounters with Saladin. The Battle of Arsuf was one of three victories Richard won over Saladin – and they had other memorable diplomatic encounters. In the chivalric literature of chansons and of chronicles, the clash of these great generals shines as an example of chivalry at its finest. The origins of the Third Crusade were notably different from those of the first two crusades, since it was called by the will of secular rulers as much as by that of the pope. Richard's participation – along with King Philip II of France and Emperor Frederick I of Germany – made the 'Kings' Crusade' one of the greatest and most glamorous of the wars of the cross – but, equally, the involvement of these monarchs was its undoing, for they were unable to put aside their fierce rivalries.

▲ *Frederick Barbarossa, King of Germany, invades Italy by sea in 1157.*

◄ *According to* jongleur *Ambroise, an eyewitness of the Battle of Arsuf, Richard was like a crossbow bolt fired against the enemy, who cut down his foes like a farmer harvesting wheat.*

ONCE MORE TO JERUSALEM
A THIRD CRUSADE IS CALLED

On 29 October 1187, in Ferrara, Pope Gregory VII issued a crusading bull known to historians from its first words in Latin, *Audita tremendi* (the first part of a Latin phrase that translates as 'On hearing of the dreadful and profound judgement inflicted on the land of Jerusalem by the divine hand'). The papal bull was issued in response to the defeat at the Battle of the Horns of Hattin in July, before news of the fall of Jerusalem had reached Europe.

The bull called the defeat at Hattin and the loss of the relic of the True Cross in the battle 'a terrible judgement inflicted by the Lord on the land of Jerusalem' and declared that the news – which had reputedly ended Pope Urban III's life, by bringing on a heart attack – had thrown his successor as pope and other church leaders into confusion and left them battered by 'such a deep horror and resounding grief that it was not apparent what we should do'. But it called for all to maintain their faith and to believe that God 'once softened by our repentance' would bring 'gladness after grief'; Christian warriors should see this as 'a chance to repent and do a good deed', offering themselves and their wealth for recovery of 'the land where Truth itself was born from the earth in order to bring about our salvation'.

Those who made the journey with 'humble and contrite heart' or who died 'in repentance of their wrongdoing and in the right faith' would earn a plenary indulgence and eternal life 'by the mercy of God Himself, on the authority of the apostles Peter and Paul' and that of the papacy. As in previous crusades, the property of those who took the cross would be protected by the Church and those who incurred debts making the journey should be free of the requirement to pay interest. The bull also urged those travelling to avoid ostentation and aim for simplicity – not to take dogs,

▲ *Pope Gregory VII is known principally for his clashes with Holy Roman Emperor Henry IV in the 'Investiture Controversy' over church appointments in Germany.*

hawks and expensive clothes but to have plain robes and equipment, to make clear that they are travelling in penitence rather than indulging idle vanity.

CRUSADE SERMONS

A Church campaign to preach the new crusade was put in train. In the British Isles, the Archbishop of Canterbury, Baldwin of Exeter, made a tour of Wales in 1188 to preach the cross. Baldwin's journey was described by the colourful Norman–Welsh churchman and chronicler Giraldus Cambrensis, or 'Gerald of Wales', in his *Itinerarium Cambriae*, written in 1191.

According to Giraldus Cambrensis Baldwin convinced 3,000 men-at-arms to take the cross. The sermons were delivered in Latin and French, sometimes with a Welsh interpreter, but even when the crowd could not have understood the words, knights and men-at-arms still rushed forward to take the cross. According to Gerald, a miracle occurred that showed God's blessing on the enterprise and the holiness of Archbishop Baldwin – in the area near Haverfordwest,

an old lady who had been blind for many years was cured when she rubbed her face with earth upon which the archbishop had stood when giving the sermon.

SALADIN TRIUMPHANT

In Outremer in July 1187, in the immediate aftermath of Saladin's victory at the Battle of the Horns of Hattin, the Muslim general's armies marched virtually unchallenged and imposed his will where they went. City after city passed out of crusader control. But the important port of Tyre was saved at the last moment following quick thinking by the charismatic European lord Conrad of Montferrat.

Conrad had sailed from Italy for Jerusalem in 1185 in order to join his father, William V of Montferrat, but he had been waylaid in Constantinople, where he had married Princess Theodora, sister of Byzantine emperor Isaac II Angelus. In July 1187 Conrad set out for the Kingdom of Jerusalem, probably fearing reprisals after he killed a rebel general named Alexios Branas when putting down a rebellion on behalf of Isaac. He set sail on board a Genoese merchant ship.

When Conrad arrived by sea at Acre on 14 July he found the place eerily quiet and cautiously dropped anchor offshore; then he and his companions saw Saladin's standards above the walls – the town had just fallen to the Muslim general. When messengers from the port approached by ship, Conrad pretended to be a merchant ally of Saladin; he promised to bring his goods ashore the next morning. But in the night he lifted anchor and inched away, setting sail for Tyre.

TYRE SAVED FROM SALADIN

There are differing versions of precisely what happened next. According to the 13th-century Old French *Continuation of the Chronicle of William of Tyre*, Conrad arrived in Tyre just as the port, which was

▲ *At Tyre, Saladin and his apparently invincible army were defeated for the first time since the Battle of the Horns of Hattin.*

▼ *The victory at Tyre, snatched as it was from seemingly inevitable defeat, was the kind of triumph against all odds that had occurred on the First Crusade and inspired later generations to try to emulate it.*

in the hands of crusader lord Reginald of Sidon, was preparing to mark its surrender to Saladin by raising his banners. But Conrad – resolute, determined and charismatic – threw the banners into the city ditch and convinced the people to transfer their allegiance to him; when they did so he led them to a last-gasp defence.

The truth may have been more prosaic. Other accounts suggest that Conrad arrived in advance of Saladin's army while Reginald was absent seeking to fortify his castle of Belfort; Conrad strengthened the town's defences and inspired its merchant community and other residents to put up a stout defence. Whatever truly happened, Saladin's attempt to take the city of Tyre was repulsed and he moved on to take Caesarea, Arsuf and Jaffa.

In November Conrad repulsed another, larger-scale attack on Tyre by Saladin, who

had blockaded the city by land with his troops and by sea using an Egyptian fleet. Saladin paraded Conrad's aged father, William, who had been captured at the Battle of the Horns of Hattin, before the walls of Tyre and threatened to kill him if Conrad did not surrender; but Conrad was unmoved, declaring that his father had already lived a long life, and even – it is said – aimed a crossbow at the old man. His bluff worked, Saladin backed down and later released William. Again Conrad drove him off, leading an assault on the Egyptian fleet, and then a brave charge out of the city gates that surprised the besiegers and forced them to retreat.

The saving of Tyre was a turning point for the crusaders. This strategically placed port was to be a vital point of access for Western ships bringing supplies and troops in order to make the Third Crusade possible. Saladin's decision not to press home his advantage by taking Tyre was one of the very few strategic mistakes he made in a long and glorious career.

KINGS OF EUROPE TAKE THE CROSS

HENRY II, PHILIP II AND FREDERICK I JOIN THE CRUSADE

At Gisors, north-west of Paris, in January 1188 a crusading sermon by Archbishop Joscius of Tyre convinced two kings, Philip II of France and Henry II of England, to take the cross. According to the account given by the English chronicler Roger of Howden in his *Chronica* (*c*.1191), the sermon was accompanied by a miracle, when the Cross of Christ appeared in the sky above the kings.

Joscius had been sent to the west by Conrad of Montferrat after Conrad had repulsed Saladin's initial assault on Tyre. Joscius sailed in a ship with black sails to spread the news of Saladin's victories and call for urgent help and, according to Arabic accounts, carried with him pictures designed to outrage the Christians in Europe – for example, one of Saladin's army horses urinating in stables he had supposedly set up within the Church of the Holy Sepulchre, and another of a 'Saracen' hitting Christ in the face.

Roger added that the kings, who had been at war, were inspired by Joscius to put aside their enmity and agreed to

▼ *Frederick Barbarossa and his crusaders are called on to liberate the Holy Land, and begin their journey in 1157.*

pursue a common goal in the Holy Land – as Roger commented: 'those who were once enemies were persuaded to become friends on that day, through his preaching and the help of God'. At their meeting the kings also agreed on distinctive crosses to be worn by their armies to help tell them apart on campaign: the English army would wear a white cross, while the French would wear a red one. The troops of Philip, Count of Flanders, who also took the cross on this day, would wear a green cross.

DECISIONS AT LE MANS

In a meeting at Le Mans in February, Henry and Philip discussed ways to finance the crusade and decided on a tax of 10 per cent on income and property for an entire year to be applied to both Church and laity. This tax became known as the 'Saladin tithe' because it was imposed to raise money for a campaign against the Muslim general. It was administered by the Church rather than by lay authorities; clerics and knights who took the cross were exempt from the tax, but those who refused either to go on crusade or to pay the tax were excommunicated. The tax was extremely unpopular, and sparked fears that it was not a one-off but the beginning of a permanent taxation of the people; Philip II was faced with such opposition that he had to issue a proclamation in summer 1189 to the effect that the tax was an extraordinary measure and would not be perpetuated.

The kings also agreed on a sober code of conduct for the crusading armies. In order to generate a penitent and suitably sombre mood, furs and other fine clothes, games of dice and swearing were all outlawed; in addition, no knight or yeoman was permitted to bring a woman with him – 'save possibly a washerwoman on foot, to be beyond suspicion'. Anyone who died on crusade would be required to give up

▲ *Clockwise from top left: King Henry II, 1133–89, Richard I, 1157–99, John, 1167–1216, Henry III, 1207–72, from Matthew Paris',* Historia Anglorum, *1250.*

the money he carried with him: it would be divided to meet immediate needs, such as maintaining his bondmen, helping the land of Jerusalem or feeding the poor.

FREDERICK TAKES THE CROSS

At Pentecost – the church festival celebrating the descent of the Holy Spirit on early Christians – in 1188, Emperor Frederick I of Germany took the cross at a special 'Court of Jesus Christ' convened in Mainz. By now in his mid-sixties, Frederick was a veteran of the Second Crusade on which he had travelled, as Duke of Swabia, in the company of his uncle, Emperor Conrad III. He had called the court the previous December, when, according to contemporary reports, he was visibly moved by a sermon at Strasburg (modern Strasbourg, now in France) that

▲ A stained-glass window in St Stephen's Cathedral, Vienna, represents Holy Roman Emperor Frederick I taking the cross.

cast Christ in the role of a feudal lord wronged by his enemies and left unsupported by his liegemen.

On that day of Pentecost, around 13,000 princes, bishops, dukes, margraves, counts, nobles as well as many lesser knights took the cross alongside Frederick and his son Frederick, Duke of Swabia. According to the author of the anonymous *Historia de Expeditione Frederici* (Narrative of Frederick's Expedition), many men were in tears as they listened to a reading of Pope Gregory's encyclical, and a sermon from Bishop Godfrey of Würzburg. Frederick put himself forward as leader and standard-bearer for the crusade. No warlike man in Germany ignored the call, said the chronicler, and those who took the cross: 'burned with a great passion for fighting. For them, life was in Christ and death was a prize to be gained.' They set the departure for St George's Day (23 April) 1189.

WAR OF WORDS

Frederick traced his descent from Charlemagne himself and in 1165 had brought about the elevation to sainthood of that great leader, the creator of a Christian empire. Frederick had also, since 1157, used the term *Sacrum Imperium* (Holy Empire) to describe his own territories; and he believed it was the necessary and rightful task of a leader of a Christian empire to come to the aid of the faithful in the East against their 'infidel' opponents. He had even in 1165 considered launching a crusade on his own initiative.

Now, according to the crusade history called the *Itinerarium Regis Ricardi* (The Voyage of King Richard), he sent a proud missive to Saladin, demanding his retreat from the Holy Land and threatening a 'trial by battle' on 1 November 1189, 'by the merit of the life-giving Cross of Christ'. He claimed that Saladin would be shocked by the ferocity and strength of the warriors of the German empire: the untamed warriors of the Rhine, young soldiers from the Danube who would never flee, the towering Bavarians and canny Swabians, Saxons expert with the sword, circumspect Franconians, Bohemians unafraid of death, men from Bologna wilder even than their own beasts. And he said that he himself could still enforce his imperial will with a sword, for his arm was not wearied by age.

The *Itinerarium* also gave details of Saladin's equally proud response, in which he boasted that only three cities – those of Tyre, Tripoli and Antioch – remained in Christian hands in all the lands of Outremer and that 'these will inevitably be captured'. He also said that he was quite happy to undergo a trial by battle but that peace was a possible outcome if the three cities were handed over; in which case, he would allow Christian pilgrims to come and go freely.

▼ Passions run high at Mainz on Pentecost 1188 when Frederick I accepted the call to take up the cross once more, together with many great men of the empire.

BARBAROSSA'S CRUSADE

THE CAMPAIGN LED BY FREDERICK I OF GERMANY

The German army under Frederick I was the first crusading force to depart, leaving on 11 May 1189. Contemporary reports claim that his army was 100,000 or even 150,000 in number – easily the largest ever to set off on crusade – and took three days to march past an observer.

DISCIPLINE AND BELIEF

Frederick, now 67, must have had a good amount of grey in the red beard that gave him his nickname 'Barbarossa', but he still cut an imposing figure at the head of his vast force. He attempted to maintain strict discipline, reportedly turning away a group of 500 small-time criminals at Vienna and accepting into the army only those who could prove their capacity to support themselves. He had absolute confidence in his ability to regain Jerusalem and the Holy Land for Christianity: in common with the soldiers of the First Crusade, he believed that the Last Days

▼ An idealized portrait from the 19th century of Frederick I Barbarossa, Holy Roman Emperor.

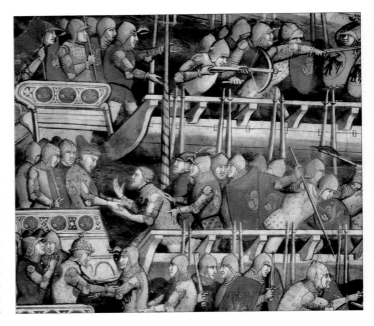

as described in the Bible were upon humankind, and that when the emperor laid his sceptre down in Jerusalem the final act would begin with a reign by the Anti-Christ prior to the triumphant Second Coming of Jesus.

BY LAND ACROSS EUROPE

The German army departed from Ratisbon (modern Regensburg, in Bavaria, Germany) and followed the overland route to Constantinople taken by the soldiers of the First Crusade almost a hundred years earlier. Frederick led the way through Hungary and Serbia into Byzantine territory. Frederick had planned ahead, and conducted prolonged negotiations with Byzantine emperor Isaac II Angelus to ensure the crusader army's safe passage across Byzantine territory, but they did not receive the warm welcome they expected. Isaac was in negotiations with Saladin, who wanted Constantinople's troops to

▲ Frederick and his vast army survived a long overland journey, with many difficulties, and then boarded ships in Constantinople to sail across the Hellespont to Anatolia.

impede the progress of the crusader army in return for support against the Seljuk Turks in Anatolia and his help in ensuring that the church in Palestine would be under Orthodox Christian control. The Byzantine emperor was also suspicious of Frederick's motives – and reports reached him that parts of the army wanted to conquer his empire for Latin Christianity.

CONFLICT WITH BYZANTIUM

In October there were several open clashes between German and Byzantine troops in the Balkans. Frederick reported in a letter to his son Henry (the future Emperor Henry VI) that the crusader army had endured 'plundering' and 'massacre', and

▲ *After setting out from Germany in a spirit of religious devotion, Frederick had a rude awakening when he encountered what seemed to be attempts by the Byzantine emperor to undermine the crusade.*

that attacks had been 'obviously instigated by none other than the emperor'. They were, he wrote, attacked by bandits, had their way blocked with great rocks and felled trees and even found castles fortified against them. Nevertheless, they progressed and spent the winter of 1189–90 in Philippopolis (modern Plovdiv, Bulgaria).

In the letter Frederick indicated that Isaac 'with little concern for his reputation' had also imprisoned German ambassadors in Constantinople and seized 'upwards of two thousand marks' of their money – and that relations had deteriorated to the extent that Frederick was planning to attack Constantinople. He asked Henry

to gather a fresh force of knights to embark by sea to help in the battle. He instructed him to send more money to Tyre, where he would collect it – and he also asked to be remembered in Henry's prayers and those of the people at home.

In the event, full-scale war between Germans and Byzantines was averted, the German army bypassed Constantinople, and crossed the Hellespont into Anatolia – on board transport ships provided by Isaac – on 28 March 1190. They marched across Anatolia and won a great victory over the Seljuks, capturing the capital of the Sultanate of Rum at Iconium (modern Konya in Turkey) on 17 May. They stayed in the city for almost a week, restocking the army with horses and supplies, before moving on towards Armenian-held Cilicia. They also captured the town of Laranda (modern Karaman) around 60 miles (100km) farther south and just to the north of the Taurus Mountains.

At this point the crusade seemed well-starred. The army had survived a difficult passage from Europe, had won a great victory and appeared to be on the threshold of great deeds in the Holy Land. But in a twist of fate on 10 June, Frederick died when he fell from his horse while crossing the River Saleph (now called the Göksu) and drowned in its icy though shallow waters. In that moment, all the energy and conviction went out of the German wave of the crusade.

Saladin and the other Muslim leaders declared that Frederick's death was the work of Allah, who had acted to deliver them from a great impending threat; to the Christians it appeared that God was not supporting their march on Jerusalem. Many Germans gave up and returned to Europe; some were reportedly so shocked that they renounced Christianity entirely.

Barbarossa's son Frederick of Swabia took control of the army and marched on to join the crusader siege of Acre, where they arrived in October 1190.

▼ *Frederick drowns in the icy River Saleph – like many crusaders before and after, he died in humiliating circumstances far from home, without having achieved the crusading mission he saw as his destiny.*

IN SICILY AND CYPRUS

RICHARD I AND PHILIP II STOP EN ROUTE TO THE HOLY LAND

The kings of France and England did not follow the German army to the Holy Land until July 1190. Although in their meeting at Gisors in January 1188 Henry II and Philip II had agreed to put disagreements to one side in the interests of Jerusalem, feuding had resurfaced.

In particular Henry II's eldest surviving son, Richard of Poitou, had allied with Philip II and invaded Henry's territory in Anjou. Henry was defeated, and was broken by this, the latest of a series of rebellions involving his sons, and he died at Chinon on 6 July 1189. He was succeeded by the Count of Poitou, who became King Richard I of England. Richard set about raising money for the crusade: he cancelled the Treaty of Falaise

▼ *On 24 June 1190, Philip II receives the royal standard in the abbey church of St Denis prior to embarking on the crusade.*

of 1174, thus freeing the Scots from their acknowledgment of English overlordship, and in return received a payment of 10,000 marks from King William of Scots.

FROM FRANCE TO SICILY

Richard and Philip II embarked together from southern France, bound initially for Sicily, where, following the death of William II of Sicily, his successor Tancred, Count of Lecce, had imprisoned William's widow, Joan of England (Richard's sister), seized her dowry and stolen a legacy intended for Richard himself.

Arriving in Sicily in September 1190, the crusader armies came into conflict with the locals; but they were given an outlet for their energies when on 4 October Richard captured and sacked the capital city of Messina. The *Itinerarium Regis Ricardi* reported that the attack was so swift and easy that it took less time than

▲ *Leaving on crusade, Richard appointed William of Mandeville, Earl of Essex, and Bishop Hugh of Durham as his regents. But William died and his position was taken by the chancellor, William Longchamp.*

a priest needs to sing the Mass; Richard spared the citizens, but his army seized vast quantities of loot. Tancred backed down, freed Joan and returned the moneys he had taken.

But Philip and Richard quarrelled fiercely about who should take most credit for the victory, with Philip enraged that Richard flew his standard above the walls rather then Philip's banner. In the end, on 8 October they made up and swore an oath to defend one another and each other's armies on the campaign ahead. Nevertheless, the differences between the two kings would dog the entire crusade.

The armies of France and England then spent the winter on the island, while their leaders continued to squabble – principally now over a marriage, for Richard had pledged to wed Philip's sister Alys, but then proposed to renege on that promise in order to marry Princess Berengaria, the daughter of the king of Navarre. According to the *Chronica* of Roger of Howden, Richard took time in Sicily to listen to the prophecies of Joachim, Abbot of the Cistercian monastery at Corazzo,

who had visions of St John the Evangelist, and declared to Richard: 'the Lord is to grant you a great victory over his enemies, and will raise your name above that of any other prince on the Earth'.

THE KINGS PART COMPANY

Finally the two kings went their separate ways. Philip left Sicily on 30 March 1191, and landed at Tyre in the middle of May. He moved on towards Acre, and joined the crusader siege of that city on 20 April. Richard made another diversion, for several of his ships – including the one carrying his intended wife Berengaria and his sister – had been caught in a storm and put in to Cyprus. There, the Cypriot ruler, Isaac Dukas Comnenus, had seized a large load of treasure that Richard was carrying and had imprisoned many of Richard's men.

Isaac Comnenus had come to power by treachery and trickery and ruled as a tyrant, so when Richard landed and

▼ Philip and Richard swore a vow like that of chivalric brothers in arms after their quarrel in Sicily. They promised to protect one another throughout the crusade. But they would soon be at loggerheads again.

ANTI-SEMITIC RIOTS IN ENGLAND

The Third Crusade was no different to its two predecessors in that the preaching of the cross sparked widespread anti-Jewish rioting. The violence afflicted England particularly, where Richard's coronation was marred by a major anti-Semitic riot in London, sparked when onlookers saw wealthy Jews apparently gaining access to the celebration. The following year violence against the Jews swept the country. The

▲ Members of the London mob run riot in a Jew's house during Richard I's reign. Crusading rhetoric drove violence at home as well as in the disputed territories of Outremer.

worst outbreak was in York, where on 16 March around 150 Jews committed suicide by setting fire to the tower in which they had taken refuge rather than face the mob in the streets below.

attacked Limassol the people welcomed him as a bringer of freedom. Isaac agreed to return the treasure and pledged to add 500 troops to the crusading army.

Once he had ensconced himself within his castle of Famagusta, however, Isaac attempted to take a hard line, ordering Richard's departure from the island. At this point, a ship arrived from the crusader camp at Acre, seeking news of Richard; on board were leading members of the Knights Templar, to whom Isaac owed a large amount of money. With their backing and encouragement, Richard led the conquest of the island, which was thereafter to be an important ally of the

crusader states in Palestine. The campaign took 15 days and, according to the *Itinerarium Regis Ricardi*, Richard found extraordinary stores of wealth that had been hoarded by the miserly Isaac – treasure was piled high in the castles of the island: the king and his knights found golden cups, silver jars, gilded saddles, precious spurs, silken cloth and fine scarlet robes, and they took them all, thinking it a gift of God to help finance the crusade.

Also during his stay on Cyprus, on 12 May, Richard married Berengaria at the port of Limassol and made her his queen. Richard finally left Cyprus and arrived at Acre on 8 June 1191.

A SICK WINTER

CRUSADERS SUFFER DURING THE LONG SIEGE OF ACRE

While King Richard and King Philip were occupied on Sicily in the winter of 1190–91, the crusader forces in the Holy Land were enduring terrible suffering as they doggedly besieged the port of Acre, while they were themselves besieged by the army of Saladin.

THE START OF THE SIEGE

The siege had begun in the summer of 1189. Saladin had imprisoned Guy of Lusignan, former king of Jerusalem, in Damascus, but in 1188 released him on condition that Guy promise to take himself overseas and never again make war against Islam. However, having sworn this oath, Guy disregarded it at once, and set about trying to rebuild his power base. He marched to Tyre, where he attempted to take control of the city but was refused by Conrad of Montferrat, who had saved the city from Saladin and saw the opportunity to establish his own territory. Then Guy, with the help of fleets from Pisa and Sicily, moved on to Acre and began a siege. A fleet of 50 ships arrived, bearing powerful Danish and Frisian warriors to bolster his army. Louis of Thuringia managed to prevail on Conrad of Montferrat to take part in the siege, and bring men from Tyre to further boost the Christian army.

▲ *Crusaders mixed with Saracens outside the walls of Acre and, by holding jousting bouts, tested in sport the fighting skills they would soon use in earnest.*

SALADIN'S ASSAULT

Saladin had considered attacking while Guy was marching south from Tyre, but he held off until the Christian army was encamped before Acre. He arrived at Acre just a few days after the crusaders at the end of August and settled in behind them. There was only desultory fighting between the two armies in September, and an atmosphere akin to that of a European

tournament developed. There was even a staged contest between two boys from the Christian army and two from the city garrison; one of the Christian youths was defeated and had to be ransomed by a crusader lord for two dinars.

Battle was joined by Christians and Saracens on 4 October. After an initial success in which the Christians drove back the centre and right wing of Saladin's army, the crusaders threw away their advantage and began looting the Muslim camp; they

▼ *Men and supplies arrived at Acre to strengthen the hand of the besieging army.*

▲ *Hunger was a recurring problem for the crusaders. According to tradition, parts of the German army on the Third Crusade lost hope and flung themselves down in the shape of the cross to await starvation.*

were then themselves forced back by a combined assault from Saladin's besiegers and the garrison of the city, who had broken out to attack. The battle was ultimately indecisive, but was certainly costly. The crusaders lost as many as 7,000 men with many Knights Templar, including their Grand Master, Gerard of Ridefort, killed. Conrad of Montferrat was isolated and had to be saved by Guy of Lusignan.

THE CRUSADERS STARVE

The siege dragged on and on. Trapped between the city walls and Saladin's army, unable to break out and forage in the countryside, the Christian army became desperately short of food. According to the *Itinerarium Regis Ricardi*, the soldiers fought over bread, and those who could afford it would pay 12 shillings for a fowl or a 100 gold pieces for a measure of wheat. They grew so desperate that they killed the finest horses for food.

A SUCCESSION DISPUTE

There were repeated outbreaks of fever and dysentery. During a stalemate in fighting in the summer of 1190, probably on 25 July, Queen Sibylla of Jerusalem died in the camp, and this sparked a succession dispute over the throne of Jerusalem.

Sibylla was the eldest daughter of King Amalric I (by Agnes of Courtenay) and was the wife of Guy of Lusignan, who had held power in the kingdom as her consort; on her death, the crown rightly passed to her half-sister, Isabella, Amalric's daughter with his second wife, Maria Comnena. But Guy refused to concede the crown and demanded to be recognized as king. Conrad of Montferrat launched an attempt to take control by marrying Isabella. At Acre, rumours circulated that Conrad was supplying food only to those in the camp who were his allies and accomplices, and that those who backed Guy of Lusignan's claim were left to starve.

In October 1190 spirits in the crusader camp were raised when the remnant of the German crusade arrived under the command of Duke Frederick of Swabia. These men were bedraggled and severely reduced in numbers, but their arrival was taken as a sign that the European armies were on their way. A little while afterwards, an English contingent arrived under the command of Baldwin, Archbishop of Canterbury. The crusaders launched a fresh assault on the city, and

knocked down part of the walls with a pair of battering rams, but the garrison held firm and the attackers made no further progress.

HARD WINTER MONTHS

The winter was very hard on the Christian army. Wells and other water sources became contaminated and disease was rife in the camp. Frederick, Duke of Swabia, Theobald, Count of Blois, Stephen, Count of Sancerre, Archbishop Baldwin of Canterbury and Patriarch Heraclius of Jerusalem all died of sickness. Count Henry II of Jerusalem (the future Henry I of Jerusalem, 1192–97) was very seriously ill for several weeks, but finally recovered.

New hope came with the spring. Duke Leopold V of Austria arrived by sea in March and took control of the army. He brought the news that King Philip II of France and King Richard I of England were on their way.

▼ *A fresh assault following the arrival of Archbishop Baldwin of Canterbury came close to success but Acre's garrison did just enough to drive back the attackers.*

THE CAPTURE OF ACRE

RICHARD I'S ARRIVAL BRINGS LONG SIEGE TO AN END

◄ *The turning point in the seemingly endless siege at Acre came with the arrival of the charismatic Richard Coeur de Lion. Sure of success, the crusaders celebrated.*

could shelter as they fired; he himself worked a crossbow and killed many of the defenders manning the walls.

The garrison fought back forcefully, using Greek fire to consume the laboriously constructed siege towers and engines, manning the battlements and clearing the ditches, but they were outnumbered and increasingly desperate. On 3 July the crusaders made a substantial breach in the walls. There was intense fighting at close quarters as the crusader army, containing many hastily armed lords, including the Earl of Leicester and the Bishop of Salisbury, tried to enter the city – but the Turks rallied strongly and held them at bay. On 4 July the city's defenders offered their surrender, but Richard was unhappy with the terms: the crusaders were asking for the Kingdom of Jerusalem to be restored to its boundaries prior to the Battle of the Horns of Hattin.

ACRE SURRENDERS

On 7 July the garrison sent a message to Saladin indicating that if he did not come to their aid they would be forced to surrender. Saladin attacked the crusaders once more on 11 July but without driving them off and on 12 July the garrison formally surrendered.

They did so without the agreement of Saladin, who reportedly wept tears of frustration and grief when he heard the news, for he had just received yet more reinforcements and was confident that a final assault might drive the crusaders off and save Acre. The garrison, moreover, had agreed punitive terms on Saladin's behalf, as negotiated by Conrad of Montferrat (or of Tyre, as he was often now known): a vast ransom of 200,000 gold dinars for the

Philip II arrived at Acre on 20 April 1191 with a Genoese fleet. He was followed on June 8, by Richard I with an English fleet carrying a force of 8,000 men. Within five weeks of Richard's arrival, the city of Acre, which had steadfastly withstood a siege since August 1189, fell to the crusader army.

Richard's reputation had preceded him to Palestine. Saladin knew from his military intelligence that although Philip II was the highest-ranking of the European kings on the crusade, Richard was the leader in terms of battle prowess and charisma, a far more powerful warrior than his rival, driven by a burning desire for warfare. For several weeks before Richard arrived, Saladin and his officers heard boasts from crusader lords in the besieging camp to the effect that when this king of England arrived, the siege of Acre would be swiftly brought to its conclusion. The day of his arrival turned into a

festival. According to the *Itinerarium Regis Ricardi*, trumpets, pipes and drums sounded out 'until the earth shook with the happiness of the Christians'; as darkness fell, people celebrated with carousing and dancing and lit bonfires that burned so brightly that the garrison of Acre thought the land around them was on fire.

SIEGE TIGHTENED

After his arrival in April, Philip II had put in train the construction of several powerful new siege engines, and Richard now personally supervised the erection and use of many more as the crusader army stepped up its attacks on the city. One of his military catapults had sufficient range to hurl great stones far over the walls and into the heart of the city; it reputedly killed 12 men with one shot. Richard fought in the front line: he had his men build a moveable protective shed beneath which the army's foremost crossbowmen lives of the garrison, 3,000 of whom would be held as prisoners; the cherished relic of the True Cross, in Saladin's possession since it had been captured at the Battle of the Horns of Hattin, would be returned, and around 2,000 Christians held prisoner by the Muslim army would be released; the city, all its possessions and the ships in its harbour would be handed over to the crusaders. Despite his anger, Saladin felt honour-bound to accept the terms agreed in his name.

The English army took possession of the city. King Philip II installed himself in the Acre mansion of the Templars, while Richard made himself at home in what had been the royal palace. Almost at once Richard quarrelled openly and fiercely with Duke Leopold of Austria – in a disagreement almost identical to the one that

▼ *Their long months of suffering at an end, the crusaders establish themselves in Acre after the garrison's formal surrender.*

had followed his capture of Messina. Duke Leopold saw himself as the commander of the German contingent on the crusade, for Frederick Barbarossa had died in Cilicia and his son Frederick, Duke of Swabia, had died during the siege; Leopold, therefore, demanded equal ranking with Philip II and Richard I. He issued an order that his standard should fly alongside that of

▲ *Saladin was impressed by the valour of Hubert Walter, Bishop of Salisbury, at Acre and later asked to meet him. On returning from crusade to England, Walter was named Archbishop of Canterbury.*

Richard on the city walls; but shortly afterwards the standard was found in the ditch, having been torn down and thrown over the wall. The result was that Leopold and the force at his command abandoned the crusade and set off for home.

KING PHILIP'S DEPARTURE

Philip II also left shortly afterwards. He had been severely ill with dysentery and also needed to settle the succession in Vermandois and Flanders, for the lord of that region, Philip of Alsace, had died in the camp at Acre and left no heirs. Philip left behind in Acre a French army of 10,000 under the command of Duke Hugh III of Burgundy and set sail for Genoa, bound for France. His departure greatly displeased Richard, who declared: 'It is a pity and a shame on my lord to leave this place without having brought to an end the enterprise that brought him here. But if he finds himself in bad health, and in fear perhaps lest he should die here, his will must be done.' His displeasure was no doubt principally caused by the knowledge that his territorial possessions in northern France would be open to interference from Philip while he himself was engaged in pursuing the crusade.

ATROCITY AT ACRE?

RICHARD I AND THE MASSACRE OF MUSLIM PRISONERS

On 20 August Richard had 2,700 Muslim prisoners from Acre beheaded on the plain in front of the city, in full view of Saladin's camp. He said that he did it because Saladin was refusing to honour the agreed terms of the surrender.

The prisoners killed included soldiers from the garrison, but also women and children. Many historians have expressed horror at the deed, contrasting it with Saladin's frequent magnanimity in victory. The Muslim army launched an attack in an attempt to stop the killing, but were driven back.

▼ *Kings Philip II and Richard I oversee the surrender of Acre and the taking of the city's garrison and people into captivity.*

It may be that Richard's decision was a justified act of war. It is certainly true that Saladin was dragging out the settlement of the ransom payment. Saladin had made an initial payment of the ransom fee on 11 August but according to the 12–13th-century Muslim historian Baha ad-Din ibn Shaddad, the general had then refused to hand over the next instalment until all the garrison prisoners had been released, and had wanted to provide a new batch of prisoners from his own camp to stand in place of the members of the Acre garrison. His motive was probably to make the settlement of the agreement drag out so long that the campaigning season would end before Richard could succeed in launching an attack on Jerusalem.

A LION IN A HURRY

Richard, on the other hand, was in a hurry. He had seen Philip II set sail for home, and had had time to consider the possible ramifications of the king of France being at large in Europe unchecked by the presence there of the king of England – Richard himself. He wanted to hasten the crusade towards its conclusion, so that he could return to manage his European affairs. He wrote to his justiciar in England from Acre on 6 August describing his victories on campaign, but indicating that he would soon be returning home – 'as soon as we have brought Syria back to its previous position'. He promised to be back in English waters by the following Lent.

▲ *Barbarous act or necessary military decision? On Richard's orders, one by one, 2,700 Muslim prisoners are put to death.*

He was in any case a decisive man who liked to act swiftly: already on the crusade he had conducted two whirlwind campaigns, one in southern Italy, where he had captured several Byzantine possessions, and one in Cyprus, where he had captured the island in just a fortnight.

He wanted to move on from Acre, and he did not have sufficient manpower to leave an army behind to guard the prisoners. Among the garrison were many crack Turkish soldiers who had fought bravely and with great skill to prolong the siege – he could not allow these men to escape or be released and then rejoin Saladin's army. Some writers have argued that the killing of the prisoners was an act of barbarity, but it can be viewed as a sensible and necessary strategic decision.

ALL THINGS FAIR IN WAR?

Moreover, it would appear from Saladin's later friendly relations with Richard that the Muslim general did not view the

killing at Acre as an act of brutality – he did not conceive a contemptuous hatred for Richard as he had done for Reynald of Châtillon. While Saladin was certainly often notable for his clemency in victory, he, too, was capable of acts of great ferocity, such as when he ordered the beheading of the captured Knights Templar and Hospitaller after their defeat at the Battle of the Horns of Hattin. On that occasion, the killing of the knights was made into an amusing spectacle, as the Muslim army jeered and laughed while untrained and unskilled army followers hacked at the knights.

Richard's actions did, however, have consequences that cannot have been good for army morale. The killing of the prisoners naturally brought an end to negotiations. As a result, the 2,000-odd Christian prisoners in the Muslim camp were not released and the sacred relic of the True Cross, captured at the Horns of Hattin and held in Saladin's camp, was not returned to the crusaders. However, the failed attack by the Muslim army left the crusaders in even stronger control of Acre than previously.

FIERCE AND RUTHLESS

Throughout his career, Richard demonstrated ruthlessness and decisiveness and a knack for making correct strategic decisions. In most ways the man known as *Coeur de Lion* was the very type of the chivalric knight – a great leader of men, charismatic, brave, strong, skilful, good-looking, hearty, and not lacking courtly accomplishments as a well-educated lover of poetry and song. But he was not the kind of knight who placed a greater importance on chivalry than on victory.

The massacre at Acre should probably be viewed in this light, seen alongside his treachery towards his father, Henry II of England, or his ruthlessness on European campaigns as another example among many of a clear-eyed desire for victory – a willingness to do whatever is necessary to win. The killing of the prisoners freed the crusader army to move on swiftly from Acre and impressed his ferocity and strength of purpose on his opponents. (Later, Saladin was unable to garrison Ascalon against Richard, for his men were too frightened by reports of Richard's behaviour at Acre to volunteer.) *Coeur de Lion's* heart was not only brave and strong, but also ferocious – and dangerous.

▼ *Ruthless in victory, Richard does away with the prisoners. He saw them as a threat that had to be eliminated.*

RICHARD'S MARCH TO JAFFA

AND A GREAT VICTORY AT THE BATTLE OF ARSUF

Richard set out from Acre on 22 August with the intention of moving swiftly on to Jerusalem. He led his army southwards along the coast to Jaffa (modern Tel Aviv-Jafo), accompanied at sea by a fleet carrying supplies and water. But Saladin's troops shadowed them all the way and launched wave after wave of skirmishing attacks. In a pitched battle at Arsuf on September 7, the crusaders drove off their persecutors, winning a resounding victory over the Muslim force.

THE MARCH

Richard imposed absolute discipline on his army. He knew that over-enthusiasm and a lack of respect for the harshness of climate and terrain had led to disaster at the Horns of Hattin: for this reason, he decreed that the army would march no more than 4–5 miles (6–8km) per day, moving only in the cooler hours of the morning and making camp each afternoon by a source of water.

On the march Richard insisted that his men kept in a tight formation, with the infantry on the landward side to fend off attacks by the Muslim army and protect the mounted knights riding in the centre of the column. The infantrymen carried large crusader shields and wore heavy armour over thick felt jerkins. According to Muslim historian Baha ed-Din, the arrows of the Turkish archers could make little impression on them: 'I saw,' he wrote, 'warriors with no fewer than ten arrows stuck in their back armour, marching on unperturbed without breaking rank.' Periodically, the infantrymen on the landward side were replaced by fresher men who had been marching on the seaward side, where there were no attacks.

In the centre of the main column was the royal standard, mounted in a wagon and guarded by an elite reserve. In front of this rode the Knights Templar and behind it the Knights Hospitaller. The rear of the army had to cope with repeated attacks, and take care not to fall behind. The Muslim force harried the column, hoping to force the crusaders to break rank, but they failed. King Richard was constantly vigilant, barking our orders, tirelessly riding out to meet attacks with his great sword shining in the harsh sun.

▼ *Richard's troops make their way in searing heat and through bare desert from Acre to Jaffa, his men under strict orders not to respond to attacks by Saladin's army.*

▲ *The crusaders fought fiercely, but it was Richard's ability to make instant tactical decisions that triumphed at Arsuf. When the Hospitallers broke rank it was a potential disaster, but with a swift general charge Richard won the day.*

There was no great crowd of camp-followers as there had been on previous crusades – only this strictly disciplined column. Baha ed-Din described the Muslims' frustration at being unable to break the self-control of the Christians: 'You could not help but admire the patience of these soldiers, who put up with the most extreme difficulties.' Richard would not allow women to accompany the army, save for a corps of washer-women who were responsible for cleaning the soldiers' linen, washing their hair and delousing them.

THE ATTACK AT CAESAREA

The crusader army reached Caesarea on 30 August. A major Muslim attack succeeded briefly in isolating the rear of the crusader column under Hugh III, Duke of Burgundy, but with the help of Richard himself they managed to drive off the attack and reunite the column. As they fought the crusaders called out 'Help us, Holy Sepulchre!'

THE BATTLE OF ARSUF

On 7 September Saladin unleashed a full-scale onslaught on the crusader army at Arsuf. His plan was to draw the Christian knights out into a series of charges, and then attack and overpower them once they were split up into small groups.

The first attack came at nine in the morning, accompanied by a fearful noise of gongs, cymbals and trumpets and by the Muslim soldiers screaming. A second attack concentrated on the Hospitallers in the rear of the army column. Each attack came in waves: first Nubian and Bedouin soldiers unleashed a storm of arrows and javelins, and then moved aside to allow a follow-up onslaught from the Turkish mounted archers who rode swiftly forward before wheeling away in the hope of drawing out a charge. Here and there along the columns were pockets of fierce hand-to-hand fighting.

All this time the crusaders continued to march forwards towards Arsuf. Richard's plan was to hold the line and keep his

▼ Richard was everywhere at Arsuf, leading his men by personal example and trying to ensure that they kept their discipline.

knights back for one overwhelming charge. This demanded extraordinary discipline, for the Christians were under extreme pressure and the natural response of many of the knights in the army was to break out and charge.

In mid-afternoon, the vanguard of the Christian army marched into Arsuf just as the Hospitallers in the rear came under very severe attack. The Hospitaller general, Garnier of Nablus, begged Richard for the order to charge but the king commanded him to hold the line. But at this point discipline snapped: the Hospitallers charged, with a great shout of 'St George!' They were followed by the French knights who were just ahead of them in the line.

Richard acted decisively, making the best of what had happened by ordering a Templar-led charge right along the line. Saladin's army was driven back, but regrouped; Richard managed to gather his knights for a second charge and the Muslim force scattered. According to the *Itinerarium Regis Ricardi*, Richard led by example: the author likened Richard's sword to a sickle, harvesting a crop of warriors: he claimed that Richard covered the battlefield with Muslim corpses.

▲ Saladin's attack was carefully planned at Arsuf. He thought he had Richard trapped, but the crusaders turned the tables on him.

The crusaders still had to weather one more storm, for Saladin's nephew Taqi al-Din led an attack on the left flank, but Richard managed to regroup his knights for a third charge. This time Saladin's army fled in disarray into the hills. Richard's knights mounted his standard on the hill where Saladin's had flown and looted the abandoned Muslim camp. Since darkness was now falling Richard ordered his men to abandon the chase.

A GREAT BUT NOT DECISIVE VICTORY

The Battle of Arsuf was a major victory. It blew a hole in Saladin's reputation for invincibility and demonstrated Richard's superb generalship and personal bravery. But it was not a victory on the scale of the Horns of Hattin, for it wasn't a decisive blow against Saladin's military strength. The Muslim general prepared to block the route to Jerusalem: Richard's triumph at Arsuf did not leave the way open to the Holy City as Saladin's victory at the Horns of Hattin had done. In the short term, instead of marching on Jerusalem Richard occupied and refortified Jaffa.

AN UNCERTAIN FUTURE
RICHARD'S NEGOTIATIONS WITH SALADIN, AND THE JERUSALEM SUCCESSION

After the immense demands of the siege of Acre, the difficult march down the coast and heroic victory in the bruising Battle of Arsuf, Richard and his army recuperated in Jaffa. Saladin went to Ascalon and broke down the fortification to prevent Richard taking it and using it as a stronghold. In October Richard opened negotiations with Saladin in search of a diplomatic solution to bring the war to an end.

With the year drawing to a close, Richard saw the difficulty of mounting a swift campaign to capture Jerusalem, given Saladin's surviving military strength and the fact that elements of Richard's own army had drifted back to Acre. He also saw that lack of manpower would make it virtually impossible to defend the Holy City even if he succeeded in capturing it, especially because many in his army were crusader-pilgrims and could be expected to return to Europe having entered Jerusalem and worshipped in the Church of the Holy Sepulchre. On 1 October 1191 Richard wrote to the abbot of Clairvaux, describing his successes at Arsuf and reoccupation of Jaffa, and look-

▼ *Richard and Saladin were exemplars of chivalry throughout the medieval period. These tiles representing the adversaries date from the 13th century.*

ing hopefully forward to future conquests. Richard indicated that he and his men were exhausted and that the land of Palestine needed reinforcement, for if they captured more territory they would need men to hold it: he asked the abbot to inspire more European lords and yeomen to travel to the Holy Land.

NEGOTIATIONS AT JAFFA
Meanwhile, Saladin sent his brother al-Adil to Jaffa to carry out the negotiations. Richard was negotiating from a position of relative strength, and initially made a remarkably bold demand: the handover of Jerusalem together with all the territory between the coast and the River Jordan, and the return of the sacred relic of the True Cross, which was still in Saladin's possession following the breakdown of negotiations after the slaughter of prisoners at Acre. Saladin returned a cautious response, noting that Jerusalem was as much a Muslim as a Christian city, that the wider territory in Palestine had been in the possession of the crusaders for only a century or so and that he was willing to hand over the True Cross if he received something of equal value in return.

Then Richard made a shockingly original suggestion to al-Adil. He proposed that al-Adil marry Richard's sister, Joan of England, who, since the death of William

II of Sicily, had been the Dowager Queen of Sicily. Richard would give them possession of Acre and Jaffa and Saladin, should he agree, would give them the remainder of Palestine: then together they would rule the entire country from Jerusalem. Richard would return to England; the war would be over. The only problem he could see, Richard said, was that the pope would not agree: in which case, Richard suggested, one of his nieces could take the place of Joan.

Saladin, remarkably enough, agreed to this proposal – although according to Baha ed-Din, only because he knew it was a practical joke. But Joan of England refused to marry a Muslim; and Richard's suggestion to al-Adil that he convert to Christianity was also rejected. The negotiations ended amicably but without lasting results.

MARCH ON JERUSALEM
Richard then marched to Ascalon and began to rebuild the fortifications that Saladin had dismantled. In the winter, when Saladin had largely disbanded his army, Richard marched the crusader force towards Jerusalem. He got within 12 miles (20km) of the Holy City in January 1192, but in terrible weather that made rivers of the roads he decided not to risk an assault; the waterlogged, mountainous terrain did not play to the strengths of the crusader cavalry and instead favoured the mobile Turkish horsemen and archers. He returned to Ascalon.

Negotiations continued. Richard felt an increasingly urgent need to return to Europe to safeguard his possessions, for he was receiving reports that his brother John was seeking to seize power in England while Philip II was eyeing Normandy. At the end of March a workable compromise seemed to have been reached: the crusaders would retain Acre, Jaffa and Ascalon and would have the relic

◄ Richard's decision to pull back from an assault on Jerusalem in 1191–92 may be a sign of his willingness to compromise.

Isabella's consort from 1192 to 1197, although for unknown reasons he was never crowned.

Rumours soon began to circulate as to who had been behind Conrad's murder, with some claiming that Richard had hired the Assassins to do the deed. But it seems unlikely, given that he did not try to force Guy of Lusignan on the kingdom but accepted the elevation of the kingship to Henry of Champagne. More likely the cause lay in conflict between Genoese merchants who had Conrad's backing and their rivals from Pisa who would have been excluded by a Genoese monopoly had Conrad succeeded, but under Henry won important concessions in Acre.

of the True Cross returned; in addition, they would have the right to visit Jerusalem as pilgrims and maintain priests there. On Palm Sunday, 29 March, Richard knighted al-Adil in a splendid ceremony.

THE JERUSALEM SUCCESSION

In April the long-running succession dispute between Guy of Lusignan (also known as Guy of Jerusalem), the husband of the deceased Queen Sibylla, and Conrad of Tyre (also known as Conrad of Montferrat), husband of Sibylla's younger sister Isabella, was decided in Conrad's favour at a meeting of a council of Jerusalem's leading knights and barons. Richard had backed Guy but Guy received no votes at all in council. Richard subsequently arranged for him to buy the Kingdom of Cyprus. But then, on April 28, before he could be crowned, Conrad was killed in the streets of Tyre by two Assassins (*see* box).

Within a week of Conrad's death Henry II, Count of Champagne, nephew to both Richard I of England and Philip II of France, had married Conrad's wife Isabella and been acclaimed King of Jerusalem. He ruled as king on account of being Queen

THE ASSASSINS

The Assassins who killed Conrad were members of a militant Shi'ite Muslim sect, founded in 1094 in opposition to the new Shi'ite Fatimid caliph in Cairo and in support of his deposed brother Nisar. They believed in terrorist murder as a sacred duty, and were known as *hashshashin* in Arabic, from their reported practice of smoking hashish before embarking on suicide murder missions. The English word 'assassin' comes from *hashshashin*.

The Assassins carried out deadly missions against Sunni and certain Shi'ite Muslims whom they considered religious enemies as well as against crusaders. Their first leader, Hasan-e Sabbah, oversaw the establishment of a string of castle strongholds in Iran and Iraq from which terrorist killers emerged on missions. In the 12th century they captured several fortresses in Syria,

► The fortress that became the Assassins' castle at Masyaf in Syria was originally built by the Byzantines.

including the celebrated castle of Masyaf, from which their Syrian chief Rashid ad-Din as-Sinan and his successors sent men out on a series of murder missions. Sinan and his successors were called *shaykh al-jabal* (mountain chieftain in Arabic), which the crusaders rendered into English as the 'Old Man of the Mountain'.

THE TREATY OF JAFFA

LAST BATTLES AND FINAL TREATY OF THE THIRD CRUSADE

In May–June 1192, when Richard and his troops came within striking distance of Jerusalem for the second time in just six months, Richard elected not to launch an assault. Subsequently, back on the coast, he won two astonishing victories over Saladin before agreeing the terms of the Treaty of Jaffa, which brought the crusade to an end.

SECOND APPROACH TO JERUSALEM

In May 1992 Richard marched southwards down the coast from Ascalon and captured the fortress of Darum. Then he marched inland towards Jerusalem and encamped in the hills about 12 miles

▼ *In war and diplomacy Richard and Saladin treated each other with respect, each aware of the other's prowess. Chivalric authors and storytellers ever since have imagined encounters between the two men.*

(20km) from the city. Two events occurred in the hills before Richard ordered a surprising retreat to the coast.

The first was that he attacked a trade caravan heading from Egypt to Jerusalem and seized rich booty, including several hundred camels and horses – according to Saladin's secretary, Imad ed-din al-Isfahani, Richard disguised himself as an Arab in order to reconnoitre the landscape as the caravan approached. On another occasion, while pursuing some Turks in the hills he looked up and saw the Holy City in the distance. This was to be the only time he saw Jerusalem – and because he had made a vow that he would look on the city only as its conqueror, he raised his shield in front of his eyes to block off the view and rode away.

After the attack on the caravan, Saladin expected an assault on Jerusalem and prepared for a siege by poisoning water sources around the city and calling his

military advisers to a council of war. But on 5 July he received reports from his scouts that the crusaders had broken their camp in the hills nearby and were marching away from Jerusalem, back to the coast. Saladin rode out to watch the retreat. Many in the crusader army were puzzled and angered by Richard's decision. It would appear that he again decided that it would be pointless to launch a major assault against a target that he could not hope to hold even if he won it.

THE BATTLES OF JAFFA

Richard retired to Acre, expecting the stand-off to continue, but Saladin launched a heavy attack on Jaffa. Here, for once, the great Muslim general lost control of his men, who ran amok looting and plundering in defiance of Saladin's orders to allow the Christians to leave the city peacefully with their possessions. Some contemporary reports suggest that Saladin urgently communicated with the Christian garrison, encouraging them to take refuge in the citadel while he struggled to impose order on his troops.

Richard meanwhile gathered a small force and sailed along the coast from Acre to Jaffa. Arriving on 31 July he anchored off the city: a priest from the garrison, seeing the royal standard, swam bravely out to the ships to let Richard know that, although the city was in Saracen hands, the garrison was holding out in the citadel and negotiating terms of surrender.

What followed was truly the stuff of chivalric legend. Richard leapt immediately from the boat and swam ashore, loyally followed by his knights. This force of just the king and 54 others succeeded against all odds in driving the Saracen forces back. Richard and his knights camped outside the city, for inside it was in ruins following its earlier sacking and the stench of corpses in the streets made it uninhabitable. At dawn on 5 August

Saladin launched an attack with 7,000 cavalry; Richard and his knights had just 15 horses between them but – supported by around 2,000 Italian crossbowmen – they went resolutely forward to defend the edge of their camp, which was marked by a line of sharpened tent pegs. That day the crusaders won another extraordinary victory, holding the camp and the city against the Saracen attack. Saladin abandoned the campaign and retreated to Jerusalem.

Richard and Saladin were both exhausted, and both fell ill in the days after the extraordinary battles of Jaffa.

▼ *Richard's heroic assault on Jaffa with just 54 knights really was an occasion when history matched the brave feats of legend.*

▲ *These stones, in the gateway to the Old City at Jaffa, witnessed the clash of armies and the great deeds of kings and knights.*

With typical chivalry, Saladin sent fruit and mountain snow to Richard to speed his recovery.

PEACE AT LAST

Negotiations for a peace settlement were reopened and the two leaders reached agreement and signed the Treaty of Jaffa on 2 September. Under its terms, there would be a three-year truce between the two sides. The Christians agreed to demolish Ascalon and not rebuild it in those three years; they were to keep the coastal lands from Acre down to Jaffa, as well as the Principality of Antioch and the County of Tripoli; they would be allowed access as pilgrims to the churches and shrines of Jerusalem; and Roman priests would be able to celebrate services in the city.

In the weeks following the agreement, hundreds of crusaders made their way to Jerusalem to fulfil their vows. But Richard refused, declaring that he could not enter the city since God had denied him the chance to do so as conqueror. He was in any case very keen to return to Europe to look after his possessions there. He set sail on 9 October.

AFTER THE THIRD CRUSADE

THE AFTERMATH AND LEGACY OF THE 1189–92 CAMPAIGN

The Third Crusade ended in 1192 without the capture of Jerusalem. The crusade did not have a dramatic conclusion, and although it succeeded in preventing the complete destruction of the Latin Kingdom of Jerusalem, there remained in many quarters a sense of unfinished business. Just three years later, in 1195, another crusade was being organized by Pope Celestine III (ruled 1191–98) and German emperor Henry VI.

▼ *Coeur de Lion's martial prowess counts for nothing as he is fatally injured by a crossbow bolt from Chalus-Chabrol castle.*

RICHARD LEAVES PALESTINE

Richard I's homeward journey from the Holy Land was a disaster. Shipwrecked in the Adriatic, he attempted to cross the lands of the Holy Roman Empire in disguise, well aware that he could not expect a hospitable welcome from either Duke Leopold of Austria (with whom he had quarrelled violently at Acre) or German emperor Henry VI (angry that Richard had recognized Tancred as King of Sicily). By rights, these lords should have offered Richard immunity from attack because he was returning from the crusades, but both were keen to punish and to profit by him.

Richard was betrayed to Leopold who passed him on to Henry. Richard languished in prison for months before being ransomed for 150,000 silver marks.

His great opponent, Saladin, died after morning prayers on 4 March 1193 in Damascus, just five months after Richard's departure from Acre. Baha ed-Din ibn Shaddad declared that the Islamic world was filled with a grief so profound that only Allah himself could plumb its depths. Famed for his generosity, Saladin died bankrupt – at his death his treasury contained a gold coin and 47 pieces of silver – not enough to pay for his funeral.

Saladin's death presented an opportunity for the crusaders at an extremely inopportune moment. The great general's army was dispersed, and his power evaporated in family squabbles as one of his sons, al-Afdal Nureddin, marched on Damascus, while a second son, al-Aziz Uthman, was besieged in Cairo by Saladin's brother, al-Adil. Had Richard I waited in the Holy Land just six months longer, he would almost certainly have been able to capitalize on Saladin's death by capturing Jerusalem and re-establishing it as a Christian city. In the event, it took al-Adil ten years to reunite Saladin's territorial possessions.

Richard was never to return to the Holy Land. He spent most of the remainder of his life fighting over his French possessions with Philip II and died in April 1199 aged 41 after being shot in the neck by an archer during a siege of the unimportant castle of Chalus-Chabrol in the Limousin.

THE 'CRUSADE' OF 1195

On 25 July 1195 Pope Celestine III issued a call to arms for a fresh crusade. His letter, as reported by English chronicler Ralph of Diceto, declared that although the most recent crusade had not entirely succeeded in its aims, Christian folk should be strong in faith that God would

'exalt in his miracles' and 'instruct their hands in battle and their fingers in fighting'. As his predecessors had done before him, Celestine promised a plenary indulgence for the crusaders' sins 'and afterwards eternal life'.

German Emperor Henry VI, the son of Frederick I Barbarossa, responded to the call. Between October 1195 and March 1196 a great throng of Germans took the cross; they departed from southern Italy for the Holy Land in spring 1197. The army, sent by Henry, Duke of Brabant, landed at Acre in September 1197 and occupied Beirut and Sidon. But Henry died of malaria in September 1197 in Messina while campaigning in Sicily; and the German crusaders, as their predecessors had in 1189, simply melted away when they heard the news of the emperor's untimely death. The crusade of 1195 ended in a hurried truce.

LEGACY OF THE THIRD CRUSADE

The Third Crusade did not succeed in achieving one of its principal targets, capturing Jerusalem, but in many ways it was a success. At the outset in 1187 Saladin appeared to be invincible and it seemed only a matter of time before the greatest of Muslim generals drove the Latin settlers out of Palestine altogether. Yet Richard I managed to inflict stunning defeats on this towering figure at Acre, Arsuf and Jaffa and in the process re-established the Kingdom of Jerusalem on a relatively secure footing. Moreover, the island of Cyprus, which Richard captured in 1191, proved to be a very valuable conquest,

▼ *Saladin died in Damascus, where he was buried close to the Umayyad Mosque.*

▲ *German crusaders capture Beirut in 1197, but the victory was to be short lived.*

since it provided a vital long-term partner for the Latin states in the Holy Land.

The Third Crusade set the pattern for future crusades to the Holy Land. After the campaign of 1189–92, crusaders no longer made their way to Palestine by way of Constantinople and Anatolia, but by sea directly to the ports of Acre or Tyre. In the first two crusades the European soldiers had chosen violence over diplomacy in every impasse, but after the use by Richard of truces and negotiated settlements with Saladin, relations between the crusaders and the Muslims were transformed. Moreover, just as the crusade had failed to capture Jerusalem, but still achieved certain valuable goals in consolidating the Latin presence in Palestine, so in future crusades the focus shifted away from the earlier narrow focus on liberating Jerusalem to a more general focus on aiding the Christian settlers in the Holy Land.

In 1198 a young, power-hungry pope, Innocent III, began to organize another crusade. The fruit of his labours would be the Fourth Crusade of 1202–04.

CHAPTER EIGHT

CRUSADES OF THE EARLY 13TH CENTURY

In the first three decades of the 13th century, popes Innocent III (ruled 1198–1216), Honorius III (ruled 1216–27) and Gregory IX (ruled 1227–41) oversaw three major crusades to the East – the Fourth of 1202–04, the Fifth of 1217–21 and the Sixth of 1228. In his 18-year reign Innocent III also proclaimed a whole series of European crusades, including two against fellow Christians (the German lord Markward of Anweiler and the Albigensian heretics of southern France), one against Baltic pagans in northern Europe and one against the Muslim Almohad caliphs in Spain. In all of these encounters, Innocent and his successors worked with their utmost force to maintain papal control, for they saw crusading as a means to extend the power of Rome.

But the popes often failed to keep control of the powerful lords and complex alliances engaged in the crusades to the East. Of the three major Eastern crusades in these years, only the Fifth can be said to have remained under papal control through the office of papal legate Pelagius. It ended in abject failure, with the agreement of a humiliating peace treaty. Of the others, the Fourth slipped entirely from the papal control and ended up as little more than a pillaging expedition, while the Sixth ended as a seeming success, with Jerusalem in Christian hands and the position of Outremer bolstered. However, these successes had been achieved by the fiercely independent Frederick II of Germany working quite unilaterally to the papacy.

▲ *Venetian and French lords take stock after the sacking of Constantinople in 1204.*

◀ *The armies of the Fourth Crusade ignored an excommunication threat from Innocent III when they sacked the city of Zara in 1202.*

FIGHTING FOR VENICE

CRUSADERS DIVERT TO ATTACK ZARA

The newly elected Pope Innocent III called for another crusade to reclaim the Holy Land in August 1198. French barons responded to the call in 1201 and, choosing to travel by sea, negotiated with the doge of Venice, Enrico Dandolo, to transport them to the Holy Land. Failures of organization and recruitment resulted in them being in such severe debt to Venice that they had to agree to divert the crusaders to fight on the doge's behalf against the city of Zara, in Dalmatia (Croatia).

INNOCENT'S CALL TO ARMS

Pope Innocent's call to arms was largely directed at knights and noblemen rather than royalty. Like many others, Innocent believed that the Third Crusade had failed to liberate Jerusalem because it had been led by kings, and principally because of the inability of Richard I and Philip II to overcome their rivalries. This time the pope set out to establish the crusade as one strictly under papal control and nominated two legates, Soffredo of Pisa and Peter of Capuano, to be leaders 'humbly and religiously' of the crusade. Innocent

▼ Venice rose to prominence as a centre for trade between western Europe and the rest of the known world – both the Byzantine Empire and Islamic territories beyond.

later authorized the preaching of the crusade by a French priest named Fulk of Neuilly, a gifted orator.

The response to Innocent's call to arms was initially underwhelming, but then in November 1199 at a grand chivalric tournament at Ecry-sur-Aisne in Champagne, the 22-year-old host, Count Theobald of Champagne, and one of the leading competitors, the 27-year-old Count Louis of Blois, both took the cross after hearing a crusade sermon by Fulk of Neuilly. (Theobald was the younger brother of Henry of Champagne, then reigning as king of Jerusalem since he was the husband of Queen Isabella of Jerusalem, having married Isabella right after the assassination of her previous husband, Conrad of Montferrat.)

Theobald and Louis were followed by other noblemen, including Count Baldwin of Flanders and Simon of Montfort, 5th Earl of Leicester. (Simon was later captain general of French forces in the Albigensian Crusade and father of the Simon of Montfort who led baronial opposition to King Henry III of England and briefly ruled the country in the 1260s.) Also among the French noblemen who took the cross was Geoffrey of Villehardouin, who wrote an account of the crusade. Count Theobald was elected leader.

▲ Earlier in his career, wily Venetian leader Enrico Dandolo had served his city as an ambassador to the Byzantine Empire. He knew the wealth of Constantinople.

NEGOTIATIONS WITH VENICE

Theobald, Louis and Baldwin appointed six envoys to negotiate the necessary practical arrangements. The envoys approached Venice, the world's leading maritime power at the close of the 12th century, and commissioned a fleet to transport the crusader army to the Holy Land. They asked for sufficient ships to transport an army of 33,500 men – a wildly ambitious number, no less than seven times larger than the force taken by Philip II in 1190. The proposed army was to consist of 4,500 knights (with their horses), 9,000 squires and 20,000 infantry.

To supply a fleet to carry this army, plus nine months' supply of food and fodder, the Venetians demanded 85,000 marks; in addition they offered to provide 50 additional armed galleys 'for the love of God', on the condition that the city be granted one-half of any plunder that was seized by, either by land or sea. The deal was agreed, and consecrated in a lavish service in St Mark's, Venice.

The envoys' overambitious planning was to have severe consequences. The envoys also secretly agreed among themselves that the initial target for the crusade should be Egypt rather than Palestine. It had been proposed before, not least by Richard I during the Third Crusade, that the key to undermining Muslim strength in the Holy Land would be found in attacking Egypt. However, the revised target was kept secret because the majority of the knights and others who had taken the cross had done so with Jerusalem as their inspiration and goal.

A NEW LEADER

In May 1201, crusade leader Count Theobald died of a mysterious malady. He was replaced by the Italian count Boniface of Montferrat. In June 1202 crusaders began gathering in Venice. Only around 11,000 men had arrived by October, partly because some had sailed directly from ports in southern France; the original target of 33,500 had been far too ambitious. The fleet of ships was ready – but the crusaders could not pay for it in full. After a prolonged stalemate, the Venetian doge offered to postpone full

▼ *Pope Innocent III felt the church had to strengthen its position against heretics within the Christian church.*

▲ *Baldwin of Flanders played a leading role in the Fourth Crusade from start to shameful finish. He was made emperor of the Latin Empire of Constantinople.*

payment of the shortfall until the crusaders were able to raise the money through looting, but only if the crusaders came to the aid of Venice by reconquering its former colony of Zara in Hungary (modern Zadar in Croatia). This was a Christian city, under the protection of the Roman Catholic king, Emeric of Hungary, who had himself taken the cross.

The crusaders effectively had no choice. The doge, Enrico Dandolo, elected to take the cross and sail with them – despite being in his 80s and virtually blind. He was an extremely capable and intelligent man, and remarkable healthy for his age.

THE ATTACK ON ZARA

The crusade fleet sailed in November 1202, bound for Zara. The papal legate Peter Capuano approved the deal as the only way to prevent the crusade foundering altogether, but Pope Innocent III wrote a letter threatening the crusade leaders with excommunication if they attacked fellow Christians. The citizens of Zara hung banners emblazoned with the cross from their windows and on the city walls in the hope of forestalling the assault. But the attack went ahead.

After a siege of five days, Zara surrendered to the crusade leaders, and accepted Venice's claim of suzerainty. The victorious army entered the city and systematically looted it. They then decided to spend the winter there before proceeding with the crusade.

ON TO CONSTANTINOPLE
CRUSADERS AGREE TO RESTORE DEPOSED EMPEROR TO THRONE

After the sacking of Zara, the crusaders took another unexpected diversion. Exiled Byzantine prince Alexius Angelus offered their leaders astonishing levels of funding and military support for the remainder of the expedition if they agreed first to sail to Constantinople and depose the emperor, Alexius III.

BYZANTINE NEGOTIATIONS

Emperor Isaac II Angelus had in 1195 been blinded, deposed and imprisoned by his own brother, who took the throne as Emperor Alexius III. The deposed emperor's son, Prince Alexius Angelus, had escaped into exile and was seeking support to restore his father to the throne. In the winter of 1202 he was a guest of Philip of Swabia, who was his brother-in-law, having married Alexius's sister Irene in May 1197.

At Philip's court, Alexius met Boniface of Montferrat, the elected leader of the Fourth Crusade, who had left his fellow crusaders in Venice before they embarked to make the attack on Zara. (Philip was the youngest son of Emperor Frederick I Barbarossa and was king of Germany; he had been elected Holy Roman emperor in 1198 following the death of Henry VI, but

Pope Innocent opposed his succession, preferring the rival claim of Otto, son of Henry the Lion, Duke of Saxony. Boniface was one of Philip's leading feudal vassals.)

Prince Alexius made a remarkable offer to Boniface: if the crusaders diverted the expedition to Constantinople in order forcibly to right the wrongs brought about by the usurper emperor Alexius III, he would provide 200,000 silver marks to meet the army's current expenses, supply food for the entire force, send 10,000 men and 20 galleys to support the planned crusading expedition against Egypt for an entire year, establish a permanent force of 500 Byzantine knights in the Holy Land – and put the Greek Orthodox Church under the authority of the pope in Rome.

Boniface of Montferrat returned to the crusaders, with Prince Alexius in his party, and news of his very generous offer. The main leaders agreed to the plan, arguing that this diversion was the only way to bring about the crusade's ultimate aims, but it was far from universally popular. Several noblemen, including the French knight Simon of Montfort, withdrew in disgust; when news of the decision reached Rome, Pope Innocent sent letters forbidding an attack on Constantinople.

However, these letters arrived after the main body of the crusade set sail for Constantinople on Easter Monday 1203, too late; in any case, the crusaders had so many reasons to move against the Byzantines that it is doubtful whether or not the letters would have had any effect.

REASONS TO ATTACK THE BYZANTINE EMPIRE

Venice had a longstanding quarrel with the Byzantine emperor, dating back to the 1170s, when Emperor Manuel I Comnenus had arrested Venetian merchants and confiscated their valuable goods. Moreover, the current usurper emperor, Alexius III, was granting preferable trading terms to Venice's rivals, Genoa and Pisa.

Boniface of Montferrat also had a quarrel with the Byzantine Empire. His younger brother Rainier had in 1179 married Maria Comnena, daughter of Emperor Manuel I Comnenus, and had been given the title 'Caesar'. Both Rainier and Maria had then been killed by poison in Constantinople in 1182 and Boniface claimed that Byzantine territory that he believed had been given to Rainier was now rightfully his.

Another important factor, although not one that can have been discussed openly, was that launching the planned attack on Egypt was not in the interests of the Venetians, who had a trading colony in Alexandria; according to some interpretations of contemporary documents, the Venetians may have secretly made a treaty in 1202 with Saladin's brother al-Adil, in power in Egypt, to divert a crusading attack away from Egypt in return for improved trading privileges there.

◀ *Zara surrenders to Venetian control. Venice had twice invaded Zara in the 12th century before the opportunity arose to impose its will on the city.*

▲ *After spurning orders from Pope Alexius III to move on to Jerusalem, the huge Venetian fleet of over 200 ships, attacked the great walls of Constantinople.*

On top of these considerations, relations had been extremely strained between the 'Latins' in the European crusader army and the 'Greeks' of the Byzantine Empire, from the time of the First Crusade.

But probably most pressing of all reasons was that the crusaders in Zara did not manage to raise enough money in looting the city to pay off their debt to the city of Venice. They needed to generate wealth, and the diversion to Constantinople, although officially being launched to restore the deposed emperor, also raised the tantalizing prospect of looting the imperial capital.

ARRIVAL AT CONSTANTINOPLE

The vast crusade fleet, consisting of 60 war galleys as well as 50 large transports and 100 horse transports, arrived at Constantinople on St John the Baptist's Day, 24 June 1203. The ships did not land before the city, but sailed on to capture and install themselves in Chalcedon and Chrysopolis on the other side of the Bosphorus.

There they were visited by an envoy from Emperor Alexius III declaring that he would provide money and supplies if they moved swiftly on towards Jerusalem, but they sent back the reply that they did not recognize his authority and that the lands he ruled belonged to his nephew who was in the crusader camp. Then the crusaders sent young Alexius to the city with ten galleys of soldiers, to ask the

inhabitants of the city, who were arrayed on its walls, whether they would recognize the rule of the deposed Isaac II Angelus and his son. They replied that they did not know these names, and jeered at the soldiers.

On 5 July – to the sound of trumpets, tabors and kettledrums – the full might of the crusader army embarked on to transports to cross the Bosphorus and begin the siege of the city. According to the eyewitness account of a crusader knight from Picardy, named Robert of Clari, the people of Constantinople armed themselves and climbed on the roofs of their houses and up the many towers of the city. They saw the vast fleet. 'It seemed to them,' Robert wrote, 'that the ocean and the land were shaking, and that the wide waves were covered over entirely with ships.'

THE SACK OF CONSTANTINOPLE

RAPE, MURDER AND LOOTING AS CRUSADERS SHAME THE CROSS

The Fourth Crusade's diversion to Constantinople, officially performed to restore the deposed Emperor Isaac II Angelus to the imperial throne, degenerated into a full-scale attack on the city, followed by three lawless days of rampant looting. The greed-driven ransacking of this historic Christian city must rival the savage slaughter of the inhabitants of Jerusalem in 1099 as the nadir of the entire crusading era.

THE FIRST SIEGE OF CONSTANTINOPLE

When the crusaders crossed the Bosphorus to attack Constantinople on 5 July 1203, the usurper emperor Alexius III led his army to the Bosphorus shore to fight, but such was the intimidating might of the crusader and Venetian fleets that the Byzantine troops fled before the crusaders landed. The knights had embarked on their transports already mounted on horseback and now were able to gallop right off the ships, along platforms lowered on to the beach. They chased the terrified Greeks as far as the city walls.

The crusaders settled in for a siege that lasted until 17 July. On that day, they launched a two-pronged attack by land and sea. The Venetians captured the Tower of Galata on the northern side of the Golden Horn, which allowed them to break the protective chain that stretched across the harbour preventing ships sailing in. The fleet then passed easily into the harbour. The aged doge of Venice rode in the foremost Venetian ship, with the city banner of St Mark before him, urging his men on, and then clambered on to land and planted the banner in the soil.

▼ *Piety was nowhere to be found as the crusaders ran amok in the historic city of Constantinople, looting, drinking, raping and wrecking treasures they could not carry.*

RESTORATION OF ISAAC II

The usurper Alexius III fled, with as many jewels and as much imperial treasure as he could take from the treasury. The Greeks of Constantinople then took former emperor Isaac II, blind and bewildered after so many years in prison, and restored him to the throne, hoping to pre-empt any actions by the Venetians. But the invaders needed Alexius to be in power, so he could make good his lavish promises to them. They engineered his election as co-emperor alongside his father. Isaac II and Alexius IV were so crowned on 1 August 1203 in the Church of Hagia Sophia.

With the treasury severely depleted, however, Alexius IV was unable to honour the promises made in Zara. He asked the crusaders to extend their stay for six more months to help him consolidate his position on the throne and to raise money from his subjects.

REVOLT OF ALEXIUS DOUKAS

The crusaders and Venetians agreed reluctantly for they could not afford to leave without Alexius's finance. They camped outside the city, but often ventured into it to seek entertainment, on one occasion starting a fire that raged for an entire week. The people of Constantinople grew restless, and rebelled against their joint emperors in January 1204: Isaac and Alexius barricaded themselves in the palace, sending a courtier named Alexius Doukas or Murtzuphlus to seek help from the crusaders. But Murtzuphlus – who was a popular figure, having taken part in number of skirmishes against the crusaders – seized his opportunity: he deposed the emperors and took the crown for himself, to great popular acclaim. He took power as Alexius V, strangling Alexius IV; the weak and aged Isaac II died in prison a few days later, probably of natural causes.

▲ *Baldwin of Flanders is elected emperor in Constantinople on 16 May, 1204.*

THE SECOND SIEGE OF CONSTANTINOPLE

Now the crusaders and Venetians had no chance of receiving the wealth and military help they had been promised. They determined to take the city by force. The pope declared that Christians could be attacked if they were actively preventing the furtherance of the crusade – and it was possible to argue that the people of Constantinople had done this by deposing the emperor who had promised to help in the holy war.

The besieging army agreed that six Venetians and six crusaders would form an electoral college to elect a new emperor, who would have a quarter of the empire. The other three-quarters would be split between Venice and the crusaders. The crusade's clergymen came up with justifications for the attack, suggesting that the people of Constantinople deserved to be punished for committing the mortal sin of murdering their anointed emperor, and

that in any case they should be forcibly brought into the Roman Catholic Church. They declared, moreover, that knights and soldiers who died in the attack would benefit from the indulgence granted by the pope as if they had carried the crusade to its conclusion.

THE CITY IS SACKED

The Venetians and crusaders embarked on a second siege of Constantinople on 6 April and took the city just seven days later, on 13 April. Emperor Alexius V fled; the crusader leaders and the doge of Venice installed themselves in his abandoned palace. The army was allowed three days of looting.

They went on the rampage, committing murder and rape, stealing indiscriminately, ransacking churches, destroying ancient objects of art, and taking sacred relics. Drunken soldiers were joined in the looting by knights, noblemen, priests and bishops. According to Geoffrey of Villehardouin, more booty was seized in the sacking of Constantinople than ever before in the entire history of the world.

THE LATIN EMPIRE OF CONSTANTINOPLE

In the aftermath, the papal legate absolved the crusaders of their vow to carry the expedition on to the Holy Land. The crusaders and Venetians set about creating a new government in Constantinople. Count Baldwin of Flanders was elected emperor and crowned in the Church of Hagia Sophia on 16 May 1204 by the papal legate. Baldwin declared himself a vassal of the Pope, and received the recognition of Rome. Thomas Morosini, a priest from Venice, was appointed the first Latin Patriarch of Constantinople. European-style feudalism was introduced, with 600 knights being granted fiefdoms.

Boniface of Montferrat had probably expected to be elected emperor himself, but he had to make do with a kingdom formed from Byzantine territory and based on Salonica (modern Thessaloniki). The doge stayed on in Constantinople overseeing Venetian interests. He died there in 1205, aged 97, and was buried in the Church of Hagia Sophia.

▼ *The bronze horses seized from the Hippodrome were sent back to Venice and erected in St Mark's Square. They are visible within the cupola of this plan.*

A NEW VIEW OF CRUSADING

CRUSADING REFORMS AND INNOVATIONS OF POPE INNOCENT III

Pope Innocent III, who reigned for 18 years from 1198 to 1216, established crusading on a new footing. He preached two holy wars in the East and proclaimed crusades against pagan Europeans, heretic Christians and political enemies as well against Muslims. In every single year of his rule, a crusade was being fought somewhere in the world, officially in his name.

PAPAL POWER

Educated in Rome, Paris and Bologna, Lothar dei Conti di Segni was elected Pope Innocent III at the age of just 37 on 8 January 1198. He had a brilliant mind, a rare gift for canon law, and a powerful desire to build on the Church reforms of Pope Gregory VII and establish the papacy as the pre-eminent religious and political force. Almost at once he set about promoting a crusade to the Holy Land. He also began negotiations with the Byzantine emperor to unite the Eastern and Western churches under papal control in Rome.

This plan was ruined when in 1202–04 the Fourth Crusade spiralled out of his control, with the army effectively serving the aged doge of Venice and diverting to Zara in Hungary and then to an attack on

▲ *Pope Innocent III, like his predecessors, proclaimed various crusades, but uniquely he sanctioned military campaigns against non-Muslim powers and heretic Christians.*

▼ *In 1209 Innocent III gave St Francis of Assisi permission to found a religious order. Francis was loyal to church and clergy and Innocent may have wanted to utilize his itinerant monks to counter heresy.*

Constantinople, but Innocent remained absolutely committed to crusading as a weapon of papal policy, both nearer to Rome as well as in the Holy Land. He declared a series of crusades in Europe, to extend the power of the papacy in political and territorial disputes, in struggles against heretics within the Church, in wars against pagan Europeans and in the continuing fight against Muslims in Spain.

Already in 1199 he had declared a crusade against Markward of Anweiler, a follower of the recently deceased Holy Roman Emperor Henry VI, who had come into direct conflict with papal policy in southern Italy and Sicily: Innocent declared Markward 'another Saladin', an enemy of Christianity who was attempting to undermine the Fourth Crusade; he promised those who fought Markward the same indulgences available to those who travelled to the Holy Land.

In 1204 Innocent launched a crusade against pagans in the Baltic region of northern Europe: in a letter to the archbishop of Bremen he offered the same indulgence available for a Holy Land crusade to those who attempted to convert Baltic pagans by force. Then, in 1208, he called a crusade against the Albigensians, a group of heretical Christians in southern France, and again promised those who fought in his service the same indulgences available for a Holy Land crusade. In this case, the indulgence would be granted in return for just 40 days of military service.

In 1212 he proclaimed a crusade in Spain against the Muslim Almohad caliphs, and that year crusader knights and infantrymen from southern France and Spain, fighting alongside the armies of Sancho VII of Navarre, Peter II of Aragon and Alfonso VIII of Castile, won a resounding victory over a Muslim army at the Battle of Las Navas de Tolosa. This was a crucial Christian victory in the centuries-long struggle against Muslims in Spain.

The following year, in 1213, Innocent began to organize the Fifth Crusade to the Holy Land and he died in 1216, while preaching the crusade in Perugia. In addition to promoting crusading in so many guises, Innocent also made a number of changes and clarifications in the financing and organization of these holy wars.

CRUSADING TAXES

Seeing that the cost of crusading put off many potential holy warriors/soldiers of Christ, Innocent set out to establish a secure financial basis for the crusading movement. In promoting the Fourth Crusade in 1199 he imposed a tax on clerical incomes – one-fortieth of their annual revenue for one year – to raise money for the expedition. He said that this would not set a precedent, but in fact it did – and clerical taxes were subsequently imposed in 1215 for the Fifth Crusade (one-twentieth of revenue for three years), in 1245, after Jerusalem had fallen to the Khwarismian Turks (another tax of one-twentieth for three years), and again in 1263 and 1274.

Innocent made a major innovation in 1213, while promoting the Fifth Crusade, when he ruled that crusade vows could be redeemed by payment of money. This meant that those Christians who could not take the cross because of age, infirmity, physical weakness or lack of equipment could pay for others to go on their behalf – and have a part in the spiritual benefit of the crusade without leaving home.

Innocent also sought to improve the arrangements for the promotion of crusades, introducing new procedures and appointments for preaching the cross. For the Fourth Crusade, he despatched Cistercian monks to give crusade sermons, while for the Fifth Crusade he sent out a group of trained reformers to promote the expedition. Innocent even set out to boost attendance at crusade sermons by offering a 'partial indulgence' (the cancellation of part of a penance due) simply for listening to a preacher's attempts to convince people to take the cross.

CRUSADER PRIVILEGES

Pope Innocent also codified and clarified the privileges available to crusaders, notably in the appendix *Ad liberandum* to the decrees of the Fourth Lateran Council of 1215. The most important was the indulgence. Previous indulgences had been given on the understanding that – by the pope's authority – God would view the crusade's sufferings on crusade as 'satisfactory', meaning that they cancelled debts due for previous sins. This sparked debate among canon lawyers as to whether any penance could be satisfactory in this way. Under Innocent III, the indulgence guaranteed a crusader that all punishment for previous sins would be remitted (both in this world and the next) whether or not as a penance it proved to be satisfactory in God's eyes; the guarantee was given on God's behalf by the pope. Other notable privileges included: a crusader's property

and dependents would be protected by the Church; a crusader would be freed of the obligation to settle debts or pay interest on them while away on crusade; he would also be exempted from feudal service, taxes and tolls for the duration of the crusade; a crusader would have the right to hospitality from the Church while on crusade; anyone who had been excommunicated would be freed from his punishment by taking the cross, and while on crusade could interact with excommunicated Christians without fear of punishment; and a crusader could take a crusade vow in place of another vow or instead of returning stolen goods.

▼ *Innocent sent a monk named Dominic to dispute with the Albigensians. In a trial by fire, Dominic's books were miraculously saved from the flames while others burned. But Dominic could not persuade them.*

THE CHILDREN'S CRUSADES

SPONTANEOUS OUTBURSTS OF ENTHUSIASM FOR HOLY WAR

According to chronicle accounts, in 1212 thousands of poor children were inspired by charismatic preachers to leave their homes in France and Germany to travel to Jerusalem on crusade and save the holy places there. This was not a holy war: none of these crusaders envisaged using force, for they believed that through faith the power of God would be enough to achieve their purpose.

FROM FRANCE AND GERMANY

There were two waves to the Children's Crusade, one issuing from northern France and one beginning in Germany. The story goes that in May 1212 a shepherd boy named Stephen from Cloyes-sur-le-Loir (near Châteaudun in the Vermandois) walked to see King Philip at Saint-Denis and reported that he had had a vision of Christ instructing him to lead a crusade to Jerusalem. Philip attempted to send the boy home, but Stephen embarked on a preaching tour of the countryside and gathered many followers among the youth and children of the area.

▼ *Christ Pantocrator (Ruler of all). Both German and French Children's Crusades were called in His name.*

He promised them that because Christ had called the crusade, He would supply food and water on the march and bring them safely to the Holy Land, and that if they followed Stephen to the south of France they would find that Christ would part the waters of the Mediterranean to enable them to walk all the way.

Around the same time, a German youth named Nicholas of Cologne mobilized a similar pilgrim army in the Rhineland. He called for the liberation of the Holy Sepulchre and, like Stephen, promised that the seas would be parted by God as they made their way to the Holy Land, demonstrating their faith by trusting in His deliverance. Stephen's followers were mainly children and youths, although there were also adults and priests in the company. People of both sexes joined up – according to the contemporary Annals of Marbach, as the crusaders marched through the countryside young people simply downed tools in the fields or abandoned the flocks they were minding and joined the march.

THE FRENCH MARCH SOUTH

The French group headed southwards towards the Mediterranean coast under Stephen's leadership. The group contained principally children and young people, mostly under the age of 15, both from very poor and more prosperous backgrounds; there were also a few priests and other adults in Stephen's following. Many died of exhaustion, illness or starvation on the way, and others simply drifted away, but when they reached Marseilles they were still as many as 30,000 in number.

The waters did not part as promised. Some pilgrims became disillusioned and wandered off, but many waited on, believing that God would still deliver them. Finally two merchants from the city, named Hugh Ferreus (Iron Hugh) and William Porcus (Pig William), offered to

▲ *Following in the footsteps of the Tafurs (the pious peasants who accompanied the First Crusade) the participants in the Children's Crusades are said to have believed that their faith would be enough to bring success.*

carry them by ship to the Holy Land and Stephen embarked with the still sizeable remnant of his following in seven ships. They were never seen again in France, but later reports (supposedly based on an eyewitness account by a survivor of the expedition) revealed that after two ships were lost in a storm near Sardinia the other merchants sailed to Bougie and Alexandria in northern Africa, where they sold the surviving children into slavery among the Saracens.

THE GERMAN CHILDREN'S CRUSADE

Meanwhile, the German contingent made its way across the Alps into northern Italy and proceeded to Genoa. Some participants settled in Genoa, others went on to Pisa and some made it all the way to Rome, where they had an audience with Innocent III. Innocent told them to return home, but to that they should preserve

pueri (Latin for 'boys') in some accounts, and this was misinterpreted by later chroniclers as a movement of children when in fact it was a migration of adults. Moreover, the largely secular movements of the poor seeking food and work were cast as pilgrimages, and even crusades, under the influence of the thriving popular cult of the Innocents. These were the children who were slaughtered, according to the Gospel of St Matthew, on the orders of King Herod, in response to a prophecy that a newborn 'King of the Jews' was destined to seize his throne. The Innocents were celebrated as the first Christian martyrs as part of a celebration of poverty and simple piety, which was also fed by memories of the poor but ferociously pious Tafurs of the First Crusade, and it may be that in the light of this cult the mass migrations of country poor were reimagined as a crusade of the Innocents.

▲ *Philip II travelled on the Third Crusade but afterwards was not interested in crusading. He did not help Innocent III in his holy war against Albigensians in southern France.*

their enthusiasm for crusading and put it to use in adulthood. From Pisa, two shiploads of German children embarked but were never heard of again.

A POPULAR LEGEND?

Some modern historians suggest that these accounts may be largely popular legends based on memories of the mass movement of country poor in the early 13th century. According to this theory, the poor forced into wandering by poverty were called

THE PIED PIPER OF HAMELIN

According to some historians, the German folktale of the Pied Piper of Hamelin has its origins in the events of the Children's Crusade. In the folktale, the people of the German town of Hamelin were plagued by rats, and accepted the offer of a vagrant in colourful clothes that he would clear the town of vermin for a fixed sum; he played a marvellous tune on his pipe and the rats followed him out of the town to the river, where they drowned. The people of Hamelin then refused to pay up the agreed fee, and so the piper returned when the folk were all in church and, playing his pipe once more, led all the town's children away. They were never seen again. The first known appearance of the piper of Hamelin is in a church window in Hamelin dated to *c.*1300, but this window – now destroyed – simply showed the piper leading away several children dressed in white; the rats were not added to the story until the late 1500s. Another theory is that the folktale is based on memories of the 13th-century migration of people to settle in eastern Europe.

▼ *The Pied Piper leads the children of the village of Hamelin on their merry dance of no return. Was he based on a folk memory of the preachers who led off the young on the Children's Crusades?*

THE FIFTH CRUSADE
CRUSADERS HUMILIATED IN EGYPT

In April 1213 Innocent III proclaimed another crusade to the Holy Land in the papal bull *Quia major*. The pope was determined to bring about the recovery of the Holy Sepulchre in Jerusalem as a symbol of papal supremacy throughout Christendom. In the event, the crusade fleet sailed to Egypt, where after taking the port of Damietta they marched to a humiliating defeat at the hands of Saladin's nephew, Sultan al-Kamil.

The crusade was promoted enthusiastically by travelling preachers, and regular processions. Innocent made the call again at the fourth Lateran Council of 1215; the departure date for the new crusade was set for 1217. Innocent died in May 1216, and his successor Pope Honorius III took over the organization of the expedition.

THE FIRST WAVE OF CRUSADERS
The first armies to depart were led by Duke Leopold VI of Austria and King Andrew II of Hungary, in 1217. They sailed to Acre, and mobilized with John of Brienne, King of Jerusalem, Prince Bohemond IV of Antioch and King Hugh I of Cyprus to fight Ayyubid descendants of Saladin in Syria – principally the great general's brother al-Adil, who had succeeded him as sultan. Very little was achieved on this expedition, although a number of sacred relics were captured. In January 1218 King Andrew headed home by way of Constantinople.

THE SIEGE OF DAMIETTA
In 1218 a contingent of German crusaders arrived in Acre. Now the target was switched to Ayyubid possessions in Egypt. In May 1218 German troops under the command of John of Brienne sailed to Egypt and besieged the port of Damietta. Their plan was to take this city as a supply base before moving on to attack Cairo.

On 25 August they captured the tower just outside Damietta, but did not push

▲ *Francis of Assisi attempts to convince al-Kamil of the merits of Christianity during the meeting he was granted with the sultan.*

on and take the city itself, preferring to wait for reinforcements – for news had reached them that a French and English army was sailing from Genoa while the Spanish cardinal Pelagius of Albano had embarked from Brindisi.

Pelagius arrived in mid-September, but struggled to impose his authority, for he was not a military man and the assembled army looked to John of Brienne as its leader. German soldiers also had another claim on their loyalty: they were expecting the arrival of Frederick II, who had taken the cross as early as 1215, but had since focused his energies on consolidating his position in Germany and Italy.

In October the English and French arrived: still the crusaders, hampered by lack of leadership and a badly organized siege, did not take the city. Their camp was flooded following storms in November and December and hit by an epidemic in which as many as 10 per cent of their number died – including English cardinal Robert of Courçon, one of the principal crusade preachers.

OFFER OF PEACE
By this time, al-Adil had died and his son al-Kamil had taken his position as sultan. In spring 1219, judging it inevitable that the crusaders would take Damietta, Sultan al-Kamil made overtures of peace – if the crusaders agreed to lift the siege of Damietta and leave Egypt, he promised to give them possession of Jerusalem, and the entire Kingdom as it had been before the Battle of the Horns of Hattin, and also to return the relic of the True Cross – which had been in Muslim hands ever since that battle. All he wanted to retain was the fortresses of Oultrejordain and the territory they controlled, so that the two main parts of his empire, Egypt and Syria, could maintain contact – for this territory he would pay tribute of 30,000 bezants. In the Holy Land, al-Kamil's brother al-Mu'azzam, the ruler of Syria, dismantled the fortifications of Jerusalem so that the Christians would not be able to defend it.

King John of Jerusalem and the barons of his kingdom urged acceptance. So did the crusader knights of Germany, France and England, for it seemed to them that the offer delivered the prize for which the crusade had been mobilized. But Pelagius made the judgement that the Holy City could not be bartered for and that the Christian army should not negotiate with the infidel. He had the support of the knights of the military orders, who were unhappy at the proposed loss of their treasured castles of Krak and Montreal in Oultrejordain, and of the Italians, who were determined to capture Damietta in order to establish a trading position there.

A SAINTLY VISITOR
The siege continued. In August or September, the saintly monk Francis of Assisi arrived in order to argue for nonviolence. He had an audience with al-Kamil and so impressed the sultan that he was allowed to preach to his subjects.

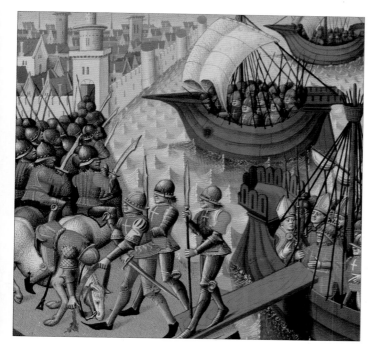

A STRONG POSITION LOST

Finally in November 1219 the crusaders captured Damietta and, true to form, sacked and looted the city. Had they marched swiftly south against Cairo they would probably have ended the rule of Sultan al-Kamil and made Egypt a Christian country. Instead they became embroiled in a quarrel over who had the right to claim Damietta, with John of Brienne declaring the town to be his possession and legate Pelagius claiming it on behalf of Rome.

The army was still expecting the imminent arrival of Emperor Frederick II, and for no less than 20 months the crusaders sat in Damietta. From Rome came official confirmation of Pelagius as commander-in-chief of the crusading army. John of Brienne returned to Acre.

In June 1221 Sultan al-Kamil made a fresh peace offer, on largely the same terms as before. Again Pelagius refused. Finally in July, Emperor Frederick's advance party arrived under the command of Duke

▲ *Crusader troops land prior to launching an assault on the port of Damietta.*

Louis I of Bavaria – the emperor himself sent orders to await his arrival. John of Brienne returned from Acre. But then, after more than 18 months of indecision

and waiting, Pelagius and the crusade leaders suddenly became decisive – and ordered a march up the river Nile towards Cairo, with the idea of making the manoeuvre before the beginning of the river's annual floods.

DEFEAT IN THE MUD

The sultan brought his troops out to meet the crusade army and the advance was stalled. Then the river began to rise and the crusaders became cut off from their supply ships by Egyptian vessels.

Pelagius saw that the campaign had gone badly wrong and ordered a retreat, but Sultan al-Kamil destroyed flood control barriers and the waters swept in, stranding the crusader troops in the thick Nile mud. When Al-Kamil launched a night attack, the crusade army suffered very heavy losses and Pelagius had to negotiate a humiliating peace treaty under which the crusaders evacuated Damietta, agreed an eight-year truce and left Egypt. All they had in return was a promise that the piece of the True Cross would be handed over – but when it came to it, the Muslims could not find this most sacred of Christian relics.

▼ *The crusaders suffered a heavy defeat as they tried to retreat following their ill-judged advance up the river Nile.*

JERUSALEM REGAINED

THE SIXTH CRUSADE OF 1228–29

The Sixth Crusade was led by Holy Roman Emperor Frederick II. Without even engaging the army of Ayyubid sultan al-Kamil in battle, he negotiated the return of Jerusalem (as well as Nazareth, Jaffa, Sidon and Bethlehem) to Christian control, although under the terms of the agreement the Temple Mount area of Jerusalem, which includes the Dome of the Rock and the al-Aqsa mosque, was to remain in Muslim hands.

KING OF GERMANY TAKES THE CROSS

Frederick II was crowned King of Germany in 1215, and in that year first took the cross as a young man of just 19 in response to the April 1213 call to arms made by Pope Innocent III. As we have seen, he was repeatedly said to be preparing to embark to take part in the disastrous Fifth Crusade to Egypt, and even sent an advance party of his force in 1221. It is probable that had he gone in

▼ *Frederick II Stupor Mundi – 'the wonder of the world' – was his own master and kept the Sixth Crusade free of papal control.*

person to Egypt he would have been able to oust the papal prelate Pelagius from control of the army and under more effective leadership the crusaders might have taken Cairo and defeated Sultan al-Kamil – and the crusade would have ended in triumph rather than disaster. However, he was embroiled in consolidating his position in Germany and Italy and did not go.

HOLY ROMAN EMPEROR – AND KING OF JERUSALEM

In 1220, before the end of the Fifth Crusade, Frederick was crowned Holy Roman Emperor by Pope Honorius III on 22 November 1220. At this point he renewed his promise to go on crusade, but it was to be 1228 before he finally arrived in the Holy Land.

By the time he did so he was notionally king of Jerusalem, for in 1225 he had married Isabella (or Yolande), Queen of Jerusalem. Isabella was the daughter of Maria of Montferrat, the previous Queen of Jerusalem, and of King John of Brienne, who had ruled as King of Jerusalem on account of his marriage to Maria. Isabella had become Queen of Jerusalem as an infant on the death of her mother in 1212. In 1225 Frederick married her in a magnificent ceremony at Brindisi Cathedral, then despatched a message to John of Brienne, who was already in his late 70s, that as a result of the marriage the Holy Roman Emperor was now also King of Jerusalem.

STUPOR MUNDI

The grandson of Frederick I Barbarossa, Frederick II was an extraordinary figure, known to his contemporaries as *Stupor Mundi*, 'Wonder of the World'. He was fluent in six languages – German, Italian, French, Greek, Latin and Arabic; he was a mathematician and philosopher and a great patron of the arts. He was worldly, ferociously intelligent and scathing of

▲ *Frederick was twice crowned king, in 1212 and 1215, before he was crowned Holy Roman Emperor in Rome in 1220.*

religion – he reportedly declared that 'Moses, Christ and Muhammad were all imposters' and intimated that the pope had been found on a dunghill. At Palermo he kept a harem in the style of Oriental rulers – and to this he despatched his young bride immediately after the wedding. This was not a man who could easily be forced to become a papal agent.

CONFLICT WITH THE PAPACY

A key reason for Frederick's repeated delaying of his crusade was that he was embroiled in a long-running struggle with Rome, both over lands in Italy and over the centuries-old issue of whether pope or Holy Roman emperor was the rightful leader of Christendom. When he first took the cross in 1215, the then pope, Innocent III, wanted to stop him going – he was determined to maintain control of the crusade and wanted to avoid the involvement of so powerful and independent a man as Frederick. Subsequent popes, however, were willing to countenance his involvement in the holy war as they believed he would bring success. Moreover, when he finally departed for the Holy Land the territories in Italy would be left unprotected.

Frederick embarked for the Holy Land in 1227, but an epidemic struck his fleet and he himself was laid low with fever, so

▲ *Gregory IX was nephew to Pope Innocent III and also attempted to maintain a strong papal authority. Frederick defied him.*

the crusaders returned to Italy. The new pope, Gregory IX, excommunicated him for breaking his crusader vows.

AN ALLIANCE WITH EGYPT

In Italy, Frederick received a diplomatic mission at Palermo from Sultan al-Kamil seeking military help against his own brother, al-Mu'azzam, and offering Jerusalem as a reward. This played right into Frederick's hands – all along he had wanted to lead a crusade on his own terms, not as an instrument of papal power but as emperor, secular ruler of Christendom. Despite the excommunication, which technically meant that he could not lead a crusade, he finally embarked. Pope Gregory issued a ringing condemnation of the emperor's actions.

He sailed via Cyprus, where he quarrelled with the regent John of Ibelin, lord of Beirut and Arsuf. Frederick imposed rule in his name by a group of five local knights (*baillis*) and then sailed for Acre, the capital of the Kingdom of Jerusalem.

SUCCESS IN THE HOLY LAND

On arrival, Frederick did not receive undivided support: he had alienated the important Ibelin group, and the Church hierarchy led by Patriarch Gerald of Lausanne followed the leadership of the

pope by being hostile. His only supporters were the barons of the Kingdom, the Teutonic knights and the German army.

Sultan al-Kamil in fact no longer needed Frederick's support, for al-Mu'azzam had died. But after Frederick made a show of force by marching down the Mediterranean coast from Acre to Jaffa with a crusader army of around 3,000, al-Kamil agreed to honour the proposed deal and Jerusalem was returned to Latin control in a treaty signed on 18 February 1229. The treaty also established a ten-year truce and guaranteed Muslims free access to Jerusalem to visit their shrines on the Temple Mount; as well as Nazareth and Bethlehem, the Christians received a corridor of land linking Jerusalem to Acre.

TRIUMPH IN JERUSALEM

Frederick marched into Jerusalem on 17 March 1229. He took part in a crowning of sorts the following day, and proclaimed himself Lord of Jerusalem. It was not a formal coronation because the Patriarch was still opposed to these events, and had remained in Acre – in fact, Frederick lifted the crown on to his own head and, according to some, used the imperial crown, not that of Jerusalem.

The treaty was generally highly unpopular on both sides. The Muslims felt cheated by their sultan – the imams in

Egypt and Damascus proclaimed a period of public mourning because Islam had been betrayed. The Christian knights felt that the treaty was far less favourable than the terms offered and turned down at Damietta. Moreover, as Pelagius and their predecessors had argued, they felt that the Kingdom of Jerusalem should have been won back by the sword and not through negotiation. The Latin settlers argued that the narrow corridor of land between Acre and Jerusalem was impracticable since it could not be adequately defended. In spite of this dissent, the fact remains that Frederick had achieved the crusade's ultimate aim by putting the Holy City back in Christian hands.

Frederick left Jerusalem in May and returned to Italy. He had to drive out papal troops commanded by John of Brienne, which had invaded his Italian territories. Later in the year the pope, humbled by defeat in battle, lifted the excommunication. But the struggle between pope and emperor was far from over – and a decade later, Frederick not only found himself excommunicated a second time, but also had a crusade declared against his territorial holdings in Italy.

▼ *At Frederick's coronation (1229) as King of Jerusalem, he is said to have placed the crown on his own head.*

KINGDOM OF JERUSALEM REBUILT
BUT RACKED BY BITTER DISPUTES

The success of the Sixth Crusade was part of a short-lived re-establishment of the crusader states of Outremer during the first half of the 13th century. Although the Christians who lived in the restored kingdom were bitterly at odds, for a short while the Kingdom appeared to have a brighter future. But in 1244 control of Jerusalem was lost once more and after this it would not be in European hands again until 1917.

CHRISTIAN DISPUTES

Almost as soon as Frederick had returned to Europe after regaining Jerusalem, in 1229, John of Ibelin overthrew imperial rule in Cyprus and assumed control himself. Frederick for his part was embroiled in fighting papal forces in Italy, and John of Ibelin established himself as the effective king of both Cyprus and Jerusalem.

In 1230 Frederick attempted to deal with this challenge to his authority, sending an army east under the command of Riccardo Filanghieri, Marshal of the Empire, but John defeated the imperial army at the Battle of Agridi in Cyprus on 15 June 1232. In Acre, moreover, the local barons sided with John against Frederick: they formed a commune and elected John their mayor. Nevertheless, Filanghieri established himself in Tyre and in Jerusalem itself.

The conflict continued after Henry of Lusignan came of age as Henry I of Cyprus; in 1234 Pope Gregory IX excommunicated John of Ibelin. John was then killed when his horse fell on him during a campaign against Muslim forces in 1236.

CRUSADE OF 1239–41

A further European crusade, not usually given a number, was called by Theobald I of Navarre (also known as Count Theobald IV of Champagne) and Richard, Earl of Cornwall. In 1239 possession of a large region of Palestine, including

▲ *During the fight for Jerusalem the sanction of the Church was at first seen as a vital component of the struggle.*

Jerusalem, came under dispute once more on the expiry of Frederick II's treaty with Sultan al-Kamil; embarking in that year, Theobald recaptured Ascalon, Beaufort and Safed, but suffered a major defeat by an Egyptian army at Gaza in November 1239 and returned to Europe in 1240 before the arrival from England of Prince Richard, Earl of Cornwall, the younger brother of Henry III of England.

The crusade of 1239–40 was a relatively minor event in the life of Theobald, who is remembered as one of the greatest

of aristocratic troubadours and wrote no fewer than 60 surviving lyrics. He was rumoured to have fallen passionately in love with the formidable Blanche of Castile (mother of 'Saint Louis', King Louis IX), and to have poisoned her husband, King Louis VIII; many of his poems are believed to be addressed to Blanche.

When Richard, Earl of Cornwall, arrived in Acre with a fine company of English knights he was welcomed by the Knights Hospitaller and stayed in their accommodation in the city. He then moved on to Jaffa and proposed to its population that they accompany him to Ascalon and help him refortify that place. This they did, and after Richard had rebuilt the defences and arranged for a garrison, he handed over control to the emperor's representative and returned to England. Also during his stay in the Holy Land, Richard negotiated the release of 33 noblemen, 50 knights and many lower-ranking Christian prisoners captured during Theobald's defeat at Gaza; he collected the unburied remains of many killed in the battle and had them buried in the cemetery at Ascalon. He finalized a treaty initially negotiated by Theobald

▼ *At Sidon the crusaders built a sea castle in the 13th century on a small island connected to the mainland by a bridge.*

▲ *This 15th-century illustration shows Christians fighting to retake Jerusalem with bowmen and siege towers to the fore.*

with Sultan as-Salih Ayyub of Egypt that settled wider borders for the Kingdom of Jerusalem than any since 1187.

The Kingdom of Jerusalem appeared to be thriving and have a sustainable future. The ports of Tyre and Acre were very rich, and the Kingdom was also less isolated than previously: Cyprus and the Kingdom of Armenia in Cilicia were Christian neighbours, offering a degree of security – Armenia had even accepted Latin Christianity and religious rule from Rome. But the Latin Christians were too badly split to take advantage of this opportunity: Tyre and Acre, for all their prosperity, existed in a state of open competition that was akin to warfare, while the Templars and Hospitallers even came to blows. In 1244 this future was swept away by the

invasion of Khwarismian Turks, who seized Jerusalem in August that year, and by a cataclysmic defeat of the Kingdom's army by the troops of Egypt at the Battle of La Forbie near Gaza.

THE BATTLE OF LA FORBIE

The sacking of Jerusalem was savage and brutal. Only 300 Christians escaped to tell the story of how the Turks swept into the city, looting and burning the churches. Christians of the crusader states reacted to the loss of Jerusalem in August by making an alliance with al-Mansur of Damascus against Sultan as-Salih Ayyub of Egypt.

An allied Christian–Syrian army drew up at La Forbie commanded by al-Mansur and Walter of Brienne, Count of Jaffa and Ascalon, against a joint force of Khwarismian Turks and Egyptians commanded by a young Turkish soldier named Rukn al-Zahir Baybars (who shortly afterwards would overthrow Sultan

as-Salih Ayyub and found the Mamluk sultanate of Egypt). The battle was launched by Templar charges on 17 October and fought all through that day and the next.

The Christian–Syrian defeat was absolutely crushing: al-Mansur had just 280 survivors out of more than 2,000 cavalry and many more infantry; the Christian knights were virtually wiped out, with only 33 Templars, 27 Hospitallers and three Teutonic knights surviving the slaughter. Among the dead was Armand of Perigord, Grand Master of the Knights Templar. His Hospitaller counterpart, William of Chatelneuf, was captured.

La Forbie was the most severe and significant defeat for the Latin Christians in the Holy Land since the Battle of the Horns of Hattin. Baybars rose to power as the first of the Mamluk sultans of Egypt in 1260 and swiftly drove the Kingdom of Jerusalem almost to extinction, reducing it to a tiny strip of coastal territory.

CHAPTER NINE

CRUSADES OF THE MID-13TH TO 15TH CENTURIES

For the most part, the news of the fall of Jerusalem to the Khwarismian Turks and the devastating defeat of the armies of Outremer and Damascus at the Battle of La Forbie had little effect in Europe, but it did provoke one very powerful man to plan a military response. In December 1244. Louis IX of France was revered by contemporaries as the embodiment of Christian chivalry, the perfect Christian ruler. He was fiercely devout, a great leader, respected by knights and men-at-arms – but even he could not bring success to the crusading cause. In fact, he led two crusades, the Seventh of 1248–54, and the Eighth of 1270. The Seventh Crusade, to Egypt, ended with a humiliating surrender. The Eighth Crusade, in Tunisia, ended in his death and the abandonment of the enterprise with only a trade treaty with the city of Tunis to show for it. The year after Louis's death saw the expedition traditionally regarded as the Ninth and last Crusade, led by Prince Edward (the future King Edward I of England). This enterprise brought about a ten-year peace treaty between Christians and Muslims in the Holy Land, but it was followed through the 14th and even 15th centuries by further crusading expeditions despatched from Europe to counter the power of the Mamluk sultanate of Egypt and then later of the Ottoman Turks.

▲ *Rukn al-Zahir Baybars destroys a Christian-Syrian army at the devastating Battle of La Forbie near Gaza in 1244.*

◄ *After four years' preparation, Louis IX of France embarked on the Seventh Crusade in 1248, heading to Cyprus and then to Egypt.*

CRUSADE IN EGYPT
KING LOUIS IX CALLS THE SEVENTH CRUSADE

King Louis IX declared his intention to lead a crusade to the East in 1245. But he certainly did not rush to war, for he spent no less than four years recruiting and preparing, raising money and even building a special port at the sleepy village of Aigues-Mortes in southern France, before he finally embarked in 1248.

Louis imposed a swingeing tax on the French Church, demanding one-tenth of ecclesiastical revenues for five years, raising 950,000 livres tournois. (The livre tournois, or 'pound of Tours', was one of a number of currencies used in France in Louis's time.) He demanded municipal grants from the towns of his royal domain, raising another 275,000 livres tournois. In all, he raised around 1.5 million livres tournois – a sum so vast that he campaigned in the East for four years before he needed to borrow more money.

FRENCH LORDS

Louis's recruitment campaign resulted in many of France's great lords taking the cross, including: Peter of Vendôme; Hugh X of Lusignan (Count of La Marche); John of Montfort; and Louis's brothers Alphonse of Poitou, Robert of Artois and Charles of Anjou. Many of these great lords' feudal dependants and blood relatives also joined the crusade. Another notable participant who joined the crusade in France was John, lord of Joinville in Champagne, who later wrote a life of King Louis that is a major source for our knowledge of the Seventh Crusade.

The army that finally embarked from southern France in 1248 numbered around 15,000 and included some 2,500 knights as well as 5,000-odd crossbowmen. As many as half of those who travelled received loans or agreed contracts

▲ *The holy warrior-king, as seen by his enemies. This image of Louis IX on horseback is from a 13th-century Egyptian or Syrian brass medallion inlaid with silver.*

from Louis, meaning that they were effectively subsidized by the king. Practical arrangements included the advance purchase of supplies and equipment, and the contracting of 36 ships from Marseilles and Genoa to carry the army.

DEPARTURE

The French crusade army left from Marseilles and from the specially built port and arsenal at the Aigues-Mortes on 25 August 1248 and sailed initially to Cyprus. They landed at Limassol on 17 September, and there united by prior arrangement with various other crusade participants, including Scottish and Italian forces, around 200 English knights led by William, Earl of Salisbury, and barons from Outremer led by Guillaume of Sonnac, Grand Master of the Knights Templar. The crusade leaders agreed that their first target should be Muslim Egypt: the plan was to defeat the sultan's army there before moving against Syria.

◀ *Louis IX of France embarks at Aigues-Mortes on the 7th Crusade. This depiction is from a mid-16th century stained-glass window in Champigny-sur-Veude, France.*

▲ *Encamped before Damietta in June 1249, Louis and his barons pray for the triumphant ending they envisaged for their painstakingly planned enterprise.*

DAMIETTA

Having overwintered on Cyprus, they embarked for Egypt on 14 May 1249. The fleet, which by now numbered as many as a hundred ships, was scattered by a storm, but the royal ships held together and arrived off the beaches near the target of Damietta (modern Damyut) in early June. They saw an Egyptian Muslim army drawn up on land. Disregarding the advice of senior campaigners to wait for reinforcements, Louis led an immediate assault that drove back the Muslim force in the course of a fierce battle on 5 June.

The Muslims retreated along a pontoon bridge of boats to Damietta and that night, in a panic, the Damietta garrison of Bedouin troops and the town's Muslim population fled. The following day, having been alerted to this development by Christians in Damietta, the French army marched in triumph, unopposed across the bridge of boats, into the port.

▶ *This 17th-century Ottoman map shows Muslim power bases around the Mediterranean as well as the movements and origins of crusaders, marking Jerusalem with an image of Christ.*

JOHN, LORD OF JOINVILLE, AND FRIEND OF LOUIS IX

John came from a family of lesser nobles from the Champagne region of France who, nevertheless, had a proud history of crusading – and is a good example of the way taking the cross became a tradition in certain families. John's grandfather, Geoffrey of Joinville, had travelled on the Third Crusade and was killed during the siege of Acre in 1189; John's father, Simon, had crusaded against the Cathars in southern France and fought on the Fifth Crusade, taking part in the capture of Damietta; he also had two uncles who had gone on crusade. John himself took the cross in 1244. In the catastrophic defeat that ended the Seventh Crusade he was later captured with King Louis and travelled with him to Acre, where he became friends with the king before returning in the royal party to France in 1254. He served as seneschal of Champagne, and lived both at the royal court and in Joinville. In 1270 he refused to take part in the ill-fated Eighth Crusade (on which Louis died): before Louis departed, John told him the enterprise was folly. He began writing his life of

▲ *This statue of Louis IX is believed to be true to life. The king was canonized in 1297, just 27 years after his death. He is revered as the perfect Christian king.*

King Louis in the 1270s, but did not complete it until 1309, when it was presented to Louis X. By this time, Louis IX had been canonized and the work was called the *Histoire de Saint-Louis* (The Story of St Louis).

A KING'S RANSOM

THE CRUSADE FAILS AND KING LOUIS IS CAPTURED

After the capture of Damietta on 6 June 1249 the sultan of Egypt, al-Salih Ayyub, offered to swap possession of the town for the Holy City of Jerusalem, as his predecessor al-Kamil had in 1219 and 1221. But Louis rejected the offer, as Pelagius had done before, on the grounds that possession of Jerusalem could not be bartered for. Louis knew, also, that al-Salih Ayyub was seriously ill with tuberculosis and that Egyptian morale was very low. He no doubt believed that with God's help the French army was poised to take complete control of Egypt as a precursor to defeating Muslim Syria and winning Jerusalem.

Initially Louis sat tight in Damietta. It was the start of the season for the flooding of the River Nile, and the king had learned the lessons of the Fifth Crusade when papal legate Pelagius and John of Brienne had been trapped in the Nile mud and forced to surrender. He waited for the waters to subside. In the interim he oversaw the reconsecration of the town's Great Mosque as a cathedral, and the establishment of an archbishopric there. In October, reinforcements from France arrived and the following month, on 20 November, Louis marched towards Cairo.

BATTLE OF AL-MANSOURAH

As the French army proceeded southwards, Sultan al-Salih Ayyub died. In mid-December the crusaders drew up on the bank of the al-Bahr al-Saghir river, opposite the fortress of al-Mansourah, where a 70,000-strong Ayyubid army was encamped. But the crusaders could not find a way across, and remained there for six weeks engaged in the construction

▲ *Louis received Robert of Nantes, the Latin Patriarch of Jerusalem, in Damietta in 1249. The king established an archbishopric in Damietta under the Patriarch's authority.*

of a causeway. Then in early February 1249, a local Coptic Christian alerted them to the existence of an undefended ford a little way downstream, and on 8 February the army's vanguard led the advance on al-Mansourah.

Under the command of Louis's brother, Count Robert of Artois, the French vanguard (with a contingent of Templars and of English knights under Earl William of Salisbury) launched a surprise attack on the Ayyubid camp. The Ayyubid troops fled and Count Robert and his fellow commanders, ignoring orders to wait, and driven by the chivalric urge to glory, rode after them into Damietta. But in the town the Egyptians were rallied by the brilliant commander Rukn al-Zahir Baybars (victor at the Battle of La Forbie) and turned on their pursuers. They cut down the small band of crusaders – who were

◄ *This celebrated portrait of St Louis was painted by Spanish-Greek artist El Greco in c.1592. In Louis's lifetime the French king was the most powerful of the monarchs of Europe.*

▲ *Scenes from a 13th-century book show Pope Innocent IV at the Ecumenical Council of Lyon in 1246 (top left), Louis (top right) receiving the blessing of the church, and the Battle of Gaza, on 12 October 1244.*

disoriented and unable to manoeuvre easily in the narrow streets – in a devastating slaughter. Most of the English knights, including Earl William and all but five Templars, were killed. Count Robert was also slain, with the members of his bodyguard. Through lack of discipline they had thrown away the advantage.

Meanwhile, the main part of the French army was still crossing the ford. Around half the army had crossed when the Egyptians, commanded by Baybars, poured out of Damietta once more to attack. A fierce battle ensued. The crusaders just about managed to hold their ground and finally the Egyptians retreated into al-Mansourah.

SIEGE OF MANY MONTHS

Louis settled in for a siege, hopeful that in the aftermath of the death of Sultan al-Salih Ayyub infighting over the succession would distract the Egyptians from the matter in hand and open the path to a victory for the Christians.

However, a new sultan, Turan Shah, arrived from Damascus to take command, and he quickly imposed his authority on the Egyptian force.

Over the following months the Egyptians effectively undermined the crusader position – principally by venturing out to destroy, one after another, the barges bringing supplies downriver from Damietta. Dysentery and typhoid spread through the crusader camp, and starvation loomed. Louis tried to reopen negotiations, but found that possession of Jerusalem was no longer on offer. His

advisers urged him to make a swift retreat, with just his bodyguard in attendance, but he refused to abandon his army of crusaders to its fate.

RETREAT – AND SURRENDER

On 5 April 1250 Louis accepted the inevitable and ordered a general retreat to Damietta, with the sick going in the front and the remnant of the army marching behind. As they limped northwards, the army was repeatedly attacked by Egyptian horsemen. On only the second day of the march, 6 April, Louis fell seriously ill and became delirious. The army was surrounded, and surrendered.

Under the terms of the surrender, Damietta was returned to the sultan. Those among the crusaders who had been reduced to weakness by disease were killed. Sultan Turan Shah decided there were too many prisoners to control and feed: and ordered that every day for a week 300 of the able-bodied Christians be marched out of the camp and executed. Louis himself was seized and marched in chains to al-Mansourah. The sultan demanded a ransom of 800,000 gold bezants, sending Louis's cloak to Damascus as proof of his triumph.

▼ *The crusade reaches a humiliating end as Louis is captured (left of picture) and then cast into a common jail (right) by his captor.*

THE EIGHTH CRUSADE
KING LOUIS'S FINAL ENDEAVOUR

In the mid-1260s devastating attacks by Egyptian sultan Baybars on Christian holdings in Syria and Palestine reduced Outremer to little more than the port of Acre in Syria. Louis IX of France was inspired by these events to launch another crusade, but it got no further than its very first engagement, the siege of the north African city of Tunis, which had been planned as a preliminary to an attack on Egypt prior to an assault on Muslim strongholds in the Holy Land.

AFTER THE SEVENTH CRUSADE
The failure of the Seventh Crusade in Egypt and the capture of Louis IX by Sultan Turan Shah in April 1250 provoked an outpouring of grief in France. The peasants of northern France rose up in a protest movement that presented itself as a crusade to free their pious king from humiliating captivity among the infidel, but which was really a social uprising and a protest against the failure of the French nobility and the Church to go to Louis's aid (see box).

Meanwhile in May 1251, on the payment of his vast ransom, Louis was released and departed from Egypt, bound for Acre. He stayed in the Holy Land for three years, effectively ruling the Kingdom of Jerusalem and holding his court in Acre. In his time there he refortified Acre, Caesarea, Jaffa and Sidon. He made several diplomatic attempts to improve the standing of the states of Outremer. In April 1254 he had to return to France on the death of his mother, Blanche of Castile, who had been serving as his regent.

OUTREMER UNDER PRESSURE
In the early 13th century Genghis Khan had led a devastating expansion from Mongolia and founded a vast empire. His grandson Hulagu inherited the Mongol territories in Persia and Armenia and in 1260 he captured Damascus.

Meanwhile, the general Baybars had risen up against Sultan Turan Shah in Egypt and founded a new sultanate of Mamluks (a military caste of former slaves converted to Islam). Baybars was originally himself a victim of the Mongols: he was a Kipchak Turk from the northern coasts of the Black Sea, who was sold into slavery in Egypt after his lands were overrun by Mongols in c.1240. In the service of the Ayyubid Egyptian sultan al-Salih, he rose to prominence, and defeated crusader armies at La Forbie and al-Mansourah.

In 1260, after taking Damascus, Hulagu sent his principal general, Kitboga, southwards to defeat Egypt. The Mongols met their match in Baybars, who led the

▲ *Angels lead the way across the waves as the saintly Louis IX embarks on crusade from the port of Aigues-Mortes in France.*

Egyptian army to victory in the Battle of Ain Jalut in Galilee on 3 September 1260. That same year Baybars plotted the death of the Mamluk sultan, Qutuz, and seized power for himself. He marched into Syria and took Damascus. He now had control both of Egypt and of Syria and united them in a single state.

In 1265 Baybars repaired and refortified the Syrian fortresses earlier destroyed by the Mongols, then launched an invasion of Outremer. That year he took the town of Caesarea and seized Arsuf from its garrison of Knights Hospitaller. The garrison surrendered on the promise that survivors would be freed, and then were slaughtered to a man. In 1266 Baybars captured Safed from the Knights Templar – again Baybars promised safe passage to members of the garrison, only to behead them. He took Toron, also in 1266. In 1268 he invaded Outremer once more, and captured Jaffa and Antioch. Both were utterly destroyed, their populations either slaughtered or sold into slavery.

LOUIS'S SECOND ATTEMPT

Baybars' devastation of Outremer inspired Louis IX to take the cross a second time, on 24 March 1267. Recruitment this time proved much more difficult than in 1245–48. Nevertheless, three years later Louis embarked from Aigues-Mortes with an army of around 10,000 men bound initially for Sardinia. He was persuaded by his brother, Charles of Anjou, to direct the attack first against Tunis, then to move against Baybars' power base in Egypt.

The crusaders landed in northern Africa in July, and besieged Tunis. Almost at once, a large part of the army became sick after drinking dirty water; Louis himself was struck down so badly that he

▲ *While in Outremer in 1251–54, Louis oversaw the building of fortifications at Caesarea, surrounded by a deep moat.*

died, on 25 August, just one day after Charles of Anjou had arrived to lend his support. By tradition, Louis's dying word was 'Jerusalem!' Louis's 25-year-old son Philip, Count of Orleans, was proclaimed King Philip III of France; Charles of Anjou took on leadership of the crusade.

The crusaders failed to take Tunis. On 30 October they lifted the siege after negotiating a favourable settlement under which Christian merchants could enjoy free trade with the city and priests and monks were given rights of residence there. About this time Prince Edward of England arrived. He moved swiftly on Acre, the only surviving crusader territory in Syria. His actions there are considered to form the Ninth Crusade.

▼ *Louis is struck down by dysentery near Tunis. He died without fulfilling his desire to reclaim the Holy City, and the legend arose that his last word was 'Jerusalem!'*

THE SHEPHERDS' CRUSADE OF 1251

French popular unrest over the capture of Louis IX in Egypt was focused into a protest by a Hungarian monk known as le Maître de Hongrie (The Hungarian Master). He declared that the Blessed Virgin Mary, Mother of Christ, had visited him in a dream with instructions to mobilize the shepherds of France and lead them in a crusade to free the saintly king from captivity.

Chronicle accounts suggest that the 'shepherd' army, which contained all kinds of rural poor, including women and children, numbered 60,000. The monk led them to Paris but Louis's mother, Blanche of Castile, who was acting as regent, sent them on their way.

(English chronicler Matthew Paris met the monk and afterwards declared him an imposter; Matthew believed that the man was a rabble-rouser, and a survivor of the so-called Children's Crusade of 1212.) The crusaders went to Rouen, where they attacked priests, and Tours, where they used violence against monasteries. Later in Amiens and Bourges they attacked Jews. At this point the regent, Blanche of Castile, gave orders that the wandering crusaders be dispersed; in a fight outside Bourges, the Master was killed and his followers then broke up of their own accord. Some of them are believed to have taken the cross and gone to the Holy Land.

SAINT LOUIS
KING LOUIS IX OF FRANCE

Louis IX led two crusades, both utter disasters. But his ascetism, the obvious strength of his religious faith, and the way he conducted himself on campaign and in negotiations meant that, remarkably, his reputation was not destroyed by his failures. He was, indeed, esteemed by both sides: by the Christians for his great leadership and his refusal to abandon his men, and by the Muslims for his noble bearing and generosity of spirit. He was canonized in 1297 by Pope Boniface VIII and is the only French king to be a saint.

A POWERFUL MOTHER
The son of Louis VIII of France and Blanche of Castille, Louis became king aged 12 on his father's death in 1226. His mother, Blanche, the powerful granddaughter of King Henry II of England and Eleanor of Aquitaine, was regent and she single-handedly secured the kingdom against baronial unrest in 1226 and an attempted invasion by the youthful King Henry III of England in 1230. Four years later, Louis came of age, began to rule in his own right and married Marguerite of Provence, but he remained under

▼ *The formidable Blanche of Castile was a powerful influence throughout Louis's life. But he defied her wishes when he went on the Seventh Crusade in 1248.*

Blanche's influence right up to her death in 1252. She served as regent a second time, just as effectively, from 1248–52, while Louis was on the Seventh Crusade; indeed, Louis returned to France from his rule in Acre in 1254 because of her death.

NEGOTIATING WITH THE ENEMY
Louis also attempted to advance the cause of Christianity in the East by attempting to make alliances against Muslim rulers. He twice sent ambassadors to the Mongols, in the belief that he could form a powerful alliance against the Abbasid caliphate in Baghdad. The first time was in 1248–49: Louis received an approach from Eljigidel, Mongol ruler of Armenia and Persia, suggesting that if Louis attacked

▲ *Louis arrives at Notre Dame, Paris, with his mother, Blanche of Castile. He owed his kingdom to her bravery and resolution during his minority.*

Egypt, Eljigidel would attack Baghdad, splitting Muslim power; he responded by sending a Dominican priest named Andre of Longjumeau as his ambassador to the court of the Great Khan Guyuk (the grandson of Genghis Khan) in Mongolia. Unfortunately Guyuk died before the envoy arrived, and his widow sent an insulting message back to Louis, demanding that he send financial tribute.

The second time was in 1253 when Louis sent a Franciscan friar named William of Rubruck to visit the Great

▶ *One of Louis's many distinctions is that he founded the* Parlement *(council of the king) in Paris. It met within the royal palace on the Ile de la Cité. On this altarpiece Louis is shown in Paris with St John the Baptist.*

Khan Mongke in Mongolia. Mongke also demanded tribute and suggested that Louis should accept Mongol authority. These were only two of several attempts by Christian powers to engage the Mongols as allies against Muslim Egypt and Syria: for while the Mongols mostly followed a folk religion based on shamanism, they had Christians among their followers and forces and were clearly enemies of Islam. Earlier, Pope Innocent IV had sent two embassies, in 1245 and 1247, and later Prince Edward negotiated with them in 1271 and Pope Gregory X did so later in the 1270s.

RELIGIOUS PASSION

Louis was celebrated for his kindness, his piety and the strength of his religious devotion. His faith did have positive consequences as well as the failed crusades and inconsequential diplomatic contact with the Mongols. One glorious product was the Sainte Chappelle (Holy Chapel) on the Ile de la Cité in Paris. He built the chapel to house two sacred relics, bought

▼ *Sultan Turan Shah returns home to a hero's welcome and fanfares of trumpets. He becomes known as the Conqueror of Louis; France's humiliation is complete.*

at inordinate cost from Byzantine emperor Baldwin II in 1239–41: these purported to be the Crown of Thorns that Christ was forced to wear after his arrest, and a fragment of the True Cross (on which Christ was crucified). These supreme relics greatly enhanced Louis's standing and that of the French crown, and made Paris the most famous city of Europe.

ON CAMPAIGN

There was no doubt as to Louis's standing as a knight and general. Prior to going on crusade, Louis proved himself in battle against French vassals. On the Eighth Crusade he fought with inspirational bravery, as reported by contemporary chroniclers. On landing at Damietta he personally led the disembarkation and planted the sacred standard of St Denis, the oriflamme, into the sand, rousing his troops to perform fearless acts of bravery by his example. Outside al-Mansourah, according to John of Joinville, Louis once again demonstrated the greatest bravery – at one point he was almost captured when six Egyptians seized his horse's bridle but he set about them with his sword and freed himself to fight on. Joinville reports that the Christians took heart at seeing their king fighting with such ferocity and

bravery. At the end of the battle, when he heard the news of his brother Robert's death and on being reminded of the victory he had won, Louis wept in the saddle.

PERFECT CHRISTIAN RULER

In his life and his death while on crusade Louis was seen by contemporaries as the perfect Christian monarch – indeed, as an embodiment of Christendom. After his death from sickness at Tunis on the Eighth Crusade, his entrails were reputedly buried at his place of death near Tunis, where a shrine raised to him still stands today. The rest of his corpse was returned to France and buried at Saint-Denis. A gilt brass tomb was raised over his remains in the late 14th century but this was destroyed and his body lost in the French Wars of Religion (1562–98). Louis was canonized in 1297. His friend and biographer John of Joinville gave evidence at the papal inquest into his life.

A mischievous Tunisian tradition however, holds that the king did not die at Tunis, but instead was inspired to convert to Islam after falling in love with a Berber princess. According to this story, he then took the name 'Sidi Bou Said'. The episode is commemorated in the name of a town in Tunisia.

THE NINTH CRUSADE
PRINCE EDWARD IN ACRE

Prince Edward of England (the future King Edward I) led an English army to the Holy Land to support the beleaguered remnants of Christian Outremer, principally Acre and Tripoli, in 1271–72. The crusade led to the signing of two ten-year truces with the warlike Egyptian sultan Baybars, and the settlement of disputes between Christians in the Holy Land – but it did nothing to secure the long-term future of Outremer. While in Acre, Edward also famously survived an assassination attempt sponsored by Baybars.

FIRST TO TUNIS
Edward had responded to King Louis IX's calling of a new crusade in response to attacks by Sultan Baybars of Egypt on the few remaining Christian strongholds in the East. He arrived in north Africa too late to take part in that crusade, which came to nothing, and after Louis IX's death of dysentery and the subsequent lifting of the

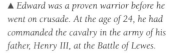

▲ Edward was a proven warrior before he went on crusade. At the age of 24, he had commanded the cavalry in the army of his father, Henry III, at the Battle of Lewes.

▼ At Acre the Knights Hospitaller built a formidable citadel, which was part of the north wall of the city. Beneath the citadel they excavated a series of large halls.

siege of Tunis in October 1270, Edward and his English knights, together with the remnant of the crusader army commanded by the late king's brother Charles of Anjou, sailed on to overwinter in Sicily before the English contingent alone pressed on to Acre. Edward travelled on crusade with his beloved wife Eleanor of Castile, whom he had married when he was 15 and she was 9 in 1254.

TRIPOLI SAVED
Sultan Baybars's capture of Antioch in May 1268 was as ruthless as any before it: the garrison and population were slaughtered or sold into slavery, the city razed to the ground. It was news of this calamity, which left the crusader County of Tripoli in a very vulnerable position, that inspired Prince Edward to take the cross. When Edward landed in May 1271, Baybars had just taken the formidable fortress of Krak des Chevaliers and was already besieging

Tripoli. But the landing of Edward's army, coupled with crusader expeditions against the Egyptian army's supply lines, caused Baybars to lift the siege and agree a ten-year truce with Tripoli.

EMBASSY TO THE MONGOLS

In June Baybars captured Montfort Castle, near Acre, from the Teutonic Knights; for once he honoured his promise to let the garrison escape alive – he marched them up to the walls of Acre before releasing them. Within the city, the knights and men-at-arms clamoured for Edward to lead a sortie against Baybars and his army – but, seeing the enormous size and strength of the Egyptian sultan's force, Edward elected to stay put. Later in the month Edward led a brief raid on St Georges-de-Lebeyne, a mere 15 miles (24km) from Acre: his army captured and looted the settlement, but the troops were badly affected by food poisoning and extreme heat.

In the same month, June 1271, Edward sent an embassy to the Mongol ruler of Iran, Iraq and parts of Anatolia, Il Khan Abagha, seeking an alliance against Sultan Baybars. While in Acre, Edward also attempted to defuse quarrels among the Christians of Outremer and Cyprus, saying that unless they could present a united front against the military threat of Baybars, they were certainly doomed. For instance, he acted as arbitrator in a dispute between King Hugh III of Jerusalem and Cyprus, and Hugh's knights, members of the powerful Ibelin family, who challenged Hugh's claim that they should fight for him in Outremer as well as in Cyprus.

THE SECOND EXPEDITION FROM ACRE

In the autumn, the Christian position in Outremer was strengthened when Edward's embassy to the Mongols bore fruit in a Mongol attack on Mamluk Syria, and reinforcements from England arrived under the command of Prince Edmund. In November, Edward led a second military expedition from Acre, marching with

▲ *Stabbed by a would-be assassin, Edward overpowered the man and so saved his own life. Acre might have been Edward's place of death, and England would have been deprived of one of its great kings.*

the support of local barons and members of the military orders around 45 miles (70km) to attack the Muslim-held castle of Qaqun. He and his troops won a victory over a Turkoman army but were unable to defeat the garrison and take the castle and retreated again to the safety of Acre. There he oversaw the building of a new tower and the foundation of a new military order, that of St Edward of Acre.

A TRUCE – AND AN ASSASSIN

The following year, in May 1272, King Hugh agreed a truce with Sultan Baybars, establishing that the Kingdom of Jerusalem would maintain its borders for ten years, ten months, ten days and ten hours. According to some accounts, Edward was unhappy at this peace treaty, and did not plan to honour it.

The following month, in any case, Sultan Baybars sent an assassin into Acre

in the guise of a Muslim seeking conversion to Christianity; on 16 June this man managed to get into Prince Edward's quarters and stabbed the prince with a poisoned dagger as he slept; Edward woke, kicked out and won possession of the dagger before killing the assassin.

In the traditional account, Edward's wife Eleanor of Castile then saved his life by sucking the poison from his wound before spitting it out. However, this part of the tale was made up; in truth what happened was that Edward's wound became so badly infected that it threatened his life, and an English doctor performed an operation to cut the diseased flesh away.

Afterwards, Edward prepared to attack Jerusalem, but the news that his father, Henry III, had died, making the prince King Edward I of England, forced him to abandon these plans and head home. On 24 September 1272 Edward and Eleanor embarked for Europe, sailing initially to southern Italy, and travelling home by way of Savoy, Paris and Gascony. They landed in England on 2 August 1274 and Edward was crowned King Edward I of England on 19 August in Westminster Abbey.

THE FALL OF TRIPOLI AND ACRE

THE END OF OUTREMER

The ten-year truces signed by Tripoli and Acre with Muslim Egypt were essentially worthless, for neither Sultan Baybars nor his successors in Cairo were the type of men to be bound by such a nicety as a peace treaty. Following the death of Baybars in 1277, sultans Qalawun and Khalil led the Mamluk Egyptian army to the conquest of Tripoli in 1289 and of Acre in 1291.

CRUSADING INITIATIVES

In the immediate aftermath of the Ninth Crusade there were further attempts in Europe to mount expeditions to come to the aid of Outremer. Pope Gregory X entered negotiations with the Mongols to mount a combined campaign in the Holy Land and preached a crusade in 1274, but the plans came to nothing following

▼ In Tripoli the forbidding Castle of Raymond of St Gilles, named for the leader of the First Crusade, was expanded by the Mamluks after they captured it in 1289.

Gregory's death in January 1276. In 1282 Louis IX's brother, Charles of Anjou, King of Sicily and in name King of Jerusalem (after he had bought the succession rights from Mary of Antioch) attempted to mount a campaign to retake Constantinople for Latin Christianity. (Constantinople had been recaptured by the Byzantine Greeks under Emperor Michael VIII Palaeologus in 1261 – see box.) But Charles had to abandon the campaign to deal with an uprising against his rule in the War of the Sicilian Vespers.

THE MAMLUK SUCCESSION

In the year of his death, in 1277, Sultan Baybars achieved two final triumphs: the defeat of a combined Mongol–Seljuk Turk army and the capture of Caesarea. When he died in June of that year, Baybars was initially succeeded by his son Baraka, who was forced to abdicate by a revolt in Egypt. He was replaced by Salamish, his seven-year-old brother – then Qalawun, established himself as regent from 1279.

▲ Acre was held by the crusaders from 1104 until 1187, when it was taken by Saladin, and from 1191 to 1291. For its last century in Christian hands, Acre was the capital of the Kingdom of Jerusalem.

EVENTS IN OUTREMER

Charles of Anjou died in 1285, and King Henry III of Cyprus was crowned King of Jerusalem at Acre on 15 August 1286. After two weeks of celebrations including an 'Arthurian Round Table' chivalric tournament, Henry returned to Cyprus leaving his uncle, Philip of Ibelin, to rule in Acre as his bailiff. Then, in 1287, Bohemond VIII, Count of Tripoli, died. The citizens of Tripoli chose to become a republic rather than accept the accession of Bohemond's sister Lucia and asked the republic of Genoa to send its fleet.

This was the impetus for Sultan Qalawun to march on Tripoli with a vast army and settle in for a siege. He had earlier moved against the remaining crusader possessions, capturing the Hospitaller fortress of Margat in 1285 and taking the main Syrian port, Latakia, in 1287. The siege of Tripoli lasted less than a month. Qalawun's troops slaughtered the population and destroyed the city and its port so that a new wave of crusaders would have nothing to inherit.

THE RECOVERY OF THE BYZANTINE EMPIRE

Following the sacking of Constantinople in 1204 during the Fourth Crusade, and the establishment there of the Latin empire of Constantinople, the Byzantine Empire moved its capital to Nicaea. There, Constantine Laskaris established a new dynasty of emperors – the Laskarid. This dynasty ruled until 1261, when the child-emperor John IV Laskaris, was deposed by an aristocrat who declared himself Emperor Michael VIII Palaeologus. Emperor Michael captured Constantinople from the final Latin ruler, Baldwin III, on 25 July 1261. Threatened in the 1270s by Charles of Anjou's scheme to reclaim Constantinople under the authority of Rome, Michael offered to engineer the

reunification of the Christian Church and to place Orthodox Christianity under papal rule. However, he was unable to force this on his outraged subjects, and had to back down, leading to his excommunication by Pope Martin IV. Michael – and Constantinople – were then saved from attack at the hands of Pope Martin's ally, Charles of Anjou, by the War of the Sicilian Vespers, which Michael himself had secretly incited. Subsequently, Michael continued to reign until his death in 1282: he established the Palaeologian Dynasty of Byzantine emperors, who ruled the empire until the Ottoman Turks caputred Constantinople under Mehmed 'the Conqueror' in 1453.

THE FALL OF ACRE

Determined to achieve the destruction of the crusader states, Qalawun next moved against Acre. But he died in November 1290 before he could effect its capture. His son and successor, Khalil, began the siege, bringing an army perhaps 75,000 strong and a huge siege train containing more than 90 mangonels and trebuchets. The siege began on 11 April 1291.

The garrison numbered 800 knights and 14,000 infantry. From Europe came a contingent of English knights sent by Edward I of England under the command of Odo of Savoy, and a contingent of French knights under Jean of Grailly. The defenders manned Acre's double line of walls, with the Templars on the northern section, the Hospitallers alongside them, the French on the southern walls and Venetians, Genoans and Pisans defending the port area. Further reinforcements under King Henry II of Cyprus and Jerusalem arrived on 4 May.

The besiegers set up their great engines: one directed at the quarter defended by the Templars, another aimed at the Hospitallers' area of walls and a third wheeled machine trained on the Accursed

Tower, on the eastern wall and defended by knights of Cyprus and Syria.

Early in the siege Frankish envoys rode into the Egyptian camp and spoke to the Sultan, asking him to have mercy on the poor and vulnerable of the city. He made them an offer: abandon the city and he would let them leave freely. They refused to negotiate, perhaps remembering the many promises broken by Sultan Baybars.

The knights of the military orders made two night-time sorties – the first (by the Templars) was essentially successful, although it did not result in the hoped-for destruction of siege equipment, but the second (by the Hospitallers) was met with fierce resistance.

The continual assault by the siege engines and the digging of sappers beneath the walls inevitably had its effect. On 15 May, following the collapse of the towers of Blois, of St Nicholas and of Henry II, the defenders were forced to abandon the outer walls and retreat to the inner defences. On 18 May Sultan Khalil ordered a general assault, which was launched before dawn to the beating of a kettledrum and accompanied by a hail of Greek fire and a storm of arrows. The

Accursed Tower was the first to be taken by the attackers, and in the bitter struggle the Grand Master of the Knights Templar, William of Beaujeu, was killed in the fighting. The attackers poured through and overran the city. Acre fell to Sultan Khalil on 18 May 1291. Only a small group of Knights Templar, in the Templars' palace, carried on the resistance – but they were forced to surrender after a week. The population of the city was put to the sword, and its buildings, including the warehouse and port, were utterly destroyed.

END OF OUTREMER

In the days following the fall of Acre, the crusader towns of Beirut, Tyre, Haifa and Tortosa were all abandoned by their defenders. A few thousand refugees managed to escape in ships bound for Cyprus, which remained in crusader hands; other survivors were sold into slavery. A little less than two centuries after the First Crusade, the Latin Christians had been expelled from the Holy Land. Outremer was a thing of the past.

▼ *William of Clermont at the forefront of the last stand in defence of the Kingdom of Jerusalem on the walls of Acre.*

THE ATTACK ON ALEXANDRIA

CRUSADES OF THE 14TH CENTURY

The fall of Acre in 1291 is traditionally taken as the end of the crusades, but people continued to take the cross for centuries afterward. Christian rulers and adventurers made a number of attempts to revive the attack on Islam in the course of the 14th century.

CRUSADING LEAGUES

In the Aegean region, Western powers such as the Knights Hospitaller, Cypriots and Venetian trading colonies attempted to form maritime crusading leagues to combat the power of Turkish emirates that had emerged along the western coast of Anatolia following Mongol devastation of the Seljuk Sultanate. These leagues had papal blessing and assembled small fleets to take the fight to the Turks by sea; they went to war under crusading indulgences and tax exemptions. The first league was formed in 1334 and defeated a Turkish fleet at Adramyttium.

A second league was established ten years later and made a significant capture

▼ *Alexandria's library was established by Ptolemy II in the 3rd century BC. By the time of King Peter's Crusade it was far from the institution it had been. The crusaders claimed that all the books were burned after Muslims conquered the city in AD642.*

by taking the port of Smyrna. In the wake of this, French lord Humbert II, Dauphin of Viennois (the region near Vienne in west-central France), attempted to gather a crusading army in northern Italy to consolidate Smyrna and then take further territory. But his efforts came to nothing, principally because of enduring hostility between the rival trading cities of Venice and Genoa.

A third league was gathered in 1359 and under the papal legate to the East, the French-born Carmelite Peter Thomas, won a victory at Lampsacus, an ancient Greek city on the eastern Hellespont (near Lapseki in Turkey). The league supported the efforts by Peter I of Cyprus to repel the Turkish coastal emirates, which were launching attacks on his territories. Gaining the fortified harbour of Corycus (modern Kizkalesi, Turkey) in 1360, he

▲ *The background to the early 14th-century crusades was the dissolution of the Knights Templar by Pope Clement V (left) in 1312. He transferred the Templars' vast wealth to the Knights Hospitaller, now on Rhodes.*

captured the port of Adalia (now Antalya in south-western Turkey) in 1361, and in 1362 led raids on Myra, Anamour, Siki and other ports along the Mediterranean coast of what is now southern Turkey.

KING PETER'S CRUSADE

Bolstered by these successes, but frustrated that the paucity of Cypriot resources prevented him doing more, he embarked on a tour of Europe in 1362, attempting with papal support to win the backing of European knights and rulers for a crusade. He visited Poland, Bohemia, Germany, France, England and the Low Countries.

The result was the embarkation of a crusading army at Venice on 27 June 1365. The enterprise was called 'King Peter's Crusade' by contemporaries.

The army sailed to Rhodes, where they joined forces with Knights Hospitaller. Peter had heard of plans for an attack from Mamluk Egypt on Cyprus and drew up a plan to pre-empt this campaign by seizing the Egyptian port of Alexandria and then negotiating to swap possession of the Egyptian port for the Holy City of Jerusalem. The combined army, embarked in a fleet of 165 mainly Cypriot and Italian ships, set sail under his command in October 1365 bound for northern Africa.

On 9 October they made a difficult landing under heavy attack from the shore: Muslim bowmen kept up a thick rain of arrows on to the crusader galleys as they neared land and warriors, undeterred by crossbow bolts fired from the ships, came into the sea up to their chests fighting desperately to drive the crusaders off. Finally a brave contingent of Peter's army established a beachhead and began to drive the Muslims back.

The retreating Mamluks closed the city gates and manned the battlements against Peter's invaders. Peter set a great fire before the gates and caused sufficient damage to enable his army to break into the city. An orgy of violence and looting followed. The crusaders rampaged through Alexandria stealing indiscriminately and even sacking the city's celebrated library.

According to the account of French musician-poet William of Machaut, more than 20,000 Saracens were killed in the attack and many others fled. The victory, he claimed, was a triumph for the Christian faith, one ordained by God and given as a reward to King Peter for his dedication to the cause of Christianity.

PETER ABANDONED

But in the aftermath of victory, Peter found that his army of adventurers did not have the stomach to stay and defend what they had won, and virtually to a man they took their booty and departed for home.

William of Machaut reports that the Viscount of Turenne made a speech warning against staying and the crusaders followed his advice. The viscount declared that King Peter did not have sufficient men to defend the city, that his army did not have food, supplies or adequate artillery and that they would soon be faced with an army raised by the sultan of Egypt, al-Ashraf Nasir, who would bring 'five hundred times five hundred thousand men' to win back the city. William notes that Peter was extremely upset, not least because before embarking on the crusade the viscount had promised to serve Peter for a year in defence of any lands conquered on the expedition. Another contemporary comment on the endeavour was made by the great poet Francesco Petrarcha (Petrarch), who wrote to his fellow writer Giovanni Boccaccio that the city of Alexandria, once taken, could have been a great base for Christianity in driving back the Saracens in Africa, but that the enterprise failed because too many of the crusaders were from northern climes – people, according to Petrarch, who begin enterprises full of energy, but cannot carry them through. The crusaders, now immeasurably richer, abandoned Alexandria and headed for home, followed by the exasperated King Peter.

PLANS TO REGAIN THE HOLY LAND

European men of letters of the 14th century drew up a range of plans for re-establishing the Kingdom of Jerusalem. The Venetian Marino Sanuto Torsello, for example, argued that the best means of achieving this end was to outlaw trade with Muslim Egypt: traders would be barred from delivering their cargoes of children, timber and iron to Egypt and from collecting cargoes of sugar, cotton and spices. He pointed out that a similar embargo on sea trade had been imposed in 1187 on trading with the empire of Saladin. He argued that this time the embargo should be maintained on land and sea.

▲ Sanuto envisaged that after a trade embargo brought Egypt low, Christian knights could win back the Holy Land.

▼ This illustration from Sanuto's treatise shows traders carrying supplies to and from the Holy Land.

PETER I OF CYPRUS
THE CRUSADER KING

Peter of Cyprus is known to history as the crusading king, who briefly in the mid-14th century made Cyprus a major participant in international affairs. He reigned for just 11 years, 1358–69, but established himself as a well-known figure of chivalry, the founder of a chivalric order and leader of holy war against Egypt of 1365. This enterprise was known by contemporaries as 'King Peter's Crusade'.

THE ORDER OF THE SWORD
Peter, sometimes also called Pierre I of Lusignan, was the second son of King Hugh IV of Cyprus and had the title of King of Jerusalem from 1358–69. Born in 1328 in Nicosia, Peter was just 19 when, in 1347, he had a religious vision that inspired him to found the chivalric Order of the Sword. According to the account given by French poet and musician William of Machaut (*see* box), Peter had a vision of a cross floating in mid-air, venerated by many as the cross on which the Good Thief hung. (The Gospels report that Christ was crucified between two thieves, one of whom railed against Christ, but the second of whom rebuked his fellow thief and addressed Christ as Lord; in later Christian tradition he was known as

the 'Good Thief' or St Dismas.) Peter heard a voice addressing him as 'Son' and urging him to wage holy war to regain the lands promised by God to the holy patriarchs; as a result, he founded the Order of the Sword for knights professing a determination to regain the promised land and for men-at-arms with the desire to save their souls. The emblem of the order was a silver sword, set with the point downward to resemble a crucifix, against a blue background and the words 'With this maintain loyalty' inscribed in gold.

Two years later Peter left secretly for Europe with one of his brothers, perhaps with the intention of trying to raise or join a crusade. But his father, King Hugh, tracked the pair down and had them brought back to Cyprus, where he jailed them for having left without permission.

SEA RAIDS
Following his father's abdication in 1358, Peter assumed power and was crowned King of Cyprus and titular King of Jerusalem in Famagusta in 1360. He achieved a number of successes against Muslim Turkish emirs along the eastern seaboard of the Mediterranean. In 1360 he was invited by the citizens of Corycos,

▲ *King Peter's Crusade in 1365 ended is disarray but Peter himself, seen here issuing orders to his men, had a great reputation a military strategist and leader.*

in Armenian Cilicia, to take control of their harbour settlement and protect them against Turkish attacks. Peter accepted and sent a Cypriot force commanded by Robert of Lusignan to defend the port. The city was then besieged by Turkish forces, but the garrison held firm and Corycos was made part of the Kingdom of Cyprus.

Peter was now seen as a threat by the Turkish emirs on the mainland, and these men united to plan a maritime attack on Cyprus. Peter, however, received news of the plan and launched a pre-emptive strike with the help of the Knights Hospitaller on Rhodes, and some European and papal forces. With a fleet of 120 ships, he attacked and besieged Adalia (now Antalya in south-western Turkey) and forced the Turks to sue for peace. He made them pay a yearly tribute to Cyprus.

TOUR OF EUROPE
The following year Peter embarked on a trip to Europe, intending to generate enthusiasm for a general crusade for the

▲ *Pope Urban V told Peter to bring the 1365 crusade to an end after it broke down, and in the wake of violent reprisals against Christian merchants in Egypt and in Syria.*

recapture of the Holy Land. He took part in a succession of chivalric tournaments and was hospitably received by monarchs and princes, but was unable to win the widespread support he had hoped for.

Nevertheless, by 1365 Peter had managed to raise an army of sorts, and he embarked on his crusade against Egypt in October of that year. As we have seen, the enterprise began well, with the taking of the city of Alexandria, but this quickly degenerated into ill-disciplined looting before the crusaders departed for home, refusing to obey Peter's command to march on Cairo. In contemporary accounts of the events, Peter's own participation was highly praised – he was represented not only as an inspirational leader, but also as a brave warrior and a

▶ *Peter was represented (back row, second from right) with Emperor Charles IV and Pope Urban V (third and fourth from right) in Andrea Bonaiuti's fresco of 'The Church Militant' at St Maria Novella in Florence.*

skilled and capable general who achieved what could have been a significant gain for Christendom if he had not been let down by greedy and self-interested troops.

Peter returned to Cyprus, where he continued to mount raids on Turkish holdings along the coasts of what is now Turkey and Syria. He raided Tripoli and was preparing an attack inland, on Damascus, but abandoned that venture after Venetian merchants – afraid of damage to trade – bribed him handsomely not to carry it through. In 1367 he made another trip to Europe, again to try to raise a crusade force, but without success. Increasingly he ruled with an iron hand: when he discovered that his wife Eleanor had conducted an adulterous affair with John of Morphou, Count of Edessa, he embarked on a bitter campaign against her favourite members of the nobility. Some began to question his sanity.

ASSASSINATION AND LEGACY

On 17 January 1369 Peter was assassinated. Two of his knights allowed conspirators – including Philip of Ibelin, lord of Arsuf, and Henry of Jubail – access to the king's bedchamber early in the morning. There, half-dressed, he was repeatedly stabbed, then beheaded and even had his genitals mutilated by an angry knight, James of Nores.

> ### WILLIAM OF MACHAUT
> Born in *c.*1300 in Champagne, the poet William of Machaut was in his mid-70s when he wrote his account of the crusade to Alexandria. He was a celebrated figure, who had served one of the great chivalric monarchs of the age, King John of Bohemia. John insisted on fighting on the French side at the Battle of Poitiers in 1356 despite being almost blind and was killed and then honoured by Edward the Black Prince, who took his emblem of an ostrich feather and motto *Ich Dien* (I serve) as his own. William wrote several poems in praise of royal knighthood and also composed many lays and ballads.

Peter's reign was brief and he died a humiliating death. His crusading endeavours achieved little – the only real effect of the attack on Alexandria was to provoke the Sultan of Egypt and damage trade. Nevertheless, because of his devotion to crusading ideals, the fact that he founded a chivalric brotherhood and cut a impressive figure in the courts of Europe (as well as when fighting during the crusade to Alexandria), he was remembered as a paragon of 14th-century chivalry.

CRUSADE TO MAHDIA

ATTACK ON TUNISIA UNITES WARRING CHRISTIANS, 1390

In 1378 the Catholic Church split, in an event known as the Great Schism: there was one pope in Rome and one in Avignon, and the schism continued until 1417 when rule by a single pope was reintroduced. The rival popes combined in 1390, however, to call a crusade against the town of Mahdia, in Tunisia, home to a corsair fleet.

CHRISTIANS DIVIDED

In 1305, at a time when Italy was riven by the papacy's conflict with the Holy Roman Empire, Pope Clement V moved the Roman curia (papal court) from Rome to Poitiers in France, and then in 1309 moved on to Avignon. In 1378 Pope Gregory XI moved back to Rome, but died the same year; there was a dispute over the succession and while Bartolomeo Prignano took power as Pope Urban VI in Rome, in France cardinals elected Robert of Geneva

▲ *John of Gaunt is received by the citizens of Bayonne. John campaigned in Europe in the 1360s–70s, fought with Edward, the Black Prince, in the Battle of Najera (1367) and led a 'crusade' to Portugal in 1386, which ended in a financial settlement.*

▼ *John of Gaunt was the fourth son of King Edward III of England and was father of King Henry IV. Lady Margaret Beaufort, mother of the first Tudor king (Henry VII) was Gaunt's great-granddaughter.*

as a rival pope to rule from Avignon. Robert took the papal name of, Clement VII, and swiftly excommunicated Urban, declaring him to be the Antichrist.

CRUSADES OF THE GREAT SCHISM

In the years following the Great Schism, supporters of the rival popes fought crusades against one another. In general terms, the Avignon pope enjoyed the support of France and her allies Scotland and Castile, while the pope in Rome had the backing of most of the rest of Europe. In 1383 Sir Henry Despenser, Bishop of Norwich in England, a supporter of Rome and a veteran of papal wars in Italy, led a crusade against Louis of Mâle, Count of Flanders and a supporter of Avignon. In a bloody campaign, beginning in May 1383, Sir Henry took Gravelines, Bourbourg, Dunkirk, Diksmuide and other coastal towns, as well as many castles and a fortified church at Veurne. He then drove off

an army raised by the Count of Flanders at Dunkirk and laid siege to Ypres. However, the crusade army became bogged down in the siege and after eight weeks, hearing that the French army under Charles VI was approaching, retreated to Dunkirk. In the end, Sir Henry left for England after a negotiated settlement and the crusade came to nothing – although the settlement with Charles VI reportedly made the bishop and his leading knights considerably richer.

A second crusade took place in 1386 when John of Gaunt, 1st Duke of Lancaster, led a campaign in alliance with Portugal on behalf of Rome against Castile. The enterprise doubled as an attempt to enforce Gaunt's claim to the Castilian throne (through his marriage to Constanza, daughter of the late King Pedro I of Castile), and before he left he was formally recognized as King of Castile by King Richard II of England. However, like its forerunner of 1383, this crusade was settled by a financial agreement under which Gaunt abandoned his claim to the Castile in return for a substantial payment.

CRUSADE OF 1390

The warring halves of Christendom were united by proposals for a crusade against Tunisia in 1390. The idea of the crusade came from Genoese traders whose Mediterranean ships had been raided repeatedly by corsairs from the town of Mahdia, Tunisia. The Genoese, supporters of Pope Boniface IX (Urban VI's successor in Rome), won the backing for the project of King Charles VI of France, who supported Clement VII in Avignon. The proposal was then enthusiastically taken up in France and won the backing of both Boniface IX and Clement VII. Contingents joined from the Low Countries, England and Spain to bolster the mainly French and Genoese army. The leader was named as Count Louis of Bourbon.

▼ *Boniface IX, second Roman pope of the Great Schism of 1378–1417, is crowned. The 1390 crusade, which had his backing, showed the benefits of Christian unity.*

The crusaders set sail from Marseilles and went by way of Genoa to northern Africa. They expected to have a fierce fight on their hands when they landed before Mahdia, but they disembarked unopposed and began a siege, with Count Louis's army surrounding three sides of the city by land and the Genoan fleet blockading the seaward wide. The inhabitants of the town waited three days before launching any attack: when it came, it was easily beaten back by Count Louis's troops, who drove the Mahdians back and reached as far as the gates of the city, fighting fiercely, but unable to force their way into the city.

After that the crusade went on for nine weeks, until finally the Genoans negotiated a peace treaty with Ahmad, emir of Tunis, under which the Tunisians would pay handsome taxes to Genoa for 15 years as well as furnishing them with 12,000 gold sovereigns to cover the cost of this campaign. The crusade turned out well for Genoa, but achieved none of its wider goals – although it certainly had benefits for Christian morale at a time of schism. Its success probably lay in the fact that it gave considerable weight to the argument that the disputes of the Great Schism would be best solved not by wars between rival camps but by creating a united front against the Turks. A further crusade would be proclaimed by Avignon and Rome in 1394 – this time against the rising power of the Ottoman Turks.

▲ *In 1417 the Great Schism was over and the Church was reunified with the deposition of two popes, the abdication of a third and the election of Pope Martin V, seen here at the Council of Constance, 1418.*

THE ENDURING SCHISM

The division within Christianity continued, however. Indeed, the two-way split became a three-way one in 1409, when patriarchs, cardinals and bishops at the Council of Pisa declared the Holy See to be vacant and elected Peter Phillarges as Pope Alexander V. Finally in 1417, at the Council of Constance, Pope John XXIII (successor to Alexander V) was deposed, the Avignon Pope Benedict XIII was deposed, Pope Gregory XII abdicated and Pope Martin V was elected as sole pope.

DEFEAT AT NICOPOLIS
THE RISE OF THE OTTOMANS

As the 14th century progressed the Christian powers of Europe were increasingly aware of the rising threat posed by the Muslim Ottoman state as it expanded from its original base in Anatolia into the Balkans and towards the lands of the mighty Holy Roman Empire. In the 1390s the Ottomans, under their great general Bayezid I, took Salonika (modern Thessaloniki) in Greece, blockaded Constantinople and invaded Hungary. The Christian response was a major Venetian–Hungarian crusade, with the backing of both the Avignon and Roman popes, in 1396. It ended in yet another crusading humiliation, a crushing victory for Bayezid and his Ottoman army at the Battle of Nicopolis.

OTTOMAN ORIGINS AND EXPANSION

The Ottomans were descended from Turkmen tribes driven from their homes in Turkestan in the early years of the 13th century by the raids of the Mongols. They took their name from Osman I, who reigned from 1299–1326, and was known

▲ *King Sigismund of Hungary was forced to retreat at Nicopolis and took refuge in Venetian shipping. He was frustrated that the crusaders, refusing to listen to the advice of those familiar with Ottoman battle tactics, brought defeat upon themselves.*

as Uthman or 'Ottoman' in Arabic. He was the son of Ertogrul, chief of a principality in Anatolia based at Söğüt (now in Turkey); Osman greatly expanded the principality, taking a series of towns including Eskisehir, Yenisehir and Bursa from the Byzantine Empire. Osman's son Orhan (r.1324–60) continued the expansion, capturing Nicaea (modern Iznik) in 1331 and Nicomedia (Izmit) in 1334.

In 1341–47 Orhan intervened in a Byzantine succession crisis, providing the military support that enabled John VI Cantacuzenus to overcome his rival John V Palaeologus. As a reward for this, John Cantacuzenus gave Orhan the hand of his daughter, princess Theodora, and allowed him to raid Byzantine lands in Thrace and Macedonia. Under Orhan, and as a result of the policy of John Cantacuzenus, the Ottomans won their first permanent holding in Europe, taking Gallipoli in 1354.

In 1361 Orhan's son, Murad I, captured Adrianople and Philippopolis in Thrace

◄ *The Ottomans became a major naval power, mostly acquiring their ships by theft. They stole an entire fleet from the Byzantines in the course of a daring night raid in 1356 led by Sultan Murad's brother Süleyman.*

and forced the Byzantine emperor (by now John V Palaeologus once more) to become a vassal. Making Adrianople his capital, renaming it Edirne, Murad then expanded deep into Serbia and Bulgaria, making local princes accept him as their overlord.

CRUSADE OF 1366

In 1366 Murad faced a crusade from Venice under the command of Italian nobleman Amadeus of Savoy. This small enterprise, which set sail with just 15 ships and 1,700 troops, was intended to restore Byzantine power in the face of Ottoman expansion and to help John Palaeologus, who was Amadeus's second cousin. Amadeus allied with Francesco I of the Aegean island of Lesbos and together they drove the Turks from Gallipoli; afterwards Amadeus, discovering that John Palaeologus had been taken captive by the Bulgarians, captured the ports of Mesembria and Sozopolis on the

Black Sea and besieged Varna, demanding his release. Finally the emperor was freed and the crusade saw no further action.

THE THUNDERBOLT STRIKES

Murad's son was Bayezid I, nicknamed *Yildirim* (the Thunderbolt) for the speed of his military campaigns. He came to power following the death of Murad in battle against Bosnian, Serbian and Bulgarian princes at Kosovo in 1389, and just two years later began a siege of Constantinople, the principal buffer between the Ottoman power base in Anatolia and Europe. He also began to extend Ottoman power towards and into Europe, capturing most of the Balkans and expelling Bulgarian tsar Ivan Shishman from his capital, Nicopolis.

A crusade was proclaimed by both Pope Boniface IX in Rome and his rival, the Avignon pope Clement VII. Kings Richard II of England, Charles VI of France and Sigismund of Hungary (who was later to be Holy Roman Emperor, 1433–37) backed the enterprise: initially the plan was for Charles and Richard to fight on the crusade, but in the event an army of 10,000 French, 1,000 English and around 6,000 from the German states gathered under Sigismund in Buda (now part of the Hungarian capital Budapest) in

▼ *The Battle of Nicopolis became a rout. Admiral of France, Jean of Vienne, fought off attackers trying to capture the French standard six times. In the end he was killed.*

TAMERLAINE AND BAYEZID

The seemingly invincible Bayezid met his match in the Turkish–Mongolian warlord Timur, or Tamerlaine. In 1402 Bayezid again abandoned his siege of Constantinople to deal with a troublesome enemy, but this time was heavily defeated by Tamerlaine at the Battle of Ankara. Bayezid was taken prisoner and kept in captivity by Tamerlaine.

Colourful contemporary reports suggested that the Ottoman sultan was kept chained in a cage but this is thought to be false. Bayezid certainly died in captivity, however, one year later; his sons, who had escaped to Serbia after the Battle of Ankara, were later able to re-establish Ottoman rule. In the 16th century English playwright Christopher

▲ *Bayezid died after a year in captivity.*

Marlowe wrote a celebrated play, *Tamburlaine the Great*, about the warlord's exploits. He was also the hero of an opera of 1724, *Tamerlano*, by Handel.

July 1396. The plan was to force the Turks from the Balkans, relieve the siege of Constantinople, and then march across Anatolia and Syria to take Jerusalem for Christ. Mircea, Prince of Wallachia, joined the crusade with a substantial army despite being an Orthodox Christian rather than a Roman Catholic; a contingent from Transylvania also joined up. Venetian and Genoese fleets and a contingent of Hospitaller knights from Rhodes also arrived to lend their support.

The army marched southwards, pillaging towns and massacring locals, before settling in to a siege of Nicopolis, the

Bulgarian capital recently taken by the Turks. Bayezid then showed why he was called 'the Thunderbolt', acting with astonishing decisiveness and speed in lifting his siege of Constantinople and marching against the crusade army. He met them in battle near Nicopolis on 25 September.

Wallachian prince Mircea, who was familiar with Ottoman tactics and had won previous victories against Bayezid, proposed that he should lead an initial assault with his skilled Wallachian light cavalry prior to a main charge by the Western army. But the crusade leaders were suspicious of his motives and instead chose to make a full-scale frontal assault. The battle was a disaster for the crusaders: although the French knights won initial successes against the Ottoman vanguard, they were overwhelmed by the main bulk of Bayezid's men; the Wallachians and Transylvanians deserted and Sigismund escaped. It was a triumph for Bayezid serving to consolidate the Ottomans in the Balkans, and leaving Constantinople even more vulnerable. Bayezid built the magnificent Ulu Mosque in Bursa to commemorate his victory in what became known as the Crusade of Nicopolis.

THE END OF BYZANTIUM
CRUSADERS FAIL TO SAVE CONSTANTINOPLE

The Ottomans repeatedly threatened Constantinople, and Western powers sent intermittent expeditions to the aid of the city. The most significant, in 1444, ended in another heavy defeat for the crusaders at Varna. Then, on 29 May 1453, the Ottomans under Sultan Mehmed II 'the Conqueror' captured Constantinople, marking the end of the Byzantine Empire.

CRUSADES OF BOUCICAUT

French knight Jean Le Meingre, Marshal of France and known as 'Boucicaut', had taken part in the Christians' defeat by Ottoman sultan Bayezid at the Battle of Nicopolis in 1396. Boucicaut was captured in the battle and later ransomed. Then, in 1399, the same year in which he established his chivalric order, the *Emprise de l'Escu Vert à la Dame Blanche* (Enterprise of the Green Shield of the White Lady), he sailed once more to the East. With 21 galleys, three transports and six ships and around 1,200 men, he succeeded in lifting the Ottoman blockade of Constantinople and rescuing the embattled Byzantine emperor, Manuel II

Palaeologus. Manuel then returned with Boucicaut to Europe to try to drum up interest for a further crusade.

In 1401 Boucicaut was made French Governor of Genoa and in 1403 he sailed to Rhodes with a fleet of 16 Genoese ships and from there led a series of raids against ports in Anatolia and Syria held by the Ottomans and the Mamluk Sultanate of Egypt. He attacked Ottoman Alanya in Anatolia, then (with the help of the Knights Hospitaller from Rhodes) raided Mamluk-held Batroun, Tripoli and Beirut.

A NEW CRUSADE

In 1443 Pope Eugenius IV (ruled 1431–47) issued a rallying call to Christians in the West to go to the aid of their brethren in the East against the Ottomans. Murad II, grandson of Bayezid 'the Thunderbolt', had re-established Ottoman supremacy after a period of decline and in-fighting following Bayezid's defeat by the Turkish-Mongolian general Tamerlaine in 1402 and his subsequent death in captivity. Murad II defeated two rivals, forced the Byzantine Empire to pay

▲ *Pope Eugenius IV did much to restore the power of the papacy after the Great Schism. The crusade he called in 1443 almost ended in success at Varna in 1444.*

tribute, and in 1430 recaptured Salonika (Thessaloniki) from the Venetians. Then he annexed Serbia in 1439.

However, the Hungarian army, commanded by King Ladislas of Hungary and his illegitimate son Janos Hunyadi, known as the 'White Knight', won victories against the Ottomans at Nis, Sofia and Snaim in 1443, on the celebrated 'long campaign', and again at Jalowaz in 1444, encouraging Christendom to dream once more of a lasting victory over Islam. A motley collection of crusaders gathered in the Balkans in 1444: the force included Hungarians, Poles, Germans, Ukrainians, Lithuanians, Croatians, Bulgarians and Bosnians. The plan was for a fleet of Genoese, Venetian and papal ships to blockade the Dardanelles to prevent Murad crossing from Anatolia into Europe to fight the crusaders; the fleet and the crusader army would rendezvous at Varna in Bulgaria, then march and sail down the coast of the Black Sea to Constantinople and relieve the siege there, pushing the Ottomans out of Europe in the process. However, the blockade of the Dardanelles failed, and Murad marched to meet the crusaders at Varna.

BATTLE OF VARNA

In the Battle of Varna on 10 November 1444 Murad's Ottoman army of around 60,000 men faced a much smaller crusade army of no more than 20,000 troops commanded by Ladislas and Janos Hunyadi. Not only were the Christians outnumbered, but they also had an unbalanced army, with very few foot soldiers and a great preponderance of heavy cavalry.

The Christians pinned their hopes on the arrival of reinforcements by sea from Constantinople. The papal legate on the crusade, Cardinal Julian Cesarini, called on the army to retreat, but they were in a difficult position, trapped by the enemy between the Black Sea, Lake Varna and the hills. The cardinal then proposed that they attempt to defend their position until they were relieved by Christian reinforcements, but Ladislas and Janos Hunyadi argued for attack – famously declaring: 'Escape is not possible, surrender inconceivable, so let us fight bravely and do honour to the arms we bear!'

The plan almost worked. The crusaders came close to victory: a group of around 500 Polish knights smashed the centre of the Ottoman deployment, breaking through the elite Janissary infantry; Sultan Murad began to flee on horseback but a soldier seized his reins to prevent him, and Murad regained his composure; Janos Hunyadi and his cavalry devastated a company of Sipahis (Ottoman cavalry) and drove them from the battlefield; King Ladislas went in pursuit of Murad, but was cut down by the Ottoman imperial

▶ *'The White Knight' Janos Hunyadi was a formidable opponent of the Ottomans for 20 years from the 1430s to his death in 1456. He was regent of Hungary in 1446–53.*

bodyguard, also of Janissaries. Ladislas was beheaded on the battlefield and, seeing the king cut down, the Polish cavalry lost heart and retreated. Janos Hunyadi escaped. King Ladislas's head was subsequently carried off to the Ottoman court.

SECOND BATTLE OF KOSOVO

In 1448 Janos Hunyadi raised another mainly Hungarian Christian army and fought Murad II again, in the Second Battle of Kosovo, which ran over two days in October. (The clash is known as the Second Battle of Kosovo to distinguish it from the earlier battle at the site between a Serbian army led by Prince Lazar and an Ottoman force under Murad I in 1389 – the battle in which Murad I died.)

Once again, as at Varna, Hunyadi was badly outnumbered by Murad II's Ottoman army, and once again he almost won the battle despite this numerical disadvantage; and, as at Varna, it was the

resilience and bravery of the sultan's elite Janissary corps that won the day. The battle began with an attack by Hunyadi's flanks that was driven back, but this was followed by a strong assault by the main part of his army. This defeated the Janissaries and reached as far as the Ottoman camp before falling back; during this latter part of the battle, with Hunyadi's forces retreating, the Janissaries recovered from their earlier setback and delivered a powerful attack that killed many of the finest Hungarian knights and forced Hunyadi himself to flee. Fighting went on with missiles and artillery fire through the night; on the next day the Ottomans launched a final and decisive attack.

The Christians' defeat in this battle left the Ottomans in the ascendant in the Balkans, with the Byzantine Empire at their mercy. Within five years, Murad II's son and successor, Mehmed II 'the Conqueror', had captured Constantinople.

THE CONQUEROR
OTTOMAN SULTAN MEHMED II

Mehmed II, son of Murad II, was celebrated as 'the Conqueror' because he achieved the long-standing Ottoman ambition of taking Constantinople. He was just 21 when he led Ottoman troops into the city on 29 May 1453. On that day the city of Constantine, founded as New Rome in AD330 to be a new capital for the Roman Empire, and for centuries the centre of the Christian Byzantine Empire, became the Islamic city of Istanbul, capital of the Ottoman Empire. The venerable 6th-century Hagia Sophia (Church of Holy Wisdom) was made into a mosque. The leaders of the West were appalled.

BOY EMPEROR

Mehmed II first came to the throne at the age of 12 in 1444. His father Murad II, having suffered defeats at the hands of the Hungarian-led Christian alliance in the Balkans, notably at Jalowaz in 1444,

▼ *Constantinople, former capital of the eastern Roman Empire, falls to Mehmed's troops. By tradition the conquest was foretold by the Prophet Muhammad.*

signed a ten-year peace treaty at Edirne in June 1444. The Western powers then broke the treaty and gathered a crusading army. Murad – who had retired to rural contemplation – returned to power and led the Ottomans to decisive victories over the Christians at Varna in 1444 and in the Second Battle of Kosovo in 1448.

EYES SET ON CONSTANTINOPLE

In 1451 Murad died, and Mehmed became sultan for a second time. Almost at once, in spring 1452, he set about preparing to capture Constantinople. He had a vast cannon cast, raised an army of no fewer than 250,000 Janissaries and built a fleet of 280 ships.

Constantine had barely men enough to defend the walls of the city when Mehmed began his siege on 6 April 1453, and the siege seemed destined to succeed. According to Niccolo Barbaro, a ship's doctor from Venice who was an eyewitness to these events, those in the city became convinced that the Ottomans would succeed after a portent was seen on the night of 22 May 1453: it was a time of

▲ *Rumeli Hisari, the great fortress Mehmed built in 1452 on the European side of the Bosphorus, was also known as 'strait blocker' because it dominated the sea.*

full moon, but the moon rose as a crescent before becoming full later in the night. Outside the walls the besiegers rejoiced, for the Ottomans held the crescent moon to be their symbol.

Mehmed delivered a stirring speech in which he reminded his troops of the greatness of their forebear Bayezid the Thunderbolt. He spoke of their suffering after Bayezid's defeat by Tamerlaine, and of how the Byzantine Empire had played, and continued to play, a major part in all their woes, constantly seeking to create dissension and set Turks against one another. And all the warriors acclaimed him and cheered his plan to attack.

THE CITY TAKEN

At Mehmed's command the Ottoman army began its assault at sunset on 28 May, with the setting sun at their backs shining directly into the faces of the defenders. The assault began with a

terrifying cacophony of pipes, cymbals and trumpets, followed by a barrage of arrows and missiles. Then the walls were attacked and close hand-to-hand fighting followed around the city perimeter. Fighting continued through the night. A Genoese soldier named Giustinianni was leading the defence of the city and when he was shot and fell down dead the defenders around him fled.

At dawn on Tuesday, 29 May 1453, Mehmed himself led a fresh wave of attacks, clasping an iron club, with the Janissaries behind him and at their back a corps of executioners ready to put to death by beheading anyone who attempted to flee. Constantine XI, last in the long line of Byzantine emperors, was killed attempting to prevent this last part of the assault.

The city secured, Mehmed later made a formal entry on horseback at around noon. He entered the Hagia Sophia; it is said by tradition that when he made his way into the Palace of the Caesars, established more than a millennium earlier by Constantine the Great, he quoted from Persian poetry: 'The spider makes his frail curtains in the grand palace of the Caesars, the owl calls softly the watches of the night in the towers of Afrasiab.'

CONQUESTS AND REFORMS

The capture of Constantinople was only the first of Mehmed's many military victories. He went on to conquer Serbia, Bosnia, Albania and Greece, and the great part of the territory around the Black Sea.

▲ *Byzantium, forerunner of Constantinople, was founded by Greek traders. Mehmed visited Troy and announced that he had avenged the Trojans when he beat the Byzantine descendants of the Greeks.*

In 1480, poised to invade Italy, he sent a vast Turkish fleet to besiege the island of Rhodes, stronghold of the Knights Hospitaller. Here he met his match, and after a three-month siege was forced to abandon the attempt to capture the island, having lost no fewer than 9,000 men in the assault. That same year he died.

As well as being a great general, Mehmed was a notable administrator. He rebuilt the city of Constantinople and brought in a new tax system, promulgated a new law code, and set up a group of advisers known as the *ulama* (meaning 'wise' in Arabic), all of whom were fluent in Arabic and Persian as well as Turkish and were learned in Islamic holy law.

Mehmed died in 1481 and was succeeded by his son Bayezid II, who led the Ottomans to a series of further triumphs against Poland, Hungary, Venice, Egypt and Persia (Iran).

◀ *After taking Constantinople, Mehmed II claimed the title of 'Caesar' for himself, implying that the Ottomans were by virtue of conquest rightful heirs of ancient Rome.*

DRACULA

In 1462 Mehmed had an encounter with Prince Vlad III the Impaler. That year Mehmed invaded Wallachia in an attempt to remove Vlad, who had raided Ottoman territory and killed 20,000 people; Mehmed brought a great army with him, and occupied the Wallachian capital, but Vlad kept up a fierce guerrilla war against the invaders. In one incident on the night of 16–17 June Vlad entered the Ottoman camp with his men and came close to assassinating Mehmed. Subsequently, Mehmed installed Vlad's brother Radu, in power. Vlad (below) was the historical basis for Dracula, the fictional vampire created by Bram Stoker in his 1897 novel.

THE MIRACLE OF BELGRADE

CRUSADERS SAVE HUNGARY, 1456

After capturing Constantinople on 1453, the Ottomans under their war-like sultan Mehmed II continued to seek new conquests, both for the glory of Islam and the enrichment of their empire. But the Christian West was encouraged once more to believe in the power of holy war when a makeshift crusading army raised by the sermons of a Franciscan friar named Giovanni da Capistrano succeeded in turning back the Ottomans at the siege of Belgrade in 1456. This event was celebrated as the 'miracle of Belgrade'.

BELGRADE FORTIFIED

The 'White Knight' Janos Hunyadi, great foe of the Ottomans in the early 1440s, was an illegitimate son of the late King Ladislas and had been regent of the Kingdom of Hungary since 1446. He foresaw that Mehmed would move to conquer Hungary, and that to do so the Ottoman

▼ Mehmed II brought a vast army, heavy artillery and a sizeable fleet to take Belgrade. The unlikely Christian victory seemed a triumph of faith that began to restore belief in the crusading enterprise.

army would have to take the border fortress of Belgrade (today the capital of the Republic of Serbia). He set about strengthening its defences and laying in provisions, and raised a sizeable garrison force that he placed under the command of his brother Mihaly Szilagyi and his own son Laszlo. He also raised a relief force and a fleet of 200 light warships. His army consisted mainly of battle-hardened mercenaries and a selection of mounted knights from the European nobility.

He was helped in these preparations by the Italian-born Franciscan friar Giovanni da Capistrano. This venerable figure had been used widely by earlier popes as a legate and had preached vehemently against heresies, notably those of the followers of Jan Hus in Bohemia; in 1454, at the age of 70, he was sent by Pope Nicholas V to preach a crusade against the Ottomans at the Diet of Frankfurt. The following year Giovanni was sent by the pope to Hungary and Transylvania to preach the crusade.

There he managed to raise an army and it marched, with Capistrano himself at the head of one division, to support Janos Hunyadi. Capistrano's army consisted of a motley crew, many of them yeomen, armed with scythes and slings, but they were driven and inspired by the preacher's words to believe that God would deliver victory in return or their faith.

SIEGE SET

Mehmed II brought an army of around 70,000 and began his siege of Belgrade on 4 July 1456. He also had 300 cannon and he used his 200 ships to prevent the arrival of reinforcements and supplies by way of the river Danube. The garrison was well armed and motivated but numbered only around 7,000.

The relief army under Janos Hunyadi and Giovanni da Capistrano arrived at Belgrade on 14 July. That same day they

▲ Franciscan friar and crusade preacher Giovanni da Capistrano raised an army of ill-armed peasants to defend Belgrade. One in a long line of militant churchmen, he led the troops himself into the battle.

managed to break through Mehmed's naval blockade of the city, sinking a total of seven large and 20 smaller Ottoman ships. They were able to bring troops and supplies into the city. Mehmed then launched a week-long bombardment by his artillery and on the evening of 21 July ordered an all-out attack.

NIGHT FIGHT

The Ottoman attack continued through the night, with desperate fighting on both sides. The Christians managed to hold the attackers at bay and a large contingent of Mehmed's elite Janissaries were put to the sword. In one celebrated incident, a Turkish soldier tried to raise the sultan's banner on a bastion of the fortress when a Hungarian soldier named Titus Dugovic attacked him and the two men fell together from the wall – Dugovic was later celebrated as a hero and his son was raised to the nobility.

On the following day the large body of peasant crusaders that Giovanni da Capistrano had raised took matters into their own hands, launching an impromptu attack on the besieging army. Giovanni da Capistrano tried to call them back, but finding it impossible to impose discipline rode into the conflict himself, reputedly declaring 'The Lord God, who brought about this beginning, will see to the end!' Janos Hunyadi also led a lightning attack, aiming to seize Turkish artillery positions. The main part of the Ottoman army fled.

OTTOMANS SHAMED

The sultan's bodyguard fought heroically, but were overwhelmed by Hunyadi's cavalry. Mehmed delivered a fatal blow to a Christian knight, but then was shot in the leg by a bowman and fell unconscious on the battlefield. Shortly afterwards darkness fell, and by night the Turks lifted the siege and retreated. They needed 140 wagons

▼ *Christians triumph at Belgrade. Pope Calixtus III ordered the church bells to be rung as a call to arms, but it became a celebration. The battle is commemorated to this day by the ringing of a noon bell.*

to bear their wounded away from the city they had expected to take with ease. One of them was Mehmed, still unconscious.

The sultan recovered in the city of Sarona. Contemporary reports tell that he was plunged into despair when he learned that the Ottoman army had been so completely humiliated and so many of his greatest warriors had lost their lives, and had to be prevented by his aides from taking his own life with poison. He then retreated to Constantinople.

▲ *In the 1480s Western powers tried to destabilize the Ottomans by supporting Cem, brother of Bayezid II, seen here meeting with the Knights Hospitaller.*

AFTERMATH OF BELGRADE

The Christian West rejoiced. The relief of the city against all odds evoked the spirit of the First Crusade, when unexpected victories convinced knights and churchmen that their battle was blessed by God. Janos Hunyadi and Giovanni da Capistrano believed that the time was a ripe for a crusading push to drive the Ottomans back, to take Constantinople and perhaps even go on to regain Jerusalem. However, neither man lived to further these ambitious plans. Both fell victim to bubonic plague: Janos Hunyadi died on 11 August, three weeks after the victory; Giovanni da Capistrano followed on 23 October.

Pope Pius II (ruled 1458–64) was inspired by the victory to call a new crusade on 26 September 1459 in Mantua. The following January he proclaimed the crusade for a period of three years. But despite the 'miracle of Belgrade' there was little enthusiasm among the powers of Western Europe and the expedition came to nothing after Pius died in August 1464.

CHAPTER TEN

THE WARRIOR MONKS

On 1 May 1187 a small Christian force of foot soldiers and 140 knights under Gerard of Ridefort, Master of the Knights Templar, encountered a Muslim Ayyubid army of 7,000 in the Battle of Cresson near Nazareth. When the Ayyubid horsemen feigned a retreat Gerard rashly ordered a charge, his knights were isolated from the foot soldiers and the two parts of the army cut down. The account in the crusade chronicle *Itinerarium Regis Ricardi* (The Voyage of King Richard) describes the extraordinary heroism and death of Templar knight Jakelin of Mailly, who reportedly fought to the last, surrounded by Muslim soldiers and entirely alone, until he sank to the ground and his soul rose at once to heaven, wearing a martyr's crown and covered in glory.

The Knights Templar and other monastic military brotherhoods – such as the Knights Hospitaller, the Teutonic Knights, the Knights of St Lazarus or the Knights of St Thomas Acon – were famed for their ferocity in battle and the powerful commitment to the crusading cause celebrated in the account of Jakelin of Mailly's death. In battle, they provided a highly disciplined, well-trained fighting force, although their leaders often were drawn by overconfidence or the desire for glory into rash and even disastrous acts. The monastic military brotherhood – consisting of men who like Jakelin of Mailly sought salvation through their exploits in religious warfare – was an institution unique to European chivalry of the Middle Ages, without counterpart in other cultures or eras.

▲ *At Cresson in 1187, Templar Jakelin of Mailly fought to the end.*

◄ *The defence of Rhodes by Fulkes of Villaret and the Knights Hospitaller, against Sultan Osman I in 1307. The Knights held the island until 1522.*

KNIGHTS OF ST JOHN

FOUNDATION AND EARLY YEARS OF 'THE HOSPITALLERS'

The monastic order of the Knights Hospitaller of St John of Jerusalem was established in the wake of the First Crusade with responsibility for the defence of the Holy Land. It had its origins in a hospital or hospice (guesthouse) founded in Jerusalem to care for Christian pilgrims, and was formally recognized in a papal bull of 15 February 1113 issued by Pope Paschal II (ruled 1099–1118).

Paschal's bull gave the order the name of the 'Hospitallers of St John of Jerusalem', but its members were often referred to as 'Knights of St John' or 'Knights Hospitaller', and over the centuries the order has also had many other names – including the 'Knights of Rhodes' and the 'Knights of Malta', reflecting the Hospitallers' residence on those islands. (The order's modern name, in use since the introduction of a new constitution in 1961, combines all these in the title of the 'Sovereign Military Hospitaller Order of St John of Jerusalem'.)

▼ *The order of the Knights of St John was founded after the First Crusade and the triumphant gain of Jerusalem.*

ORIGINS OF THE HOSPITAL

The hospital in Jerusalem was established by merchants from Amalfi and Salerno in Italy in 1023, with permission from Caliph Ali az-Zahir of Egypt, who ruled Jerusalem at the time. Benedictine monks served the establishment, housing and caring for the pilgrims who came to see the holy sites in Jerusalem. The hospital

▲ *The brothers built the imposing Church of St John of the Hospitallers in Sidon in the 13th century. Today it is a mosque.*

became associated with St John because it stood close to the site of the monastery of St John the Baptist.

The Jerusalem hospital, in fact, had a long history prior to the 11th century. Its forerunner was established as early as AD600 by a certain Abbot Probus, on the authority of Pope Gregory the Great (ruled 590–604), and was intended from the start to house and care for Christian pilgrims to the Holy Land. Then, in *c*.800, Charlemagne, the King of the Franks, promoter of learning and 'August Emperor', who wanted to establish himself as ruler of all Christendom, expanded the hospital and installed a library there. But in 1010 the hospital was destroyed as part of the demolition of many Christian shrines – including the Church of the Holy Sepulchre – ordered by the sixth Fatimid caliph of Egypt, Al-Hakim bi-Amr Allah. The building raised by the Italian merchants in 1023 was the replacement for the earlier hospital.

▲ *Raymond du Puy was the order's second Grand Master but the first to use the title. He was the man who established the Hospitallers on a firm footing. He fought in the siege of Ascalon in 1153.*

FOUNDER OF THE ORDER

In the immediate aftermath of the capture of Jerusalem by the soldiers of the First Crusade in 1099, a Christian knight or merchant named Gerard Thom became guardian, or superior, of the hospital. Later known as 'Blessed Gerard', he founded the religious order of St John of Jerusalem, under the Benedictine rule, and then travelled to Europe to raise money and gather support – crucially winning the backing of Pope Paschal II. Paschal decreed that the order would not be subject to the authority of the King of Jerusalem, but was to be subservient only to the papacy; he granted it exemption from paying tithes to the Church and the right to own its religious buildings.

Gerard also established associated hostels for pilgrims at cities in Provence and Italy that were on the pilgrim route to the Holy Land. In the Holy Land, the warrior

▶ *The Knights Hospitaller wore the eight-pointed Maltese cross. This example is on a coin issued by John of Brienne, King of Jerusalem in the years 1210–1225.*

monks of the order branched out from housing and caring for pilgrims into providing them with an armed escort on dangerous parts of their journey, when they were liable to attack by bandits or enemy soldiers.

SECOND GRAND MASTER

Gerard was succeeded as Grand Master of the order in 1120 by French knight Raymond du Puy of Provence. Raymond was related to Adhemar of Le Puy, papal legate on the First Crusade, and was the son of the leading crusade knight Hughes du Puy, who fought as a general of Godfrey of Bouillon and was named Governor of Acre. Over 40 years as Grand Master (1120–60), Gerard established the order as a significant military force: he divided the brothers into military, medical and clerical divisions; he established the

order's first infirmary in Jerusalem, close to the Church of the Holy Sepulchre; and he moved the order from the Benedictine to the Augustinian rule.

Gerard also made the eight-pointed cross of Amalfi in Salerno the order's symbol, in honour of the hospital's founders from that town. This symbol later became known as the Maltese cross because of the residence of the Hospitallers on the island of Malta after 1530. The knights went into battle wearing black surcoats marked in white with the eight-pointed cross.

EQUESTRIAN ORDER OF THE HOLY SEPULCHRE OF JERUSALEM

The Equestrian Order of the Holy Sepulchre of Jerusalem is a chivalric order that, like the Order of the Knights of St John, traces its history back to the time of the First Crusade. At that time, Godfrey of Bouillon, the first ruler of the Kingdom of Jerusalem, gathered a body of knights to protect the canons in the Church of the Holy Sepulchre. They fought under the banner of a red cross on a white background. In 1113 Pope Paschal II gave the order official recognition, and in 1122 Pope Callixtus II granted it status as a lay religious order with the duty to defend the Church of the Holy Sepulchre and the city of Jerusalem against attack by Muslims.

▶ *Godfrey, lord of Bouillon, first leader of the Kingdom of Jerusalem, is recognized as the founder of the Equestrian Order.*

HOSPITALLERS SAVE RHODES

KNIGHTS OF ST JOHN DEFEAT MEHMET THE CONQUEROR

After the loss of Jerusalem in 1187 the Knights of St John removed to Acre and, following the fall of Acre in 1291, took up residence on the island of Cyprus, so maintaining a presence in the East. The Hospitallers did not stay long in Cyprus. Within 20 years they had transferred to the island of Rhodes, where they would remain for more than 200 years, in that time twice defeating seaborne armies – one in 1444 from Muslim Egypt and a second in 1480 from the Ottoman sultan Mehmet II 'the Conqueror'.

ESTABLISHMENT ON RHODES

On being driven from the Holy Land following the fall of Acre in 1291, the leading figures in the hierarchy of the Hospitallers saw that the sea would inevitably play an important part in the order's future. The admiral of the Hospitaller fleet, Fulkes of Villaret, joined the inner council of the order in 1299. In 1307 the knights captured Rhodes, in part to curb the operations of Muslim corsairs who used the island as a base of operations for raiding Christian shipping in the East, but also perhaps with an eye to establishing their own landholding.

The knights found it difficult to maintain their independence from court politics on Cyprus and elected to move permanently to Rhodes in 1310. By now Fulkes of Villaret was Grand Master. The order also took control of a number of small neighbouring islands, including Bodrum and Kastellorizo. Using these bases, the Hospitaller knights waged a determined sea war against Muslim corsairs from northern Africa who preyed on Christian shipping in the western Mediterranean. (These ruthless Muslim operators were also known as 'Barbary pirates' because the north African coast from which they emanated was called the Barbary coast.)

The Hospitallers also took part in the various minor crusades of the 14th cen-

▲ *The Ottoman fleet, commanded by Palaeologos Pasha, approaches Rhodes, at the top right of this picture. The island appears secure behind stout walls.*

tury, notably those of 1345 in which Smyrna was captured; 'King Peter's Crusade' of 1365, which degenerated into the sacking of Alexandria; and the Nicopolis Crusade of 1396.

A NEW ORGANIZATION

In this period, the order also became immeasurably richer: after the Knights Templar were disbanded in 1312, all their property was assigned to the Hospitallers by Pope Clement V (ruled 1305–14). The Hospitallers organized their new territory

well, dividing their landholdings into eight *langues*, or 'tongues' (Provence, Italy, Germany, France, England, Castile, Auvergne and Aragon), each with its own prior and with key positions of authority in the order distributed among the langues. In this way, the Knights Hospitaller avoided difficulties caused by national feelings at a time when such feelings were increasingly powerful in Europe.

On Rhodes the brothers of different langues lived in their own *auberges*, or hostels, within an enclosed area of the city known as the *collachium*. They fortified both the city and the island's main harbour and established a commercial area, as well as inviting Latin and Greek farmers from the mainland to settle.

ATTACK ON RHODES

In 1426 Cyprus was conquered by Muslim Egypt and Rhodes was more than ever isolated and vulnerable. In 1435 the warlike Egyptian sultan Baybars planned an invasion of Rhodes, and the Knights brought reinforcements in from Europe at full speed, but the threat came to nothing. In 1444 the Egyptians tried again, mounting an invasion of the island and a month-long siege of the town of Rhodes.

In 1480 Ottoman sultan Mehmet II 'the Conqueror' launched a major attack on Rhodes – ostensibly because Muslims on the islands had reported being persecuted, but really as part of military expansion towards southern Italy. A vast Ottoman fleet, reputedly carrying 70,000–100,000 men, appeared off Rhodes in May. It was commanded by Palaeologos Pasha.

On the island, the garrison, under the command of Grand Master Pierre d'Aubusson, had just received reinforcements of around 2,000 foot soldiers and 500 knights from France. D'Aubusson had been vigilant and had prepared well against possible attack, laying in substantial supplies and military equipment.

The Ottomans settled in to a siege. Coming under attack from the citadel, where the garrison was ensconced, the Ottomans launched an assault: they succeeded in building a bridge from the boats in the harbour to the citadel walls but as their men began to pour across it to attack, this makeshift structure collapsed and thousands were drowned in the ensuing panic. A second attack was more successful and some of the Ottoman troops succeeded in raising the sultan's standard on the walls.

HEAVENLY ARMY

Accounts differ as to what happened next. According to the version given by Flemish writer Guillaume Caoursin, the Ottomans were terrified by a vision of the Virgin Mary and a saintly army in the sky above the citadel. Caoursin reports that the Knights had raised banners showing Christ, the Virgin Mary and St John the Baptist on the walls of the citadel, but that when the Ottoman attack was at its height a golden cross appeared in the clear sky above these banners, together with a miraculous image of the Virgin Mary carrying a spear and a shield and next to her a man in simple clothing standing before a great host of warriors of light. The Ottomans were paralyzed with fear and the Hospitallers were able to cut them down and drive them back.

The Ottoman account, however, suggests that their soldiers were poised for victory when their commander issued the order that there was to be no looting since the wealth of the citadel, and the merchants in the town, belonged to the sultan. This apparently caused the Ottoman warriors to stop fighting and many were slain in their moment of wavering.

OTRANTO PUNISHED

In the wake of this defeat, the Ottoman fleet lifted the siege of Rhodes and sailed away on 28 July 1480. On the island, the merchants, farmers and knights of the Hospitaller garrison rejoiced at their delivery by a seeming miracle from a force of such size. The Ottomans, for their part, sailed on and wreaked a terrible vengeance for the frustration at Rhodes on the people of Otranto in Italy. Having overrun the port, they killed Archbishop Stefano Agricoli in the cathedral and slaughtered 800 citizens of the town who refused to convert to Islam.

▼ *The Ottoman forces preparing for battle outside the walls of Rhodes in 1480. Their attack failed, reputedly after an appearance by the Virgin Mary.*

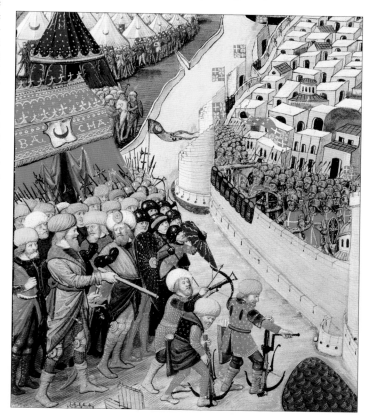

SULEYMAN TAKES RHODES
BUT THE HOSPITALLERS HOLD MALTA

In 1522, the Hospitaller garrison on Rhodes was forced to surrender after a six-month siege by Ottoman sultan Suleyman I 'the Magnificent' and his army. The Hospitallers departed Rhodes to take up residence on Malta.

PREPARATIONS FOR THE SIEGE
Philippe of L'Isle-Adam was elected Grand Master of the order in 1521 and began at once to prepare for the defence of Rhodes. He sent out an appeal throughout Europe for reinforcements to defend this outpost of Christendom, but received no response save a small contingent from Venice and Crete. He laid in a year of provisions and organized the defence of the town's reconstructed walls and bastions with most particular care, assigning the protection of different areas to groups of knights.

▼ *The Hospitallers had a powerful fleet and were a force to be reckoned with at sea.*

The Ottoman fleet arrived on 26 June under the command of Mustafa Pasha; Sultan Suleyman sailed in around a month afterwards to take command. The Turks launched a concerted assault on a section of the town walls defended by knights of Aragon and England, using both artillery and the digging of mines. This went on for as much as a month, with little progress, but on 4 September the Ottoman attack opened a breach almost 40ft (12m) across beside the bastion of England. The Ottomans gained control of this area, but then a fearless Hospitaller assault led by English knight Nicholas Hussey managed to force the Turks back.

GENERAL ATTACK
On 24 September the Turks mounted a general assault on the town, with particular concentration of fire against the bastions of England, Italy, Provence and Spain. Twice in one day the bastion of

Spain was captured by the Ottomans and then retaken by the Hospitallers. After hours of fierce fighting, with the garrison's powerful cannon killing vast numbers of Ottoman warriors, the attack was at last called off. Suleyman was enraged and ordered the execution of Mustafa Pasha because he had failed to take the city despite his vast numerical advantage; the sultan was persuaded to spare Mustafa, but he replaced him with Ahmed Pasha.

The Ottomans launched another powerful attack in late November, but it was driven back once more. However, the Knights and the townspeople of Rhodes were close to exhaustion and by mid-December were ready to negotiate terms of peace. A truce was called on 11–13 December, but when the townspeople asked for further reassurances regarding their safety, Suleyman ordered the artillery attacks to begin again. His troops took the bastion of Spain on 17 December – and from this point on there seemed no doubt the city would eventually be taken.

PEACE AT LAST
On 20 December Grand Master of L'Isle-Adam requested another truce and on 22 December a peace treaty was agreed under which the Knights who wished to depart would be allowed 12 days to leave the island in peace, with their weapons and religious relics, while the islanders would be permitted to leave for up to three years. Suleyman was very impressed with the fight put up by the Knights and the bearing of Grand Master of L'Isle-Adam. After the peace negotiations, the sultan is reported to have said of of L'Isle-Adam 'it gives me no pleasure to force this fearless old man from his home' and when he entered Rhodes he dismissed his imperial bodyguard, declaring that he had his safety guaranteed on the honour of the Grand Master of the Hospitallers, and that this was 'worth more than all the world's

armies'. A further tribute to the heroism and faith of the Hospitallers came from Holy Roman Emperor Charles V, who declared: 'Nothing in the world was ever so well lost as Rhodes.'

IN MALTA

After leaving Rhodes, the Knights Hospitaller took up residence in Sicily, but in 1530 moved on to Malta, which was given them as a fief, along with the nearby island of Gozo and the port of Tripoli in north Africa, by Holy Roman Emperor Charles V (r.1519–56). In return, they were required to send one falcon a year to the Viceroy of Sicily and to celebrate Mass for Charles on All Saints Day.

From their new base they launched regular attacks on Muslim shipping, and fought a running war against the Muslim corsairs who operated from north Africa across the Mediterranean. In 1551 the corsair Turgut Reis and the Ottoman admiral Sinan combined in an attack on Malta: they did not take the main island, but captured Gozo, and, also during the same campaign, drove the Hospitaller garrison from Tripoli. In response the Knights greatly expanded and strengthened fortifications on Malta. In 1559, the Knights took part in an expedition organized by

▼ *Jean Parisot of Valette masterminded the defence of Malta. He was a veteran of the Hospitallers' campaigns in Rhodes.*

Philip II of Spain to drive Turgut Reis from Tripoli. It was a significant enterprise – involving more than 50 galleys and 14,000 men – but ended in a heavy defeat in the Battle of Djerba in May 1560.

THE ASSAULT ON MALTA

Nevertheless, the Hospitallers kept up their attacks on Muslim shipping, and in 1565 Suleyman determined to stop them once and for all. A vast Ottoman war-fleet landed a force of around 40,000–50,000 men on Malta in mid-May. Grand Master Jean Parisot of Valette had sent out a summons to members of the order around the world, but even so its defending garrison numbered no more than around 6,000. He further strengthened the fortifications on the three main forts of Malta – St Elmo, Fort St Michael and Fort St Angelo.

The Ottomans could not use the mining that had worked so well on Rhodes because the fortresses on Malta were built on solid rock. Instead they relied on their mighty artillery, training their guns on the fortress of St Elmo at the entrance to the Grand Harbour. The Ottomans launched three major attacks on St Elmo, on 3, 10 and 16 June, and each time were driven back by the determined defenders; the attackers suffered very heavy losses, and many of the elite Janissary troops were killed. But finally on 23 June, in another major attack, the entire defending garrison of that fort was killed – even the

▲ *In the defence of Malta the Hospitallers fought with heroic courage.*

wounded men who had fought heroically to the last, sitting on chairs on the ramparts. The fort was taken.

Next the Turks attacked the Senglea Peninsula to the south of Fort St Angelo. There was fierce fighting over several days in early August, but the Ottomans were driven back. Another attack on Fort St Michael and the town of Birgu on 7 August seemed to have brought the Turks close to victory when they made a breach in the walls, but they had to retreat to defend their camp against a daring attack by Hospitaller cavalry from Mdina.

THE OTTOMANS DEPART

Further attacks on Fort St Michael and on Mdina also failed and in early September the Ottomans abandoned the attack when a relief force arrived from Sicily. The holding of Malta against seemingly impossible odds was an extraordinary and famous victory that ranked alongside any of the Hospitallers' other feats.

The Knights Hospitaller continued to fight for Christendom at sea and in land wars in eastern Europe and on Crete. They were to remain on Malta until 1798, when they were finally driven out by French general Napoleon en route to Egypt, on the expedition that was to discover the Rosetta Stone.

KNIGHTS OF THE TEMPLE OF SOLOMON
FOUNDATION OF THE KNIGHTS TEMPLAR

The military brotherhood of the Knights Templar was founded in the aftermath of the First Crusade, initially for the care of Christian pilgrims travelling to Jerusalem. The order received the official blessing of the Church at the Council of Troyes in 1129 and this was confirmed and many privileges granted to the order by Pope Innocent II in 1139.

French knights Hugues of Payens and Godfrey of Saint-Omer, both veterans of the First Crusade, took on the responsibility of protecting pilgrims on the road between the port of Jaffa and the Holy City, and in c.1120 proposed the formation of a religious brotherhood to perform this task. King Baldwin II of Jerusalem gave them his backing and provided space for a headquarters in the former al-Aqsa mosque on Temple Mount. At the time, this building was believed to stand on the ruins of the biblical Temple of Solomon and the brotherhood took the name of the 'Poor Knights of Christ and the Temple of Solomon'. Initially there were nine knights in the brotherhood and they had very few resources; their emblem, which shows two

▼ *With the backing of Bernard of Clairvaux, the Templars received the ceremonial blessing of the Roman Catholic Church at the Council of Troyes in 1129.*

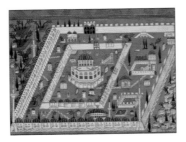

▲ *In crusader Jerusalem the al-Aqsa mosque was used as a palace. The Knights Templar were given space in one wing.*

knights mounted on a single horse, reflects their poverty-stricken beginnings. They took vows of poverty, chastity and obedience and agreed to share all their property.

BERNARD OF CLAIRVAUX
In 1126 Hugues of Payens, by now known as *Magister militum Templi* (Master of the Temple Soldiery) travelled to Europe to raise finances and seek Church support. He had a powerful ally in the Cistercian monk Bernard of Clairvaux, founder and first abbot of the Cistercian Abbey of Clairvaux in north-eastern France, who was also nephew to Andre of Montbard, one of the initial members of the brotherhood. Bernard wrote a pamphlet called *De Laude Novae Militiae* (In Praise of the New Soldiery), in which he set up the Templar knights as ideal exemplars of chivalry and contrasted their Christian poverty and religious devotion with the lack of these qualities in the secular knights of the day, men who expended their God-given energy in private quarrels driven by greed.

The pamphlet took up the imagery used by St Paul in his *Epistle to the Ephesians*, which urged readers to put on 'the whole armour of God' and 'the breastplate of righteousness', to use 'the shield of faith' and 'the helmet of salvation' and fight with 'the sword of the spirit'. Bernard

FOUNDER MEMBERS
Hugues of Payens was initially a vassal of (and cousin to) Count Hugues of Champagne in France and fought alongside his suzerain on the First Crusade, probably in the army of Godfrey of Bouillon. In addition to Godfrey of Saint-Omer, there were seven other founding members of the order: Payen of Montdidier; Archambaud of St Agnan; Andre of Montbard (Bernard of Clairvaux's uncle); Geoffrey Bisot; two knights known as Gondamer and Rossal; and an unknown knight – who may perhaps have been Count Hugues of Champagne himself. Legend tells that the image on the Templar seal of two knights on a single horse (seen below) in fact represents the actual practice of Hugues of Payens and Godfrey of Saint-Omer, who shared a horse because in the early days of the order they could not afford one each.

wrote of the new 'fearless knight, secure in every direction, who dons the breastplate of faith to protect his soul just as he dons an iron breastplate on his body'; he added that with this 'double armour' knights need fear nothing, and urged them to go forward in safety, with undaunted spirits, to fight back those who oppose the Cross of Christ.

Hugues of Payens, almost certainly with Bernard's help, drew up a rule for the new order, which was to be committed to protecting pilgrims and the holy places in Jerusalem, and this was approved at the Council of Troyes in January 1129. Five Templars, led by Hugues of Payens, attended the council and received the rule from Bernard. The rule was based on that of the Cistercians.

On his trip of 1128–29, Hugues of Payens also visited England and Scotland, where he established the first Templar house in London and also one close to Edinburgh on land granted to the order by King David I at Balantrodoch (now known as Temple, in Midlothian).

ROBERT OF CRAON

Hugues of Payens died in 1136 and was succeeded as Grand Master by Robert of Craon. Robert won papal approval for the order in 1139. In his bull *Omne Datum Optimum*, Pope Innocent II confirmed the order's rule and granted the Templars exemption from local laws and taxation and also from all secular and religious authority save that of the papacy. He wrote: 'since your religious order and your

ancient institution is praised throughout the whole world … you should be regarded especially as part of God's knighthood.' By this date, the order was well established, having already received several substantial gifts of land and finance from the nobility of Europe, many as a result of Bernard of Clairvaux's tract in praise of the order.

The Templars gained further significant privileges in the papal bulls *Milites Templi* of 1144 (issued by Pope Celestine II, who ruled 1143–44) and *Militia Dei* of 1145 (issued by Pope Eugenius III, who ruled 1145–53), which permitted them to build

▲ *Burgundian nobleman Jacques of Molay is inagurated into the Knights Templar. He became Grand Master in 1292, and was also the last Grand Master, for the order was accused of heresy and dissolved in 1312 under his leadership.*

their own places of worship, to bury their dead in the grounds of these establishments and to gather taxes on Templar property once each year. In 1147 Eugenius III granted the knights to right to wear a red splayed cross (one with spreading ends) on their white surplice. The sacred design was sewn above the heart.

▼ *The Templars meet, with great ceremony, in Paris in April 1147, shortly after they were granted privileges by the Church.*

ORGANIZATION

The head of the order was the Grand Master. Major decisions were taken by the Grand Chapter, a council of leading officers. Only the Grand Chapter could agree treaties or declare war. Its officers included the Marshal, in charge of military affairs, and the Seneschal, in control of administration, plus eight provincial masters in Aragon, Apulia, England, France, Poitiers, Hungary, Portugal and Scotland.

KNIGHTS TEMPLAR IN THE FIELD

BRAVE BUT OFTEN RECKLESS

The Knights Templar were famed for their bravery and martial prowess – as exemplified by the extraordinary heroism of Jakelin de Mailly, who fought until he was the last knight standing at the Battle of Cresson (1187). However, as a self-contained unit within crusader armies they often fought for the glory of the order above all other considerations. Within the order discipline was extremely strict – and this made the Templars a formidable fighting unit; but in a campaigning army they often undermined overall discipline by acting on their own initiative, seeking their own glory at the expense of strategy.

AT ASCALON

One celebrated example occurred during King Baldwin III of Jerusalem's siege of Ascalon (modern Ashkelon in Israel) in 1153. Baldwin brought a vast army, including the Templars and Hospitallers

▼ *Jakelin of Mailly, who reputedly fought on single-handedly when overwhelmed by Ayyubid troops at Cresson (1187) was the paragon of Templar bravery in battle.*

and all the great barons of the Kingdom of Jerusalem, as well as a contingent of pilgrims and Patriarch Fulcher of Jerusalem carrying a piece of the True Cross; but the city was well garrisoned and supplied with food to endure a long siege. Thus, it was particularly galling that when chance (or some might say the hand of God) gave the crusaders an opportunity, the self-interest of the Templars worked directly against the crusader army's long-term interests.

The Egyptian garrison attempted to burn down one of the crusaders' siege towers but the wind blew the flames back on the city defences and started a conflagration that made a section of the wall collapse. This part happened to be the one assigned to the Templars to attack. The Templars' Grand Master, Bernard of Tremblay, led an assault with 40 of his elite knights but did not tell King Baldwin. He even mounted a guard to prevent other crusaders joining the assault. Some accounts suggest that this was because the Templars wanted to have the glory all for themselves; according to chronicler William of Tyre, Bernard wanted to have

the spoils of the city to enrich the order's coffers. In the event, the 40 knights were overwhelmed by the garrison, the breach was repaired and the crusader army lost its advantage. The heads of Bernard and the Templar knights were displayed on the city walls.

AT AL-MANSOURAH

Another often cited example of Templar rashness in conflict was at the Battle of al-Mansourah during the Seventh Crusade when, following success in a surprise attack on the enemy camp, the Templars and members of other brotherhoods swept into the town of al-Mansourah against the orders of crusade leader King Louis IX of France. Their attack was a failure and jeopardized the entire campaign. All but five Templar knights were killed.

AT HATTIN

The Templar leadership also played a significant – and disastrous – role in the events leading up to the cataclysmic crusader defeat at the Battle of the Horns of Hattin in July 1187. Following Saladin's attack on 2 July on the Castle of Tiberias, King Guy of Jerusalem encamped with a vast army at Sephoria, around 18 miles (29km) away from the castle; initially Guy and his military council were minded to attack Saladin, but Sephoria was a strong defensive position and Count Raymond of Tripoli, who was master of Tiberias and knew the land, urged caution. Raymond insisted that even if he were to lose his castle, and his wife who was within it, he would prefer this outcome to putting the entire Kingdom of Jerusalem at risk by launching an ill-timed and ill-advised assault in difficult terrain.

The council accepted his advice, but that night Templar Grand Master Gerard of Ridefort managed to persuade King Guy to launch an assault on Saladin's army – by convincing him that Raymond was a

traitor who had agreed a secret deal with Saladin. The army made a reckless advance, was surrounded by Saladin's troops, and suffered a devastating defeat. The relic of the True Cross was captured and the military strength of the Kingdom of Jerusalem was annihilated.

THE MIGHT OF THE CROSS

At the Horns of Hattin – as at the Battle of Cresson shortly beforehand – Gerard placed his confidence in the might of the cross and showed himself willing to risk all in order to win glory. The Templars and other warrior brotherhoods took pride in waging war by the sword against the armies of Islam and had no time for the methods of negotiation and diplomacy that were increasingly favoured by the lords of the Kingdom of Jerusalem.

In 1148 at the Council of Acre, Templar Grand Master Robert of Craon was one of the voices urging an attack on Damascus while local lords argued rather for building an alliance with Mu'in ad-Din Unur, emir of Damascus, against the Zengid lords of Syria, notably the formidable Nur ed-Din of Aleppo: the resulting siege of

▼ *In 1299 Templar Grand Master, Jacques of Molay, fought the Mamluks in Armenia.*

▲ *The Templar chapel at Cressac, south of Angouleme, France, is decorated with scenes of the Templars fighting in Syria.*

Damascus was a disaster and brought the Second Crusade to a miserable end. In 1172, similarly, the Templars refused to back an alliance between King Amalric of Jerusalem and the Muslim Assassin sect against Nur ed-Din: they were annoyed that the proposed alliance would damage their income, for Templar taxes on Assassin villages were to be waived, and a body of Templar knights murdered a group of Assassins shouting 'No diplomacy with the infidel!' Their action effectively scuppered the deal. According to one chronicler, King Amalric was so angry that he declared his intention to ask the pope to dissolve the Templar order.

In the later crusades in Egypt, the Templars were likewise among those who refused to enter negotiations for the return of Jerusalem on the grounds that the Holy City must be won by the sword and the Christian knights must not negotiate with those of Islam. On the Fifth Crusade the Templars backed the papal legate Pelagius against King John of Jerusalem and the barons of his kingdom when Pelagius turned down the offer of Sultan al-Kamil in Egypt to give possession of Jerusalem and the entire Kingdom of Jerusalem as it

had been before the Battle of the Horns of Hattin if they would return Damietta and leave Egypt.

BROTHERS AT WAR

Such was the rivalry between Templars and Hospitallers over glory and resources that they became effectively enemies on sight. In the 13th century a Templar would draw his sword when he encountered a Hospitaller in the streets; in 1242, the two orders were actually drawn into a sword battle in the streets of Acre. In this period the Templars and Hospitallers secretly worked against one another in their dealings with the enemy.

BRAVERY AT ACRE

In 1291 in the siege of Acre, the last great military engagement of the Kingdom of Jerusalem, the Templars were defending the northern part of the city walls and showed all the bravery and indomitable fighting spirit of old. The Grand Master, William of Beaujeu, gave his life in the struggle at the walls and even after the city fell on 18 May the Templars carried on the fight for a full ten days from their headquarters within the city. By the time they were finally overrun by the invading army, attacks had reduced the Templar palace in Acre to a ruin, and it collapsed, killing defenders and attackers alike.

TEMPLAR BUILDERS
CASTLES AND CHURCHES

The Templars were involved in building from the first years of the brotherhood. When King Baldwin II of Jerusalem gave the founding Templars the Temple Mount as their headquarters in c.1120 he allowed them to develop the area as they pleased. In 1139 a key privilege granted to the order was the freedom to build their own churches and graveyards. In the early-to-mid 12th century they began to build castles to help in the protection of pilgrims and Christian sacred sites in Outremer.

TEMPLAR CASTLES

On the road to Jerusalem from Jaffa, the Templars manned the Castle of Castrum Arnaldi, first erected by the Patriarch and citizens of Jerusalem in c.1130 but subsequently given to the knights. Protecting the southern route to Jerusalem they had the Castle of Le Toron des Chevaliers, or Latrūn: built by Count Rodrigo Gonzalez of Toledo in Spain in 1137–41, during an armed pilgrimage to the Holy Land, and then given to the Templars. Midway between Jerusalem and Jericho, the Templars built a castle at Cisterna Rubea, complemented by a tower close to Jericho.

▼ *The Keep of the imposing Templar castle of Chastel Blanc at Safita (north-westen Syria) has walls 9 feet (3 metres) thick.*

The Templars were responsible for protecting the mountains to the north of Antioch, the area known as the Amanus March, and they built or garrisoned a number of impressive castles in the region. These included the Castle of Gaston (now known as Baghras), which the Templars manned from c.1154. They lost it to Saladin on 26 September 1188 and he dismantled the fortress, but the Templars regained the repaired castle in 1216. Shortly afterwards, however, they burned it when they had to retreat from the army of Egyptian sultan Baybars.

In Galilee the Templars themselves built the Castle of La Fève before 1172 and perhaps a good deal earlier. When this fortress was captured by Saladin in 1187, it was praised by an Islamic chronicler as 'the finest castle and most strongly fortified, the best supplied with men and munitions ... for the Templars this was a powerful castle, a place of refuge and a pillar of strength'. He added that it had a fine pasture and a fountain, and was regularly used by the Templars as a meeting place and a pasture for their horses. We know that the Castle of La Fève was used as a base for armies on campaign. From La Fève, Templar knights under the command of Gerard of Ridefort rode to defeat at the Battle of Cresson.

▲ *The impressive five-towered Monzon Castle, on a hilltop in Aragon (in northern Spain), was given to the Templars in 1143.*

The Templars also manned the fortress of Gaza, originally built by King Baldwin III of Jerusalem, who gave it to the knights in 1149 as a base for raids against the Muslim garrison in Ascalon and to protect the Kingdom of Jerusalem's southern frontier against attacks from Muslim Egypt. At a crossing of the upper River Jordan, the Templars began building the formidable

▼ *The Templars built fortifications in Europe as well as in the Holy Land. Their vast castle at Ponferrada in the kingdom of Léon was constructed in c.1290.*

▲ *Building began on the Temple Church in London in 1166, and finished in February 1185. A statue outside shows the Templar symbol, two knights riding on one horse.*

▲ *The imposing Convent of Christ in Tomar, Portugal, was built by Gualdim Pais, provincial master of the order, in 1160. The Templars were fighting against the Moors.*

Castle of Le Chastellet or Jacob's Ford. The position of the castle was a potential threat to Saladin because it guarded the only crossing of the Jordan and the way necessarily taken from Saladin's territory to the Kingdom of Jerusalem; the sultan offered King Baldwin IV a bribe of 100,000 dinars to tear the castle down and when he was refused he prepared to attack. The castle was still unfinished when the attack came in August 1169 and Saladin's sappers were able to bring the incomplete outer wall down. His men poured through the tun-

nel they had excavated and killed 800 of the garrison. Another 700 Templars were executed by Saladin. He dismantled the remains of the castle before he left.

TEMPLAR CHURCHES

The Templars understood that the former al-Aqsa mosque, which they had made their Jerusalem headquarters, was built on the remains of the Temple of Solomon, and they called it the *Templum Solomonis* (Temple of Solomon) or *Templum Domini* (Temple of the Lord). The temple itself, or

perhaps the Church of the Holy Sepulchre in Jerusalem, was the inspiration for a number of Templar churches with round naves in Europe.

These included the Church of the Holy Sepulchre, or 'Round Church', in Cambridge, England, built in 1130, and the Templars' own London headquarters, Temple Church in central London. Originally this building was lavishly decorated within; it was the order's second London base, built when the brotherhood moved from a smaller headquarters in High Holborn, also in central London, and it had a very grand consecration service performed by no less a figure than Patriarch Heraclius of Jerusalem on 10 February 1185, probably in the presence of King Henry II.

The Templars did not build only round churches – the chapel at their castle of Chastel Pelerin (built *c.*1218), now in Israel, had 12 sides and that at Safad Castle (built 1240–60) also had many sides; nor were the Templars the only creators of round churches – the Knights Hospitaller also built chapels and churches in this form. The majority of Templar churches, moreover, are rectangular and undecorated, in line with Bernard of Clairvaux's call for simple architecture.

TEMPLAR BANKERS

The Templars pioneered many methods of banking still in use today. Because the Templars received lavish gifts and had privileges exempting them from taxation, they grew immensely rich and became established as money lenders, providing funds for many monarchs and the Church to finance cathedral building. They used their network of monastic houses, or preceptories, to facilitate the safe transfer of funds for merchants: funds could be paid in at one Templar preceptory, and the credit note issued could be cashed at another preceptory halfway around the world. Money lending or usury was forbidden for Christians, so Templars did not call the fees they charged 'interest' – instead they compared the activity to being a landlord and called the charge 'rent'.

DOWNFALL OF THE TEMPLARS

ACCUSED OF HERESY AND DISBANDED

In the early 14th century the Templars came under a fierce and sustained attack on charges of heresy, pressed particularly by King Philip IV of France (r.1285–1314). The order was dissolved by papal bull *Vox in excelso* of 1312, issued by Pope Clement V (ruled 1305–14).

After the fall of Acre in 1291 the military monastic orders faced an uncertain and difficult future: with no possessions to defend in the Holy Land, their purpose was unclear; the Teutonic Knights and the Hospitallers established monastic states, in Prussia and Rhodes respectively, but the Templars did not. The Templars also faced criticism for the lavish lifestyle of some members, funded by wealth generated from banking and property; they were also subject to attack because many people were in debt to them.

▼ *After executing Jacques of Molay in early 1314, Philip ruled for only a few months. He met an untimely death, mauled by a boar while out hunting in November 1314.*

▲ *Arrested at dawn. Grand Master Jacques of Molay and thousands of French Templars are taken into royal custody.*

MERGER PROPOSAL

One popular solution was the merger of the Templars and the Hospitallers. This proposal was made by, among others, Norman lawyer and pamphleteer Pierre Dubois and by Majorcan novelist, poet and author on chivalry Ramon Llull. King Philip IV of France was strongly in favour, seeing an opportunity to escape his very substantial debts to the Templars, and he proposed that the kings of France should become hereditary masters of a combined order; under this plan, Philip was to lead the knights of the combined order on a new crusade to recover the Holy Land.

In 1305 Bertrand of Goth, Archbishop of Bordeaux, was elected Pope Clement V. He was strongly under the influence of King Philip IV of France, and he established the papal curia not in Rome but in France, first at Poitiers and then, from 1309, at Avignon. In 1306 Clement summoned the two Grand Masters, Jacques of Molay of the Templars and Fulk of Villaret of the Hospitallers, to Poitiers to consider the merger; Jacques arrived in 1307 but Fulk was delayed. Clement raised the

matter with the Templar Master and also discussed accusations of heresy against the Templars that had been made by former Templar knights Esquin of Floyan, Bernard Pelet and Gérard of Byzol. It would appear that Clement was convinced that the charges were false, but he asked Philip IV to investigate.

ON TRIAL

Philip IV saw an opportunity to bring about the downfall of the Templars, cancel his vast debts, and engineer the merger of the monastic orders that he favoured. Philip issued secret orders and in dawn raids on Friday 13 October 1307, 5,000 Templars in France, including Jacques of

---

TEMPLARS IN AMERICA

Some rather fanciful accounts suggest that Knights Templar were in fact the first Europeans to sail to the New World of North America (after the Vikings in *c*.1000). The theory goes that the Templars sailed from Scotland (or perhaps from their port of La Rochelle in western France) after the downfall of the order and settled in Nova Scotia (Latin for 'New Scotland') in 1398, and then moved on to New England in 1399 – almost a century before the voyages of Christopher Columbus, the Genoan explorer usually credited with discovering America. There are gravestones in Nova Scotia that bear crusader crosses, and a hand-cut gravestone in Westford, Massachusetts, is marked with Templar imagery. The Templar Rossyln Chapel in Scotland is reportedly decorated with carvings in stone of American plants such as the *aloe vera*; the chapel was completed in 1486, six years before Columbus's first voyage in 1492.

Molay, were arrested on charges of heresy, blasphemy and sodomy. The accusations centred on the Templars' secret initiation ceremony: it was alleged that an initiate was required to spit on the cross, to deny Christ three times and to kiss the officer who admitted him. There were also claims that initiates worshipped a pagan idol and that knights were not permitted to refuse to have sexual relations with one another. Most Templars admitted to these or similar charges under severe torture.

On 22 November Clement called on all Christian rulers to arrest Templars and to take possession of their assets. He also commanded the French Templars to be released from imprisonment and be given into the care of papal commissioners. In hearings before a papal committee beginning on 24 December 1307 Jacques of Molay and other senior Templars retracted their confessions on the grounds that they had been extracted under torture.

Trials began in 1309 and ran on and off for five years. Before the commission in November 1309 Jacques of Molay declared that he wanted to mount a defence of the order, but had doubts that he could – since he was illiterate and the order did not contain a single lawyer; he

▼ Philip IV used his influence over Pope Clement V to bring about the downfall of the Templars, to whom he was in debt.

▲ The condemned Templars are executed in Paris on 18 March 1314. In 2001 a document uncovered at the Vatican revealed that Pope Clement had secretly absolved Jacques and other Templars in 1308.

put his faith in the pope and seems to have believed, perhaps with the confidence of the innocent, that he and his men would be cleared in the end. Under questioning he declared that the Templars had always been generous in charitable donations, that Templar liturgy was more beautiful than that in any other churches, and that in no other order had the knights shed their blood more readily in defence of the cross of Christ.

One accusation against the Templars that was most widely confessed was that they spat on the cross and denied Christ during their initiation ceremonies. Some historians suggest that this claim may have been true, and was perhaps required as a demonstration of the initiate's total loyalty to the order – overriding all other claims, even that of religious faith.

At the Council of Vienne in 1312 Pope Clement issued the bull *Vox in excelso*, dissolving the Templars, and a second bull, *Ad Providam*, transferring most of the Templars' assets to the Knights Hospitaller. However, a paper found in Vatican archives in 2001 suggests that privately Clement absolved Jacques of Molay, the Templar order and all its knights of guilt.

JACQUES OF MOLAY EXECUTED

On 18 March 1314 at a trial hearing in Paris, Jacques of Molay and leading templar Geoffrey of Charney, Preceptor of Normandy, publicly withdrew their confessions once more and were sentenced to death as relapsed heretics by burning at the stake in central Paris. On his own insistence, Molay was tied facing the cathedral of Notre Dame, and with his hands raised in prayer; legend recounts that at his death he declared that Pope Clement and King Philip would soon meet him before the throne of God. Both men were indeed dead by the end of the year.

Of the remaining Templars some joined the Knights Hospitaller; others probably quietly returned to the secular world. Still others fled beyond the reach of papal power – to Switzerland or to Scotland, which had been excommunicated; some, perhaps, sailed to America (see box). In Portugal, the Templars carried on as the Knights of Christ, and in Spain as knights of the Order of Montesa.

▼ Rosslyn Chapel in Midlothian, Scotland, reputedly has Templar connections and secret coded decorations, but many scholars dispute the link to the Templars.

TEUTONIC KNIGHTS
GERMANIC BROTHERHOOD

The German order of the Teutonic Knights was established in Acre in the late 12th century and granted approval by Pope Celestine III (ruled 1191–98) in 1192. In the 13th century the order established itself in Prussia, initially as part of a crusade against pagans in the region and subsequently against the non-Christian people of central and northern Europe. The order suffered a crushing defeat at the hands of a Polish–Lithuanian force at the Battle of Tannenberg in 1410 and became gradually secularized.

ORIGINS AND FOUNDATION
The earliest origins of the order of the Teutonic Knights lie in a hospital for German pilgrims run in Jerusalem from *c.*1140 by German knights under the overall control of the Knights Hospitaller. It was known as the *Domus Teutonicorum* (House of the Germans). In 1189–90 during the siege of Acre on the Third Crusade, German merchants from Lübeck and Bremen set up a sister German hospital in the crusader camp. After the

▼ The Teutonic Knights' Montfort Castle was originally so called from the French for 'strong mountain'. The Knights' name for it, Starkenberg, means the same in German.

▲ Holy Roman Emperor and sometime King of Jerusalem, Frederick II, seen here receiving a delegation of Arabs in 1230, was a major patron of the Teutonic Knights. His chancellor, Petrus of Vinea, pictured on the left, was a Master of the Order.

capture of Acre in 1191 the hospital was established as a permanent institution in Acre, known as the Hospital of St Mary of the German House in Jerusalem. Initially a simple monastic brotherhood, as recognized by Pope Celestine III in 1192, it became a military order with the approval of King Amalric II of Jerusalem in 1198.

The Teutonic Order received substantial grants of land from popes Celestine III and Innocent III in the Latin Kingdom of Jerusalem and in Germany, Italy and elsewhere. It was Innocent III who, in 1205, granted the knights the use of their white habits, or surplices, decorated with a black cross. The order based its organization on that of the Knights Templar and its head was known as the Grand Master.

MONTFORT
The order's original base was in Acre, but in 1220 the brotherhood bought the Castle of Montfort, or Starkenberg, to the north-east of the city and on the route between the Mediterranean coast and Jerusalem. From 1229 this was the principal seat of the Teutonic Grand Masters, as well as the home of the order's treasury and archive. In 1266 the Knights repelled an attack by Mamluk sultan Baybars, but when he returned in 1271 the garrison surrendered at the end of a seven-day siege. Baybars for once honoured his promise made during negotiations to allow the knights to leave Montfort with their belongings. They returned to Acre.

IN TRANSYLVANIA
Hermann von Salza, Grand Master of the Teutonic Order in 1210–39, was a close friend of Holy Roman Emperor Frederick II. Under von Salza's leadership, the brotherhood began to transfer its operations from the Holy Land to central Europe.

▲ *The Teutonic Knights' days of glory ended when, under Grand Master Ulrich von Jungingen, they were roundly defeated at the First Battle of Tannenberg in July 1410.*

In 1211 the Teutonic Knights entered the service of King Andrew II of Hungary (r.1205–35) and settled on land he gave them in Burzenland, Transylvania; his aim was to establish a buffer against the border incursions of the nomadic Turkish Cuman people. However, when the Teutonic Knights attempted to establish an independent principality on the territory by appealing to Pope Honorius III (ruled 1216–27) to be placed under his authority rather than that of the Hungarian crown, King Andrew expelled them from the country.

IN PRUSSIA

In 1226 the Teutonic Knights answered a call from Duke Konrad I of Masovia in Poland to fight on his borders against the pagan Prussians who had been provoked to violent uprising by the first Prussian Crusade of 1221. Over 50 years between 1233 and 1283 the knights fought with great ferocity for the conversion of the Prussians. From 1245 the order even had the power to grant crusade indulgences in this struggle without prior papal approval.

The Teutonic Knights governed Prussia as a sovereign 'monastic state' under charters from the Holy Roman Emperor and the papacy. They founded several fortress settlements including Konigsberg (now in the Russian enclave of Kaliningrad Oblast, situated between Poland and Lithuania), Elbing (modern Elblag in northern Poland), Allenstein (modern Olsztyn in north-east Poland) and Memel (modern Klaipeda in Lithuania). But they faced sustained and brutal opposition from pagan Prussians, who (according to the order's chronicles) would 'roast' captured knights in their armour over fires 'like chestnuts'. The order also tried to expand eastwards to convert Russia to Roman Catholicism, but suffered a devastating defeat at the hands of Alexander Nevsky in the Battle of Lake Peipus, 1242.

MARIENBURG

The knights maintained their presence in the Holy Land at Acre but following the fall of that port in 1291 and the final collapse of Outremer, they briefly made their main base in Venice, Italy, from where they planned ways to retake the Holy Land. In 1309, however, they built a vast castle in Prussia named Marienburg (Mary's Castle)

▼ *Teutonic Knights encounter pagan east German farmers during their attempts to impose Christianity in the region.*

in honour of the Virgin Mary. This place (now Malbork in Poland) was thereafter their main base. In the 14th century they waged a long war against pagans in the Baltic, in the area known as Livonia (now Lithuania, Latvia and Estonia).

The knights were also engaged in wars against Poland, because their expansion cut the country off from its access to the Baltic Sea, and with Lithuania even after that country's conversion to Christianity in 1387. In 1410 Poland and Lithuania joined forces and defeated the Teutonic Knights at the Battle of Tannenberg. The brotherhood ceded territory to Poland, and further landholdings in 1466 following defeat by the Poles and the knights' own Prussian vassals in the Thirteen Years War (1454–66). The order survived in East Prussia, but the Grand Master held the land as a vassal of the Polish king.

DECLINE AND REBIRTH

In 1525 Grand Master Albert of Brandenberg dissolved the order and founded a secular duchy in Prussia under his own rule. Gradually over the ensuing 400 years, the order's territories were ceded to secular authorities. In 1809 the French emperor Napoleon dissolved the order entirely and seized its remaining holdings. However, the Teutonic Knights enjoyed a rebirth in Vienna in 1834 as an ecclesiastical body engaged in charitable work.

WARRIORS OF THE RECONQUISTA
SPANISH AND PORTUGUESE ORDERS OF KNIGHTHOOD

A number of military brotherhoods were formed in Spain and Portugal as part of the *Reconquista* (Reconquest), the 770-year war waged between 722 and 1492 to win back those countries from Muslim control.

The first Spanish military brotherhoods were formed shortly after the establishment of the Knights Hospitaller and the Knights Templar in 1110–20. In the 1130s a number of Templar foundations were made in Spain, and on his death in 1134 King Alfonso I *El Batallador* (the Warrior) of Aragon and Navarre left the entire kingdom of Aragon to be shared between the Templars and Hospitallers.

The bequest was annulled, and in the event the Templars and Hospitallers took on the care and defence of a number of castles both in Aragon and elsewhere in Spain; however, they were generally not keen to be drawn into the war against Muslims in Spain because their main interest was to use European landholdings to raise money and men to fight for the cross in the Holy Land.

THE ORDER OF CALATRAVA
In 1157 the Templars told King Alfonso VII of León and Castile that for this reason they were abandoning the Castle of Calatrava in southern Castile. At this point

Raymond, Abbot of the Cistercian monastery of Fitero, offered to man and defend the castle with Cistercian lay brothers; he had been persuaded to do so by a former knight turned monk named Diego Valasquez. The monks held Calatrava until Raymond's death in 1163, after which some withdrew to the monastery of Cirvelos. The remainder stayed on, elected Don Garcia as their first Grand Master and established the Order of Calatrava.

The order was recognized as a militia by Pope Alexander III (ruled 1159–81) on 26 September 1164. The brothers' rule,

▼ *The Knights of Calatrava had monastic beginnings, but repeatedly proved their worth in battle against the Moors.*

▲ *King Alfonso IX of the Spanish kingdom of León conquered Alcantara on the River Tagus from the Moors and gave it into the protection of the Knights of Calatrava. The town's imposing Convent of St Benedict was built later, in the 16th century.*

based on that of Cistercian lay brothers, was approved in 1187 by Pope Gregory VIII (pope for less than two months in 1187). It included the requirement that the brothers keep silent when eating and sleeping and sleep in their armour. Unlike the Templars and Hospitallers, the order was subject to secular authority and its Grand Master took an oath of loyalty to the King of Castile.

The Knights of Calatrava had mixed fortunes on the field of battle. Alongside the Castilian army they suffered a heavy defeat at the hands of the Moors at the Battle of Alarcos in 1195 and as a result lost the Castle of Calatrava; the survivors settled in the Cistercian monastery of Cirvelos, and then built a new stronghold at Salvatierra in 1198. They also lost this castle to the Moors in 1209, but in 1212 recaptured Calatrava and then fought in the great Christian victory of that year at the Battle of Las Navas de Tolosa. After which they built a new headquarters, Calatrava La Nueva just 8 miles (12km) from their original home.

▲ A Spanish nobleman wears the cross of Alcantara on his court clothes. By the 16th century, when this portrait was painted, the knights no longer lived as monks.

THE ORDER OF ALCANTARA

The knights of the Order of Alcantara, which grew from a brotherhood established in the 12th century in the Kingdom of Leon, came under the protection of the Order of Calatrava in *c.*1218. Its knights were originally called the Knights of St Julian of Pereiro: according to tradition, St Julian was a hermit who inspired a group of knights to build and garrison a castle on the River Tagus. They were known to have existed in 1176 and were recognized by Pope Celestine III in 1197; in 1218 they took over the defence of the Castle of Alcantara from the Order of Calatrava. Like the Calatrava brothers, the Alcantara knights followed the Cistercian rule.

THE ORDER OF AVIZ

The Portuguese knights of the Order of Aviz were also under the protection of the knights of Calatrava. Originally known as the Brothers of Santa Maria of Evora, the Order of Aviz had possession of the town of Evora, taken from the Moors in 1211; they subsequently took possession of the Castle of Aviz and named themselves after it, the Knights of St Benedict of Aviz. They

followed the Benedictine, then the Cistercian rule. The knights of Calatrava passed control of a number of their castles in Portugal to the Order of Aviz.

THE ORDER OF SANTIAGO

Established in *c.*1170, the Order of Santiago had its origins in a brotherhood of knights founded to protect pilgrims travelling to the shrine of Saint James (Santiago) at Compostela. Also known as the Order of Saint James of Compostela, it had it headquarters at Uclés in Castile. It followed the rule of the canons of Saint Augustine. The order was unusual in that, unlike other military orders, from the start the knights of Santiago had the right to marry. In the mid-13th century the knights of Santiago won a great reputation fighting in the campaigns of King Ferdinand III of Castile (reigned 1217–52) against the Moors in southern Spain and they played a notable part in the siege and capture of Seville in 1247–48.

▼ Knights of the Order of St James of Compostela were granted their first monastic rule in 1171 by Cardinal Jacinto, who later became Pope Celestine III.

OTHER SPANISH ORDERS

The Order of the Knights of Our Lady of Mountjoie was established by Spanish knight Count Rodrigo and received official approval from Pope Alexander III (ruled 1159–81) in 1180. It was named after the hill of Mountjoie, the 'hill of joy' from which the men of the First Crusade first saw Jerusalem. The brothers – all Spaniards – had their headquarters on Mountjoie and also had landholdings in Castile and Aragon and had responsibility for protecting pilgrims there. Their emblem was a red-and-white cross.

The brotherhood had difficulty with recruitment and was renamed the Order of Trufac in 1187. Several of its knights were killed at the disastrous Battle of Hattin in 1187 and the remainder left the Holy Land and settled in Aragon. In 1221 King Ferdinand of Aragon merged it with the Order of Calatrava.

Other Spanish brotherhoods included the Order of Montegaudio, founded in Aragon in *c.*1173; that of Saint George of Alfama, established in *c.*1200; and that of Saint Mary of Spain, created in *c.*1270. The Order of Montegaudio merged with the Knights Templar in 1196. The Order of Saint Mary of Spain combined with the Order of Santiago in 1280. The Order of the Blessed Virgin Mary of Mercy was established in 1218 in Barcelona.

KNIGHTS OF ST THOMAS
THE HOSPITALLERS OF ST THOMAS OF CANTERBURY AT ACRE

The English military brotherhood of the Knights of St Thomas of Canterbury at Acre was established after the capture of the city by crusader armies led by King Richard I of England (r.1189–99) and King Philip II of France (r.1180–1223) in 1191. Some sources suggest its founder was a certain William, chaplain to the Dean of St Paul's Cathedral, London, although there is also evidence that the knights celebrated no less a figure than Richard Coeur de Lion himself as their founder. Their brotherhood was named in honour of Saint Thomas Becket, the Archbishop of Canterbury who had been slain in his own cathedral by English knights in 1170 and canonized in 1173 (*see* box). The order survived for around 340 years, until it was wound up by King Henry VIII of England (r.1509–47) as part of the Dissolution of the Monasteries in 1538.

▼ *The Fifth Crusade was mainly against Ayyubid Egypt, but its initial stages took place in the Holy Land, and at this time Peter Roches established the Knights of St Thomas as a military order.*

CARING FOR THE SICK
In its first years the brotherhood was a religious rather than a military order, dedicated to caring for the wounded and sick, burying the knights who had died in the wars of the cross and seeking to raise funds in order to ransom Christian warriors who had been taken prisoner by Saladin and his Muslim generals. The

◄ *Peter Roches, Bishop of Winchester and the man who transformed the St Thomas brotherhood from monks to knights, founded Titchfield Abbey in Hampshire in c.1222.*

brothers took vows of poverty, chastity and obedience like their counterparts in other monastic orders. In Acre they built a church and a hospital, both dedicated to St Thomas of Canterbury.

The brotherhood was made into a military order by Peter Roches, Bishop of Winchester, when he was in the Holy Land for the Fifth Crusade of 1217–21. He established the brotherhood under the rule of the Teutonic Knights with the backing of the Latin Patriarch of Jerusalem and leading magnates of Outremer. The brotherhood was recognized by Pope Gregory IX (ruled 1227–41) in 1236. The order became more generally known as the Knights of St Thomas Acon (the last word being an anglicized form of Acre). In the first 80 years or so of its existence, the brotherhood had a prior as its senior figure, but from *c*.1279 – reflecting increasing militarization – the pre-eminent individual was the master.

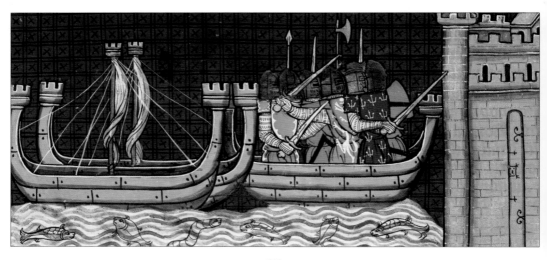

Historians are not certain why members of religious brotherhoods initially dedicated to providing medical and other care for pilgrims and soldiers became themselves soldiers. It is likely that the constant shortage of warriors in Outremer was an important incentive for the brothers to take up arms and further the Christian cause themselves. Bishop Peter Roches would surely have been encouraged in his militarization of the Order of St Thomas of Acre when he sought the counsel of Outremer's leading barons, for these men faced a constant struggle to find enough soldiers to fight their wars and maintain hard-won territories.

The brothers fought in defence of Christian holdings in the Holy Land and, in particular, to protect Acre. They did not become wealthy. In 1279 they were forced to appeal to King Edward I of England (r.1272–1307) for funds. But they did succeed in establishing a house in London and various provincial quarters in both England and Ireland.

▼ *Mercers Hall in Ironmonger Lane, London, stood on the site of the former Hospital of St Thomas Acon, which was destroyed in the Great Fire of London (1666). The hall as shown here was itself destroyed by German bombs in May 1941.*

THE CULT OF ST THOMAS BECKET

King Henry II of England (r.1154–89) elevated Thomas Becket to greatness, making him Chancellor in 1155 and Archbishop of Canterbury in 1162 but the pair quarrelled over Henry's attempts to impose his authority on the Church and, despite an apparent reconciliation, four knights claiming to be acting on Henry's wishes killed Becket in Canterbury Cathedral on 29 December 1170. The whole of Christendom was outraged and in 1173 Pope Alexander III (ruled 1159–81) canonized the archbishop. Becket's cult was immediately very strong and his tomb at Canterbury became a major draw for pilgrims. For his part, Henry II strongly denied having ordered the murder of his archbishop, but was forced to make a public demonstration of penance at the saint's tomb in July 1174.

▲ *Two murderous knights violate the sanctuary at Canterbury Cathedral and slay Thomas Becket at his prayers.*

IN CYPRUS

After the fall of Acre in 1291 the brothers removed, with the Knights Templar, to Cyprus. There they built the fine Church of St Nicholas in Nicosia. But very difficult times followed. In the early 14th century the London house of the Knights of St Thomas was reported to be in ruins and the brothers had to fight off two proposed takeovers, firstly by the Knights Templar and secondly by the convent of Bonhommes at Ashridge, Hertfordshire.

In *c.*1320 the master of the order in Cyprus, Henry of Bedford, removed to London and established himself in power there. He sent a deputy to rule in Cyprus, but the brothers rejected this man and there was a spilt in the order. Overall power briefly returned to Cyprus after Henry's death, but in *c.*1360 it was finally confirmed in London; there are no records of a master in Nicosia after this date.

From this period onwards, the brothers appear to have abandoned their military role and exchanged the rule of the Teutonic Knights for that of the monastic rule of the Augustinians. They concentrated on charitable and educational work in London, where they established St Thomas of Acres grammar school in the city in *c.*1450. The order was dissolved by Henry VIII in 1538 in the Dissolution.

MERCERS

Henry put the brothers' London hospital and chapel up for sale and the buildings were bought by the Worshipful Company of Mercers. Incorporated under royal charter in 1394, the Worshipful Company of Mercers was established as a trade association for merchants in the cloth trade, especially importers of velvet and silk and exporters of wool. The Mercers had already established links with the Knights of St Thomas and had been worshipping in the brotherhood's London chapel for some years. This was destroyed in the Great Fire of London in 1666, but a statue of Christ was salvaged and reused both in the second Mercer's Hall and Chapel (destroyed in World War I) and in its modern replacement.

THE ORDER OF ST LAZARUS

AND OTHER MINOR CHIVALRIC ORDERS

A number of smaller chivalric orders complemented the major brotherhoods of the Knights Templar, the Knights Hospitaller and the Teutonic Knights. Among these, as we have seen, was the brotherhood of the Knights of St Thomas at Acre. Others included the Order of St Lazarus of Jerusalem, established *c*.1123, and the Order of the Sword, founded by King Peter of Cyprus in 1347.

THE ORDER OF ST LAZARUS

Another group of knights in the Holy Land who were dedicated to relieving the suffering of pilgrims and soldiers in the wars of the cross belonged to the Order of St Lazarus of Jerusalem, which specialized in the care of lepers. Like the Order of St John (Hospitallers), St Lazarus grew into a military order from a brotherhood offering hospitality and medical care. Under the Templar rule, any Templar knights who contracted leprosy were required to transfer to the Order of St Lazarus, and

▼ *The Knights of St Lazarus are named after the man raised from the dead by Christ, as told in the Gospel of St John.*

▲ *Henry II of England was an important patron of the Order of St Lazarus. His effigy is at Fontevrault Abbey, France.*

these Templars trained the St Lazarus brothers in military ways. The Order of St Lazarus of Jerusalem was established as a military brotherhood in *c*.1123.

The order became very wealthy, and was left endowments by European kings including Louis VII of France (r.1137–80), Henry II of England (r.1154–89) and Holy Roman Emperor Frederick II (r.1220–50). The order followed the Augustinian rule. Knights of the Order fought at the Battle of La Forbie in 1244 against the alliance of Khwarismian Turks and Sultan as-Salih Ayyub of Egypt (r.1240–49), in the army of the Seventh Crusade led by King Louis IX of France (r.1226–70) and at the fall of Acre in 1291.

The order received papal recognition under Augustinian rule in 1255 in the reign of Pope Alexander IV (ruled 1254–61), and was granted the same privileges and exemptions as the principal monastic orders in 1262 under Pope Urban IV (ruled 1261–64). Its numbers were swelled after 1265 when Pope Clement IV (ruled 1265–68) issued an order that Catholic clergy send all lepers to the houses of St Lazarus.

After the loss of Jerusalem in 1187, the Knights of St Lazarus (like the Hospitaller counterparts) removed to Acre. Then, following the fall of Acre in 1291, the Order

of St Lazarus disappeared from the East altogether while the Hospitallers as we have seen took up residence on Cyprus. The Knights of St Lazarus continued to maintain leper hospitals in Europe.

THE ORDER OF THE SWORD

The future Peter I of Cyprus, the titular King of Jerusalem in 1358–69 and the monarch known as the 'Crusading king', led a military expedition in 1365 against Muslim Egypt. He founded the chivalric brotherhood of the Order of the Sword

▼ *Those afflicted with leprosy, who entered the Order of St Lazarus, were required to pass their worldly goods to the brothers.*

▲ *Mary the mother of Christ, was honoured in the brotherhood of Our Lady Of Bethlehem, established to counter the power of the Ottomans in the mid-15th century.*

in 1347. In a powerful mystical experience, Peter had a vision of a floating cross and heard a voice urging him to liberate the Holy Land: the order he formed was for knights and men-at-arms prepared to dedicate themselves to freeing Jerusalem and other parts of Outremer from Muslim control. Its emblem was a silver sword, point down, against a blue backing inscribed with the words 'With this maintain loyalty'.

THE ORDER OF OUR LADY OF BETHLEHEM

After the Ottoman Turks under Sultan Mehmed II 'the Conqueror' (r.1444–46, 1451–81) captured Constantinople in 1453, Pope Pius II (ruled 1458–64) established the Order of Our Lady of Bethlehem on the island of Lemnos in the Aegean Sea. Its knights were charged with defending the island against the Ottomans and countering the Turks' activity in the Aegean and Hellespont. The knights of the order wore a white surplice with a red cross and followed a rule similar to that of the Knights Hospitaller.

Pope Pius suppressed a number of orders, including that of St Lazarus, in order to provide the knights of Our Lady of Bethlehem with property and revenues.

But the enterprise came to nothing when the Ottomans succeed in capturing Lemnos. The orders Pius had suppressed were re-established.

OTHER GERMANIC ORDERS

A number of minor Germanic military-monastic orders of knighthood were established in the 13th century. The Order of Dobrzyn, also known as the *Fratres Milites Christi de Prussia*, (the Prussian Cavaliers of Christ Jesus), was created in the 1220s by Christian of Oliva, the first Bishop of Prussia, in order to fight against raids on Masovia by pagan Prussians who had risen in defiance of Duke Konrad I of Masovia's efforts to force them to convert

to Christianity. The establishment of the order was approved by Pope Gregory IX (ruled 1227–41) in 1228. The order was granted possession of the town of Dobrzyn and surrounding regions (Dobrzyn Land). The order initially had 15 German knights in membership under the command of Master Brunon. In 1235 the majority of the knights joined the Teutonic Order.

The monastic order of the Livonian Brothers of the Sword was established by Albert of Buxhoeveden, third Bishop of Riga in Livonia, in 1202 and was granted official sanction by Pope Innocent III in 1204. Bishop Albert wanted the German warrior monks to help in the forcible conversion to Christianity of pagan Curonians, Livonians and others in the region. The knights, who were also known as 'Christ Knights', 'Sword Brethren' and 'The Militia of Christ of Livonia', made their headquarters at Fellin (modern Viljandi in Estonia) and the remains of their Grand Master's castle can still be seen there. They suffered a heavy defeat by Lithuanians at the Battle of Schaulen in 1236 and in 1237 most of the members joined the Teutonic Order.

▼ *Two minor Germanic orders – those of Dobrzyn and of the Livonian Brothers of the Sword – were established by bishops.*

CHAPTER ELEVEN

THE EUROPEAN CRUSADES

Christian wars were waged against Muslims in Spain from as early as the 8th century, and against the pagan peoples of northern Europe from the time of the Second Crusade (1147–49) up until the 14th century. In southern France the Albigensian Crusade of the 13th century brutally attacked the Cathars, who were denounced as heretics by the papacy; in Bohemia the Hussites (followers of Czech nationalist preacher Jan Hus) were likewise declared heretics and attacked by crusaders in 1420–32; and in Italy during the 12th–14th centuries, several holy wars were called against enemies of the Catholic Church.

Many of these wars were thinly disguised secular struggles – those in Italy, for example, were fought to promote the territorial interests of the papacy. They were different in kind to the crusades in the Holy Land, and would probably have been fought even if the ideology of crusading was not deployed. One of them, the war to reconquer Spain, predated the crusading era, for it began in the immediate aftermath of the Muslim conquest of the Iberian Peninsula in the early 8th century. Yet, once available, crusading rhetoric and the apparatus of crusade indulgences and taxes were enthusiastically applied to this Spanish struggle from the time of the First Crusade in the 1090s. The call to fight for the cross also gave an added force and charge to all the struggles termed as the Northern Crusades against Muslims, heretics or pagans.

▲ *King Alfonso XI of Castile waged war against Muslims in Spain with such determination he was called 'the Implacable'.*

◀ *After the conquest in 1492 of Granada, the last remaining Muslim territory in Spain, Ferdinand and Isabella receive Arab tributes.*

THE RECONQUISTA
THE STRUGGLE IN SPAIN

◄ At the Battle of Guadalete (711) in the far south of the Iberian Peninsula, invading Muslim cavalry routed the Visigoths.

The *Reconquista* – from the word in Spanish and Portuguese for 'reconquest' – was the struggle by the Christians of Europe to retake the Iberian Peninsula from its Moorish rulers. The Reconquista lasted a full 750 years, from the early 8th century, when Muslim Arabs and Berbers captured the peninsula from the Visigoths, to 1492, when the combined armies of Aragon and Castile conquered the city of Granada, the last Muslim territory in the peninsula. These Iberian wars were promoted as holy wars by popes who offered crusading privileges to those taking part in the struggle.

VISIGOTHS AND MUSLIMS
In the 5th century AD the Visigoths, an East Germanic tribe, took power in the Roman province of Hispania (incorporating the whole of the Iberian Peninsula and part of southern France) under the auspices of Rome. After the fall of the Roman Empire in the west, the Visigoth territory became an independent territory.

A Muslim army of Arabs and north African Berber tribesmen invaded the southern part of the peninsula in 711 and in five years captured most of the large

Visigoth kingdom. The Muslims then attempted to push on northwards but were defeated by Odo, Duke of Aquitaine, at the Battle of Toulouse in 721 and by Frankish leader Charles Martel in the Battle of Tours in 732. Thereafter they largely abandoned attempts at northward expansion and settled in what is now Spain and Portugal.

Only in the north of the Iberian Peninsula did the Visigoths maintain a foothold. The Visigoth nobleman Pelayo established the Kingdom of Asturias, which was subsequently to be an important base for the reconquest of Spain. His defeat of a Muslim army in the Battle of Covadonga (722) is often identified as the first conflict of the Reconquista.

AL-ANDALUS AND THE MOORS
The Muslim state in the Iberian Peninsula was known by the Arabic name al-Andalus – and its people were known by the Christians as 'Moors'.

Al-Andalus was at first nominally subject to the Umayyad caliph in Damascus, Syria. 'Caliph' was the title for the leader of Islam as a successor to the founder of the faith, the Prophet Mohammad; the

Umayyads were the successors of the fourth caliph, Mu'awiyah, a member of the Umayyad clan of caravan merchants.

In 750 the Umayyad caliph Marwan II was defeated by a rival leader, Abu al-Abbas, who established the Abbasid caliphate. Abu al-Abbas was known as *as-Saffah* ('the Bloodshedder') on account of the ruthlessness with which he eliminated his rivals, but one prominent Umayyad, Abd ar-Rahman, escaped to Spain and established himself in Córdoba. His successors were in theory subordinate to the Abbasid caliphs, who were now based in Baghdad, in Iraq, but were in practice independent and ruled as emirs of Córdoba. When Abbasid power declined sharply and their realm fell into anarchy in the early 10th century, the then emir, Abd ar-Rahman III, declared himself the

▼ The Arabs capture Córdoba. Under their rule it became one of the world's largest cities, home to as many as 500,000 people.

independent caliph of Córdoba in 929. Historians call al-Andalus the Umayyad caliphate province from 711 to 750, the Emirate of Córdoba fom 750 to 929, and the Caliphate of Córdoba from 929 to 1031. After 1031, the caliphate broke up into small Muslim kingdoms.

ST JAMES THE GREAT

Descendants of King Pelayo of Asturias seized territory in Galicia (the north-west part of the peninsula). In the reign of King Alfonso II of Asturias (r.791–842), the bones of St James were reputedly discovered at Compostela, which became established as one of Europe's foremost pilgrimage sites. St James the Great was one of Christ's 12 Apostles and traditionally brought the Christian Gospel to the Iberian Peninsula. According to legend, his bodily remains were brought to what is now Spain by sea after his death. In 844 the saint then supposedly made a miraculous appearance to lead the Christian army of King Ramiro I of Asturias (r.842–50) against the Moors of Córdoba in the Battle of Clavijo.

PROGRESS IN THE RECONQUISTA

Gerona and Barcelona were taken from the Muslims in 785 and 801 by Carolingian armies from France, and the region of Catalonia became part of the Carolingian realm known as 'the Spanish March'. After 850 the Christian buffer between southern France and the Iberian Peninsula established by the Kings of Asturias was expanded to the valley of the River Duero. In 913 the rulers of Asturias moved their seat of power from Oviedo to León and the kingdom became known as León. Christian kingdoms were also established in Pamplona and Aragon.

In 1002 the caliphate of Córdoba collapsed and divided into around 30 small *taifa* (successor) kingdoms that were to prove vulnerable to the continuing Christian recovery. In 1029 the independent kingdom of Castile was founded in what had been a county within the kingdom of León.

ALFONSO VI AND EL CID

King Alfonso VI of León temporarily reunited his kingdom with Castile, reigning as king of Castile and León from 1072, until his death in 1109. When he captured Toledo in May 1085, he appeared to be on the brink of a major onslaught against the taifa kingdoms: in 1077 he had declared himself Emperor of Spain. But the beleaguered rulers of the taifas appealed to the Muslim Almoravids of north-west Africa, and Almoravid armies defeated Alfonso at Sagrajas in 1086 and Ucles in 1108.

In this period, Don Rodrigo Diaz of Vivar, the Spanish knight celebrated as 'El Cid', performed his great feats of chivalry. He was cast into exile by King Alfonso in 1081, entered the service of al-Mu'tamin, Moorish king of Saragossa, and then fought for al-Mu'tamin and his successor al-Musta'in II for almost ten years, before returning to Alfonso's service and capturing the Muslim kingdom of Valencia in 1090–94; he ruled Valencia until his death in 1099, when it was captured by the Almoravids. (León and Castile remained reunited until 1157.)

▼ *In the legendary Battle of Clavijo, a Christian army was vastly outnumbered by the Moors but triumphed nonetheless after a miraculous appearance by St James.*

CRUSADING PRIVILEGES

War against Muslims in Spain was promoted as crusading, with privileges identical to those offered for military service in the Holy Land, from the 1090s onwards. In 1095 Pope Urban II (ruled 1088–99) urged the Spanish to respond to his call to crusade by fighting the Muslims in their own land rather than by travelling to Palestine. In 1123 Pope Callixtus II (ruled 1119–24) declared a crusade in Spain at the same time as he called a fresh military expedition to the Holy Land.

At the time of the Second Crusade during 1145, Pope Eugenius III (ruled 1145–53) also called a crusade in Spain, guaranteeing King Alfonso VII of León and Castile (r. 1126–57) the same indulgence he had given to the French crusader knights. In 1147 crusader armies from England, Scotland, Normandy and Germany stopped in Spain and Portugal en route to the Holy Land and helped to recapture the city of Lisbon; around the same time, as part of the crusading campaign, Alfonso VII of Castile and Count Ramon Berenguer IV of Barcelona conquered Almeria in south-eastern Spain from the Moors. The next major crusading activity in the Iberian Peninsula was to come in 1212.

THE SPANISH CRUSADE OF 1212
AND OTHER 13TH-CENTURY CRUSADES IN SPAIN AND PORTUGAL

In 1212 Pope Innocent III (ruled 1198–1216) proclaimed a crusade in Spain against the Almohad caliphs. The Almohads had ousted their Almoravid predecessors and defeated the kingdom of Castile in the Battle of Alarcos on 19 July 1195. With the support of troops from the Spanish kingdoms of Aragon and Navarre and with crusaders from France, King Alfonso VIII of Castile (r.1158–1214) won a resounding victory over the Almohads at the Battle of Las Navas de Tolosa, one of the greatest and most important Christian victories in the entire period of the Reconquista.

RISE OF THE ALMOHADS
The Almohads were originally followers of a Berber religious teacher named Ibn Tumart from the Atlas Mountains of

▼ King Alfonso VIII led the army of Castile and a vast force of crusaders and Knights Templar to victory over the Almohads at the Battle of Las Navas de Tolosa in July 1212.

Morocco. Ibn Tumart established the Almohads as a religious order dedicated to bringing purity back into the faith of Islam, and after declaring himself the *mahdi* (a promised Islamic redeemer) in 1121, he led armed resistance against the Almoravid caliphs ruling in northern Africa. His successor, Abd al-Mu'min, defeated the Almoravids by 1147 and made himself Emir of Marrakech in 1149; another Almohad leader, Abu Ya'qub Yusuf (r.1163–84), conquered the Almoravid empire in Spain and established a capital in Seville.

Meanwhile King Alfonso VIII of Castile led resistance to the Almohads in Spain. In 1190, following a defeat, Alfonso was forced to agree an armistice, but when this expired in 1194 he attacked the Almohad province of Seville. Almohad caliph Abu Yusuf gathered an army and inflicted a heavy defeat on Alfonso near the fortress of Alarcos, making the Castilian king retreat to Toledo.

In the aftermath of this defeat, the Almohads took a great deal of territory – capturing Trujillo, Talavera, Cuenca, Ucles and the fortress of Calatrava, stronghold of the Spanish monastic military brotherhood the Order of Calatrava. These Muslim successes forced the border between Muslim and Christian Spain many miles northwards, until it lay in the hills just south of Toledo.

Alfonso's ally Rodrigo Jiménez of Rada, Archbishop of Toledo, sought Church backing for a crusading response. Pope Innocent III issued a call to arms, and in 1212 crusaders – including Frankish knights under Archbishop Arnold of Narbonne and members of the military-monastic brotherhood of the Knights Templar – arrived at Toledo. They marched southwards, accompanied by the armies of Aragon, León and Castile. They captured Calatrava, Alarcos and Benevente before they met the Almohad army.

GLORY OF NAVARRE
According to legend, King Sancho VII of Navarre broke into the Almohad caliph's camp at the climax of the Battle of Las Navas de Tolosa. The story goes that the caliph had surrounded his tent with a defensive barrier made of slaves chained together, but that Sancho cut through the barrier and burst into the tent. To celebrate his feat of arms, Navarre changed its coats of arms to one showing a golden chain, below.

LAS NAVAS DE TOLOSA
The Almohad caliph, Muhammad al-Nasir, gathered his army on the plains of Las Navas de Tolosa. The Christians, trying to reach them though the mountain pass of La Llosa, found it heavily guarded, but then with the help of a local shepherd found a different route through the Despenaperros Pass.

After a prolonged stand-off, the two armies clashed. King Alfonso led the Christian forces into battle, and they won a famous victory – killing, wounding or capturing no fewer than 100,000 of the Almohads at the cost of 2,000 of their own men dead or wounded. Tradition has it that King Sancho VII of Navarre (r.1194–1234) humiliated the Almohad emir in his tent following an act of great

▲ *King Ferdinand III of Castile and León receives homage from a Moor after taking Seville in 1248. The city had been in Moorish hands since its conquest in 712.*

bravery (*see* box). The Almohad caliph, al-Nasir, fled to Marrakech in Morocco, where he died shortly afterwards. Alfonso went on to capture the southern towns of Baeza and Ubeda.

CHRISTIAN TRIUMPHS

In the following years, the victory at Las Navas de Tolosa proved to have been a truly significant one, for the Almohad empire fell apart in dynastic struggles after 1224 and without strong leadership was unable to hold back the armies of the Christian reconquest. King Alfonso IX of León (r.1188–1230) captured Caceres (1227) and Merida and Badajoz (1230), opening the way to the recapturing of Seville. Ferdinand III, who reigned as King of Castile 1217–52 and of León 1230–52, captured Córdoba in 1236), Jaen in 1246 and Seville in 1248. (Ferdinand is celebrated as San Fernando after he was canonized on 4 February 1671.)

King Alfonso X of Castile and León (r.1252–84) defeated the Muslim emirates in Niebla and Murcia. (Alfonso was the

father of Eleanor of Castile, beloved wife of King Edward I of England, and it was at his court that the law code known as the *Siete Partidas*, or Seven-Part Code, was composed; he was a great patron of learning and is remembered as Alfonso 'the Wise' or 'the Learned'.)

King James I of Aragon (r.1213–76) captured the Balearic Islands (1229–35) and the kingdom of Valencia (1233–38). Both these campaigns were crusades. James was renowned as *El Conquistador* (the Conqueror). In Portugal, King Sancho

II (r.1223–47) reconquered from the Moors a number of cities in Alentejo (south-central Portugal) and the Algarve (the southernmost part of the country). By the close of the 13th century, the kingdom of Granada was the only part of the entire peninsula to remain under Muslim rule.

▼ *Knights embark by sea for the Holy Land on crusade. The illustration is from a book made for Alfonso X of Castile and León, a great patron of court learning who also played his part in the Reconquista.*

THE CONQUEST OF GRANADA
FINAL STAGE OF THE RECONQUISTA

In the 14th and 15th centuries the Muslim kingdom of Granada in southern Spain was the only surviving part of al-Andalus. In theory subordinate to the kingdom of Castile, its ruler a feudal vassal of the King of Castile from the time of King Ferdinand III onwards in the mid-13th century, its days seemed numbered. But remarkably, Granada survived until 1492 when the might of a united Spain, formed by the union of Castile and Aragon, finally brought to an end almost 800 years of Muslim rule in Spain.

MUSLIM HOLY WAR

In Morocco, the Marinids ousted the Almohads, with the aid of Christian mercenaries, in the mid-13th century, taking Fes in 1248 and Marrakech in 1269. The Marinids were fundamentalist Muslims who declared a jihad on the Kingdom of Castile in 1275 and formed an alliance with the Nasrid sultans of Granada; Marinid soldiers helped Granada to protect its borders and even won back some fortified settlements that had fallen to the Christians. The Nasrid sultans ceded the Spanish city of Algeciras to the Marinids.

▼ *Crusading monarchs. This stained glass window celebrates the capture of Malaga by Ferdinand and Isabella's army in 1487.*

SIR JAMES DOUGLAS AND THE BATTLE OF TEBA

King Alfonso XI 'the Implacable' of Castile (r.1312–50) took up the battle against Granada. In 1330 he defeated Sultan Muhammad IV of Granada at the Battle of Teba in Andalusia. In this battle Sir James Douglas, friend of Robert the Bruce, King of Scots, was killed. Douglas had departed from Scotland bearing the Bruce's embalmed heart in order to fulfil his promise to the late king to carry it to the Holy Land; en route he had diverted to Spain to help Alfonso in his struggle against Granada. After the battle, Douglas's body and the Bruce's heart were returned to Scotland, where they were buried.

In the immediate aftermath of his victory at Teba, Alfonso captured the nearby Castle of the Star and installed knights of the military monastic brotherhood of the Order of Santiago as its garrison. Two years later in 1332, in Vittoria, the king founded the chivalric Order of the Sash.

BATTLE OF RIO SALADO

In 1340 Alfonso – together with King Afonso IV 'the Brave' of Portugal (r.1325–57) – defeated a large Marinid army at Rio Salado. The Marinids had amassed a vast army and they crossed the Straits of Gibraltar to mount an invasion with the

▲ *King Ferdinand I of Aragon, the ruler celebrated as 'He of Antequera' after he captured that town from the Muslims as part of the Reconquista, issued this ducat during his brief reign in Aragon, 1412–16.*

aim of establishing their own permanent kingdom in Spain. They captured Gibraltar, defeating a Christian fleet, then moved inland to meet the two Christian kings near Tarifa on the Salado river.

Following a resounding victory over the invaders, Alfonso proceeded to attack Algeciras, which he retook after a two-year siege in 1344. This siege drew Christian volunteers from all over Europe. The defeat of the Marinids at Rio Salado marked the end of the last attempted Muslim invasion of Spain and seemed to clear the way for a final push against Granada. After 1350, however, Alfonso's successors were distracted from the Reconquista by civil war in Castile, and Granada made a number of inroads into Christian territory, taking the city of Jaen, among other strongholds.

In the first part of the 15th century, the Spanish Christian kingdoms moved once more against the Muslim presence. In 1410 the future King Ferdinand I of Aragon (r.1412–16) captured the fortified town of Antequera from Granada while he was regent for his nephew, the infant King John II of Castile. For this feat, he was

▲ After the end of the Reconquista in 1492, the Jews were expelled from Spain by decree of Ferdinand and Isabella.

elected to the throne of Aragon and was known as *El de Antequera* (He of Antequera). In 1430 Ferdinand's nephew King John II of Castile (r.1406–54) launched a campaign against Granada that culminated in a victory over the Nasrid sultan Muhammad IX at the Battle of Higuerela, in July 1431.

For almost 50 years thereafter there was no major offensive against Granada. Spanish military brotherhoods, such as the orders of Calatrava and of Santiago, and leading Castilian noblemen conducted a raiding and skirmishing war along the frontier between Castile and Granada, intermittently joined by crusaders seeking glory, riches and crusading privileges.

BIRTH OF SPAIN

In 1469 Ferdinand, heir to the throne of Aragon, married Princess Isabella, heir to the throne of Castile. He became king consort in Castile in 1474 when Isabella became queen following the death of her brother King Henry IV of Castile, and when Ferdinand succeeded his father,

King John II of Aragon (r.1458–79), in 1479, the couple ruled a united kingdom of Aragon and Castile. This marked the birth of the nation of Spain. Within three years they moved against Granada and in a ten-year war, 1482–92, won the final victory of the Reconquista. Ferdinand and Isabella made sure that their army was

equipped with the latest artillery guns and cannon. They promoted the campaign as a religious war – on several occasions Isabella led prayers on or near the field of battle, declaring her burning desire that God's will be performed; soldiers came from several European countries to join the crusade. In Spain, money was raised to cover expenses through the imposition of crusade taxes and the sale of crusade indulgences. The crusaders besieged and captured Ronda in 1485 and took Loja the next year. In 1487 they captured Malaga and in 1489 Baza.

They laid siege to the city of Granada in 1491. After their camp was destroyed by fire, they rebuilt it in stone in the shape of a giant cross, had it painted white and named it Santa Fe (Sacred Faith). At the end of 1491 Sultan Boabdil surrendered the city. Ferdinand and Isabella made a formal entry into Granada on 2 January 1492 and oversaw the reconsecration of the city's main mosque as a church.

▼ At the gorgeous Alhambra palace in the city of Granada, Sultan Boabdil consults with advisers in 1492, prior to surrendering to the army of Ferdinand and Isabella.

THE ALBIGENSIAN CRUSADE

WAR ON HERESY

In 1208 a papal legate named Pierre of Castelnau was murdered in the Languedoc region of southern France and Pope Innocent III (ruled 1198–1216) declared a crusade against the Cathars of that region, who were viewed as heretics by the Catholic Church. The Cathars were subsequently called the Albigensians (from the town of Albi that was inaccurately identified as their headquarters).

The Albigensian crusade lasted 20 years, from 1209 to 1229, and although it began as a religious war aimed at curbing what the Church hierarchy saw as a popular and dangerous heresy, it became little more than an exercise in territorial expansion by northern French barons. The

▲ *The seal of Raymond VI of Toulouse. It was his vassal who murdered Pierre of Castelnau and provoked Pope Innocent to declare his crusade against the Cathars.*

▼ *St Dominic worked for years to convince the Cathars that their beliefs were heretical. After the celebrated trial by fire, in which Cathar books burned while orthodox Catholic volumes were spared, he gave one of the orthodox books to the Cathars.*

religious victory over the Cathars when it came was achieved not in battle but through the efforts of the Dominican Inquisition (a tribunal to investigate heresy), established in 1233. Military action against the Cathars continued inter-

mittently until 1255. The Cathars were driven from France into Italy, where they died out and were heard of no more after the end of the 14th century.

CATHAR BELIEFS AND BACKGROUND

The Cathars took their name from the Greek word *katharos*, meaning 'pure'. They were dualists, believing in two gods – an ultimate embodiment of goodness, and a lesser and evil creator god who had made the material world. They believed the material world therefore to be evil: the human soul was naturally good and trapped in this evil creation; people should seek salvation through extreme asceticism. Cathars avoided meat and animal products, were sexually chaste, lived in poverty and were pacifists.

Cathars divided themselves into two groups: 'the perfect' and 'the believers'. The perfect passed through an initiation ceremony called the *consolamentum* and

lived lives of extreme asceticism, devoting their energy to contemplation. The believers were not required to attain the very high standards of asceticism and religious devotion attained by the perfect.

ROOTS IN GNOSTICISM

Cathar beliefs may have derived from ancient Gnosticism, a dualist faith system popular in the Mediterranean and Middle East from the last centuries BC onward, but suppressed in the Christian Roman Empire from the 4th century AD. Like Cathars, Gnostics believed in dual divinities. The highest god was good and the lesser one evil; the evil one had created the material world. Humans were divine souls trapped in the material world, from which they could only escape through *gnosis* or knowledge held by the elite. The Cathars did not place strong emphasis on spiritual knowledge, but they did have an initiation ceremony, and an initiated elite.

BOGOMILS AND PAULICIANS

The Cathars certainly had links with the Gnostic-influenced Christian groups of the Bogomils and the Paulicians. The Bogomils had emerged in the 10th century in Bulgaria and spread from there into the Byzantine Empire, as well as into Italy and France: they were dualists, who rejected the doctrine of Christ's divine birth and the veneration of the Virgin Mary and declared that reverence for the cross and for saintly relics was no more than idolatry.

The Paulicians had their origins earlier, in the 7th–9th centuries, in Armenia: they rejected the Old Testament, veneration of the Virgin Mary, worship of the Cross and the sacraments of Baptism and Communion. The Cathars for their part denied the divinity of Christ and declared him to have been an angel come to earth; they said that his apparent sufferings and death as a human being were an illusion. Cathar teaching also rejected the doctrines of purgatory and hell and that of the resurrection of the body, arguing in favour of reincarnation.

▲ *Pope Innocent III sent out wandering preachers to bring heretics back to the true faith. He gave St Dominic and St Francis (shown here) his blessing to do this work.*

The Cathars were first established in Flanders, northern Italy and western Germany in 1000–50. They expanded in 1140–70, particularly under the influence of a resurgent Bogomil Church that sent missionaries throughout Europe; historians also believe that soldiers and pilgrims on the First Crusade picked up dualist ideas and brought them back to Europe in the early 12th century. In the 1140s the Cathars established themselves as a church: their first bishop in *c.*1149 was in northern France, but soon afterward he was joined by counterparts in Lombardy and in Albi. By 1200 they had five bishops in France and six in Italy.

SERIOUS THREAT

Remarkably, in the Languedoc Catharism became a popular religion – unlike many sects, attracting a wide following among the nobility, educated townspeople and the peasantry. Cathars attacked the wealth and corruption of the Church, while rejecting the authority of Catholic priests and of the pope; they posed a threat to the very structure of society, for they rejected the taking of oaths that was one of the central features of the feudal system. Moreover, the fact that they had many followers among both nobility and peasantry served to undo the natural, God-given social hierarchy that orthodox believers saw in the feudal system.

Pope Innocent III initially tried to bring the Cathars back to orthodoxy by peaceful means, sending preachers – including Dominic Guzman (later St Dominic), founder of the Dominican Order – to attempt to convert the heretics. The preachers had little success. Innocent then found that local nobles and even bishops were protecting the Cathars. In 1204 he suspended the bishops and replaced them with papal legates, and he demanded that Philip II of France (r.1180–1223) force the nobles to return to Catholicism. Philip refused to take action. Innocent demanded that the powerful local count, Raymond VI of Toulouse, take action but he, too, refused and was excommunicated.

In January 1208 Raymond held a meeting with the papal legate, Pierre of Castelnau, which ended angrily. The following day Pierre of Castelnau was murdered by one of Raymond's vassals. Pope Innocent III declared war, issuing a call to a crusade against the Cathars.

Innocent offered a full crusade indulgence to all who responded to his call to take up arms against the Cathars. He also declared that they would have the right to seize the land of the heretics, which attracted a number of northern French barons to the cause. It should be noted that the indulgence offered to the anti-Cathar crusaders was remarkably generous – the annulment of sins was being offered for a mere 40 days campaigning (the normal period of feudal military service) and for a war fought in nearby southern France rather than for a potentially very hazardous journey over land and sea to the Holy Land.

MASSACRE OF THE CATHARS

TWENTY YEARS OF BRUTAL WAR, 1209–1229

The crusade armies raised against the Cathars by Pope Innocent III won a series of brutal victories in 1209–15, in which local people – both Cathars and Catholics – were slaughtered in their thousands. During the next ten years, many of these bloody victories were overturned by rebels, but in 1226 King Louis VIII of France (r.1223–26) entered the fray on the side of the Church and following his death in November that year, his son Louis IX (r.1226–70) took up the fight. The Languedoc region was conquered by 1229 and peace was finally agreed in the Treaty of Paris that year.

COUNT RAYMOND RECANTS

In 1209 a crusade army of around 10,000 massed in Lyon and marched south under the leadership of papal legate Arnaul Amalric, Abbot of Cîteaux. Suddenly persuaded of the error of his ways, Raymond VI of Toulouse agreed at last to move against the Cathars and was reconciled to the Church in a ceremony before carvings of the Passion of Christ on the west front

At the Battle of Muret on 12 September 1213, Simon of Montfort's small crusader force roundly defeated the much larger army of Peter II of Aragon and Raymond of Toulouse. Peter was killed in action.

of the Benedictine abbey church of Saint-Gilles. The crusaders then marched towards Montpellier; Raymond-Roger Trencavel, viscount of Béziers and Albi and a vassal of Raymond VI of Toulouse, attempted to make peace with them but was refused an audience. He fled back to Carcassonne to arrange its defence.

THE SLAUGHTER AT BÉZIERS

The crusade army marched to Béziers, where it arrived on 21 July 1209. The soldiers demanded the surrender of the Cathars and the submission of any local Catholics; both groups refused. But the crusaders gained access to the town when an attempted sortie by the defenders went wrong and they burned Béziers to the ground and savagely killed every man, woman and child.

According to one account, soldiers asked the Abbot of Cîteaux how they would tell Cathars from Catholics and the abbot replied: 'Kill them all. God will recognize his own.' Afterwards the Abbot wrote gleefully to the Pope: 'Our soldiers spared neither rank, nor sex, nor elderly. About 20,000 people lost their lives … the entire city was put to the sword. Thus did God's vengeance vent its wondrous rage.'

CATHARS EVICTED FROM CARCASSONNE

Many settlements were terrified into submission and surrendered to the army. The crusaders marched on Carcassonne and took it after a two-week siege on 15 August 1209. The Cathars were forcibly evicted, having been stripped naked to humiliate them. At this point, French nobleman Simon of Montfort took charge of the crusade army and was granted territory that included the Cathar strongholds of Carcassonne, Albi and Béziers. (Simon of Montfort, a veteran of the Fourth Crusade, was the father of Simon of Montfort, 6th Earl of Leicester and main

▲ *Fighting during the siege of Carcassonne. In the rear the Cathars emerge from the city to take on the besieging crusaders.*

leader of baronial opposition to King Henry III of England; the 6th Earl was the effective ruler of England in 1263–64 and is remembered as a pioneer of parliamentary democracy.)

Town after town surrendered or was conquered by the crusader army over the following months. In June–July 1210 the city of Minerve put up a brave resistance but finally surrendered on 22 July; many Cathars accepted Catholicism, but fully 140 remained defiant and were burned at the stake. In 1211 Raymond of Toulouse was again excommunicated after he fell out with Simon of Montfort. In May hundreds of Cathars were burned at the stake and Aimery of Montréal was hanged after his castle fell to Montfort.

The crusaders besieged Raymond in Toulouse, but the siege failed and the army withdrew. Raymond then led a successful rebellion, capturing Castelnaudary from Simon of Montfort and 'freeing' more than 30 towns for the Cathar cause.

THE BATTLE OF MURET

In 1212, however, much of Toulouse was captured. In 1213 King Peter II of Aragon (r.1196–1213), famous victor over the Moors at the battle of Las Navas de Tolosa, led an army in support of Raymond, who was his brother-in-law. With Raymond, he besieged Montfort in Muret, but was defeated and killed in the ensuing battle. The Aragonese army broke and fled on seeing their king slain.

In 1214, Raymond was forced to flee to England and his lands were given by the pope to Philip II, who became involved in the war. In 1214–16 Montfort captured the remaining Cathar strongholds and also ceded his lands to Philip II.

CATHAR RESURGENCE

In 1216 the tide began to turn. In that year, Pope Innocent III died and was replaced by Honorius III (r.1216–27), who was not so strongly committed to waging war on the Cathars. Raymond returned from exile and captured first Beaucaire and then, in 1217, Toulouse. Montfort besieged him there and was killed in fighting outside the city on 25 June 1218, his head crushed by a stone hurled from a mangonel. The Cathar side made a number of gains, including

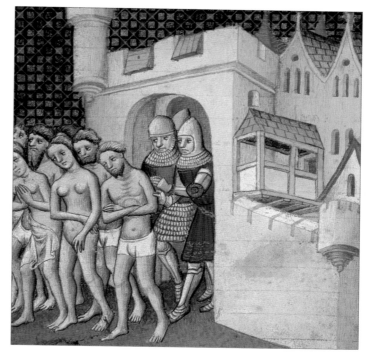

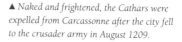
▲ *Naked and frightened, the Cathars were expelled from Carcassonne after the city fell to the crusader army in August 1209.*

Castelnaudary, Montreal and Fanjeaux and, in 1224, Carcassonne. Raymond VI of Toulouse had died in 1222 , and been succeeded by his son, another Raymond; and Philip II had died, in 1223, and been succeeded by King Louis VIII. Amaury of Montfort, son of Simon, offered his claim to territory in the Languedoc to the new French king, who took up the challenge.

Louis led a new crusade army into the region in June 1226. Many castles and towns surrendered without a fight but it took a three-month siege to capture Avignon. That same autumn, Louis VIII died and was succeeded by his son, Louis IX, at the age of just 12. Louis VIII's widow, Blanche of Castile, acted as regent and ordered the continuation of the crusade under the command of Humbert of Beaujeu. The crusaders crushed Cathar resistance, taking Labécède in 1227 and Toulouse in 1228.

A peace treaty was finally agreed in 1229 under which Count Raymond was recognized as ruler of Toulouse, but was forced to agree to hand his castles over into royal control, to dismantle the defences of Toulouse and to attempt to suppress the Cathars.

▼ *The Cathar stronghold of Carcassonne had grown from a Roman fortification, and parts of its northern walls date from when France was under Roman rule.*

THE CATHAR INQUISITION

THE FAITHFUL BESIEGED – WITH SECRET TREASURE?

In 1233 Pope Gregory IX (ruled 1227–41) established a papal Inquisition (or investigative tribunal) staffed by Dominican friars charged with stamping out the Cathars. Many of the heretics were burned at the stake, while others fled the Inquisition to northern Italy. A few Cathar communities survived in isolated fortresses in the Pyrenees but these were gradually captured by the royalist forces. The Castle of Montségur was taken in March 1244 after a nine-month siege, while the small fort of Quéribus, probably the last surviving Cathar stronghold, was taken in August 1255.

The Dominican Inquisition was given substantial powers to stamp out heresy by burning Cathars where they were found and even in some cases digging up the bodies of former heretics to burn them. In a letter of 1233, the pope denounced the preachers of the Cathar faith as 'evil min-

▼ *An enthroned Pope Gregory IX hears the report of a Dominican inquisitor.*

▲ *The mountaintop Castle of Quéribus may have been the Cathars' last refuge. It was rebuilt by the French as one of five castles that guarded the French border with Spain.*

isters of Satan … they appear to be pious but they entirely deny all virtue. Their sermons are smoother than the oil of crushed olives; but they are as dangerous as javelins and their words have a sting in the tail like that of a scorpion.' He urged the Dominican priors to 'root out … the wickedness of heresy', 'to work assiduously against all who receive, help or defend any who are excommunicated'; he encouraged them to 'lay sentences of interdict' on the lands of those behaved in this way. But he also encouraged them to give absolution to those that 'wish to come back to the unity of the church'. He made a promise that all who came to listen to the sermons of the friars would be granted freedom from 20 days' penance.

CATHAR REVOLTS

The Cathars continued to resist. They drove the friars of the Inquisition out of Narbonne, Toulouse and Albi in 1235. Another Raymond, son of Roger Trencavel, led a revolt in 1240 and attempted to capture Carcassonne. But he was driven off and then besieged by the forces of King Louis IX in the Castle of Montréal. Raymond escaped and fled into exile in Aragon. (Later he surrendered to Louis, and accompanied the king on the Seventh Crusade.)

In 1242 Count Raymond VIII of Toulouse tried to mount a revolt in alliance with the English, but the campaign faltered, the English were defeated by Louis IX at Taillebourg and the rebellion came to nothing. Count Raymond surrendered to Louis and asked for his excommunication to be lifted. Many Cathars took refuge in mountain strongholds such as Montségur. The Council of Béziers determined in the spring of 1243 to attack the castle there as an attempt to wipe out Catharism once and for all.

SIEGE OF MONTSÉGUR

The Castle of Montségur was perched atop a rock at an altitude of 3,900ft (1,200m) in the Languedoc near the Pyrenees Mountains. It was built on the ruins of an earlier fortress by Raymond of Pereille in c.1210. According to some accounts, it was the headquarters of the Cathars in the Languedoc region.

▲ *Roman Catholic monks rejoice at the burning of the Cathars at Montségur.*

From May 1243 to March 1244 it was besieged by a royalist army of around 10,000 commanded by Hugh of Arcis, Louis IX's Seneschal of Carcassonne. On 1 March 1244 the defenders, offered terms of surrender, asked for a two-week truce to consider them; in return they provided hostages whose lives would be forfeit if the defenders tried to flee. On March 14, the defenders reportedly celebrated a festival coinciding with the spring equinox. On the next day the truce expired, and around 220 Cathars, all members of their initiated elite group 'the perfect', were taken down the mountainside and burned as heretics in a large stockade at the foot of the hill. In the two-week period, an additional 25 of the Cathars had joined the ranks of 'the perfect' and were therefore put to death.

ESCAPE WITH TREASURE?

In the final days of the siege, it is said that four of the castle defenders slipped unnoticed though the siege lines carrying some unidentified treasure. This treasure may have been esoteric writings, Cathar riches or, as some claim, the Holy Grail.

One tradition claims that the Knights Templar when building on Temple Mount in Jerusalem discovered extraordinary treasure that they then passed to the Cathars, and that these treasures were among those smuggled out of Montségur. Some writers claim that the castle may have been the actual Holy Grail castle celebrated in chivalric romances and poems such as *Parzival* by Wolfram von Eschenbach (written only decades earlier, in 1200–10) – where the Grail castle is called Monsalvat, strikingly similar to Montségur. (The Castle of Montségur that survives today is not the one that was occupied by the Cathars, for that fortress was entirely destroyed by the royalist army in 1244. The building seen today was built over the ensuing centuries and has many characteristics typical of the 1600s.)

The few surviving Cathars gathered in another hilltop stronghold at Quéribus. When a French army was despatched to deal with them in 1255 they fled the castle without a fight and left the country, dispersing to take refuge either in Aragon or in northern Italy.

LINKS TO TEMPLARS?

One reason that the Knights Templar came under such fierce attack in the early 14th century was that they were accused of fraternizing with and protecting heretics. The sixth Templar Grand Master, Bertrand of Blanchefort (Grand Master 1156–69) was reputedly from a Cathar family and from his time the Templars accepted Cathars into the order. The Templars accepted many heretics into their ranks because recruitment was always difficult, but they had a significant number of Cathar members from France. During the Albigensian Crusade the Templars gave refuge to Cathars fleeing the crusaders – and allowed them to bury their dead in their Templar graveyards.

▼ *Was the Cathar fortress at Montségur in south-western France the original Grail castle? The current castle was erected on the ruins of the Cathar one in the 1600s.*

THE BALTIC CRUSADES
HOLY WAR AGAINST NORTHERN PAGANS

The Baltic Crusades were military campaigns against the pagan peoples on the southern and eastern shores of the Baltic Sea. They were cast as wars of religion but were often fought to gain territory for local bishops and feudal lords. The Baltic Crusades are often said to have started in the 1190s when popes Celestine III and Innocent III called what became a standing crusade. Its purpose was to support the Catholic Church in the region of Livonia (now Estonia, Lithuania and Latvia), but as early as 1147 crusading privileges had been officially granted to Saxon, Danish and Polish Christians fighting against the pagan Wends of the Baltic.

THE WENDISH CRUSADE

In 1147 when Bernard of Clairvaux was preaching the Second Crusade to the Holy Land on behalf of Pope Eugenius III, he was told by the north German Saxons that they were not willing to travel to the Holy Land but wanted to conduct a holy war against the pagan Wends in the Baltic. Eugenius sent out the *Divina dispensatione*

bull, on 13 April 1147, guaranteeing those fighting on this Baltic crusade the same benefits as those who took the cross to fight in the Holy Land. Bernard himself wrote of the crusaders' attack on the Wends: 'We expressly forbid that for any cause they should agree peace with these people until either their false religion or their nation has been destroyed.'

Papal legate Anselm of Havelberg was put in command of an army that included Danes and Poles as well as Saxons. Some of these crusaders were genuinely fighting in order to convert the pagans, but many bishops and lords were primarily seeking to increase their landholding in the region.

◄ *The Wends of the Baltic region were descendants of Slavic tribes who settled in eastern Germany in the 5th century AD. King Wandalus was a mythical ancestor, and was supposedly originally a Trojan.*

▲ *The Baltic Crusades had begun as much as 50 years before Pope Celestine III called a crusade in Livonia following the failure of a Church mission to the region.*

The campaign followed the annexation by Count Adolph of Holstein of Wendish lands, which he had parcelled out among Christian immigrants from western Germany. Wendish leader Niklot led an invasion of Wagria (now eastern Holstein in northern Germany) and Adolph fought back with part of the crusader army. This part of the campaign was swiftly over, and ended in a peace treaty, but other crusaders attacked Dobin and Demmin. At Dobin, the members of the Wendish garrison were baptized following a siege. The crusade army marching on Demmin sacked a castle and pagan temple at Malchow, but their siege of Demmin was unsuccessful and so they marched on into

Pomerania on the Baltic coast where, reaching the Christian city of Stettin (now in Poland), they were greeted by Bishop Albert of Pomerania and Prince Ratorbor I of Pomerania and then disbanded.

The crusade achieved a few conversions, but many of these Christianized Wends reverted to their own religion after the crusaders left. It had the effect of strengthening Christian landholdings in the region and of weakening the resistance of the local people to future campaigns.

THE CRUSADE IN LIVONIA

Before Celestine and Innocent unleashed the power of the crusading machine on Livonia in the 1190s, the Church had made peaceful efforts to convert the local populace. In the 11th century Adalbert, Archbishop of Bremen in 1045–72, had sent missionaries into the region, but with little effect. In 1180 an Augustinian monk called Meinhard led missionary work at Uxhull (modern Ikskile) on the River Dvina (now called the Daugava) and established himself as bishop.

▼ *Prince Niklot, who fought against the crusade army in 1147, had renounced Christianity and reverted to paganism. He is an ancestor of the dukes of Mecklenburg, and is honoured with this statue in their castle at Schwerin, north-eastern Germany.*

▲ *The Livonian Brothers of the Sword fought in Finland in 1232 on the orders of Pope Gregory IX. After they merged with the Teutonic Knights in 1236, they still had their own Master. He was subject to the Grand Master of the Teutonic Knights.*

After Meinhard's successor, Berthold, reported that the mission to Livonia was close to failure, Pope Celestine III called a crusade in the area. A Saxon crusading army led by Berthold won a battle against the Livonians in 1198, but Berthold was killed. Subsequently the crusaders went home and the missionary monks had to abandon their work after the Livonians issued death threats against them.

In 1199 the Archbishop Hartwig of Bremen appointed his nephew Albert of Buxhoeveden as Bishop of Livonia, with instructions to conquer the region and impose Christianity on its people. Albert embarked on a tour to preach a crusade in Livonia, and Pope Innocent III issued a papal bull guaranteeing those who fought in Livonia the same crusading privileges as knights and men-at-arms fighting in the Holy Land. At the bishop's request, Innocent also dedicated the Baltic region to the Virgin Mary, in order to encourage recruits to the cause, and the area is still sometimes known as 'Mary's Land'.

In 1200 Albert landed at the mouth of the River Dvina with a crusade army of around 1,500 men aboard a fleet of 23 vessels. In the next year he abandoned his mission station at Uxhull and founded the trading settlement of Riga at the mouth of the river. Previous efforts at conquest had foundered when temporary crusading armies disbanded, so in 1202 he founded the military order of the Livonian Brothers of the Sword to ensure a continuous military presence. (Albert founded the Cathedral of Riga in 1215; he was later named a Prince of the Holy Roman Empire, with Livonia as his fief, and was known as a 'Prince-Bishop'.) The Livonian Brothers of the Sword suffered a heavy defeat at the hands of a Livonian army in 1236 and the order's few survivors joined the Teutonic Knights.

For more than 25 years, until his death in 1229, Albert was engaged in the conquest of Livonia. He converted some of the locals – for example the Livs accepted Christianity when Bishop Albert guaranteed them military protection against incursion by rival Lithuanians and Estonian tribes; he also achieved the conversion of some Latvians. Otherwise he achieved his goals by military means. By c.1230 the conquest and conversion of Livonia was complete.

▼ *The seal of the Livonian Brothers of the Sword. They were called* Fratres militiae Christi Livoniae *in Latin.*

IN PRUSSIA AND LITHUANIA

EUROPEAN CRUSADES OF THE TEUTONIC KNIGHTS

Over a period of 50 years of brutal campaigning from *c.*1230 onwards, the military brotherhood of the Teutonic Knights imposed Christianity on the pagan peoples of Prussia. The Teutonic Knights, who had been founded in the Holy Land but were seeking to establish themselves in central Europe, entered Prussia under an agreement that allowed them to keep their initial landholding and all that they conquered. As a result they built up a substantial territory, which they ruled as a sovereign monastic state, answerable only to the Holy Roman Emperor and the papacy. In the 14th century, having conquered Prussia, they led a series of campaigns against Lithuania. These campaigns attracted knights from France and England to test their chivalric attributes in battle.

In 1209 Christian, a Cistercian monk from the monastery of Oliva (modern Oliwa, part of Gdasnk in northern Poland)

▼ *Grand Master of the Teutonic Knights. The brotherhood needed shrewd leadership as it attempted to find a new role and a new base in Europe in the 1200s.*

HENRY BOLINGBROKE'S CRUSADE

In 1390, after taking part in the celebrated Jousts of St Ingelvert near Calais, Henry intended to lead a small army of around 120 men on a crusade against Muslims in Tunisia, but because he was not granted safe conduct through France he joined the Teutonic Knights on a *reysen* against the Lithuanians. With 32 knights and squires he sailed to Danzig (now northern Poland), arriving on 10 August and joining the knights' march up the River Niemen. He took part in the siege of Vilnius from 4 September and after its failure returned to the Teutonic Knights' headquarters at Marienburg (now Malbork in Poland), where he remained for the winter, enjoying the feasting, hunting and other

▲ *Henry Bolingbroke (right) accompanies King Richard II as he enters London.*

chivalric entertainments. He departed at the end of March 1391. We know from royal records that the expedition cost him no less than £4,360.

---

was appointed by Pope Innocent III to lead missions in Prussia. He was named the first Bishop of Prussia in 1212. The mission came under repeated attacks from pagan Prussians and in 1217 Pope Honorius III (r.1216–27) called a crusade in the region.

The Prussians launched another major attack in 1218, in the course of which they sacked no fewer than 300 churches and cathedrals. A crusade army gathered in Masovia (now eastern Poland) from 1219 onwards and engaged the enemy without fighting a major campaign; the bishopric of Prussia was given a number of territories by Christian lords, meanwhile, in the area of Chelmno Land (now central Poland). The Prussians launched another devastating attack on Chelmno Land and Masovia in 1223.

Bishop Christian and Duke Konrad I of Masovia decided to establish an intimidating and permanent military presence to deter further Prussian raids. In 1225–28, on the border between Masovia

and Prussia (modern Dobrzyn Land in Poland), Christian established the Order of Dobrzyn, also known as the *Fratres Milites Christi de Prussia* or 'the Prussian Cavaliers of Christ Jesus'. At around the same time, Konrad invited the Teutonic Knights to help defend his borders against the Prussian raiders.

TEUTONIC KNIGHTS

The Teutonic Knights had been founded in 1192 as a monastic brotherhood in charge of a German hospital in Acre and then become a military brotherhood in Outremer in 1198. At the start of the 13th century they had established a presence in eastern Europe, entering the service of King Andrew II of Hungary in 1211, but after a disagreement Andrew had expelled the brothers from the territory he had granted them in Burzenland, Transylvania.

When Duke Konrad invited the Teutonic Knights to Masovia, the brotherhood was still heavily committed in Outremer: the first contingent of Teutonic

Knights despatched to Masovia numbered just seven knights and around 100 squires and sergeants. From an initial base at Vogelsang, south of the River Vistula, they concentrated on establishing timber fortresses along the line of the river. Reinforcements, numbering around 20 knights and 200 sergeants, arrived at Vogelsang in *c*.1230. They campaigned only when German and Polish crusaders arrived to swell their numbers. By 1232 the Knights and crusaders had defeated the Prussians in Chelmno Land.

Pope Gregory IX (ruled 1227–41) called for crusaders to back the Teutonic Knights in their struggle and a crusade army of 10,000 men gathered in the summer of 1233. In 1233–34 they won significant territorial gains, consolidated with fortresses at Marienwerder (now Kwidzyn in northern Poland) and Rehden (modern Radzyn Chelminski).

On these foundations the Teutonic Knights built a great edifice. In the course of many long and bloody campaigns over no less than 50 years they gradually defeated the Prussians. There were several Prussian uprisings: in 1242, most seriously in 1260–74, and again in 1286 and in 1295, but by the end of the 13th century the Knights had imposed their authority completely on Prussia.

ASSIMILATING OTHER ORDERS

The Order of Dobrzyn did not have a long or glorious existence. The initial membership was just 15 knights, and at its largest order had only 35 knights. In *c*.1235 most of the knights joined the Teutonic Order. In the following year, 1236, the Livonian Brothers of the Sword, the brotherhood established by Albert of Buxhoeveden in 1202, was comprehensively defeated by an army of pagan Samogitians at the Battle of Saule and was also assimilated by the Teutonic Knights.

MONASTIC STATE

The Teutonic Knights had moved to Prussia on the understanding that they would be given a base in Chelmno Land

as a permanent territory of their own and would be allowed to keep any land they conquered. This agreement was not recognized by Duke Konrad or Bishop Christian, but was guaranteed by Holy Roman Emperor Frederick II in the 'Golden Bull of Rimini' of 1226 and by Pope Gregory IX in the 'Golden Bull of Rieti' of 1234. The Knights governed the territory they carved out for themselves in Prussia as a 'monastic state'. They were subject only to the Holy Roman Emperor and the papacy.

14TH-CENTURY CRUSADES

Throughout the 14th century the Teutonic Knights led a series of crusading campaigns against the pagan Lithuanians. Following the fall of Acre in 1291 to the Mamluks, the great knights of Europe had no outlet in the Holy Land for their crusading ambitions and they saw the Teutonic Knights' annual manoeuvres in Lithuania as an opportunity to prove their martial prowess, have a taste of crusading glory – and perhaps relive some of the storied exploits of past knights of the cross.

The Teutonic Knights ran their campaigns like adventure holidays, laying on feasts, courtly hunting expeditions and prizes. Knights came from all over Europe – especially from England and France – to take part; in Chaucer's *The Canterbury Tales* his Knight takes part in one of the Teutonic adventures. The campaigns were called *reysen* (voyages): those who took

▲ *The Teutonic Knights built a vast castle as their new headquarters at Marienburg (Mary's Castle) in Prussia in 1309.*

part had to cross a 100 mile (160km) wide area of swampland and forest, which they called 'the wilderness' before engaging the enemy.

It was in the interests of all involved in the *reysen* to maintain the pretence that these annual chivalric adventures were genuine crusades, fought to bring the Christian faith to an obdurately pagan people. The campaigns became so popular that they continued even after the Lithuanians were converted to Christianity in 1386. For all that fantasy played its part, the military element, it must be stressed, was real enough – the fighting when it came was as brutal as in any war, and prisoners taken were treated with contempt since they were pagan.

Among the many great names connected to the *reysen* were French knight Jean Le Meingre, Marshal of France and known as 'Boucicaut', who fought on three campaigns in Lithuania as a young man, and King Henry IV of England, who in his youth (while Henry Bolingbroke, Earl of Derby) took part in a campaign of 1390 that culminated in the siege of the Lithuanian capital, Vilnius. He subsequently looked back with great pleasure on the experience; he was still talking of the Teutonic Knights with warmth and affection some 17 years later, in 1407.

CRUSADES AGAINST THE HUSSITES
BOHEMIA UNDER ATTACK

◄ *Hus defends his beliefs at the Council of Constance. His execution fanned discontent in Bohemia and led to the Hussite Revolt.*

Five crusades were launched against the Hussites in Bohemia in 1420–32. Followers of a university lecturer and preacher, Jan Hus, who had been burned at the stake for heresy in 1415, the Hussites were inspired by the beginnings of Czech nationalist feeling and challenged the rule of King Sigismund of Hungary in their homeland. None of the crusades achieved its goal and Sigismund was forced to agree a compromise in 1436.

HUS
Jan Hus was Dean of the philosophical faculty at Prague University from 1401 and a supporter of reform of the Roman Catholic Church in Bohemia. He established himself as a popular preacher through his sermons in Czech (rather than Latin) at the Bethlehem Chapel in Prague and was a leader of a national reform movement. He was excommunicated by Pope Alexander V (ruled 1409–10) in 1409 after refusing to accept a papal ban on preaching in private chapels. He was called to the Council of Constance in 1415

and promised safe conduct, but while he was there he was condemned as a heretic and burned at the stake.

His execution sparked protests in Bohemia, where Bohemian knights and nobility made a formal protest, the *protestatio Bohemorum*, and offered support and protection to people persecuted for their religious faith. When King Wenceslaus IV of Bohemia died in 1419, his half-brother King Sigismund of Hungary (later Holy Roman Emperor, 1433–37) claimed the throne. The Bohemian nobles rejected his claim, however, and installed their own government, starting the 'Hussite Revolt', which had the support of reforming clergy and townspeople as well as the nobility.

THE FIRST CRUSADE (1420)
In a bull of 17 March 1420 Pope Martin V (ruled 1417–31) called a crusade against the Hussites, to be led by Sigismund with the support of German princes. Sigismund marched an army swelled by crusaders from all over Europe towards Prague, and besieged the Hussites there at the end of

June, but without success. He had himself crowned king of Bohemia in the fortress of Hradcany Castle, but was defeated by the Hussites on 1 November near Pankrac. The Hussites gained control of most of Bohemia after Sigismund withdrew.

HUSSITE DEMANDS AND DIVISIONS
Following the siege of Prague in 1420, Hus's successor at the Bethlehem Chapel, Jakoubek of Stribo, drew up the Four Articles of Prague, which helped establish common ground for the Hussite movement. They called for: freedom in preaching; support for the doctrine of Ultraquism, which required that the faithful should be given both bread and wine in the communion service; the clergy to adopt a lifestyle of poverty; and mortal sins to be prohibited and punished.

▼ *Jan Zizka, inspirational Hussite leader and a great general, commands the rebels in an attack on a small town in Bohemia.*

▶ *Sigismund I of Hungary leads an army against the rebels during the Second Anti-Hussite Crusade, early in 1421. The venture ended in a heavy defeat for the crusaders at the Battle of Nemecky Brod.*

Almost from the beginning, however, the Hussites were split into two camps. Moderate Hussites were called 'Utraquists' from their support for the doctrine of Ultraquism; but there was a more radical wing, often known as 'Taborites' after the city of Tabor. Led by Jan Zizka, the Taborites believed the Millennium or New Age of Christ was at hand and called for a return to innocence and the establishment of a communist-style society in which servants and masters would be no more.

THE SECOND ANTI-HUSSITE CRUSADE (1421)

A German army arrived in Bohemia in August 1421 and besieged Zatec, but after a failed attempt to take the town retreated to avoid an approaching Hussite army. After Sigismund joined the crusaders at the end of the year, he seized the town of Kutna Hora, but on 6 January 1422 was utterly defeated by a Hussite army led by Jan Zizka at the Battle of Nemecky Brod.

THE THIRD CRUSADE FAILS

In 1422–23 there was civil war between the rival Hussite groups in Bohemia: on 27 April 1423 a Taborite army led by Jan Zizka defeated the Utraquist forces at the Battle of Horic. A third crusade had been called, meanwhile, and an army gathered, but it came to nothing amid dissension, and the force dispersed without even attempting to invade Bohemia.

Zizka won further victories over the Utraquists in 1423–24, but died of the plague on 11 October 1424 as he was preparing an invasion of Moravia. Chronicle accounts report that his last wish was for his skin to be made into drums, so that he could continue to lead his men into battle. His soldiers were so distraught at his passing that from that time they called themselves 'the Orphans'.

THE FOURTH AND FIFTH CRUSADES (1427 AND 1431)

Under the leadership of Zizka's successor, Prokop the Great, the Hussite army conducted a series of military raids – which they called 'beautiful rides' – into neighbouring territories. Two further crusades in 1427 and 1431 came to nothing. On the first occasion a crusader army under Frederick, Margarve of Brandenburg, and Cardinal Henry Beaufort, Archbishop-elect of Trier, was defeated at Tachov. In this battle, the crusaders attempted to use the Hussite tactics of the Wagenburg, but were were defeated. On the second crusade, a large crusader force entered Bohemia but fled before a Hussite army under Prokop.

PEACE AT LAST

Internal Hussite conflicts were brought to an end at the Battle of Lipany (or Cesky Brod) on 30 May 1434 when the Taborite army under Prokop the Great was roundly defeated by an alliance of Utraquist nobles and Catholics (the 'Bohemian League'). Finally, with more moderate Hussites having won the day, a peace was agreed with Sigismund on 5 July 1436.

HUSSITE BATTLE TACTICS

A key to the Hussite success in battle was the use of *wagenburg* (war wagon) tactics. Horse-drawn war wagons were set in a defensive circle, and a ditch dug around the formation. Each wagon had a crew of 22 foot soldiers and bowmen: eight crossbowmen, two gunners, eight men armed with pikes and flails, two drivers and two shield carriers. In the first phase they used the wagons as a defensive barrier, from behind which they fired their small cannon and handguns; usually the enemy knights were drawn into an attack and the wagenburgers were able to cause carnage among them. The second stage was to burst out from behind the wagons and attack the enemy on the flanks with pikes while the gunners kept up the barrage of fire from behind the wagons.

▶ *Military historians see the* wagenburg *as the forerunner of the tank.*

CRUSADES IN ITALY

WARS IN THE PAPAL INTEREST

In the 12th–14th centuries a series of crusades were called against Christian princes and noblemen who had been declared enemies of the Catholic Church in Italy. Many of these enterprises were in fact thinly disguised attempts to enforce the interests of the papacy.

TERRITORIAL CONFLICTS

In the 12th century the popes established themselves as secular rulers of a strip of territory across the middle of what is now Italy – bound to the north by a collection of independent city-states in Tuscany and Lombardy, and to the south by the Kingdom of Sicily, which at this time included the southern part of the mainland as well as the island of Sicily. As early as the 1120s, crusading indulgences were offered to those fighting the opponents of the papacy, King Roger II of Sicily, for example, who had a crusade declared against him by Pope Honorius II.

▼ *Farinata degli Uberti, a 13th-century Ghibelline leader from Florence, fights the pro-papal Guelphs at the Battle of Serchio.*

In the 12th and 13th centuries, Italy was divided between the Guelphs (those who supported the papacy) and the Ghibellines (who supported the rule in Italy of the Holy Roman Emperors). The conflict between Holy Roman Empire and papacy in Italy went back to the investiture conflict between Holy Roman Emperor Henry IV (r.1084–1106) and Pope Gregory VII (ruled 1073–85) over control of church appointments. The names of the Guelphs and Ghibellines probably derived from rallying cries used at the Battle of Weinsberg (1140) between the house of Hohenstaufen, who called the name of a castle, 'Waiblingen!' (later Ghibelline) and the rival house of Welf, who shouted 'Welf!' (later Guelph), which had the support of the papacy.

MARKWARD OF ANWEILER

At the close of the 12th century Pope Innocent III (ruled 1198–1216) called a crusade against Markward of Anweiler, a former follower of Hohenstaufen emperors Frederick I 'Barbarossa' and Henry VI. Markward was appointed Margrave of

▲ *This coin was issued by the Ghibelline government of Genoa, northern Italy.*

Ancona and Count of Abruzzo by Henry; his service to the emperor in Italy brought him into territorial conflict with the papacy and he was excommunicated by both Celestine III and Innocent III.

Following Henry's death he entered the service of the emperor's brother, Philip of Swabia, by whom he was granted the lordship of Palermo in Sicily. In 1198 Henry VI's widow, Constance of Sicily, died, placing her son, the future Emperor Frederick II (r.1212–50), in the care of Pope Innocent III. Markward challenged the pope, however, and established himself as guardian of the heir and Regent of Sicily.

In 1199 Innocent declared a crusade against Markward, likening him to the greatest of defenders of Islam by calling him 'another Saladin' and claiming that Markward was working in alliance with Muslims resident in Sicily and attempting to undermine preparations for the Fourth Crusade, which had just been proclaimed. Knights who joined up to fight Markward were to receive the same indulgences as those who travelled to the Holy Land on crusade; Innocent declared that because Markward was attempting to hinder the crusade, fighting him was as crucial as actually going to Jerusalem.

▲ *Prominent Ghibelline Ezzelino III da Romano was* podestà *(magistrate and representative of the Holy Roman Emperor) in first Verona, then Vicenza, then Padua.*

When he had earlier excommunicated Markward, Innocent had placed him under anathema, cursed him and damned him to hell. For all that, however, and although he suggested that Markward was in league with Muslims, in calling the crusade Innocent did not accuse Markward of being a heretic, and so the cause of the war remained transparently political rather than religious; many historians identify it as the first purely political crusade. The crusade itself did not really come to anything, although an army under Walter of Palear, Chancellor of Sicily, fought against Markward in 1202 as a result of Innocent's call to arms.

CRUSADE OF CHARLES OF ANJOU

For the next 70-odd years, the papacy preached a series of crusades in Italy, most aimed at countering the power of Emperor Fredrick II and his Hohenstaufen descendants in Sicily. Most notable was the holy war waged in Sicily in 1265 by Charles of Anjou, brother of King Louis IX of France.

Following Frederick II's death in 1250 and the death of his heir Conrad in 1254, Frederick's illegitimate son Manfred

(Conrad's brother) had seized power in Sicily and declared himself regent, then entered an alliance with the Saracens to defeat a papal army at Foggia. Pope Alexander IV (ruled 1254–61) excommunicated Manfred, and his successor, Urban IV (ruled 1261–64), offered the crown of Sicily to Charles of Anjou.

Urban's successor, Clement IV (ruled 1265–68), had Charles declared King of Sicily in Rome in May 1265. Charles led his army on campaign and defeated and killed Manfred at the Battle of Benevento on 26 February 1266 to become King of Sicily in fact as well as in name.

WARS OF THE SICILIAN VESPERS

Charles was driven out of Sicily in 1282 and the people allied themselves with the royal house of Aragon. Almost 20 years of fighting followed, known as the Wars of the Sicilian Vespers (1283–1302), and in this period the papacy called a series of crusades in an attempt to restore the rule of Charles and his Angevin descendants. (Charles's descendants were known as the Second Angevin Dynasty, since the first was that otherwise known as the House of Plantagenet, established in England by King Henry II in 1154.) None of these crusades succeeded and, in 1302, the

Treaty of Caltabellotta divided the old Kingdom of Sicily into a mainland portion, to be ruled by the Angevins (and subsequently known to historians as the Kingdom of Naples), and the island of Sicily itself, to be ruled by Aragon.

CRUSADES OF AN EXILED PAPACY

In 1305, the papacy established itself in France, first at Poitiers and then from 1309 at Avignon. Through the period of the papacy's French exile (until 1378), various popes in exile declared crusades against the Ghibellines in Italy. Crusades were launched against the Ghibelline Visconti lords of Florence, for example, in the 1320s and 1360s. But none of these crusading initiatives succeeded in defeating the Ghibellines.

During the ensuing Great Papal Schism of 1378–1417, when there were rival popes in Rome and Avignon, the two sides used crusades against one another with no success. After this date, the holy war as an instrument of papal policy was little seen, found only occasionally in the 16th century under popes such as Julius II.

▼ *War of the Sicilian Vespers. The people of Sicily rise up against Charles I and his French followers on the island in 1282.*

AFTERWORD
THE END AND LEGACY OF CRUSADING

On 7 October 1571 in the naval battle of Lepanto in the Ionian Sea, the ships of the Christian 'Holy League' commanded by Don John of Austria inflicted a heavy defeat on the fleet of the Ottoman Empire. The Holy League was an alliance of the papal states, Spain, Venice, Genoa, the Duchy of Savoy and the Knights of Malta (as the Knights Hospitaller were by then known). The league was formed by Pope Pius V (ruled 1566–72) to try to wrest control of the Mediterranean from the Ottomans – seemingly all-powerful in the region – after Sultan Selim II (reigned 1566–74) had invaded Cyprus in 1570.

The victory was celebrated as a great triumph for Christendom. The day of the battle, 7 October, was named the feast day of *Santa Maria della Vittoria* (Saint Mary of Victory) by the Catholic Church; in his

▼ *No longer an invincible force? Christian ships drive the Ottoman fleet to destruction at the celebrated Battle of Lepanto, 1571.*

▲ *Religious or national war? Pope Sixtus V gave King Philip II of Spain's war against Queen Elizabeth I of England in 1588 the status of a crusade in support of true faith.*

novel *Don Quixote* (first published 1605), Spanish author Cervantes wrote that Lepanto 'revealed to all the nations of the world the error under which they had been labouring in believing that the Turks were invincible at sea'. For all that, the victory proved to have little or no long-term strategic effect, for Selim went on to conquer Cyprus in 1571 and in 1574 he drove the Spanish out of Tunisia, where they had made conquests at the start of the century. Nevertheless, Lepanto was important in that it gave a great boost to Christian morale in their long struggle against the Ottomans, which already by that date stretched back more than 200 years to the crusade of 1366, led by Venice, against Sultan Murad I.

The crusading spirit thus remained resolutely alive through the 16th century, and even survived well into the 17th. As late as the 1680s, Pope Innocent XI (ruled 1676–89) formed a new Holy League after the Ottomans besieged Vienna in 1683. The new League included the Holy Roman Empire, Poland, Muscovite Russia and the Venetian Republic and its campaign, culminating in a great victory at the second Battle of Mohacs (Hungary) in 1687, had definite crusading overtones.

▲ *The beautiful Alhambra palace and fort was the residence of the Granada's Moorish kings in Spain. Via the Islamic courts of Spain, classical learning passed to Christian Europe and helped power the Renaissance.*

AUTHORITY TO CALL WARS

Historians generally identify Lepanto as the last major encounter with the Ottomans explicitly preached and financed (through taxes and the sale of indulgences) as a crusade. Yet all authorities agree that it is impossible to pinpoint a single end date for the era of the crusades. Crusading died gradually away, as the authority for calling and organizing wars passed from the pope and the Catholic Church to kings, princes and other heads of state.

The Protestant Reformation played an important part in this process. Beginning in the 16th century, the Reformation split the Church and undermined crusading. Protestants did not accept the basic premises of crusading – that the pope had the authority to call a war or that Jerusalem needed liberating. German theologian Martin Luther declared that there was no call to free Jerusalem from Muslim control – what did the city contain but an empty tomb?

Protestants, in fact, became the object of crusades. In 1588 Spanish forces were offered crusading privileges to fight in the Spanish Armada against Queen Elizabeth I of England – the crusade in this instance being the war waged by Catholic Spain against Protestant England. In this atmosphere, Francis Bacon, the Elizabethan-Jacobean philosopher and statesman was scathing of crusades and crusaders, writing that the wars were 'the rendezvous of cracked brains that wore their feather in their head instead of their hat'.

EFFECTS OF THE CRUSADES

It is clear that the crusades formed a highly significant period in the long and bloody history of the Holy Land. They contributed to the region's legacy of religiously motivated violence, a legacy whose effects are still tragically felt today. They also have a powerful resonance in the long history of distrust and hatred between some Christians and some Muslims.

Certain historians argue that the crusades decisively changed the course of history in the East. According to this argument, crusader attacks on the Byzantine Empire and, in particular, the capture and sacking of Constantinople in 1203 by the armies of the Fourth Crusade, weakened the empire to such an extent that it was

▼ *As in many crusading conflicts before, the Christian victors at Lepanto attributed their triumph to the intervention of the saints, in this case saints Peter and Paul, in battle.*

unable to resist the later onslaught of the Mamluks of Egypt and the Ottoman Turks – far from strengthening the position of Christianity in the East, the crusades catastrophically undermined it.

Others hold that this argument, which characterizes the Mamluks and Turks as a tide from the East that might have been stopped and driven back by a stronger Constantinople, is mistaken. These historians point out that the Byzantine Empire would probably have been too weak to withstand the Mamluks and Ottomans even without the events of 1203 and that crusader activity resulted in enduring Christian possessions in the East (such as Cyprus) that proved to be important bases for the struggle against the Ottomans.

In Europe, meanwhile, the crusades had a significant effect. Crusading endeavours brought both the Iberian Peninsula and the Baltic region within Christendom, in the first place by reconquering land from the Moors and, in the second, by defeating pagan tribes. The crusades also contributed significantly to the growth in wealth and power of the maritime republics of what is now Italy – cities such as Venice and Genoa, whose merchants carried armies and pilgrims to the East and grew rich on the trade in exotic goods, such as spices, sugar and oranges, that they carried back to Europe from the Holy Land and ports in the Byzantine

Empire. It is no accident that it was in the city-states of Italy, made wealthy by trade, that the European Renaissance began.

By comparison, the crusades had a less permanent effect in the Holy Land and region. While the remains of buildings erected by crusaders, military brotherhoods and settlers of Outremer can still be seen in places, by and large their other

▲ *Venice grew rich on goods from the East –*
including the loot brought back after the
sacking of Constantinople by the soldiers of
the Fourth Crusade in 1204.

▼ *Latterday crusade? A 19th-century*
painting imagines Christopher Columbus's
landfall in the Americas as the coming of a
Christian army driven by faith.

achievements and endeavours were swept away by the Mamluks in the 13th century. The one truly enduring legacy was cultural, in focusing the attention of Christian Europe on the Holy Land, in encouraging the demonization of non-Christians and in contributing to the creation of a legacy of religious violence in the region.

CONTACT BETWEEN WEST AND EAST

One important side effect of the crusades, evidenced by the success of the trade carried on by Venetian, Genoan and other ships, was the establishment of increased contact between Europe and the East. Many now familiar foodstuffs – including spices (such as pepper, ginger, cloves and cinnamon) and fruits (such as dates, figs and oranges), as well as rice, almonds and cane sugar, according to some accounts – first came to Europe as a result of this trade. Returning traders, pilgrims and crusaders also introduced to European homes glass mirrors of the kind used in Constantinople and rugs and carpets like those found in the castles of Outremer.

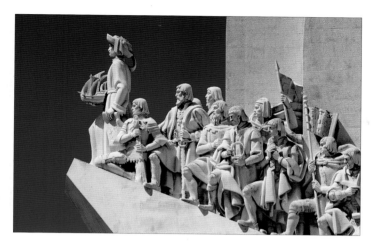

▲ *The Monument to the Discoveries in Lisbon celebrates Henry the Navigator and other Portuguese who contributed to the explorations of the 15th–16th centuries.*

Some accounts claim that the game of chess, which originated in India and spread to the Persian Empire, was popularized in Europe by crusaders, travellers and traders returning from Outremer. Contact between Europeans and Arabs was made not only in the Byzantine Empire and the Holy Land but also in the Iberian Peninsula – itself, as we have seen, a crusade venue.

ANCIENT WISDOM

Contact with Arabs and Moors was, moreover, the route by which a great deal of classical philosophy and science made its way into Europe, where it powered the Renaissance of the 14th–17th centuries. Prior to the crusading era, when Muslim Arabs overran the lands of the Middle East in the 7th and 8th centuries, they found manuscripts and books from the days of ancient Greece and Rome; they were careful to preserve this knowledge, translating many volumes from Greek into Arabic.

Europeans came into contact with this knowledge in the Iberian Peninsula and via the Greek scholars of the Byzantine Empire; many of these Greeks fled to Europe to escape the Ottoman conquest of Constantinople in 1453. One of these was the theologian and collector Cardinal Basilius Bessarion (1403–72), who had been Latin Patriarch of Constantinople: he brought a priceless collection of books to Italy and gave them to the republic of Venice. They today form the core part of the well-known Library of St Mark's.

CASTLES AND CITIES

The crusades also had an effect on the military and sacred architecture of Europe. The monastic military brotherhoods, such as the Knights Hospitaller and the Knights Templar, were great builders. The Templars, as we have seen, built a great number of churches, many round in form as a homage to the *Templum Solomonis* (Temple of Solomon) in Jerusalem, their original headquarters. The brotherhoods also developed the concentric design in castles – the fortress had two sets of walls, a taller set within, around the 'inner bailey', and a lower outer set, around the 'outer bailey'.

We know that the future King Edward I of England was profoundly impressed by Krak des Chevaliers, the Knights' Hospitaller concentric castle near Homs in Syria, which he inspected while travelling on the Ninth Crusade (1271–72) and later, in association with his builder Master James of St Georges, used the design in his Welsh fortresses, such as Beaumaris Castle in North Wales.

The crusade era also saw the rise of cities. Just as the maritime cities of Italy thrived, so throughout Europe the spread of towns and cities was driven by trade. In addition, kings such as Richard I of England sold off rights of self-government to municipal boroughs as a way of raising money for their wars. Some historians also suggest that the repeated failures of the crusading armies served to undermine feudalism and contributed to its decline as a form of social organization.

CRUSADING'S NEW FRONTIER

In the 15th and 16th centuries, the exploration of Africa and the Americas was in part informed and inspired by crusading ideology. Portuguese explorations of Africa and the Atlantic, organized and financed by Prince Henry the Navigator, were explicitly driven by crusading ideals – Henry was intrigued by the story of Prester John (the legendary Christian king, believed by many of Henry's contemporaries to reside in the East or in Africa and to be preparing a great war against Islam), and one reason for Henry's exploration of Africa was to seek help in the conquest of Muslim powers in the Holy Land.

The adventurer Christopher Columbus was sponsored in his voyages to the West Indies and central and southern America by Ferdinand and Isabella of Spain, who approved his exploration in 1492 immediately after their conquest of Granada. Columbus later declared that the wealth discovered in central America could fund a new crusade to the Holy Land. The Conquistadores who swept into Mexico and Guatemala, were driven by a desire for gold and land, but also by a fervour for religious conversion informed by the Reconquista. The energy, spirit of adventure and religious devotion that had sustained centuries of crusading fed into these voyages of discovery across the great oceans and thus made an enduring mark in the countries of the 'New World'.

INDEX

Abbasids 25, 31, 118, 119, 120, 182

Acre 6, 7, 14, 15, 17, 60, 75, 78, 91, 97, 111, 128, 129, 171, 180, 181, 184, 185, 223

  Council of Acre 15, 112–13, 213

  fall 186, 187, 188, 206, 216, 219

  massacre 146–7

  siege 142–3, 144–5, 213, 218

Adhemar, Bishop of Le Puy 42, 43, 53, 59, 65, 70, 74, 79, 86, 205

al-Afdal Shahanshah 34, 74, 77, 83

Afghanistan 25

Albert of Aix 62

Albigensian crusade 131, 157, 164, 227, 234–5

Aleppo 14, 110, 111, 113, 116

Alexander III, Pope 15, 220, 221, 223

Alexandria 129, 188, 189, 191

Alexius I Comnenus 14, 38–9, 41, 44, 50, 52, 54–5, 62, 69, 72, 74, 75, 76, 77, 92, 93, 96, 97

  siege of Nicaea 56, 57

Alfonso VI of León 229

Alfonso VIII of Castile 128, 164, 230

Alfonso IX of Castile 129

Alfonso X of Castile and León 25

Alfred the Great 23

Almohads 128, 157, 164, 230

Amalric I of Jerusalem 15, 88, 118, 119, 121, 122, 124, 143, 213

Anatolia 14, 15, 24, 26, 38, 49, 50, 51, 56, 58

  march across 62–3

Anna Comnena 16, 50, 51, 52, 62, 72

Antioch 6, 14, 15, 26, 60, 62, 63, 65, 74, 75, 129, 181

  Bohemond of Taranto 72–3

  capture of 68–9

  defeat of Kerbogha 70–1

Nur ed-Din 118–19

  siege 34, 66–7, 77, 92

armour 59, 104–5

Arnulf of Choques 14, 33, 82–3, 86

Arsuf 14, 75, 97, 129, 180

Artuqids 15, 100

Ascalon 15, 17, 60, 97, 212

Assassins (hashhashin) 151, 213

Ayyubids 168, 170, 173, 128, 178, 180, 203

Baghdad 24, 25, 31, 116, 118, 119

Balak 102

Balderic of Dol 40, 41, 44

Baldwin I of Jerusalem (Baldwin of Boulogne) 14, 15, 49, 61, 62–3, 80, 82, 85, 86, 87, 92, 95, 96, 97, 103

Baldwin II of Jerusalem (Baldwin of Le Bourg) 14, 15, 73, 78, 86, 92, 93, 102, 103, 210, 214

Baldwin III of Jerusalem 15, 103, 111, 112, 118, 214

Baldwin IV of Jerusalem 15, 89, 121, 122, 215

Baldwin of Flanders 128, 158, 159

Baldwin V of Jerusalem 15, 122

Baldwin VI 89

Balian of Ibelin 122, 123, 124, 125

Baltic crusades 8, 15, 126, 157, 164, 240–1

battles

  Ager Sanguinis (Field of Blood) 15, 100–1, 102

  al-Mansourah 178–9, 180, 212

  Arsuf 7, 128, 133, 149

  Ascalon 14, 60, 77, 83

  Cresson 203, 212, 213, 214

  Dorylaeum 14, 58–9, 60, 62, 72, 73, 77, 92, 104, 105

  Harenc 14, 67

  Harran 93

  Horns of Hattin 6, 7, 15, 17, 33, 95, 99, 122–3, 124, 125, 134, 135, 144, 145, 147, 148, 149, 168, 212–13, 221

  Jaffa 152–3

  Kosovo, Second 197

  La Forbie 128, 173, 175, 178, 180

  Las Navas de Tolosa 128, 164, 220, 230–1, 237

  Lepanto 7, 248, 249

Manzikert 25, 26, 38

Montgisard 15, 121

Muret 237

Nicopolis 129, 194, 195

Rio Salado 232–3

Tannenberg 218

Teba 129, 232

Varna 197

Bavaria 35

Baybars, Rukn al-Zahir 95, 128, 129, 173, 175, 178–9, 180–1, 184–5, 186, 207, 214, 218

Bayezid I 129, 194, 195

Bedouins 31

Beirut 15, 17, 74, 75, 87, 97, 187

Belgrade 200–1

Belvoir 95

Berenguer of Barcelona 15

Bernard of Clairvaux 15, 35, 106–7, 114, 115, 210–11, 215

Bethlehem 7, 8, 14, 32, 78, 170, 171

Béziers 236

Blanche of Castile 172, 180, 181, 182–3

Bogomils 235

Bohemia 8, 244–5

Bohemond of Taranto, Prince of Antioch 6, 14, 16, 19, 40, 49, 52–3, 54, 55, 56, 57, 58, 59, 62, 63, 66, 67, 68, 70, 72–3, 74, 76, 75, 77, 82, 86, 92, 93

Bolingbroke, Henry 242, 243

Boniface of Montferrat 159, 160, 163

Boucicaut, Jean Le Meingre 196, 243

Bush, George W. 10

Byzantine Empire 6, 7, 14, 24, 25, 26–7, 29, 38–9, 46, 49, 52, 54, 56, 66, 67, 72, 73, 87, 91, 92, 96, 249

  Fourth Crusade 160–1, 249

  Ottomans 196–7, 198–9

  recovery 187

  Second Crusade 108, 109, 114, 115, 116

  Third Crusade 138–9

Caesarea 14, 60, 61, 75, 88, 90, 91, 97, 129, 180

Cairo 7, 25, 79, 118, 119

Calixtus II, Pope 15

cannibalism 66, 69, 74, 77

caravans 89, 90, 95, 122

Carcassonne 236, 237, 238

Cathars 10, 126, 128, 129, 131, 227, 234–5, 236–7, 238–9

Catholic expansion 130–1

Celestine III, Pope 128, 154, 155, 218, 221, 240, 241

Charlemagne 22, 23, 27, 137

Charles of Anjou 186, 187, 247

Children's Crusades 166–7, 181

chivalry 44

Christ 9, 11, 12, 17, 21, 22, 30, 32, 33, 35, 41, 43, 47, 65, 138

Christianity 22–3, 82–3

  Eastern Church 26–7, 29

  Great Schism 192, 193, 247

Cicero 21

Cilicia 87, 92

Clement V, Pope 129, 206, 216, 217

Clermont 6, 7, 12, 14, 23, 29, 37, 40–1, 42, 44, 45, 46, 47, 53

Clovis I of the Franks 22

Columbus, Christopher 250, 251

Conrad III of Germany 6, 15, 107, 108–9, 110, 112, 113, 114, 136

Conrad of Montferrat 134–5, 136, 142, 143, 144, 151, 158

Constantine the Great 26, 30, 32–3

Constantinople 6, 7, 8, 14, 15, 24, 26, 27, 29, 39, 44, 46, 47, 49, 56, 92, 96, 97, 109, 187

  Fourth Crusade 128, 160–1, 162–3, 249

  Ottomans 196, 197, 198–9

  People's Crusade 50–1

  Prince's Crusade 52, 53, 54–5

corsairs 192, 193, 206

Council of Acre 15, 112–13, 213

Council of Troyes 8, 15, 210, 211

County of Edessa 14, 63, 85, 86, 87, 92–3, 99

County of Tripoli 85, 86–7, 99, 184

cross, taking the 9, 11, 12, 35, 42–3, 44, 106–7, 134, 136

Crusade of 1101 96–7

Crusade of 1212 230–1

Crusade of 1239–41 172–3

Crusade of 1366 194–5

Crusade of 1390 193

Crusade of 1443 196–7

  ancient wisdom 251

  architecture 251

  contact between East and West 250–1

▼ *A knight at communion.*

▲ *Antioch under siege.*

crusader pilgrims 9, 34–5
crusading privileges 165, 229
effects 249–50
exploration 251
Great Schism 192–3, 247
interpretations of the crusades
  9–10
relevance 11
resonance 10–11
weapons and tactics of the Saracens
  104–5
crusading leagues 188
Cyprus 7, 155, 172, 185, 187, 206,
  207, 223

Daimbert of Pisa 14, 86
Damascus 6, 14, 15, 25, 31, 87, 97,
  102, 112
Nur ed-Din 116, 117
siege of Damascus 113, 114, 213
Damietta 7, 128, 168–9, 177, 178,
  179, 213
Danishmends 24, 56–7, 58, 73, 86,
  92
David, King 11, 17, 20, 30
defenders of the faith 22–3
diplomacy 22
Douglas, Sir James 129, 232
Dracul, Vlad 199
Dubois, Pierre 216
Duqaq, Sultan 14, 67, 77

Edessa 15, 38, 45, 111
capture by Imad ed-Din Zengi
  102–3, 106
Edgar the Atheling 67
Edward I 7, 8, 94, 129, 175, 181,
  183, 187, 223
Ninth Crusade 184–5, 251
Egypt 7, 8, 15, 60, 74–5, 77, 78, 79,
  83, 118, 119, 160, 171, 207
Fifth Crusade 168–9, 213
Mamluks 173, 175, 180, 186

Seventh Crusade 176, 177, 178–9
Eighth Crusade 7, 8, 129, 175
Louis IX of France 180–1
El Cid, Rodrigo Diaz de Vivar 229
Eleanor of Aquitaine 107, 110, 111,
  112, 115, 182
Emicho of Leisingen 14, 47, 52
England 44, 53, 67, 115
Enrico Dandolo, Doge of Venice 158,
  159, 161, 162, 163, 164
Ephesus 38
Equestrian Order of the Holy
  Sepulchre 15, 205
ergotism 47
Eugenius III, Pope 6, 15, 106, 108,
  114, 211
Eugenius IV, Pope 196
European crusades 108, 126, 164,
  227

Fatimids 6, 14, 24, 25, 31, 34, 74–5,
  77, 83, 118, 120
Ferdinand and Isabella 10, 129, 131,
  227, 232, 233
Ferdinand III of Castile and León 128,
  221, 232
feudalism 88–9, 90, 251
Fifth Crusade 7, 8, 128, 157, 165,
  168–9, 178, 213
First Crusade 6, 8, 12, 29, 30, 31, 34,
  37, 99, 115, 126, 227
Battle of Dorylaeum 58–9
capture of Jerusalem 80–1, 82–3
first-hand accounts 62
march across Anatolia 62–3
march on Jerusalem 74–5, 78–9
motives of crusaders 44–5
People's Crusade 6, 14, 16, 37,
  46–7, 49, 50–1, 56, 69
Princes' Crusade 49, 52–3, 54–5
routes of the First Crusade 16
siege of Antioch 34, 66–7
siege of Nicaea 56–7
taking Antioch 66–7, 68–9, 70–1
timeline 14–15
Flanders 46, 53
Fourth Crusade 7, 8, 155, 157
route of the Fourth crusade 130
France 8, 35, 44, 45, 46, 47, 53, 82,
  109, 115, 176, 180, 181
Francis of Assisi 168
Frederick I Barbarossa, Holy Roman
  Emperor 6–7, 128, 133, 136–7,
  138–9
Frederick II, Holy Roman Emperor 7,
  8, 128, 157, 168, 169, 170–1, 172,

218, 243
Frederick of Swabia 107, 108–9, 112
Fulcher of Chartres 37, 40, 41, 42,
  54, 55, 58, 59, 62, 75, 81, 85, 100,
  102
Fulk of Jerusalem 15, 102, 103, 111,
  112

Gelasius II, Pope 15
Genoa 7, 53, 91, 97, 129, 160, 193,
  249, 250
Germany 34, 35, 46, 47
Gesta Francorum 6, 40–1, 42, 58, 59,
  62, 70, 76, 80, 81, 82, 83
Ghibellines 246, 247
Gideon 20
Giovanni da Capistrano 200, 201
Gnosticism 235
Godfrey of Bouillon 6, 14, 16, 19, 49,
  52, 54–5, 56, 57, 58, 59, 67, 73,
  75, 76, 77, 79, 80
Equestrian Order of the Holy
  Sepulchre 205
Kingdom of Jerusalem 60–1, 82,
  83, 86, 88, 90, 92, 103
Great Schism 192, 193, 247
Gregory VII, Pope 28–9, 164
Gregory VIII, Pope 6, 125, 128, 134,
  137, 220
Gregory IX, Pope 128, 157, 171, 172,
  222, 238, 243
Gregory X, Pope 183, 186
Guelphs 246
Guibert of Nogent 40, 41, 42–3, 44,
  46, 69, 74
Guy of Lusignan 15, 17, 122, 123,
  128, 142, 143, 151

Haifa 97, 187
Henry I of Jerusalem 143
Henry II 115, 128, 136, 182, 215,
  223
Henry IV 242, 243
Henry IV Holy Roman Emperor 28–9,
  55, 60
Henry the Navigator 251
Henry VI Holy Roman Emperor 128,
  154, 155
Henry VIII 222, 223
heretics 126, 164, 200, 227,
  234–5, 244
Holy Lance 14, 62, 65, 70, 71, 73,
  77, 82, 83
Holy Sepulchre 9, 17, 30, 31, 33, 34,
  60, 75, 82–3, 90, 125, 205
holy war 19, 20, 40–1

Christianity 22–3
jihad 11, 99, 100, 104, 105, 116,
  121, 123, 232
Last Judgement 21, 43
theories of just and holy wars 21
Honorius III, Pope 157, 168, 170,
  219, 237
Hugh III of Jerusalem 129, 185
Hugh of Vermandois 14, 49, 52, 54,
  59, 60, 74, 77, 96
Hugh of Payens 97, 210, 211
Hungary 46, 52, 128, 196
Ottomans 200–1
Hunyadi, Janos 196, 197, 200, 201
Hus, Jan 244
Hussites 129, 200, 227, 244–5

Iconium 128, 139
Iftikhar al-Daula 78–9, 83
Ilghazi 15, 99, 100–1, 102, 105
Imad ed-Din Zengi 15, 99, 116
Innocent III, Pope 7, 8, 15, 128, 155,
  157, 164–5, 210, 211, 218
Albigensian Crusade 234, 235,
  236, 237
Baltic crusades 240, 241, 242
crusader indulgences 165
crusading taxes 165
Fifth Crusade 165, 168
Fourth Crusade 158, 159, 160, 170
Innocent IV, Pope 128, 183
Isabella of Jerusalem 128, 143, 151,
  158
Islam 24–5
Sufism 117, 123
Italy 8, 44, 53
papal crusades 246–7

Jaffa 79, 148, 149, 152–3, 170, 180,
  181
Jakelin of Mailly 203, 212
Jeremiah 19
Jerusalem 6, 7, 8, 9, 11, 14, 15, 16,

▼ *Crusaders attack Jerusalem.*

▲ The keep of Saladin's castle.

19, 26, 30, 31, 39, 126
Church of the Holy Sepulchre 30, 31
city plan during First and Second Crusades 17
Dome of the Rock 31, 125, 170
Fifth Crusade 168, 213
First Crusade 54, 56, 57, 58, 65, 66, 72, 73, 74–5, 76, 77, 78–9, 80–1, 82–3
hospital of St John 204
King of Jerusalem 88, 89, 90
Last Judgement 21, 43
pilgrimage 32, 34, 35, 47, 53
recapture by Saladin 124–5
Richard I the Lionheart 150–1, 152, 153
Sixth Crusade 157, 171, 172, 173
Temple Mount 170, 171
Urban II's speech 41, 42
Jews 11, 30, 31, 80, 91
persecution of 10, 14, 15, 47, 52, 60, 107, 141, 181
jihad 11, 99, 100, 104, 105, 116, 121, 123, 232
John Lord of Joinville 176, 177
John of Gaunt 192, 192–3
John of Ibelin 171, 172
Joshua 20, 79
Judas Maccabeus 19, 20, 30

al-Kamil, Sultan 7, 168, 169, 170, 178, 213
Kerbogha, Sultan of Mosul 14, 65, 68, 69, 70–1, 72, 73, 77
Khalil, Sultan 129, 186, 187
Khwarismians 7, 128, 173, 175
Kilij Arslan 56–7, 58, 59, 77, 96, 102, 110
Kilij Arslan II 110, 117
King Peter's Crusade 129, 188–9, 190–1
Kingdom of Jerusalem 6, 7, 8, 11, 14,

15, 16, 33, 38, 45, 85, 86, 99, 115, 120, 121, 122, 123, 154, 155, 213
Godfrey of Bouillon 60–1, 82, 83, 86, 88, 90, 92, 103
plans to regain the Holy Land 189
Saladin 120, 121, 122, 123
Sixth Crusade 172–3
Kings' crusade 107
knights 43, 44–5
Knights Hospitaller 8, 9, 15, 87, 89, 112, 117, 123, 129, 147, 148, 172, 173, 181, 184, 186, 187, 196, 203, 204–5, 215, 217, 220
Battle of Arsuf 133, 149
crusading leagues 188
King Peter's Crusade 189, 190
Krak des Chevaliers 94–5, 251
Malta 208, 209
Rhodes 206–7, 216
Knights of Christ 219, 221
Knights of Our Lady of Mountjoie 15, 221
Knights of St Lazarus 8, 203, 224
Knights of St Thomas Acon 8, 203, 222–3
Knights Templar 8–9, 15, 17, 89, 97, 112, 117, 123, 129, 143, 147, 148, 173, 176, 187, 203, 220, 221
al-Mansourah 212
America 216, 217
Ascalon 212
banking 215
castles 214–15, 251
Cathars 239
churches 215
downfall 206, 216–17
foundation 210–11
Horns of Hattin 212–13
negotiation and diplomacy 213
rivalry with Hospitallers 213
siege of Acre 213
Krak des Chevaliers 15, 85, 87, 93, 94–5, 168, 184, 251
Kurds 119

Last Judgement 21, 43
'Latins' and 'Greeks' 22, 26, 161
Leopold of Austria 145, 154
Lisbon 15
Lithuania 243
Livonia 240, 241
Livonian Brothers of the Sword 128, 225, 241
Llull, Raymon 216
Louis IX of France 7, 8, 9, 126, 128–9, 175, 178, 182–3, 184, 186,

238, 239
Eighth Crusade 180–1
Seventh Crusade 176–7, 177–8
Louis of Bourbon 129, 193
Louis VII of France 6, 15, 106, 107, 108, 109, 110–11, 112, 113, 114, 115

Maarat al-Numan 14, 69, 74, 77
Magyars 23
Mahdia 129, 192, 193
Malta 7, 9, 204, 208, 209
Mamluks 128, 129, 173, 175, 180, 185, 186, 189, 249
Manuel I Comnenus 108, 109, 110, 111, 114, 115, 116, 119, 160
Margat 95, 186
Marienburg 129, 219, 243
Markward of Anweiler 157, 164, 246–7
massacres 47, 68, 80–1, 92, 146–7, 173, 181, 184, 186, 187, 236
Mehmed II the Conqueror 197, 198–9, 200, 201, 206, 207
Melisende of Jerusalem 15, 102–3, 111, 112
Mercers, Worshipful Company of 223
merchant enclaves 91
military orders 8–9, 89, 203
Molay, Jacques 129, 211, 216–17
Mongols 129, 180, 182–3, 185, 186, 188
Montfort 218
Montreal 88–9, 95, 168
Montségur 238–9
Moors 10, 14, 15, 126, 128, 129, 249
Reconquista 128, 130–1, 220, 221, 228–9, 231, 232–3
Muhammad 11, 24, 25, 30, 31
Muslim empires 24–5, 26
Nazareth 7, 170, 171
Nicaea 14, 16, 24, 38, 50, 51
siege 56–7, 58, 60, 76, 92
Nine Worthies 20
Ninth Crusade 7, 8, 129, 175, 181, 184–5
Normans 23, 28, 38, 52–3, 58, 72, 105
Nur ed-Din 15, 99, 110, 111, 113, 115, 116–17, 118–19, 120, 121, 213

Odo of Bayeux 53
Old Testament 19, 20
Order of Alcantara 221
Order of Aviz 221

Order of Calatrava 15, 220, 221
Order of Dobrzyn 243
Order of Montesa 217, 221
Order of Our Lady of Bethlehem 225
Order of Santiago 15, 221
Order of St Edward of Acre 185
Order of St Lazarus 15, 224
Order of the Sword 190, 224–5
Orthodox Church 9, 63, 89, 160
Otranto 207
Ottomans 7, 8, 175, 129, 193, 194–5, 248, 249
attack on Malta 209
attack on Rhodes 207, 208–9
Belgrade 200–1
Mehmed II 197, 198–9, 200, 201, 206, 207
Oultrejordain 88, 168
Outremer 85, 86–7, 114, 115, 129, 157, 172, 175, 184, 185, 250
Baybars 180–1
fall of Outremer 186–7, 219
government of the crusader states 88–9
life in the crusader states 90–1

pagans 108, 126, 157, 164, 218, 219, 227, 240–1, 249
Palestine 6, 7, 16–17, 25
papacy 9, 28–9
authority to call wars 249
crusades in Italy 246–7
papal indulgences 7, 29, 37, 43, 128, 165
Paris 183
Paschal II, Pope 8, 14, 15, 96, 204, 205
Patriarch of Jerusalem 89
Paulicians 235
Peace of God 43, 44
Pelagius 7, 8, 157, 168, 169, 170, 178, 213
penance 33
People's Crusade 6, 14, 16, 37, 46–7, 49, 50–1, 56, 69
Peter Bartholomew 14, 70, 71, 82
Peter I of Cyprus 129, 188–9, 190–1
Peter the Hermit 14, 37, 46–7, 49, 50, 51, 67, 79, 92
Petrarch 189
Philip I of France 40, 52, 60, 93
Philip II of France 6–7, 128, 133, 136, 140, 141, 142, 143, 144, 145, 146, 154, 158, 167, 222
Philip IV of France 129, 216–17
Philip of Ibelin 186, 191

Pied Piper of Hamelin 167
pilgrimage 9,12, 17, 30–1, 32–3, 115
  crusader pilgrims 9, 34–5
  German pilgrimage of 1064 34, 35
  persecution of pilgrims 31
  pilgrimage as penance 33
Portugal 8, 108, 217, 220, 221
Prester John 106, 107, 251
Princes' Crusade 49, 52–3, 54–5
Principality of Antioch 14, 38, 45, 77, 85, 86, 87, 99, 100, 116
Protestantism 249
Prussian Cavaliers of Christ 128, 225
Prussian crusades 219, 242–3

Qalawun, Sultan 129, 186, 187

Radulph of Caen 74, 77, 92, 93, 105
Radwan 14, 67, 72
Raymond du Puy de Provence 112, 205
Raymond IV of Toulouse 14, 16, 37, 49, 53, 55, 57, 58, 59, 62, 66, 67, 74, 75, 77, 79, 80, 82, 83, 96, 107, 112
  County of Tripoli 86–7
Raymond of Antioch 15, 106, 110, 111, 114, 116
Raymond of Tripoli 15, 122, 123, 212–13
Raymond VI of Toulouse 234, 236, 237
Reconquista 128, 130–1, 220–1, 228–9, 231, 232–3, 251
Reformation 249
relics 33, 183
Renaissance 250, 251
Reynald of Châtillon 88–9, 95, 117, 122, 123, 147
Rhineland 14, 15, 47, 60
Rhodes 9, 196, 204, 206–7, 216
Richard Earl of Cornwall 172–3
Richard the Lionheart 6–7, 128, 133, 140–1, 142, 143, 144, 145, 155, 158, 159, 222, 251
  Battle of Arsuf 133, 149
  death 154
  Jerusalem 150–1, 152, 153
  march to Jaffa 148
  massacre at Acre 146–7
  negotiations with Saladin 150
Robert II of Flanders 14, 19, 39, 41, 44, 53, 55, 56, 67, 76–7, 79, 83
Robert of Craon 112, 211, 213
Robert of Normandy 14, 16, 40, 49, 53, 55, 56, 59, 67, 74, 75, 77, 79, 80, 82, 83

Robert the Bruce 129, 232
Robert the Monk 6, 40, 41, 42
Roger of Antioch 100–1, 102, 105
Rome, ancient 21, 26, 27, 30
Roosevelt, Franklin D. 10
Rum 14, 16, 38, 50, 56, 87, 108, 139

St Ambrose 21
St Augustine 21
St George 6, 76, 77, 121
St James the Great 229
St Peter 9, 26, 27
St Peter 9
St Thomas Becket 222, 223
Saladin (Salah ed-Din Yusuf) 6, 7, 15, 33, 89, 95, 99, 118, 119, 120–1, 154, 214, 215, 222
  conquests 16–17
  Frederick Barbarossa 137, 139
  negotiations with Richard I 150, 152, 153
  recapture of Jerusalem 124–5
  'Saladin tithe' 136
  Third Crusade 128, 133, 134–5, 142–3, 144–5, 146, 147, 149, 150
  victory at Horns of Hattin 122–3
salvation 6, 43
Sancho VII of Navarre 128, 164, 230
Saone 17, 95
Saracens 23, 85
Saragossa 15
Sardis 38
Second Crusade 6, 8, 35, 85, 99, 106–7, 108–9, 126, 227
  Council of Acre 112–13
  progress to Attalia 111
  recriminations 114–15
  siege of Damascus 113, 114, 213
Seleucids 20, 30
Seljuks 6, 14, 15, 24, 25, 26, 29, 31, 38–9, 49, 56, 58, 63, 65, 66, 67, 73, 74, 77, 87, 93, 96–7

▼ Saracen knights, 1337.

▲ Philip I and Tancred (right).

Mongols 188
Second Crusade 100, 101, 105, 108, 110, 111, 115
  Third Crusade 128, 139
Seventh Crusade 7, 8, 126, 128, 175, 180
  Louis IX of France 176–7, 177–8
Shepherd's Crusade of 1251 180, 181
Shi'ites 24, 25, 31, 118
Shirkuh 99, 116, 118, 119, 120
Sibylla of Jerusalem 15, 122, 128, 143
Sidon 15, 17, 85, 97, 170, 173, 180
Sigurd I of Norway 14, 15, 97
Simon of Montfort 158, 160, 236, 237
Sixth Crusade 7, 8, 128, 157, 170–1
slavery 50, 51, 124, 187
Spain 7, 8, 14, 15, 53, 97, 108, 128, 157, 164, 217, 227
  Armada 249
  crusade of 1212 230–1
  Islamic expansion 25
  Reconquista 128, 130–1, 220–1, 228–9, 231, 232–3
Stephen of Blois 14, 40, 53, 55, 56, 57, 59, 62, 65, 66, 68, 69, 96
Sufism 117, 123
Suleyman I the Magnificent 208–9
Sunnis 24, 25, 31, 117, 118, 120
Syria 6, 7, 14, 25, 66, 100, 116, 118, 168

tactics 104–5
Tafurs 69, 74, 166, 167
Tamerlaine 195
Tancred de Hauteville 14, 15, 22, 53, 55, 56, 57, 58, 59, 62–3, 67, 74, 75, 77, 78, 79, 80, 81, 83, 87, 100
  literary hero 93
  Prince of Galilee 86, 88, 92–3
Tarsus 62–3, 87, 92, 111
Taticius 56, 67
Teutonic Knights 8, 89, 128, 129,

173, 185, 203, 216, 218–19, 222, 223, 242–3
Theobald I of Navarre 172, 173
Third Crusade 6–7, 8, 126, 128, 134–5, 136–7
  aftermath and legacy 154–5
  siege of Acre 142–3, 144–5, 213, 218
  Treaty of Jaffa 152–3
Tortosa 14, 75, 187
trade 89, 91, 122, 160, 249–50
Transylvania 218–19
Tripoli 15, 45, 75, 82, 129, 184, 185, 186
Truce of God 43
True Cross 14, 17, 32, 33, 82, 83, 97, 122, 123, 134, 145, 147, 150, 168, 169, 183, 212, 213
Tunis 7, 8, 129, 175, 180, 181, 184
Tunisia 25, 129, 175
Turan Shah 179, 180
Turkomans 185
Tyre 15, 17, 91, 97, 134–5, 187

Umayyads 25, 31, 228–9
Urban II, Pope 6, 7, 9, 10, 12, 14, 16, 22, 23, 26, 34, 72, 96
  declaration of plenary indulgence 29, 37, 43
  Eastern Church 27
  speech at Clermont 40–1, 42, 44, 45, 46, 47, 53

Venice 7, 15, 53, 91, 97, 158–9, 160–1, 249, 250, 251
  attack on Constantinople 160–1, 162–3
Vézelay, France 15, 106
Vikings 22, 23
Visigoths 228

Walter Sans Avoir 14, 46, 49, 50
War of the Sicilian Vespers 186, 187, 247
wealth 44–5
weapons 104–5
Welsh crusader castles 94, 251
Wends 15, 108, 240–1
William I the Conqueror 23, 28, 49, 53
William of Machaut 189, 190, 191
William of Tyre 61, 78, 103, 110, 113, 115, 118, 121, 122, 134

Zara 7, 128, 157, 158, 159, 160, 161, 162, 164

▲ *The formidable citadel of Aleppo.*

▲ *German crusaders capture Beirut in 1197.*

Charles Phillips would like to dedicate this book, with
thanks and love, to his parents Gay and David Phillips.

This edition is published by Hermes House, an imprint of Anness
Publishing Ltd, Hermes House, 88–89 Blackfriars Road, London SE1 8HA
tel. 020 7401 2077; fax 020 7633 9499

www.hermeshouse.com; www.annesspublishing.com

If you like the images in this book and would like to investigate using them for
publishing, promotions or advertising, please visit our website
www.practicalpictures.com for more information.

Publisher: Joanna Lorenz
Editorial Director: Helen Sudell
Executive Editor: Joanne Rippin
Designer: Nigel Partridge
Illustrations: Simon Smith
Editorial reader: Jay Thundercliffe
Production Controller: Steve Lang

ETHICAL TRADING POLICY

Because of our ongoing ecological investment programme, you, as our customer, can
have the pleasure and reassurance of knowing that a tree is being cultivated on your
behalf to naturally replace the materials used to make the book you are holding.
For further information about this scheme, go to www.annesspublishing.com/trees.

PUBLISHER'S NOTE

Although the advice and information in this book are believed to be accurate and true
at the time of going to press, neither the authors nor the publisher can accept any legal
responsibility or liability for any errors or omissions that may have been made.

PICTURE ACKNOWLEDGEMENTS

ART ARCHIVE, pp5bm, 7, 12, 21t, 22t, 23t, 23b, 27t, 27b, 28t, 28br, 29, 40t, 32b,
35, 38br, 41b, 42b, 42b, 42t, 43tr, 44b, 45b 50, 51b, 54b, 54t, 57t, 68, 71t, 73t, 84,
94b, 95tr, 95b 254b, 115, 123t, 128, 129, 133, 136b, 137t, 137b, 139b, 141t, 158b,
159b, 163b, 170b, 171t, 173b, 176b, 176t, 177tr, 177b, 181t, 182b, 190, 193t, 198b,
199bl, 200t, 204t, 205b, 206, 209t, 213t, 215tr, 220t, 224tr, 224br, 226, 236b, 236t,
224br, 226, 236b, 236t, 238t, 238b, 240t, 244b, 245t, 245b, 246t, 247t, 247b, 252b.
BRIDGEMAN ART LIBRARY: pp7b, 9b, 10t, 12, 20b, 21b, 24t, 25t, 25b, 26t, 26b,
28bl, 30t, 31t, 31b, 32t, 33, 34t, 34b, 36, 38t, 39t, 39b, 40b, 41t, 43tl, 44t, 45b, 46b,
46b, 47t, 48, 49, 51tl, 51tr, 53, 54b, 55t, 56b, 56t, 59t, 60, 61t, 62t, 62b, 63b, 64,
66, 67t, 67b, 69t, 69b, 70t, 70b, 71b, 74t, 75b, 76, 77t, 79b, 80, 81bl, 82b, 82t, 86b,
89t, 89b, 90, 91t, 92b, 93, 95tr, 96t, 96b, 97t, 97b, 98, 100, 101t, 103b, 104b, 105t,
106, 107tl, 107b, 107tr, 108t, 109t, 109b, 111t, 111b, 112t, 112b, 116t, 117t, 119t,
119r, 120b, 121b, 122t, 124b, 127, 132, 134, 135t, 135b, 140b, 141b, 142t, 142b,
143b, 145t, 146, 147b, 148b, 149t, 149b, 150, 151b, 152b, 153t, 153b, 154, 155t,
156, 158t, 160, 161, 162, 163t, 164t, 164b, 165, 166t, 167b, 169b, 169t, 169b, 170t,
172, 173t, 177tl, 178tl, 178t, 179t, 180t, 183t, 183b, 184t, 186b, 187, 188t, 188b,
189t, 189b, 191b, 192t, 192b, 193b, 194b, 195, 196, 198t, 200b, 202, 203, 204b,
205tl, 205tr, 207t, 208, 209b, 210bl, 210t, 210br, 211b, 211t, 212b, 213b, 214bl,
214t, 216bl, 214t, 216b, 216t, 217t, 220b, 221t, 221b, 222t, 222b, 223b, 223t,
224bl, 224t, 225t, 225b, 227, 228t, 228b, 229b, 230b, 231t, 231b, 232b, 232t, 233t,
233b, 234t, 234b, 235, 237t, 240b, 242b, 242t, 243, 244t, 246b, 248t, 248t, 248b,
249b, 250t, 250b, 253t. AKG pp2, 3tl, 3bm, 3br, 4tl, 4bl, 6t, 6b, 7t, 8b, 9t, 10b, 11t,
15b, 18, 30b, 38br, 52t, 57b, 58, 72t, 73b, 75t, 79t, 81t, 83br, 83, 88, 93t, 99, 103tr,
108b, 110, 113t, 114, 116b, 117b, 118b, 120t, 122b, 123b, 124t, 125l, 125t, 138b,
138t, 139t, 143t, 144, 145b, 147t, 151t, 156, 166b, 167t, 168t, 171b, 174, 178b,
179b, 181b, 185, 186t, 191t, 194t, 197, 199t, 199r, 207bl, 207br, 214br, 217bl,
218b, 218t, 219tl, 219b, 239t, 239b, 241lb, 252t. ANCIENT ART AND
ARCHITECTURE: 14t, 52b, 61t, 94t, 140t, 159b, 181b, 217br, 255. ISTOCK: pp11b,
86t, 87, 91, 101b, 155b, 184b, 215tl, 237b, 249t, 251.

NOTES

NOTES